China BUSINESS

Compiled by Ma Ke, Li Jun, etc.

Translated by Song Peiming and Zhu Youruo

CHINA INTERCONTINENTAL PRESS

图书在版编目（CIP）数据

中国商务／马可，李俊主编；宋佩铭等译．—北京：
五洲传播出版社，2004．1
ISBN　7-5085-0413-5

Ⅰ．中…　Ⅱ．①马…　②李…　③宋…　Ⅲ．商务－
概况－中国－英文　Ⅳ．F72

中国版本图书馆 CIP 数据核字（2004）第 000064 号

顾　　问　赵启正
策　　划　李　冰
主　　编　郭长建
副 主 编　宋坚之　吴　伟

撰　　稿　马　可　李　俊　何　方　王学文　文　江
翻　　译　宋佩铭　朱攸若
责任编辑　冯凌宇
编辑助理　苏　谦
装帧设计　郑方红
图片提供　www.photocome.com

出版发行　五洲传播出版社
地　　址　北京北三环中路 31 号
邮　　编　100088
电　　话　(010)82008396　82008228
网　　址　www.cicc.org.cn
制　　作　北京天人鉴设计制作有限公司
印　　刷　利丰雅高印刷（深圳）有限公司
版　　次　2004 年 1 月第 1 版第 1 次印刷
定　　价　188.00 元

Location of China in the World

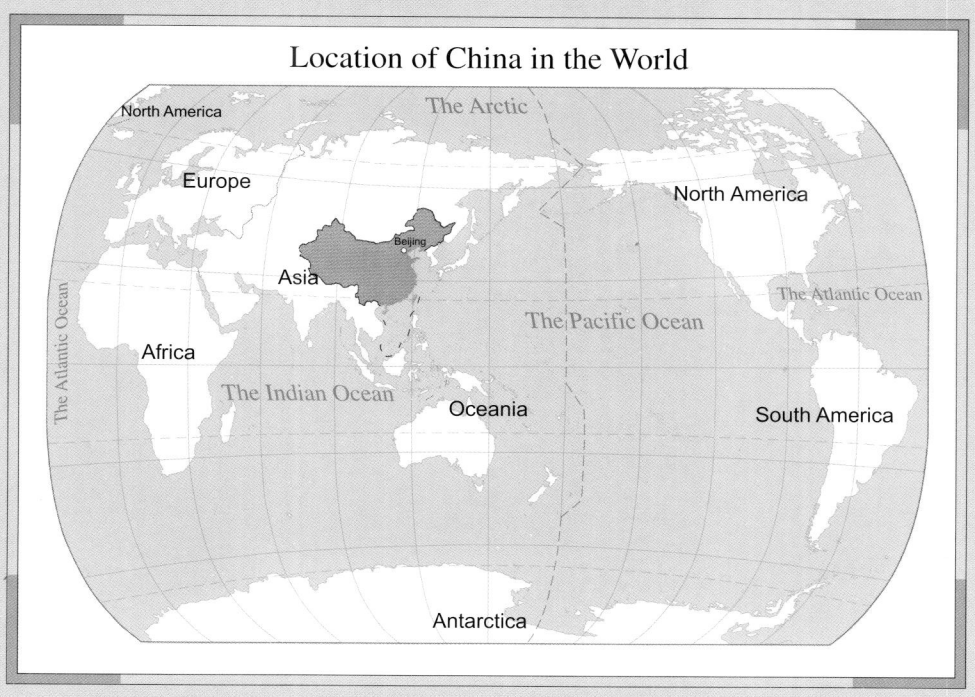

City Time Differences

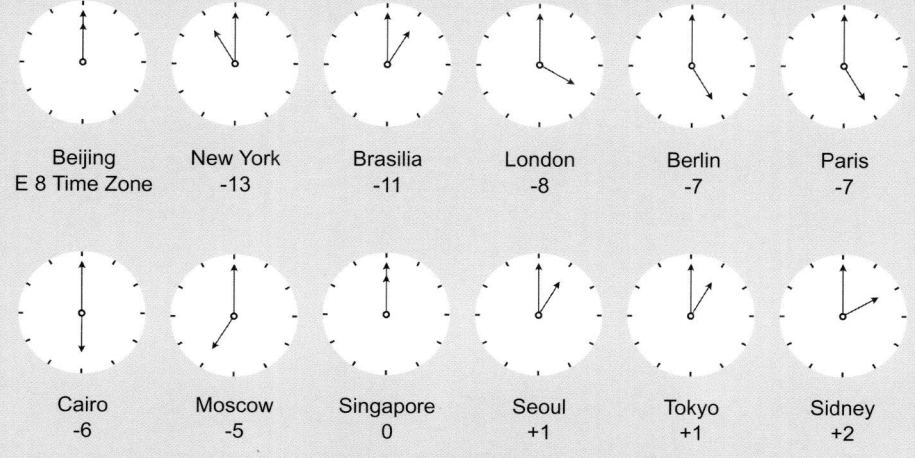

Beijing E 8 Time Zone	New York -13	Brasilia -11	London -8	Berlin -7	Paris -7
Cairo -6	Moscow -5	Singapore 0	Seoul +1	Tokyo +1	Sidney +2

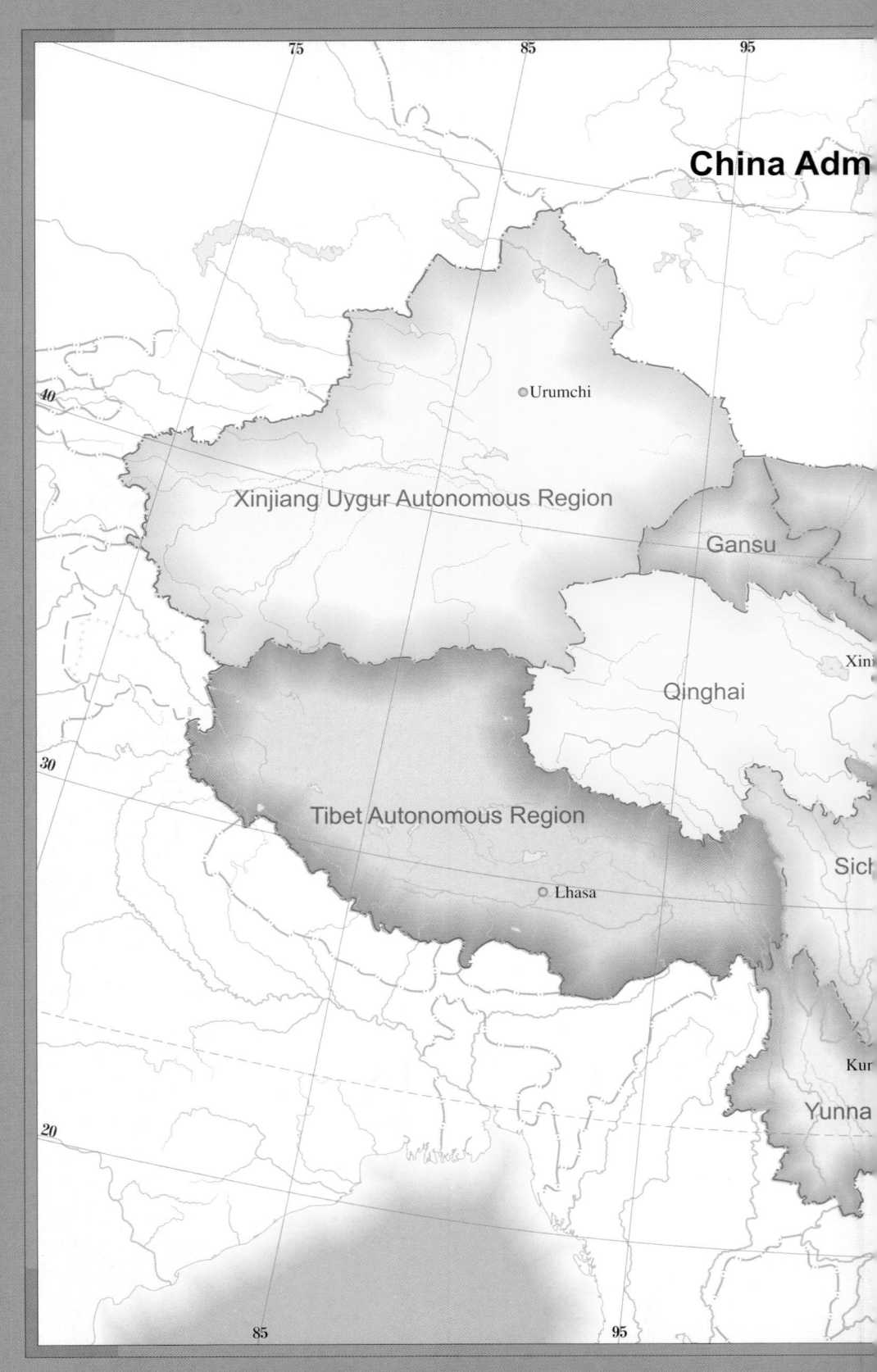

China Adm

75 85 95

40

Urumchi

Xinjiang Uygur Autonomous Region

Gansu

Qinghai

Xin

30

Tibet Autonomous Region

Sich

Lhasa

Kur

20

Yunna

85 95

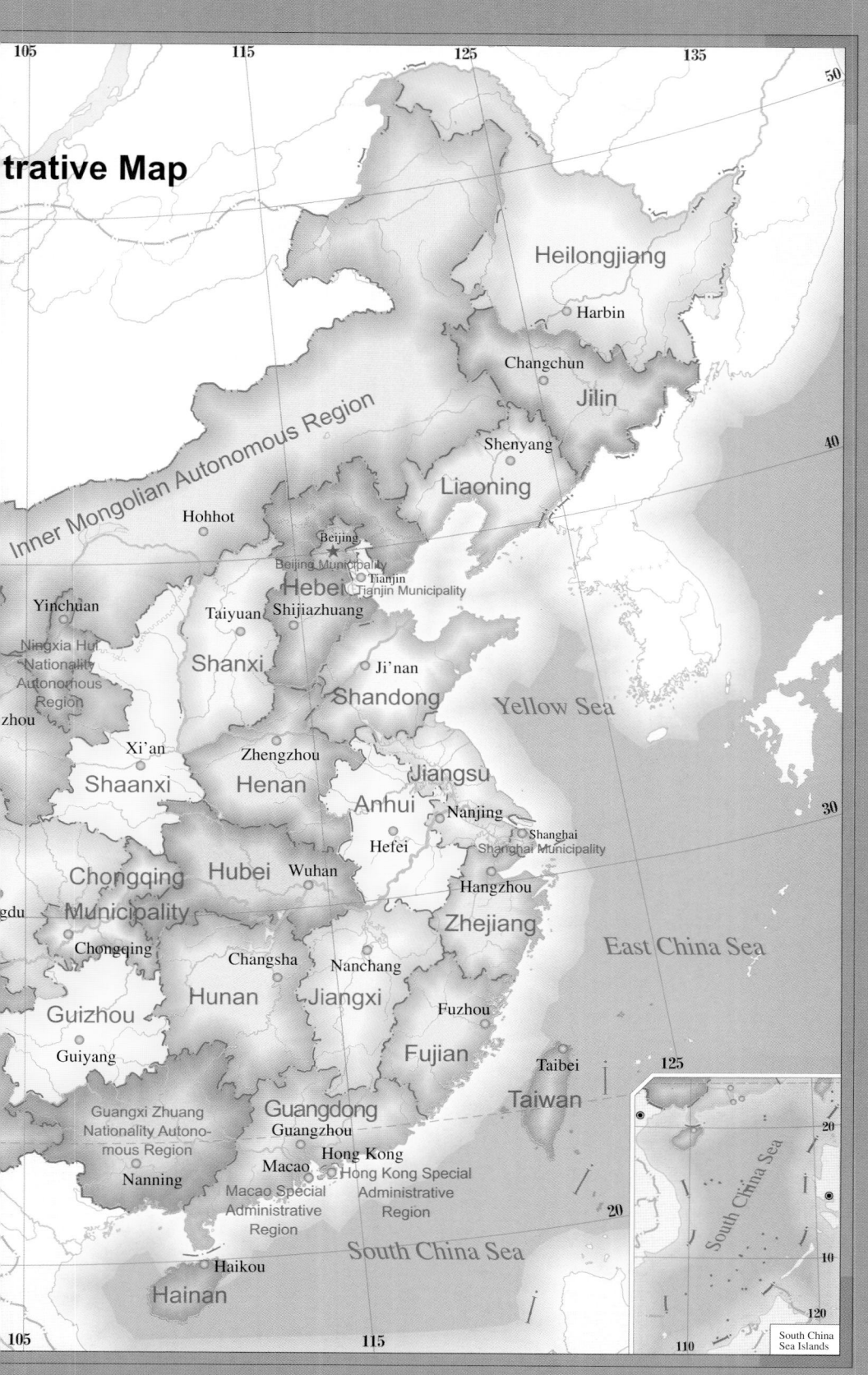

trative Map

105 115 125 135 50

Heilongjiang

Harbin

Changchun

Jilin

Shenyang

Liaoning 40

Inner Mongolian Autonomous Region

Hohhot

Beijing
Beijing Municipality
Tianjin
Tianjin Municipality

Hebei

Yinchuan

Taiyuan Shijiazhuang

Ningxia Hui
Nationality
Autonomous
Region

Shanxi

Ji'nan

Shandong

Yellow Sea

zhou

Xi'an

Zhengzhou

Shaanxi

Henan

Jiangsu

Anhui

Nanjing

Hefei

Shanghai
Shanghai Municipality 30

Chongqing
Municipality

Hubei Wuhan

Hangzhou

gdu

Zhejiang

Chongqing

Changsha Nanchang

East China Sea

Guizhou

Hunan

Jiangxi

Fuzhou

Guiyang

Fujian

Taibei 125

Guangxi Zhuang
Nationality Autono-
mous Region

Guangdong

Guangzhou

Taiwan

20

Nanning

Macao

Hong Kong

Hong Kong Special
Administrative
Region

South China Sea

Macao Special
Administrative
Region

20

South China Sea

Haikou

Hainan

105 115

110

10

120

South China
Sea Islands

CONTENTS

Foreword 6

Business Background 10
Geography 10
Population 15
Politics 18
Society 25
Finance 40
Communications 48
Telecom 54
Energy 57

Industries and Markets 62
Economy in General 62
Industrial Policies 65
Agriculture and Farm Produce Market 72
Industry and The Market For Industrial Products 78
Service Sector and Policy For Its Development 119
Market for Consumer Goods 139
List of Industries, Products and Technologies Currently
Encouraged by the State for Development 155

Foreign Trade 176
An overview 176
Right of Import-Export Management 181
Administration of Imported and Exported Commodities 185
Policies on Customs Duty 190
Policies on Processing Trade 190

Foreign Investment 196
Current Situation of Foreign Investment 196
Forms of Foreign Investment 198
Basic Policy on Foreign Investment 206

Special Economic Zone and Development Zone 215
Establishment of Foreign-Invested Enterprises 226
Taxation Policies Governing Foreign-Invested Enterprises 232
Land, Labor and Foreign Exchange Management 235
Provisions on Guiding the Orientation of Foreign Investment 245
Catalogue for the Guidance of Foreign Investment Industries 250

Intellectual Property Rights 276
Laws and Statutes Concerning Intellectual Property Rights 276
Application for Trademark and Patent Rights 280
Commitment for the Protection of Intellectual Property Rights 282

Around China 288
A Survey 288
Urban Development 356
The Western Development 360
List of Advantageous Industries for Foreign Investment in Provinces,
Autonomous Regions and Municipalities Directly under the Central
Government in the Central and Western Parts 377

Commercial Activities 388
Acquisition of Commercial Information 388
Work and Life 392

Appendix: Organs and Websites 399
Central Organs 399
Local Information 406
Sector Information 413
Trade and Investment 416
Society, Media and Tourism 427
Embassies in China 431
Long Distance Call Area Codes of Main Cities and Regions in China 448

FOREWORD

A certain day in the year of 2001, the president of a foreign company paid a visit to China intending to sell some technical know-how related to insurance to the Chinese. However, what made him surprised was that instead of selling something to China he bought from China a set of computer software related to insurance business management.

"If you know nothing about what is happening in China, it means you are ignorant about it." Many foreign businessmen who have been to China say so. Then what is really happening in China?

At least in the latest twenty years or so, China has seen the most rapid development of economy in the world. Just take a look ahead of you, what meets your eyes is high-rises, modern plants, a metropolis suddenly emerging on the horizon, and freeways extending thousands of kilometers. But all this is only the front cover of the "Story of China". What attracts you most will be the overall economic transformation—from planned economy to market-oriented economy—and the construction of an open and democratic society ruled by laws.

Twenty years ago, almost none could forecast the China of today. In those days, everything should be arranged by the state, from enterprise production to the people's life. The then China was almost short of everything except human beings and coupons were a must to buy anything. It was also during those days, the door of China was open to the outside world and groups of businessmen and entrepreneurs entered. The story that follows sounds quite logical. China becomes a big nation for foreign trade and a piece of hot land for foreign businessmen's investment as well. It seems that China is to be the "manufacturing center" of the world.

The fact that China uses a period of twenty years to cover a distance that takes other countries to do so for 100 years or so is a great achievement itself. If you have

The night China gained WTO membership

Overseas retail businesses aim at Chinese markets

not gone through the process, what you can see is only the exciting results or disheartening problems—the problems a developing country is sure to face with. The key issue is that the time spent for China to solve these problems is much shorter than many other countries. Some transnational corporations say that they have plants all over the world but the efficiencies of the plant in China are the best.

Once China was eulogized as "a country with the ground paved with gold" just like a myth but China was also suspected that its "economy is going to collapse". No matter what the world opinions are, a strong trend can be seen, i.e. foreign funds keep on pouring into China under the situation of global economic concession. That is the strength of market.

China, a market with strong attraction, is well worth a survey from various angles.

So far as purchasers are concerned, products "Made in China" are no longer primarily processed commodities. Instead, they are surging high towards high-tech products and their advantage of products, "cheap but good", is consistent.

To suppliers, though the Chinese people are not wealthy yet, China, as a big nation with the largest population in the world, is consuming quite a large volume of products, manufactured either at home or abroad. The Chinese people, open-minded and self-confident, know how to enjoy foreign commodities and their services. In 2001, an expert of economic analysis reminded merchants of various countries in one of his research reports that "in case you have not seen any Chinese tourists yet, please be ready to receive them in your store as you can make money out of them for fifty years".

To investors, China, having entered the WTO, is available with even free and standardized investment environments.

The Chinese people, under ever-changing environments, have come to see that many principles and ideas left from the past are no longer applicable to solving the present issues. The new environments need you to know yourself as well as the others and will make you readjust yourself in time. The present China is more challengeable than any period in the history but is also more attractive than any other places in the world to do business with. This growing nation has attracted 25 million people in the world outside of China to learn the Chinese language. No matter out of what considerations, they have stepped onto the short cut to contact China by doing so.

This book "China Business" is not only for the purpose of listing various kinds of details for those intending to do business with China, but also helping the readers to understand the business environments in China, such as the real picture, the economic plan in the next few years and the actual operational status of business activities. The book will also provide the readers with the fundamental knowledge to appraise the Chinese market and to be engaged in this market. To speak the truth, even if more information is contained in this book, these issues still cannot be clearly stated. Therefore, in the appendix of this book we list quite a number of valuable internet websites and a list of periodicals and organizations, institutions, and diplomatic missions so that our readers can get more and prompt information and different views and statements from the websites.

The large numbers of information and data quoted in the book are mainly from government systems, such as the relevant publications of the State Statistical Bureau and the trade reports of the State Economic and Trade Commission. The credit should go to the government with higher and higher diaphaneity and the society with more and more developed information. Anyhow, what should be pointed out here is that the business environments and various kinds of data mentioned in this book, unless otherwise stated, include only the Chinese mainland, not involving Hong Kong, Macao and the Taiwan area.

When young, we all heard a fairy tale about a pony wading across the river: an old ox says the river is too shallow but a little sheep says it is too deep. For the gigantic dragon of China that is surging swiftly upward, what we provide here is merely odd bits of information. Only by stepping into the water, we are sure, can you really know whether the river is too deep or too shallow.

BUSINESS BACKGROUND

The ancient Chinese alleged that favorable climatic, geographical and human conditions were the factors affecting the result of winning or losing a battle and the rise and fall of a family or a nation as well. To do business in China, one must know business environments, including natural, social, political and economic environments. Due to the extensive content involved, it's impossible for us to give a systematic interpretation in one chapter. That is why the background is raised first and large amount of content is dispersed in the following respective chapters. A careful reader may have already noticed that the whole book, in fact, is talking about the business environments in China.

GEOGRAPHY

Where is China? China is in the east part of Asia and on the west coast of the Pacific Ocean with all its territory lying to the north of the equator. Viewed from the map, China looks like a crowing roaster. The distance between the south and north inside the territory is 5,500 kilometers. When the Northeastern region of China is freezing cold and people are carrying out various kinds of touring and trading activities like ice and snow festivals one by one, Guangdong and Hainan Provinces in the south are still as warm as spring. The distance between the east and the west is 5,200 kilometers with the time difference of over four hours. When the people of Shanghai in the eastern region start to work at eight or nine o'clock in the morning, Urumchi, the westernmost capital city of Xinjiang, has just woken up. Don't expect anyone to answer your phone call at such an early hour like this unless it is an extraordinary call. Everywhere in China, the Beijing time is used as the standard time. Beijing is located at the E8 time zone, eight hours earlier than the Greenwich time.

New Business Card of Shanghai: Pudong

How large is China? The land space of China, almost as large as Europe, is around 9,600,000 square kilometers, the third largest country in the world. Along the land boundary of 22,000 kilometers there are fifteen neighboring countries. China adjoins the Democratic People's Republic of Korea in the east; Russia and Mongolia in the northeast and north respectively; Kazakhstan, Kirghizstan, Tadzhikstan, Afghanistan and Pakistan respectively in the west; and India, Nepal, Sikkim, Bhutan,

Myanmar, Laos and Viet Nam respectively in the southwest and the south. On the eastern part and southeastern part of China is the coastline with the length of 18,000 kilometers, neighboring six countries, the Republic of Korea, Japan, Philippines, Brunei, Malaysia and Indonesia, separated apart from each other by the seas from the north to the south. The total population of these twenty-one neighboring countries amounts to two billion. With the population of China added, it makes a half of the world. A Chinese saying goes "Neighbors are dearer than distant relatives". The neighborhood relationship also applies to the neighboring countries. The diplomatic policy China pursues is a good-neighbor friendly policy and China has established diplomatic relations with all the peripheral countries.

Around 98% of the territory of China is located between 20^0 and 50^0 north latitude, around 50% of which belongs to damp and semi-damp area with adequate rainfall and sunlight, and plenty of resources of living things. When looking around the world, one can see that most of the land around the line of 30^0 north latitude is the so-called "Tropic" desert, arid and dry, a land of desert and semi-desert. On the contrary, the same line in China, the Yangtze River Valley, is a densely-populated region with a splendid view of green mountains and blue waters. Though the northwestern re-gion is arid and dry with desert here and there, it has rich resources of oil and gas, a land of treasures now. The east faces the Pacific Ocean, providing excellent condi-tions for ocean shipping, sea fishery and oceanic industries.

In the total land space of China, 33% is mountain region, 26% plateau, 19% basin, 12% plain and 10% hills. Though the mountain regions are not advantageous to traffic and agricultural development, they are rich in resources of forest, grassland, minerals, water energy and tourism.

Qinling Mountain—Huaihe River is the demarcation line of the climate between the south and north in China. In summer, the whole nation is generally hot and rainy and there is no big difference in temperature between the south and north. In winter, most regions in China are cold and dry and the temperature difference between the south and the north is very obvious. Precipitation is mainly in summer time. In the south, the rainy season is longer, concentrated in May ~ October while that in the north is shorter, concentrated in July ~ August. The distribution rule of the precipita-tion region is that in the east there are more raining days than in the west, decreasing gradually from the southeastern coastline regions to the northwestern inland regions. The difference of climate in various places is rather obvious. For instance, the winter in the northeastern region is long and severe. Harbin, the capital of Heilongjiang Province, has always been known as an "ice city" while Hainan Province in the south has a long summer with no winter at all, imbued with a strong flavor of tropical

The Great Wall remains the same, but China has changed.

scenery. Kunming, the capital of Yunnan Province in the southwestern region, is like spring all the year round, renowned as a "spring city".

China is rich in natural resources. So far the mineral products with the reserves verified amount to 156 varieties. Many nonferrous metal minerals such as tungsten, lead, zinc, titanium, tin, smithsonite, nickel, and rare-earth metal rank first or at the forefront in the world; nonmetal minerals such as gypsum, barite, phosphate rock, mica, asbestos and kaolin also rank at the forefront in the world; and among the energy resources, the reserves of verified coal, petroleum and natural gas are rather impressive and the reserves and availability of the hydraulic power rank first in the world too.

In line with the differences of the economic development and geography, the whole country can be divided into three economic regions: the eastern, the middle and the western. The eastern region, mostly plain and hilly land, is in the vicinity of seas with profound industrious foundation, fairly perfect infrastructures, higher level of science and technology, better culture and education, and sound management and administration. Since the reform and opening-up, the Central Government has given more favorable policies to the eastern region. Special economic zones, open cities along the coast and economic development zones are mainly scattered in this region.

The middle region is located at the hinterland of China. The economic development in this region is slower than that in the eastern region but the industrial foundation is still good enough, having rich energy resources and natural resources of nonferrous metals and ferrous metals, and petrochemical industry. It has a number of cities and regions with high-developed industries and science and technology and is the main production region of grains, cotton and edible oils.

The western region, covering around 70% of the land area of the whole country, has very remarkable reserves of energy and minerals such as hydraulic energy, petroleum, natural gas, coal, rare-earth minerals, and nonferrous metals. The western region adjoins more than ten nations and regions, an important passageway leading from China to some other countries in Asia and some countries in Europe and having the regional advantages to develop economic and trade cooperation with the peripheral nations. Nevertheless, due to various reasons in the fields of natural conditions, history, culture, policies and systems, the western region is still rather underdeveloped. In the year of 2000, the Central Government started to carry out the western development strategy on a large scale, giving it much consideration in favorable policies and fund investment. The development of infrastructure construction in the respects of communications, energy, and telecom in the western region is so fast that one can see changes with each passing year.

A Chinese saying goes "A certain area of water and soil raises a certain kind of people in that area". When doing business in China, one has to consider the differences of nature, economy, society and culture in various parts of China. Just for a few examples. In case of selling bicycles, don't go to the mountain city Chongqing and when one takes an insurance policy on property in some places along the coastline of southeastern China, typhoon should be considered. According to a survey, the infiltration rate of skin-care cream in Beijing and Tianjin is both over 60% while in Shanghai and Guangzhou both lower. The main reason is that the demand for skin-care

New packing of Coca-Cola on festival market, showing Da Afu, a traditional Chinese mascot in the form of a clay figurine

cream in the damper climate of the south is lower than that in the dry climate of the north. Let's cite another example. In 2002, a kind of new car for family use was simultaneously promoted by a certain foreign automobile manufacture into the markets of Beijing and Guangzhou but met with different responses. Over 50% of the people surveyed in Beijing held that the space inside the car was too limited but the air-conditioning was satisfactory. But a higher percentage of people in Guangzhou expressed their approval for the interior space of the car but was not happy with the air-conditioning. The reason for such a difference is because of the people living in different regions of the south and the north. Generally speaking, the stature of the northerners is taller and bigger than that of the southerners so they prefer larger space in the car. However, the climate in the south is warm and humid than that in the north so the southerners place a higher demand for the air-conditioning.

In General, the economy in the south of China is more developed than that in the north. All the five special economic zones are in the south and most of the national pilot reforms also start from the south. Quite a number of people think that the southerners often have a higher sense of commodity concept and management consciousness, a more practical consumption philosophy, and a more complete and sophisticated understanding towards commodities and comparison consciousness than the northerners. It seems that all this is related to the cultural differences between the south and the north. For instance, the main staple food in the north is wheat and the northerners consume a large volume of meat and dairy products while that in the south is mainly rice and the southerners are very particular about delicious food and cooked dishes. As to disposition and sense of beauty, there is also a saying that "the southerners are mild and tender while the northerners firm and upright".

Another Chinese saying goes that "As there is no same wind within a distance of ten kilometers, there are no same customs and habits within a distance of one hundred kilometers". If one wants to get the backing of favorable climatic, geographical and human conditions, one has to learn about the background differences of social development in China and to know about the characteristics in the aspects of nature, economy, culture and geography. A number of foreign businessmen have come to know the regional disparity of the market in China and count on, comparatively speaking, the native talented people.

POPULATION

In November 2000, China conducted the fifth national population census. It showed that the total population on the mainland was 1,265,830,000, ranking first in

Age Composition of Chinese Population in 2001

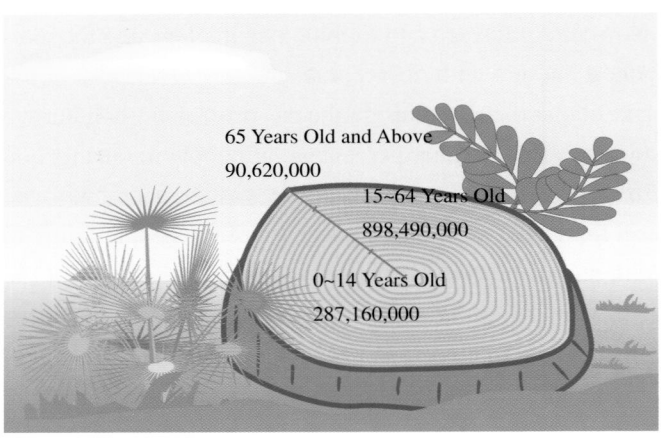

65 Years Old and Above
90,620,000

15~64 Years Old
898,490,000

0~14 Years Old
287,160,000

the world. Starting from twenty years ago, China put into effect the family planning policy to control the population growth. In general, a couple in the city rears only one child while in the rural areas or in the areas of ethnic nationality, usually two kids. What is related to the family planning, more or less, is that the family is too fond of the only child, even to the extent of spoiling. The parents are often never closefisted to spend money on the only child's life and education and those smart businessmen are always gazing at this huge "cake". Though the natural population growth in China has dropped to a medium level, the annual population growth is still huge enough due to the massive cardinal number. During the 1990~2000, almost 12,000,000 babies were added to the population annually.

At the end of 2000, the population over 65 years old was 88,110,000, accounting for 6.96% of the total population. This percentage was close to 7%, a standard for an aged society commonly acknowledged throughout the world. So China has entered an aged society and support of the elderly becomes a prominent issue. The traditional family way of taking care of the old cannot meet the demand any longer and more and more aged people have moved to the home for the aged. The medical care, cultural entertainment, and nursing for the old are being developed into a new industry.

The ratio of male and female sexes in China is 106.74, a little higher than the average world level (101.44). A sample survey of 1‰ made in 1999 showed that the sex ratio of the population between 0~4 years old was very high, reaching around 119. Generally speaking, the life span of the female population is longer than that of the male. Starting from the age group of around 69 years old, the male population of China is less than the female. With the growth of age, the ratio of male and female is further decreased. At present, the expected average life span of the national population is 71.

In the total population of China, the population in cities and towns composes 36.22% while that in rural areas, 63.78%. Due to the low level of urbanization, surplus manpower in rural areas is still rather high. Since 1990's, the flowing speed of rural population to cities and towns has been moving faster. In 2001, big cities and medium and small cities and towns as well conducted a further reform for household registration system, lifting the policy restriction for rural inhabitants transformed into registered permanent residents in cities and towns. It can be foreseen that the pace of future population urbanization will be sped up. In 1990's, the proportion of city and town population in China rose 0.91 percentage point per year on the average. It is expected that the same growth rate will remain the same at the beginning of the 21st century. According to the prediction of the United Nations, the city and town population of China in the year of 2030 can be increased to 884,000,000, 59.1% of the total population, corresponding approximately to the average world level at that time.

The population between 15~64 years old in China is 880,000,000, just at the period of "population bonus". Quite a number of foreign businessmen coming to China to make investment and run plants are attracted by this abundant and cheap manpower. With the development of education, the laborers' quality will be further improved and the advantages of the manpower in China can be long maintained.

For over 20 years, the average household population of China has tended to go

Basic Status of Chinese Population in 1990 and 2000

Index	1990	2000
Total Population (00,000)	113368	126583
Male	58495	65335
Female	54873	61228
Sex Ratio	106.60	106.74
Family Size (Head/Household)	3.96	3.44
Population of Various Age Groups (%)		
0~14 Years Old	27.69	22.89
15~64 Years Old	66.74	70.15
65 Years Old and Over	5.57	6.96
Population of Educated People at Various Levels per 000,000 people (Head)		
University and Above	1422	3611
Senior High and Polytechnic School	8039	11146
Junior High	23344	33961
Elementary	37057	35701
Illiterate Population and Illiteracy Rate		
Illiterate Population (00,000 People)	18003	8507
Illiteracy Rate (%)	15.88	6.72
Urban and Rural Population (00,000 People)		
City and Town Population	29971	45844
Rural Population	83397	80739

UN Prediction of Population Changes in China during 2000~2050

	2000	2005	2010	2020	2030	2040	2050
Total Population (000,000,000)	12.78	13.26	13.72	14.54	14.96	15.04	14.78
Birthrate (‰)		14.6	14.2	13.6	11.7	11.1	10.8
Natural Growth Rate (%)		0.75	0.69	0.58	0.28	0.06	-0.18
Population over 65 (%)	6.8	7.5	8.1	11.5	15.7	21.3	22.6

down due to the development of economy, the growth of population urbanization, the speed of population flowing rate, the increase of divorce rate and the unmarried population at the marriageable age. At present, the average population per family is about 3.44 heads in cities and towns and 3.65 heads in rural areas. With more and more youth and adults forming their own core families and less and less aged people left in the empty nests, there are less and less traditional extended families for several generations living under the same roof and the independent living space for family members are expanded. Anyhow, the family relations based on blood and marriage are still very close. Quite a few product ads and business activities often make an issue of "affection" and "courtesy".

The average population density of China is approximately 130 people per square kilometer but the distribution is very uneven. The population density is over 400 people per square kilometer along eastern coastal areas; over 200 people per square kilometer in the middle areas; less than 10 people per square kilometer in the western plateau areas. Big cities are very densely populated while rural areas very sparsely populated. Shanghai Municipality is the most densely populated city in China with over 2,500 people per square kilometer. The population density of Beijing Municipality is 750~900 people per square kilometer and that of Tibet, Inner Mongolia and Xinjiang in the west is sparse, less than 50 people per square meter.

POLITICS

In China, in addition to the Communist Party in power there are eight other political parties called by a joint name democratic parties.

The Communist Party of China (CPC) was founded in July 1921, now having over 64,000,000 members. All those who have no prejudice against the CPC can see that it was because of its leadership, there were "two revolutions" in the 20th century. The result of the first revolution was the founding of the People's Republic of China in 1949 and the people won independence and freedom. It was from then on that the CPC has become a party in power, having the national regime under its control. The "second revolution" is the reform and opening-up which are still in progress, the achievements of which are perfectly obvious to anyone.

The leadership of the state affairs exercised by the CPC embodies mainly in the leadership of political principles, political orientation and important decision-making of the whole nation and in the recommendation of important cadres to the state regime.

The supreme leading body of the CPC is the National Congress of the CPC and the Central Committee produced by the National Congress. The National Congress of the CPC is convened once every five years while the Central Committee should convene a plenary session at least once a year. The Plenary Session of the Central Committee elects the Political Bureau of the Central Committee, the Standing Committee of the Political Bureau of the Central Committee, and the Secretary-general of the Central Committee as well as decides the members of the Secretariat of the Central Committee. The Secretary-general of the Central Committee is responsible for convening the meetings of the Political Bureau of the Central Committee and the meetings of the Standing Committee of the Political Bureau of the Central Committee and for taking care of the work of the Secretariat of the Central Committee. The National Congress of the CPC particularly attracts the attention of all countries in the world as it involves the future decision-making and major personnel changes of China.

China exercises the system of multi-party cooperation and political consultation under the leadership of the CPC. Before the state takes any important measures or makes any decision for major issues related to the national economy and the people's livelihood, the CPC will carry out consultation beforehand with all nationalities, all circles, all political parties and groups, and nonparty democratic personages, reach unanimity of understanding and then make the decision. There are two main forms for multiparty cooperation and political consultation. One is the Chinese People's Political Consultative Conference (CPPCC) and the other is the consultative meeting and forum convened by the Central Committee of the CPC and the Party Committee in the localities at different levels with the presence of personages from democratic parties and nonparty democratic personages.

The official newspaper of the Central Committee of the CPC is the "People's

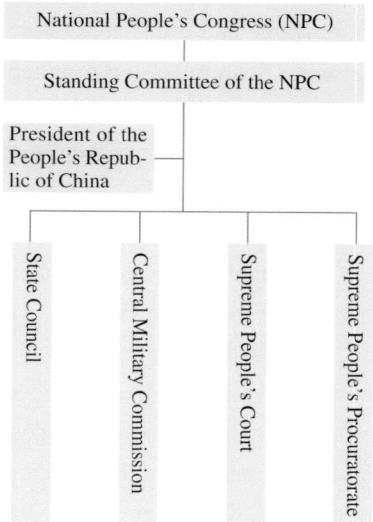

Setup Diagram of State Institutions of Central People's Government

National People's Congress (NPC)

Standing Committee of the NPC

President of the People's Republic of China

State Council

Central Military Commission

Supreme People's Court

Supreme People's Procuratorate

Daily". As it plays the role of the "mouthpiece", quite a few people are used to inferring the readjustment of the policies of China and changes of situation on the basis of the news released on the paper. In fact, the policies of China are more and more stable and transparent and the media competition such as newspapers, TV and networks is tougher and tougher. Both governmental and nongovernmental organs have their respective information organs and one can obtain all kinds of information easily and conveniently from different channels, whether one is at home or abroad.

State Institutions

The state institutions of China include:

Organs of State Power   The NPC and the People's Congress in the localities at different levels are the organs of state power. The NPC is the supreme organ of state power. Its standing body is the Standing Committee of the NPC. Compared with the congress or parliament of most countries in the world, the NPC is also a kind of parliamentary organ. Its fundamental powers of office can be outlined as the legislative power, the power to make decisions for major issues, the power to select suitable persons for different posts, and the power to make supervision. The term of office for each session of the NPC is five years. The Congress is held once a year, generally around the middle ten days of March every year.

President of the State   President of the state is the head of the state. The President represents the state when contacting foreign countries and exercises the functions and powers in accordance with the decisions of the NPC and its Standing Committee.

State Administrative Organs   The State Council and the people's government in the localities at different levels are the state administrative organs. The State Council is the Central People's Government, the supreme state administrative organ. The State Council consists of the premier, vice premiers, members of the State Council, ministers of various ministries, directors of various commissions, auditor general, and secretary-general, practicing the system with the premier in charge.

State Military Leading Organ   The Central Military Commission is the state military leading organ.

State Judicial Organ   The Supreme People's Court is the state judicial organ.

State Procuratorial Organ   The Supreme People's Procuratorate, the People's Procuratorate in the localities at different levels and special People's Procuratorate are the state procuratorial organs.

All administrative organs, judicial organs, and procuratorial organs are produced by the People's Congress, are responsible for and supervised by the People's Congress.

Tiananmen Gate Tower in Beijing

Government

One of the characteristics of the leading system of the Chinese administrative organs is that the administrative head is held responsible. In the work, the administrative head at different levels enjoys the power of all-round leadership corresponding to his respective level, the power of making the final decision, the power of personnel nomination, and the power of all-round responsibility.

During the period of planned economy, the government held too much power under its control, exercising the power particularly in the form of administration examination and approval. It was in charge of many things that it should not and could not take good care of. In recent years, due to rapid development of economy and the needs to enter the WTO, the government at different levels has carried out reforms in the system of administrative examination and approval, got rid of the heavy administrative burden of an all-round government during the planned economy, and devoted itself to improving services and a better management of public affairs. Now, more and more electronic platforms handling official businesses and government affairs in a concentrated way have emerged in China with the purpose of improving administrative efficiencies so that people can obtain more convenient and better government services than any time in the past.

Setup Diagram of Organizations under State Council

State Council

General Office of the State Council

Ministries and Commissions

Ministry of Foreign Affairs
Ministry of National Defense
State Development and Reform Commission
Ministry of Education
Ministry of Science and Technology
Commission of Science, Technology and Industry for National Defense
State Commission for Nationalities Affairs
Ministry of Public Security
Ministry of State Security
Ministry of Supervision
Ministry of Civil Affairs
Ministry of Justice
Ministry of Finance
Ministry of Personnel
Ministry of Labor and Social Security
Ministry of Land and Resources
Ministry of Construction
Ministry of Railways
Ministry of Communications
Ministry of Information Industry
Ministry of Water Resources
Ministry of Agriculture
Ministry of Commerce
Ministry of Culture
Ministry of Health
State Commission for Population and Family Planning
People's Bank of China
Auditing Administration

Organizations Directly under the State Council

General Administration of Customs
State General Administration of Taxation
State General Administration of Environmental Protection
Civil Aviation Administration of China
State General Administration of Radio, Film and Television
State General Administration of Physical Culture
State Statistical Bureau
State General Administration for Industry and Commerce
State General Administration of Press and Publications
State Bureau of Forestry
State Administration for Quality Supervision, Inspection and Quarantine
State Food and Drug Administration
State Bureau of Intellectual Property Rights
State Tourism Bureau
State Bureau of Religious Affairs
Counselors' Office of the State Council
Bureau of Government Offices Administration of the State Council

State Bureaus under the Jurisdiction of Ministries and Commissions

State Grain Administration
State Tobacco Monopoly Bureau
State Bureau of Foreign Experts Affairs
National Bureau of Oceanography
State Bureau of Surveying and Mapping
State Bureau of Postal Service
State Bureau of Cultural Relics
State Administration of Traditional Chinese Medicine
State Administration of Exchange Control

After the WTO accession, the Chinese government faces two transitional periods. The first one is a legal transitional period, a period of 5~7 years for the Chinese Government to reduce its tariffs and readjust its economic policies, which is clearly stated in the terms for China to enter the WTO. The other is a transitional period for transformation, a period for the Chinese Government to adapt itself to the overall requirements of the WTO rules and to establish step by step a transparent and opened government ruled by laws. The task of the legal transitional period is mainly to carry out the policy readjustment, cut down the tariff barrier and the non-tariff barriers while the task of transitional period for transformation is to establish a government system and an operational system that is in compliance with the overall requirements of the system of the WTO rules.

For twenty years or so since the reform and opening, China has always been exploring how to found a government with high-efficient operation and has carried out four major administrative reforms. The latest reform starting from 1998 has made China change basically the administrative management system and organizational institutions formed during the period of traditional planned economy. The State Council has readjusted and reduced the special economic departments and the province-level government maintains no longer the special economic management departments for industry and commerce. The comprehensive economic departments have been changed into departments for macro readjustment and control. The government functions have been changed into taking care of macro planning, policy guidance, enforcement of laws and supervision, and organizational coordination with concentrated force as well as supplying public goods and services for enterprises and the public.

The reform of the system for administrative examination and approval, which is of great concern to investors both at home and abroad and operators as well, is an important content for the reform of government organs. Starting from the central government, the State Council has redefined the responsibilities and competence of the various departments and cancelled quite a few items for administrative examination and approval, returning the functions belonging to enterprises and social intermediate organizations to the enterprises and the social intermediate organizations themselves, and returning the affairs to be taken care of by the localities to the localities themselves. The organizational reforms of the local government started in 1999 have sorted out and revised a number of local statutes and government rules and regulations, cancelled, simplified and reformed numbers of items for administrative examination and approval. For those items that can be operated with market mechanism to replace administrative examination and approval, the forms of public invitation for bidding and bid submission and auction are used while for those items that examination and approval should still be maintained, the procedures for examination and approval are simplified so that the time needed can be shortened.

At the same time, the government administration brought into the open in the main form of electronic administrative affairs is practiced nationwide. A lot of so-called "restricted information" or "confidential information" not for public eyes in the past have now become public information. From government websites, one can conveniently and quickly check the relevant government proclamation, trade information, statistical data, and guide to the process of going through government formalities.

With the all-round opening to the outside world, competitions in various parts of China have obviously become tougher and the services to foreign businessmen better in the fields of foreign trade and economic cooperation. The reform and opening-up are still underway. Profound changes have taken place in many places. Just take Pudong, Shanghai for instance. To anyone who wants to start a business or run a company, what he has to do is only to sign his name and affix the official seal on a copy of "Commitment Paper" issued by the industrial and commercial department instead of going through numerous examinations and approval formalities. Only by making commitment to the related matters listed in the "Commitment Paper", that is the conditions, standards and requirements for founding an enterprise stipulated by the Chinese laws, statutes, rules and regulations, and the relevant technical specifications, can the applicant get the business license and corresponding licenses with ease, within seven working days to the maximum.

Division of Administration Regions

The whole country is divided into province, autonomous region and the munici-pality directly under the central government. The province-level administration unit is the highest administration region of the locality under the direct jurisdiction of the State Council and county is the fundamental administration region. The administra-tion regions in-between the province and the county are the prefecture or city under the jurisdiction of the province. The county exercises control over villages and towns, and the township is the administration region at the grass-roots level. Under the general and specific policies of "one country, two systems", the two special adminis-trative regions, Hong Kong and Macao, exercise the policy of "Hong Kong people administering Hong Kong" and "Macao people administering Macao", enjoying a high degree of autonomy with the exception of national defense and foreign affairs. Taiwan has been the Chinese territory from time immemorial. In 1949, the CPC

Schematic Diagram of Administration Division

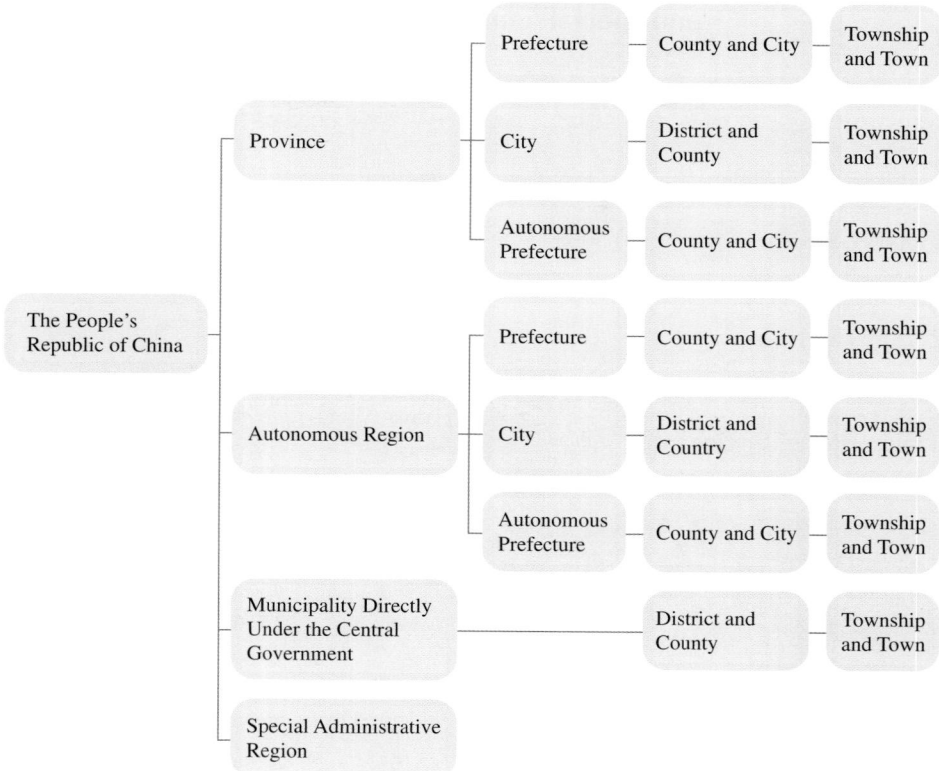

overthrew the rule of the KMT and the KMT regime withdrew to Taiwan. Even to this day, Taiwan and the motherland mainland have not been unified yet.

With the reforms, the Central Government has authorized quite a number of authorities and responsibilities to the subordinate governments at different levels. This measure has made the local governments more powerful and the transfer of power to locality by the Central Government makes the economic benefits of locality no longer depend on the decision of the Central Government but resolved primarily by the local governments themselves.

SOCIETY

Reform and Opening-Up

After the founding of the People's Republic of China in 1949, China practiced a highly-concentrated planned economic system. Starting from 1978, China has made a fundamental reform, transforming the system from planned economy into market-

A list of Province, Autonomous Region, Municipality Directly under the Central Government and Special Administrative Region

Name	Government Location	Space (00,000 km²)	Population at End of 2001 (00,000 Heads)
Beijing Municipality	Beijing	1.68	1381
Tianjin Municipality	Tianjin	1.13	1004
Hebei Province	Shijiazhuang	19.00	6699
Shanxi Province	Taiyuan	15.60	3272
Inner Mongolia Autonomous Region	Hohhot	118.30	2377
Liaoning Province	Shenyang	14.57	4194
Jilin Province	Changchun	18.70	2691
Heilongjiang Province	Harbin	46.90	3811
Shanghai Municipality	Shanghai	0.62	1614
Jiangsu Province	Nanjing	10.26	7355
Zhejiang Province	Hangzhou	10.18	4613
Anhui Province	Hefei	13.90	6328
Fujian Province	Fuzhou	12.00	3440
Jiangxi Province	Nanchang	16.66	4186
Shandong Province	Ji'nan	15.30	9041
Henan Province	Zhengzhou	16.70	9555
Hubei Province	Wuhan	18.74	5975
Hunan Province	Changsha	21.00	6596
Guangdong Province	Guangzhou	18.60	7783
Guangxi Zhuang Nationality Autonomous Region	Nanning	23.63	4788
Hainan Province	Haikou	3.40	796
Chongqing Municipality	Chongqing	8.20	3097
Sichuan Province	Chengdu	48.80	8640
Guizhou Province	Guiyang	17.00	3799
Yunnan Province	Kunming	39.40	4287
Tibet Autonomous Region	Lhasa	122.00	263
Shaanxi Province	Xi'an	20.50	3659
Gansu Province	Lanzhou	45.00	2575
Qinghai Province	Xi'ning	72.00	523
Ningxia Hui Nationality Autonomous Region	Yinchuan	6.64	563
Xinjiang Uygur Autonomous Region	Urumchi	160.00	1876
Hong Kong Special Administrative Region	Hong Kong	0.1092	
Macao Special Administrative Region	Macao	0.0024	
Taiwan Province		3.60	

oriented economy, which is called a "Second Revolution".

The history of reform and opening-up in China can be successively divided into two major stages.

The first stage was from 1978 to 1991. From 1978 to 1984, the reform focusing on rural areas was carried out and an experiment of power expansion for enterprises, establishing four special economic zones and opening-up fourteen harbor cities along the coast, was also simultaneously carried out in the city. From 1984 to 1991, an all-round reform focusing on the city, a pilot reform for the state-owned enterprises, was carried out, which opened up further the Yangtze River Delta Area and established Hainan Special Economic Zone and Shanghai Pudong New Area.

The second stage started in 1992 and is still undergoing. This is a stage of system creation of the reform with the target of establishing a system of socialist market-oriented economy. This reform lays emphasis on establishing a modern enterprise system for the state-owned enterprises, on macro system reforms as well as reforms for banking, financial and foreign trade system, on further deepening the reforms for housing and social security systems and transforming government functions as well, and on carrying forward the opening-up from the coastal areas to the inland so that after the WTO entrance, a situation of opening to the outside world in an all-dimensional and multi-ranging way can come into being.

The reform and opening-up in China are carried out in a progressive way. The reforms starting from rural areas are being moved step by step to urban areas; the price reform starting from "double-track system" is being gradually geared up and led finally to market price. At the same time of readjusting state-owned economy in a strategic way, non-public ownership is being developed and a mixed economy is being established with the public ownership as the basis and coexistence of various ownership forms. State-owned enterprise is being reformed progressively from mainly depending on government and policies to mainly depending on market and law, spurring the establishment of modern enterprise system. The opening-up is to be pushed step by step from the southeastern coastline to other coastal areas, boundary areas and inland areas. And the reform of economic system takes the lead to promote gradually the reforms in other aspects.

After the reforms of twenty years or so, China has initially established a system of socialist market-oriented economy. The outstanding signs are as follows:

First of all, the market has obviously played a role of fundamental function in the disposition of resources. During the period of planned economy, the restrictions controlled by the state over enterprises were so strict that enterprises had no right at all to make their own decisions. Since 1979, the reforms with the purpose of enlarging the power of enterprises to make their own decisions for production and management have been gradually enfolded and continuously developed in depth, developing from enlarging the power by depending on the means of policy to creating its own dynamic operational mechanism through the system. The enterprise has become a producer and manager of commodities, independent in management and assuming sole responsibility for its profits or losses. Simultaneously, the position with the human being as the main body of the market has been established, showing mainly in great improvement of decision-making power of laborers in their economic activities, and consumers' demands have become the basic guidance for social economic activities.

In 1988, China started the marketization process of production essential factors. In 1990's, the speed of this process went up rapidly and land, funds, and manpower promptly entered the market. All this promoted the extraordinary development of real estate market, stock market, bond market and labor market. Scientific and technical market and information market also gradually came into existence.

The reform has made industrial sectors open gradually, lowering or eliminating the entrance thrash and price control laid down by the government. At present, the industrial products with price under control are only iron and steel, petroleum and a few other products and agricultural products, only a few major crops like grains and cotton, are purchased by the state with price under the state control. After fulfilling the purchasing quota laid down by the state, farmers are allowed to sell their surplus farm produce in accordance with the market price.

Second, the unitary public ownership economy that was practiced for a long time has been reformed into a new situation of economy with public ownership as the main body to develop jointly an economy of diversified ownerships. Now the composition of the GDP is divided into three parts, namely, the state economy, the mixed economy and the private economy.

Third, a system of macro indirect regulation and control has taken shape. China has changed the practice of macro management mainly with direct management and the management in kind, practiced during the planned economy period. The mode of macro regulation and control has changed from direct to indirect regulation and control and gradually from simply depending on means of administration to mainly depending on economic and legal means through market channel to regulate economy. Administrative mandatory plans were step by step eliminated and a new administration mode is finally formed with market as the basis and guidance planning as the dominant factor.

The last but not the least is that a social security system has achieved significant development. Before the reforms, a unit in which one works is usually "a small society". Medical care, retirement and housing were almost all taken care of by the state and the unit, and the employment system practiced at that time was unified care and unified distribution and the workers had no unemployment insurance. Since 1980's, China has started to establish a social security system taken care of jointly by the state, the unit in which one works and the individual himself. Today, the social security system has covered the workers, the retired veteran workers and retired workers in most cities and towns, and in some areas even the farmers moving to the city for employment are also covered. All cities have universally established the system to ensure residents' minimum income.

Since China entered the WTO in November 2001, the economic relations with foreign countries have also entered a new stage. The limited opening-up in certain realm and sphere in the past has been turned into an all-dimensional, multi-tiered and wide-ranging opening; the strategy of gradient opening with characteristics of pilot and experiment has been turned into an overall opening strategy; and the government-guided opening-up with planning and administration decree as the basis has been turned into a market-guided opening-up with the market and comparative superiority as the basis.

Shenzhen, a City Booming with Reform and Opening-up

In the next few years and even in a quite long period in the future, China's WTO entry will be the most important impact on the reforms of the Chinese economic system. In 2001, the Chinese government declared to carry out reforms in the traditional monopoly industries such as electrical power, telecom, civil aviation and railway, primarily involving the content of reforms in division of government and enterprise, transformation into company, market access, decision of price, cooperation with foreign countries, competition, and supervision.

What is going on at the same time to break up the administrative industrial monopolization is the transformation of government functions. This is to establish, on

The Data Reflecting Changes of Ordinary People's Life

Heavier Purse

Urban and Rural Residents' Balance of Savings Deposit

1990	2002
712 billion yuan	8,691 billion yuan

More Personal Cars

Proportion of Personal Car Ownership in Total Amount of Autos Nationwide

1990	2001
Around 15%	Around 45%

Decreasing Engel's Coefficient

	1990	2002
Cities and Towns	54.2%	37.7%
Rural Areas	58.8%	46.2%

Higher Educational Level

Entrance Rate of Universities and Colleges

1990	2002
3,4%	13%

Longer Average Life Span

Expected Average Life Span

1990	2000
68.55 Years Old	71.4 Years Old

More Holidaymakers

Number of Chinese Citizens Traveling Abroad

1990	2002
3,000,000 Person-times	16,602,000 Person-times

More Living Space

Residents' Average Living Space

	1990	2001
Cities and Towns	6,7 m²	10,3 m²
Rural Areas	17,8 m²	25 m²

Faster Ways of Telecom

By September 2002
Fixed-line Phone
214,000,000 Subscribers
Mobile Phone
207,000,000 Subscribers

the basis of accurate determination of the government functions over sector management, an effective organizational structure of the government supervision to provide a guarantee with system for the development of infrastructure and public utilities and for fair competition of all investors. For the time being, one of the important aspects for the transformation of government functions is to reform the system of administrative examination and approval. It mainly uses the form of registration and record entrance under the guidance and monitor of the corresponding government departments so that the operational costs, particularly the "transaction costs", of the market-oriented economy can be decreased by a big margin.

The progressive reform and opening-up in China have always maintained the stability of the state and the society. The common people universally hold an attitude of approval for the reform and opening-up and are generally optimistic towards the prospect of social development.

Social Strata

In December 2001, the Chinese Academy of Social Sciences issued a "Study Report on Contemporary Social Strata of China". The report had an analysis of the contemporary social strata of China and divided the Chinese society into ten strata. They are the state and social management stratum, the manager stratum, the stratum of private business owners, the stratum of special technical people, the stratum of office workers, the stratum of self-employed industrial producers and commercial businessmen, the stratum of commercial service workers, the stratum of industrial workers, the stratum of agricultural laborers, and the stratum of jobless, unemployed and semi-unemployed people.

The division of the social stratum in China tends to be more and more the division of occupations. The social economic differences between the physical and non-physical laborers, and the managing and non-managing people are expanding. The changes mainly include the following aspects: the stratum of agricultural laborers is gradually diminishing, constantly moving towards other social strata; the number of commercial service workers and staff members is growing and so is the number of industrial workers because of rural industrialization; the social intermediate stratum is rapidly expanding, making the structure of the Chinese social strata change from original pyramid shape into spindle shape; and the stratum controlling and operating economic resources is in the making and growing in strength. The phenomenon of the development of social strata structure in China, just like that of the economic development, is obviously unbalanced with different regions. As the mid-western regions are less developed in economy, the social strata structure is also simpler.

Street Scene

The report said that in the future the social strata structure in China would not have big changes in its composition. The possible changes are chiefly in the size of individual stratum, of which the stratum of special technical people, the stratum of commercial service workers, the manager stratum, and the stratum of private business owners will greatly expand.

Before the reform and opening-up, most of urban residents were employed by enterprises owned either by the whole people or by the collective. There was no big difference in wage incomes and the ways of life were more or less the same. But since the reform and opening-up, the social flow has sped up and there is a wide range for occupation choice, which gradually falls in three parallel categories, namely, politics, industry and commerce, and professional work (such as education, scientific researches, medical workers, law, art, sports, etc.). With the recognition of the market-oriented economy, a variety of economic forms, individually-run, self-employed, privately-owned, foreign-funded, and Sino-foreign joint-ventured, have been rapidly developed and a number of wealthy people have emerged.

The update of social ways of life will inevitably cause the change of family life. The traditional family life with parents as the core is changing without one's knowledge. The generation of the only child born in 1970's ~ 1980's has stepped onto the social stage on a large scale. With economic independence, their life style of pursuing the new, the peculiar, and the changing holds an important position in the family. The market-oriented economy provides an excellent opportunity for young people to bring their talents into full play and to grow up to be somebody rapidly. The economic income of large numbers of young people has exceeded that of their parents and their enthusiasm and boldness to go after new ways life also exceed those

Data

Chinese People's Concept of Job Hunting
Affected by Economic Benefits

With the rapid economic development in China, Chinese people's concept of job hunting is changing. People are more concerned about economic benefits when choosing a job. A survey made by China Economic Situation Monitoring Center in 2002 showed that nowadays the three sectors people were most eager to pursue were finance / economy, high-tech, and commerce / logistics, comprising 60.3%, 50.3%, and 29.6% respectively. Compared with the result of the survey made at the beginning of 2000, the most popular sectors remained almost the same. The only difference was that popularity of high-tech sector moved from third place to second place and that of the commerce / logistics from second place to third place. The work in government / political parties and groups, which had been regarded as impressive and dignified, only made up 19.6% of the total proportion, ranking sixth. It's not difficult to see from this example that people's job hunting is more interested in economic benefits, i. e. the sector that really benefits rather than that sounds dignified.

The result of the survey shows that the various measures taken and efforts made by the government to raise the income of the urban citizens are effective. More than half of the people, i. e. 58.2%, are happy with the present income, 4% very happy, 24.6% basically happy, and 33.2% just so-so. Anyhow, 20.6% are not very happy and 17.1% are very unhappy.

When asked about the factors that decide the economic income, 34.2% of the people hold that personal ability / technique counts, 20.6% think that it is up to the economic efficiencies of the unit where one works, 18.1% deem that the economic level of the state decides everything and only 9% assume that position / title is the decisive factor. Under the great impact of the market-oriented economy, the factor used to decide the person's income, position / title, has been replaced by personal ability. This shows that people are more concerned about their own credentials.

of their parents. The white-collar generation with higher academic credentials and higher income has noticeably changed their way of life and may be rated as the vanguard in leading the tide in vogue.

The indisputable fact that higher academic credentials will bring about higher benefits in the tide of knowledge economy inspires unprecedentedly people's enthusiasm to go in pursuit of knowledge and improve their own educational level so as to adapt themselves to the challenge of competition. The "trend of going through exams", for university and college, for postgraduate, for doctorate, for computer grade, and for English band as well as for various kinds of advanced studies and training courses – all this prevails among the young people in the city. "Knowledge recharging" has become an important part in the life of city dwellers.

Construction of Legal System

During the first thirty years after the founding of the New China, a series of statues were laid down in succession. But due to the fact that what practiced at that time was a system of planned economy, the process of legal system construction was rather slow and the laws and statues in the field of economy were particularly lacking. Since the reform and opening-up, China has entered a rapid legislation time rarely seen in the history of world legislation with the construction of legal system at the head.

On December 11, 2001 China entered the WTO. Seen from the surface, China's entry into the WTO involves primarily the laws and rules related to trading and investment, but its impact is by no means limited only in these aspects. The system philosophy of "doing business in line with international conventional practices" and the game rules of "justice, opening-up and transparency" brought up by the WTO accession are spurring China to manage state affairs according to the law.

China's WTO entry has raised even higher demands for the construction of legal system in China. The first is to set up a transparent legal system so that the laws and rules related to trading and investment could be easily understood by other parties. The second is that these laws and rules should be exercised on the basis of equality, justice and rationality. And the third is that a judicial examination system should be established to examine the administrative behaviors.

Since 2001, China has sorted out the laws and statues related to foreign investment and revised the content not in conformity with the WTO rules. The most important ones are the basic laws and statues related to foreign investment, such as the "Law of the People's Republic of China on Joint Ventures Using Chinese and Foreign Investment", the "Law of the People's Republic of China on Cooperative Joint

Ventures Using Chinese and Foreign Investment", the "Law of the People's Republic of China on Wholly-Owned Foreign Enterprises" and the revision of details for implementation. Before entering the TWO, the legislative body had already revised the "Copyright Law", the "Trademark Law" and the "Patent Law", strengthened the protection of intellectual property rights and optimized the legal system environments in these respects.

In addition to revising and perfecting a number of laws that are not in conformity with the demands of the market-oriented economy, China has also unveiled and perfected a series of policies, laws and statutes for foreign investment, and promulgated the statutes involving the opening of service and trading realm in the fields of intermediary agent, tourism, telecom, medical establishment, finance, investment, and recovery of terrestrial and off-shore petroleum resources. The State Council has promulgated a number of administrative statues in the form of rules and regulations such as the"Anti-dumping Regulations of the People's Republic of China", the "Anti-subsidy Regulations of the People's Republic of China" and the "Regulations of Social Security Measures of the People's Republic of China".

Following the committed timetable of market opening, China is at present readjusting the structure of those administrative monopoly sectors and restructuring the government control system. Correspondingly, China is sorting out those laws and statutes that are not favorable to breaking up the monopoly and practicing competition, and is establishing a legal system that is in conformity with the philosophy of modern control. The related departments of the state are modifying or are ready to modify the "Electric Power Law", the "Aviation Law" and the "Railway Law", and are speeding up the legislation process of the "Telecom Law" and the "Petroleum and Natural Gas Law".

On the nationwide scale, China is giving an energetic impetus to managing the administration according to laws. In 2001, the most attractive measure taken in the field of administration law was that the State Council sorted out in an all-round way the administration statutes promulgated and implemented in the past and declared that 221 administration statutes were either annulled or invalid. Corresponding sorting was also done in various local governments and departments.

For creating even better judicial environments, China passed the amendment of the "Judge Law" and the "Prosecutor Law" in 2001. From 2002, all those trying to hold the post of judge, prosecutor and attorney-at-law should go though the centralized judicial examination held by the state to achieve the requisite qualifications. This is sure to bring about an even deeper reform in judiciary. In 2002, the Supreme People's Court drew up a plan for the court of China to undertake the judicial examination obligation corresponding to the WTO rules so that the independence and public conviction of the administrative judgment can be further heightened.

The Great Wall was not built in a day. Compared with those countries with the legal system comparatively well established, the legal environments of China are still to be improved. For several thousand years, China was under the traditional rule by man, lacking the foundation of the rule by law. The real construction of legal system started only around half a century ago, particularly since the reform and opening-up. Anyhow, in the short period of a few decades, China has had laws and regulations to go by for the fundamental aspects of the social life. To run the state affairs according to the laws has been defined as the general plan for managing the state affairs. This philosophy has been widely disseminated in the whole society. A virtuous relationship between the legislation and execution of the law is being gradually formed. Compared with many other countries, China spent much less time to obtain these achievements.

Education

China practices nine-year compulsory education system. During 1991~2001, the rate of going to elementary school for school age children reached 97.8~99.1%. The urban area in big cities and the economically developed area along the coast have started to make senior-high education universal.

MBA, One of the Most Popular Academic Credentials in China in Recent Years

More and more people are receiving university education in China. In 2001, the rate of colleges and universities enrollment was 11% and the university student at school was 14% of the total number of the young people at the same age. For meeting the ever-increasing demand for intermediate and senior talented people raised by the rapid economic development, colleges and universities have expanded the number of enrollment in recent years with the range of expansion over 20% each year. In 1998, the enrollment of institutions of higher learning nationwide was 1,080,000 students and in 2001, it was expanded to reach 2,680,000. According to the plan of the Ministry of Education, the enrollment will keep on expanding in 2001~2005.

In 2001, China worked out an "Outline of 10th Five-Year (2001~2005) Plan for National Economy and Social Development" (the "10th Five-Year Plan" for short), defining the overall target for national economy and social development in the following five years. The primary expected target for educational development is as follows:

Elementary education will leap onto a new stage of nationwide universal education. The scope of population coverage for nine-year compulsory education will be expanded, striving to make elementary education basically universal in the outlying poverty-stricken areas in the mid-western region and the minority nationality regions and the gross rate of junior-high students at school over 90% all over China.

The junior-high students in cities and towns after completing junior-high education can basically enter senior-high school. Efforts will be made to make senior-high students at school (including ordinary education, vocational education and adult education) reach 46,000,000 on the basis of 27,000,000 in 2000 so as to make the gross rate of senior-high students at school rise from 44% to around 60%, basically achieving the target for junior-high students after completing junior-high education to enter senior-high stage.

By speeding up development paces of institution of high learning, the students at school are expected to increase from 11,000,000 in 2000 to 16,000,000, the number of postgraduates to 600,000, and the gross rate of colleges and universities enrollment over 15%.

Educational informatization will be basically realized. Efforts will be made to speed up the establishment of nationwide informatization network that covers various levels and various kinds of education. In 2005, campus network will be set up in all institutions of higher learning in China, and the Internet will be linked to all colleges and universities, overwhelming majority of senior-high schools and part of junior-high and elementary schools; and distance learning network will basically cover all junior-high stage education and part of elementary school.

The communication between ordinary education and vocational education will be strengthened. A framework of lifelong educational system will be established by promoting the mergence between school education and outside school training and developing and perfecting adult education and training, and the forms and systems of distance learning and self-study examination.

For realizing the above-mentioned targets, the "10th Five-Year Plan" puts for-

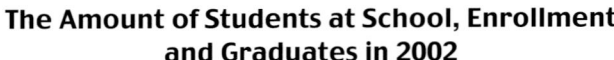

The Amount of Students at School, Enrollment and Graduates in 2002

(Unit: 00,000 People)

	Postgraduate Student	Institution of High Learning	High School	Elementary School
Students at School	50.1	903.4	9415	12157
Enrollment	20.3	320.5	3371.2	1952.8
Graduates	8.1	133.7	2601.3	2351.9

ward that in 2005 the state financial expenditure on education will account for 4% of the GDP.

Science and Technology

At present, China has already formed a quite complete system for scientific research and technical development with scientific and technical development level, as a whole, ranking at the forefront of developing countries. In 2001, the number of full-time scientists and engineers engaged in R&D reached 700,000 people/year and the amount of patent authorization to domestic residents reached 165,000 items. China has resolved a batch of key technical issues in the construction of national economy, achieved a rather great development in high-tech studies and industrialization, and produced a fairly important influence worldwide on basic researches.

In 1995, the Chinese government declared to carry out the strategy of "reviving the nation through science and education" and put forward the strategic target for scientific and technical development: in 2010, the scientific and technical strength in major branches of learning and some domains of high-tech will approach or reach world advanced level; the ability of creation by acting on our own will improve by a big margin and the key technology and systematic design technology of major industries will be mastered; and the production technology in major industries will approach or reach world advanced level, and the production technology of some newly-developed industries will reach world advanced standard.

During the "10th Five-Year Plan", the targets for developing science and technology in China are as follows:

There will be a big raise of technological level in industry and international competitive power. The technical standard in the main realms of agriculture, industry and service sector will reach the standard of the mid-1990 developed countries and some realms will be among the world advanced rank.

There will be some breakthrough in basic researches and strategic high-tech researches. In 2005, some major scientific fields and strategic technical fields will approach or reach the world forward position and a number of creative scientific

research achievements with great international influence will be made.

Scientific and technological support will be provided for the coordination and development of population, resources and environments. A comparatively perfect scientific and technical working system will be established to protect the ecological environments, to improve population quality, to raise living quality, to increase the efficiency of resources utilization and to heighten the ability of reducing and preventing disasters, social security and services so as to speed up the rapid development of various social undertakings and related industries.

There will be an obvious growth in science and technology by the whole society. In 2005, the proportion of R&D funds invested in science and technology by the whole society will be raised over 1.5% of the GDP; the investment in R&D made by enterprises will account for the proportion of over 50% of the investment made by the whole society; and the investment in R&D made by high-tech enterprises will account for over 5% of the annual sales income.

Scientific and technical talents will be able to meet the continuous demands for development. In 2005, the full-job scientists and engineers engaged in R&D activities nationwide will be over 900,000 people/year.

The infrastructure of science and technology will be perfected step by step. Several new items of major scientific engineering with international standard will be established and a number of first-rate bases for scientific researches with international level will be completed as well so that basic conditions and infrastructures for scientific researches can be obviously improved, resources can be shared by all and the ability to ensure scientific and technical activities can be heightened.

FINANCE

The structure of banking system of China is like this. Under the central bank, the state-owned commercial bank is the nucleus of the financial market and the others are the non-bank institutions controlled by state capital, such as trust and investment company, securities company, insurance company, and financial company. In addition, there are also the branch banks of foreign-funded banks and representative offices. The banking industry, securities industry and insurance industry in China are run and supervised according to their respective sectors.

In accordance with the present statutes, the main principles for separated operation of financial industry are that the commercial bank, the securities company and the insurance company are not allowed to hold each other's stock shares and their business scopes are not allowed to be crossed with each other; commercial bank, securities company and insurance company are not supposed to hold the stock shares of trust and investment company but trust and investment company is allowed to hold stock shares of securities company; and trust and investment company, as a non-financial group company, is allowed to make investment in commercial bank, securities company and insurance company.

Banks

The bank system of China includes central bank, policy bank, commercial bank exclusively owned by the state, stock-system commercial bank, city commercial bank and urban and rural credit cooperative, trust and investment company, and other non-bank financial institutions.

The central bank is the People's Bank of China, a state organ under the leadership of the State Council to manage national financial undertakings with stabilization of currency and supervision of banking as its main duty. In 1998, the People's Bank of China carried out important reforms in its organ setup. Instead of setting up branch banks in line with administrative areas, several branch banks going beyond the province, autonomous region and municipality directly under the Central Government are set up all over China. In the provincial capital city with no branch bank set up, a banking supervision office was set up as the agency of the branch bank responsible for supervising bank and non-bank institutions within its jurisdiction. The central branch bank of the provincial capital city is no longer under the jurisdiction of a

A Forest of Bank Signs, Both Foreign and Chinese, along a Street in Pudong, Shanghai

Stock Market and Stock Speculators

certain province. This is advantageous to the People's Bank to get rid of administrative interference and gives it full play to exercising its supervision duty.

The policy bank is a specialized bank to provide fund support to the economic policy of the state. Its administrative principle is to exercise fund management in a planned way, to finance and use the funds in a directional way, to strive for self-balance, and to maintain the capital in running business instead of making profits. At present the policy bank is a step to promote the reform of commercialization of the special bank. There are three policy-related banks for the time being: the state development bank, the import and export bank of China and the agricultural development bank of China. The primary prospective borrowers are policy-related projects and their matched engineering of the basic industries and the pillar industries that have been approved by the state to set up the project, medium- and large-sized capital constructions, and technical transformation. The agricultural development bank of China is primarily to undertake the banking business related to the agricultural policies laid down by the state, acting on the financial funds to support agriculture. The import and export bank of China is primarily to provide export credit for exporting large-scale complete sets of equipment and mechanical and electrical products. During the operational process of the project, the policy bank generally entrusts the commercial bank to undertake the operation of concrete business.

The commercial bank is a main component part of the Chinese banking system, which mainly consists of two parts. One part is the state commercial bank transformed from the original specialized bank, including the Industrial and Commercial Bank of China, the Bank of China, the Agricultural Bank of China and the China Construction Bank. These state-owned commercial bank are the leading force in the present Chinese banking system, having huge assets and a large network of banking establishments, but the problem of non-performing loans formed in the history is rather glaring. The other part is the other commercial banks newly set up or restored after the reform and opening-up. Due to the fact that at the initial state of operation they were not restricted by the specialty division but practiced standardized management instead and they did not have heavy burden of non-performing creditor's rights, their business size is expanding with each passing day. They have become a new force in the system of commercial banks in China, comparatively close to the conventional commercial banks in the world.

There are various kinds of banking business available in China. Take the credit funds of the commercial bank for instance, the loan scope includes short-term working loan, technical transformation loan, fixed assets loan, and consumption loan; the business scope includes Chinese currency business, foreign exchange business and intermediate business; and the business varieties have developed from simple deposit, loan, and transaction to comprehensive banking services such as investment consultation, personal management of money matters, on-line banking and E-business.

In the aspect of measures for readjustment and control, since 1998, the People's Bank of China has rescinded the loan quota for state-owned commercial banks and practiced a new management system of "planned guidance, self balance, proportional management and indirect readjustment and control" on the basis of promoting the management of assets and liabilities proportion and risk management. The people's bank mainly uses the tools of financial policy, such as the rate of reserve against deposit, interest rate, open market operation, foreign exchange operation and re-discount to readjust the amount of currency supply.

The terminal target of the Chinese money policy is to maintain stability of the RMB currency for promoting economic growth. To maintain stability of the RMB currency does not mean to keep the prices fixed but to maintain relative stability of the prices in the domestic market and the RMB exchange rate from the considerations of actual conditions of China. From October 1997, the general price level in China started negative growth and in 1998 signs of deflation started. For coping with this situation, the Chinese government adopted the policy of expanding demands, carried out active financial policies and at the same time other policies were comprehensively used to readjust and control the macro economy. At the same time to use the policy tool of diverse currencies to readjust and increase the currency supply, a number of credit policy measures were unveiled to expand domestic demands and promote the readjustment of economic structure. Expected effects were achieved.

Securities Business

In late 1980's, varies kinds of securities businesses in China grew out of nothing, developed from small to large and from a regional market swiftly into a nationwide market with considerable size. At present, the securities market include bond certificate market, stock market, fund market and commodity futures market. The business undertaken by the securities management organs includes sale of securities, self-operation of buying and selling securities, agent of securities transaction, securities mortgage and financing, company's financial consultant, enterprise reorganization, acquisition and integration, and fund and assets management. The securities management institutions are not allowed in any form to manage deposit business, to pay interest for the margins, and undertake any lending business with the exception of securities mortgage loan

There are two securities exchanges in China, namely, the Shanghai Securities Exchange and the Shenzhen Securities Exchange. At present, the stock delivery volume of the Shanghai Securities Exchange is the third largest securities exchange in Asia, only behind Tokyo and Hong Kong. The negotiable securities that are allowed to be listed in the securities exchanges mainly include varies kinds of bond securities issued by the state, various kinds of construction bond securities issued by provincial people's government or the local government corresponding to the provincial level, various kinds of bond securities issued by financial institutions, enterprise bond securities publicly issued nationwide, and stocks and various kinds of right-benefited vouches.

China practices centralized and unified supervisory system and the China Securities Regulatory Commission (CSRC) is the management institution of the securities market. Securities company and trust and investment company have set up their respective business institutions in medium and large cities of China and their major technical means and ways all reach world advanced level. All stocks and funds are issued and transacted without any paper and all the securities management institutions follow the unified technical standard.

Financial Market

Financial market is a place for financing funds and buying and selling negotiable securities, generally composing of two parts: the monetary market and the capital market.

Before the reform and opening-up, what China practiced was planned economy and capital was disposed by plans. Therefore, there existed basically no genuine financial market. But since the reform and opening-up, China has cultivated and standardized the financial market in an active way and has established and perfected step by step a monetary market, a bill market, a market of treasury bond and bond repurchase, and a stock market.

Monetary Market   The monetary market is the main place for the central bank to readjust and control finance. The monetary market of China includes inter-bank borrowing market, bond repurchase market, and the market of buying and selling ready bills, of which the most important one is inter-bank borrowing market.

The inter-bank borrowing market refers to the behavior of short-term fund financing between financial institution with legal person qualifications and branch institution of non-legal person financial institution authorized by legal person with the purpose of regulating money supply and temporary fund balance. The inter-bank borrowing in China was developed in 1986. Today, the main transaction body of the inter-bank borrowing market has been expanded from the initial sixteen head offices of commercial bank to a few hundred various kinds of financial institutions, including head offices of commercial bank and their authorized branch banks, insurance companies, securities companies, securities investment funds firms, and the united cooperatives of rural credit cooperatives. The total sum of deposits and assets of all the members accounts for over 95% of the Chinese financial system.

Foreign Exchange Market   During the period of planned economy, what China practiced was a highly-centralized foreign exchange administration system. It

Promotion Activities of Stores for Complimentary Insurance on Condition of Patronage

Yearly Average Exchange Rate between RMB and Chief Foreign Exchanges
(Intermediate Price)

Unit: RMB/Yuan

Year	US$ (100)	Japanese Yen (100)	H.K.$ (100)
1993	576.20	5.2020	74.41
1995	835.10	8.9225	107.96
1997	828.98	6.8600	107.09
1999	827.83	7.2932	106.66
2000	827.84	7.6864	106.18
2002	827.70	6.6237	106.07

was reformed later. The main content of the reforms is to combine planned administration with market regulation, to reduce mandatory foreign exchange planning, to expand guided foreign exchange planning, to establish foreign exchange regulation market and to make use of the function of market regulation. Since 1994, China has realized the merge of official exchange rate with the exchange rate of the regulation market, forming a unitary and manageable floating exchange rate system on the basis of market supply and demand. In December 1996, exchange of the RMB under the frequent item was realized and now even exchange of the RMB under the capital item is also partly realized.

The international revenue and expenditure of China has always been maintained in a good state and the exchange rate of RMB stable. In August 2002, foreign exchange reserve reached US$ 253 billion. China's share in the International Monetary Fund has been raised from the eleventh to the eighth place. So far, the RMB of China is still not a free convertible currency yet and the exchange rate between the RMB and the US dollar is around 8.27: 1. With the growth of foreign exchange reserve, China will relax step by step the control over capital transaction so as to promote the convertibility of the capital item.

Stock Market   In the past ten years the stock market of China has traveled the path for some developed countries to travel for several decades. In 1992, the securities market of China was only at an initial pilot stage in Shanghai and Shenzhen but in September 2002, the listing companies within the boundaries of the Chinese territory reached 1,212 with the total market value of 4,500 billion yuan, accounting for approximately 50% of the GDP.

During the economic system reform and opening to the outside world, the reform in financial system was once long considered lagged behind and restricting the development of enterprises. But after the economic crisis in Southeast Asia, quite a number of people rejoiced to see that the financial opening-up in China was not out of control but some were worried about the increasing hidden danger of the non-performing creditor's rights. It can be clearly seen that the development of Chinese financial market is a complicated process full of disputes. Compared with other countries, the financial market of China had quite a large room but also gigantic potentiality for development. The profit space produced by the existing distance has made China one of the few markets with profitable prospects. This is the most fundamental reason why foreign-funded financial institutions are swarming into China. With their accession, they bring about competition mechanism into China. The market share varies with various companies, some going up and some coming down, but the absolute volume of the market business will constantly grow. After entering the WTO, the financial sector of China is further quickening its steps in reform and opening-up and is blending with the process of international financial competition and cooperation on an even larger scale and an even deeper depth. In May 2002, the president of the People's Bank of China delivered a speech at the Congress of the World Savings Bank Association to the effect that:

The reform of state-owned commercial bank must be sped up in line with the requirements of establishing a system of modern financial enterprises. The target is to transform the four state-owned commercial banks with sole investment into modern large-scale competitive commercial banks within five years or a little longer. The state-owned commercial banks with sole investment, in case of availability of necessary conditions, will be reformed into stock-system commercial banks with the state holding the shares. The present main task is to perfect the structure of legal person control, lower the ratio of non-performing loans and digest the financial burden left over by the history so that the capital sufficiency rate can meet the international criteria.

The level of laying down and executing monetary policy will be raised. A steady monetary policy will be kept executing and the strength to support economic development with finance will be further strengthened so as to prevent deflation and maintain the currency stable. The floating range of interest rate will be expanded so as to promote the reform of marketization of RMB interest rate in a steady way. The connection between the currency market and the capital market will be further standardized so as to pursue diversification of financing channels and proper proportional relationship and to support a healthy development of capital market from the system.

The financial supervision level will be heightened and the interests of depositors, investors and nationwide taxpayers will be maintained. During a rather long period in the future, China will still carry out the practice of divided management and divided supervision for the sectors of bank, securities and insurance. Since 2002, the measure of five-level classification management for the loan quality of all commercial banks has been carried out and the system of retrieve and cancel after verification of the reserve fund for bad account has been established in reference to international common practice. Cautious accounting system will be practiced so as to raise the actual profit level of commercial banks. The transparency of information disclosure will be improved.

The manageable floating exchange rate system decided by market supply and demand will be further perfected. Under the prerequisite of maintaining RMB basically stable, a mechanism will be gradually formed to perfect the RMB exchange rate. With the growth of foreign exchange reserve, the control over capital transaction will be gradually lifted so as to promote the exchangeability of capital item.

COMMUNICATIONS

In China, the slogan "In order to get wealthy, pave the road first" like this can be seen in many places. Since the reform and opening, the state has adopted the forms of government investment, collection of social funds and utilization of foreign funds to increase more investment and give corresponding policy support to road construction with artery railway, freeway, hub airport and international shipping center as key

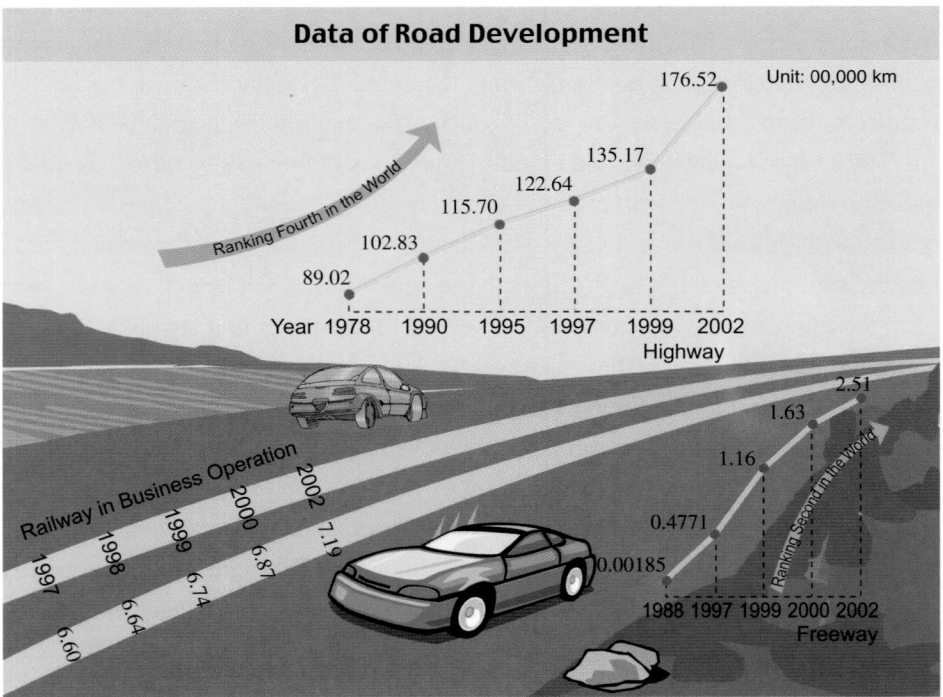

Data of Road Development

Unit: 00,000 km

Highway:
1978 — 89.02
1990 — 102.83
1995 — 115.70
1997 — 122.64
1999 — 135.17
2002 — 176.52

Ranking Fourth in the World

Freeway:
1988 — 0.00185
1997 — 0.4771
1999 — 1.16
2000 — 1.63
2002 — 2.51

Ranking Second in the World

Railway in Business Operation:
1997 — 6.60
1998 — 6.64
1999 — 6.74
2000 — 6.87
2002 — 7.19

points.

Take freeway as an example. The first freeway in China's mainland was completed and open to traffic in 1988 but at the end of 2002 the freeway in China reached 20,000 kilometers, ranking second in the world. It only took a little more than a decade for China to finish the same course that generally took developed countries to go through for forty years. Today, the time needed for driving from Shenyang to Beijing is shortened from the original seventeen hours to six hours. The southwest highway is a thoroughfare leading to the sea. One can go through Sichuan first, then enter Guangxi by Guizhou, and finally reach the coastal city Beihai directly. Now it takes only twenty hours or so but it used to take a few days.

Of course, what China can be proud of is not only highway but also railway and civil aviation. Generally speaking, a fairly perfect transport system is available in China now. The system includes airport and seaport facilities with advanced technology, the highway system that radiates in all directions, convenient railway system and many important inland river channels, basically forming a high-speed channel framework for passenger transport with Beijing, Shanghai and Guangzhou as centers.

Comparatively speaking, the traffic network in east area is denser and transport is more convenient. Though west area is backward, the infrastructure construction, communications included, has been listed as one of the key projects in its development. Those ambitious schemes and investment plans with huge amount of funds are being gradually realized. Railway or highway open to traffic is frequently reported in the news.

Railway Transportation

For quite a long time, railway transportation has been the main force of transport sector in China. But in recent years, due to the development of highway and civil aviation, the share of railway in the transport market is dropping. Compared with 1980, the rotation volume of cargo transport handled by railway in 2001 dropped from 48 to 31.4% and the rotation volume of passenger transport from 60.6 to 36.8%. In spite of this, in the various kinds of transport, the rotation volume of cargo transport and passenger transport handled by railway still ranks first in China.

At the end of 2001, the railway of China in business operation reached 70,100 kilometers, running through thirty provinces and regions all over China with the exception of Tibet. Now the state is speeding up the construction of the Qinghai-Tibet railway, which is expected to be open to traffic in 2007. The completion of this railway will be of far-reaching significance to the promotion of economic and social

Engineering Equipment Ready for Being Shipped
for Construction of Qinghai-Tibet Railway

development in Tibet.

The Chinese railway network is mainly composed of a few artery railway lines that run through the south and north in lengthwise and the east and west in breadthwise, in addition to many branch railway lines and local railways and a dozen lines that link up with Russia, the Democratic People's Republic of Korea and Viet Nam. At present, the railway distribution is not very even, mainly in northeast area and east coastal areas. The state is speeding up the construction and transformation of artery railway lines, giving priority to the central west areas, paying special attention to solving insufficient transportation capacity in the southwest areas and improving the modernization of the artery line facilities.

Since 1997, railway has successfully increased the train speed for four times on a large scale so that the speed of passenger train has been raised for 25% on the average. With the impact of speed, the railway sector has also quickened its step into the market. Different kinds of trains are in operation one by one, such as high-speed train, start-at-dusk-and-arrive-at-dawn train, tourism train, holiday train and special train for luggage and packages. The service is continuously being improved. According to the "10th Five-Year Plan" of the Ministry of Railway, railway will have two more speed increases before 2005. At that time, a network of high-speed transport for railway passengers covering the main cities nationwide will be initially completed and the maximum speed of special passenger train will reach 200 kilometers/

hour and the speed of ordinary passenger train on busy lines will universally reach 160 kilometers/hour.

Highway Transportation

China has a well-developed highway network, reaching 99% villages and towns and 19% of administrative villages. In 2002, the total highway reached 1,700,000 kilometers. Compared with 1980, the rotation volume of cargo transport handled by highway in 2001 rose from 6 to 13.8% and the rotation volume of passenger transport from 32 to 54.2%.

In 1985, Chinese mainland started to build the first freeway. Since then, it has developed at a very rapid pace and artery freeways running to all directions have been completed one by one. In 2001, freeways have run through all provinces (autonomous regions and the municipalities directly under the Central Government) with the exception of Tibet. Not only have the freeways promoted the rapid development of long-distance bus with sleeping berth, special transport with refrigeration truck to preserve freshness, container and ultra large cargo but also brought about competitions with railway and civil aviation in passenger transport market. As a result, consumers can gain more substantial benefit from the competitions.

The national artery composed of high-grade highway mainly for auto use has become the main framework of highway network. At present, the national artery runs through all provincial capitals and links up all big cities with population of over one million and most of the cities with population of over half a million. In addition to the ever-developing infrastructure of highway transportation, excellent equipment for highway transportation is also available in China. Highway transportation is developing towards the direction of large scale and specialization.

Waterway Transportation

The waterway transportation sector of China includes deep-water freight transportation for foreign trade and domestic trade, and cargo transport of big rivers and inland rivers. Ordinary cargo is usually shipped by cargo liners arranged by public transport department while dry and bulk cargos mainly by special freighters.

Waterway transportation is mainly distributed along the coastal areas in the east and south areas. Compared with 1980, the rotation volume of cargos handled by waterway transportation increased from 42 to 53.2% in 2001 while that of passengers decreased from 5.7 to 0.8%.

The total length of inland river is 110,000 kilometers, of which the channels that can navigate for 1,000-tonnage ships are over 7,800 kilometers. The main inland channels are the Yangtze River, the Pearl River and the Heilongjiang River. There are over 8,000 dock berths at the main ports, over 40 of which are 10,000-tonnage berths. The important river ports are Chongqing, Wuhan, Nanjing, Shanghai, Guangzhou and Harbin.

The rotation volume of cargos handled by ocean shipping accounts for 70% of that handled by waterway transport. Over 85% of China's foreign trade cargos are handled by ocean shipping. The coastal navigation line can be divided into north navigation area with Dalian and Shanghai as the center and the south navigation area with Guangzhou as the center. There are 60 harbors along the coastal areas and 640 berths for 10,000-tonnage ships. At the end of 2001, there were seven big harbors with annual cargo-handling capacity over 100 million tons, i.e. Shanghai Harbor, Guangzhou Harbor, Ningbo Harbor, Tianjin Harbor, Qinhuangdao Harbor and Dalian Harbor. Eight harbors can handle over one million TEU's annually, of which Shanghai Harbor and Shenzhen Harbor ranked fifth and eighth respectively in the world. Harbor construction, particularly the construction of multi-functional and comprehensive large-scale hub harbor, has always been the key issue in the development of waterway transportation in China. The main harbors along the coast are all generally linked up with inland hinterland by high-grade highway and artery railway. A shipping system for international containers, linked up with ocean shipping, harbor loading and unloading and inland scatter and transport, has basically taken shape.

Home sedans speeding along the streets

Civil Aviation Transportation

Ten years ago, to travel by plane was a sign for the Chinese to show position or wealth. But now, it is something very common. The frequency of flights between big cities is very high. Take the flight from Beijing to Shanghai for instance. There are over forty flights a day, one flight every ten minutes or so on the average. The modes of booking plane ticket are also many and varied, such as E-ticket and on-line ticket.

In 1990, there were only 385 domestic airlines in China. But in 2001, there were 143 civil aviation airports and 1,143 airlines, 134 international and 1,009 domestic. The civil aviation of China, taking Beijing, Shanghai and Guangzhou as hubs, flies to all the main cities at home and many cities abroad. In 2001, the total rotation volume of air transport of the CAAC reached 14.1 billion ton/kilometers, ranking sixth in the world. In the total rotation volume of passenger transport, the proportion of the CAAC accounted for 8.2%.

China is in possession of an airport network with fairly considerable size for air transportation of domestic and international cargos. So far as business volume is concerned, the three largest airports are the Beijing Capital International Airport, the Shanghai Hongqiao International Airport and the Guangzhou Baiyun International Airport. In addition, there are also quite a number of airports, large, medium and small, distributed in various provinces, cities and regions nationwide.

In October 2002, the CAAC declared to separate government functions from enterprises and founded three major air transport groups, China Air Group Corp., China Eastern Air Group Corp., and China Southern Air Group Corp.

The main targets for the development of communications and transportation in China during the period of the "10th Five-Year Plan" are as follows:

Five systems of transportation will be developed and perfected, namely, rapid transport of passengers between cities, transport of passengers in big cities, transport of containers, transport of large volume of goods and materials, and transport of special goods. The development of intelligent communications will be sped up with informatization and networking as the basis. The construction of infrastructure for postal service will be continuously strengthened. The reforms of management system and management mechanism of communications and transportation with the separation of government functions from enterprise management as the basis will be sped up. Railway will practice "separation of net from transport", civil aviation airports and harbors will be lowered to the locality for management, and air transport enterprises will be reorganized to form big groups.

In line with the analysis of demands and calculation with various ways, the average annual growth rate of Chinese cargo transport in the period of the "10th Five-Year Plan" will be around 3.5%, of which 2% for railway, 5.7% for highway and 3% for waterway, around 5.5% for cargo handling capacity of the main ports along the sea, and around 13% for air transportation; and the growth rate of passenger transport will be around 7%, of which 4.6% for railway, 7.9% for highway and 8~10% for air.

In the respect of highway, the construction of national artery highway network with "five in lengthwise and seven in breadthwise" will be sped up, linking up the "three in lengthwise and two in breadthwise" in an all-round way. The construction of the eight new thoroughfares in the west will be started, perfecting the highway network structure and improving the depth of the highway network extension. In 2005, the highway length opening to traffic will reach 1,600,000 kilomoters, of which 25,000 kilometers are freeway.

In the respect of railway, the main railway throughway of "eight in lengthwise and eight in breadthwise" will be built and reformed, expanding the western railway network, quickening up the technical reform of the existing railway lines and raising train speed. The Qinghai-Tibet railway, the Beijing-Shanghai high-speed railway and the railways leading out of the territory in northwest and southwest will be built. In 2005, the railway in business operation will reach 75,000 kilometers. Track transport in big cities will also be developed.

In the respect of water transportation, the construction of large-scale container transport system at the main hub harbor along the sea, the transport system for specialized bulk cargos and sea-going channels of the main harbors will be strengthened, and the international shipping center in Shanghai will be constructed. In 2005, deep-water berths along the coastal harbors will reach 800. The construction of main water transport channels for the Yangtze River, the Pearl River and the Beijing-Hangzhou Grand Canal will be strengthened and inland river navigation will reach 110,000 kilometers, 8,800 kilometers of which are over 1,000-tonnage channels.

In the respect of civil aviation, priority will be given to the construction of branch airports and special favor will be given to west regions, perfecting the hub airport and artery airport and improving the technical equipment for air traffic control.

TELECOM

Telephone is available all over China, villages and towns. In China, there is no worry for telecom issue.

In 1991, the rate of telephone popularization was only 1.29% but at the end of

September 2002 it went up to 30% (of which 40% in urban areas) with 207,000,000 fixed-line subscribers, ranking first in the world. In 1990, there were only 18,000 mobile phone subscribers all over China but at the end of September 2002, subscribers reached 190,000,000, ranking first in the world and maintaining the trend of monthly increase of 5,000,000 new subscribers. In 1992, China started to construct, on a large scale, data communication network for public use, covering over 90% of counties and cities at present and becoming one of the largest public data communication networks in the world. At the end of 2001, Internet users surpassed over 36,000,000.

At the same time with an admiring speed of telecom development, both the service and price of telecom have had great changes. In 1995, the cost of installing a telephone for home use was around 3,600 yuan but now only 200~300; in 1996, a mobile phone cost around 7,000 yuan but now less than 2,000. The network of mobile phone in China has covered over 95% of counties and cities in China. Mobile communication network, data network and IP phone business have opened mobile wandering business with over 90 countries and regions, while Internet wandering business with over 160 countries and regions. Since 1990's, the Chinese telecom industry, having broken away from monopolization by reforms and reorganizations,

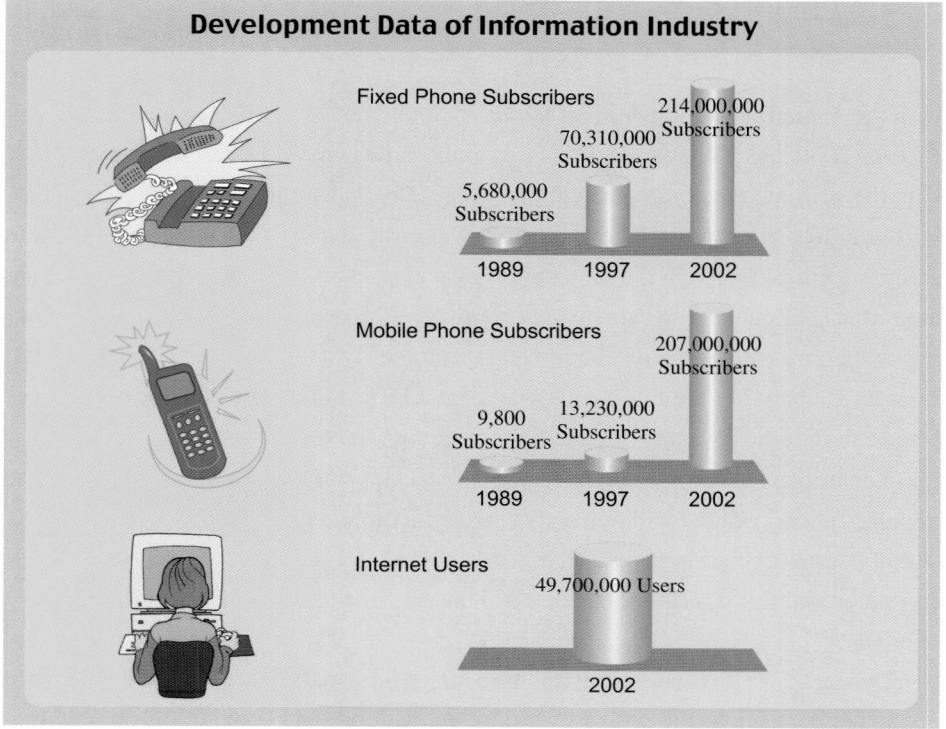

Development Data of Information Industry

Fixed Phone Subscribers
- 5,680,000 Subscribers — 1989
- 70,310,000 Subscribers — 1997
- 214,000,000 Subscribers — 2002

Mobile Phone Subscribers
- 9,800 Subscribers — 1989
- 13,230,000 Subscribers — 1997
- 207,000,000 Subscribers — 2002

Internet Users
- 49,700,000 Users — 2002

Part of Traditional Postal Business Being
Gradually Replaced by E-mail

has formed a situation of competition between several key enterprises and a large number of small and medium enterprises in the market of telecom and information service and is capable of providing several kinds of telecom services and facilities. Users are able to enjoy various kinds of telecom service, such as voice, data, written works and graphics.

In recent years, rapid development has been achieved in the application of information technology in China and the information technology and network technology are widely penetrating into various realms. In accordance with the related report, the NIQ of China in 2000 was 38.46. In the two years from 1998 to 2000, the NIQ rose 48.6%, an average annual growth of 21.9%, much faster than the national economic growth of 7~8%. The appearance of E-government affairs and E-business helps enterprises to lower costs and improve efficiencies. More and more cities, by using digital technology and network technology, are improving their management and investment environments. More and more people are receiving education, obtaining information and placing orders for something with Internet. Internet is changing the traditional way of working and business mode of Chinese people so that their way of life and habit is being affected.

According to the "10th Five-Year Plan", at the end of 2005, the rate of phone popularization in China will reach 40%, the total mobile phone subscribers over 260, 000,000, ranking first in the world in network size and capacity; social possession of computer will reach 60,000,000 sets; and the rate of popularization of Internet users over 8%.

During the "10th Five-Year Plan" five major information projects will be carried out so as to speed up the progress of national economy and social informatization.

These five major information projects are the project of developing information resources, the project of information infrastructure, the project of informatization application, the project of E-business and the project of information products. The project of developing information resources is to form initially an overall pattern for the development of information resources by constructing the project of fundamental national condition information, the project of macro economic information, and the project of public information resources. The project of information infrastructure is to make information infrastructure adapt itself to the needs of informatization construction by constructing the project of high-speed broadband networks, the project of mobile information networks, the project of urban informatization, and the project of informatization security system. The project of informatization application is to unfold and deepen in an all-round way the application of informatization by constructing the project of E-government affairs, the project of electronic medium, the project of network education, the project of social security informatization, and the project of the informatization of comprehensive improvement. The project of E-business is to make Chinese economy more competitive by constructing the project of E-business demonstration, the project of financial informatization, and the project of enterprise informatization. The project of information products, the last but not the least, is to improve by a big margin the supplying ability of information products by constructing the project of digital television, the project of integrated circuits, and the software project.

ENERGY

At present, a quarter of the world population still has no electricity for their daily life but China made electricity popularized in twenty years. Particularly from 1998, China made huge investment in three years for major infrastructure construction of power energy, such as popularization of electricity in rural areas, construction of new power grid for agricultural use, and reform of grid in urban areas. A few years ago, it was quite common to restrict use of electricity by cutting off the supply but now a policy of encouragement to use power is practiced instead. According to the data issued by the State Statistical Bureau, the energy generated nationwide reached 1,478 billion KWh at the end of 2001, ranking second in the world in both installed generator capacity and generated power, and over 98% of rural households were supplied with power.

The price of power in China increases basically from the west to the east successively. In the next few years, the state will keep on making investment in power construction. When the "West-to-East Power Transmission" project, which is still under construction, is completed, not only will more power be supplied but the price of power will also be kept down nationwide.

However, what has achieved rapid development is not only electric power. The entire energy industry of China has made considerable progress. At present, the energy consumption in China ranks second in the world.

In energy resources, China is rich in coal deposits, mainly distributed in North China and the northwest areas, and particularly abundant in Shanxi, Shaanxi and Inner Mongolia. The coal resource in Shanxi makes up over one-third of the total coal resource in China. High-energy consumption industries such as thermal power generation, iron and steel, and building materials are developing rapidly with the impact of investment, providing excellent demanding environments for the growth of coal production. Since 1989, coal output in China has been ranking first in the world. In 2001, the raw coal for output reached 964 million tons.

The reserve of hydraulic power in China is around 680 million kilowatts, ranking first in the world but most of them is not developed and utilized yet. The distribution of areas with resource of hydraulic power is very uneven, 70% in the southwest area. Calculated in line with rivers, the waterpower resource of the Yangtze River water system makes up 40% of the whole nation and that of the Yalu Tsangpo River water

Night Scene of Oilfield

system comes the second. The electrical energy production of the Yangtze River Three Gorges Hydroelectric Station, the largest hydroelectric station in the world beginning to construct in 1994, will reach 84.7 billion KWh annually. In 2003, the first generating set will start to generate electricity and the entire project will be completed in 2009.

The petroleum resources of China are mainly distributed in the Northeast, North China and Northwest, and the continental shelf along the coast also has considerate petroleum reserve. In recent years, great achievements have been made in both exploration and development of petroleum and natural gas. Restricted by possible supplied volume of resources, the domestic production is short of supply. Large volume has to be imported every year to meet the demand of economic growth.

The distribution of energy resources in China is uneven. The vast mid-western area is very rich in reserves of hydraulic energy and coal while the coastal area in the east with economy comparatively developed is poor in energy resources. China is speeding up the construction of energy development and energy base in the mid-west area, of which the two major projects are the "West-to East Power Transmission" and the "West-to-East Natural Gas Transportation".

China is a big nation in energy production and consumption in the world. In 2001, the total volume of energy production was 1.17 billion tons of standard coal and the total volume of consumption was 1.32 billion tons of standard coal. In the production composition of energy, raw coal plays the main role, making up 67.7%; then comes crude oil, 20.6%; and finally hydraulic power and natural gas, comprising 8.3% and 3.4% respectively. In the consumption composition of energy, it is more or less the same with coal making up 67%, petroleum 23.6%, hydraulic power 6.9% and natural gas 2.5% respectively. In addition, nuclear power has grown out of scratch and production ability of new energies, such as solar energy, wind energy and geothermal energy, is also improved to a certain extent.

The rapid growth of energy production tends to ease up in general the contradiction of energy supply and demand in China. Besides, the continuous optimization of energy structure has contributed a lot to the improvement of energy quality and efficiency of energy utilization and the atmospheric environments as well. The improvement of modernization level of energy industry has also brought about development of machinery manufacturing industry, electronic industry and other related industries at home. With the reform, the marketization level of Chinese energy sector has been further enhanced and the management system and price system are gradually adapting themselves with international practice. Coal price is basically no longer under control and the price of crude oil and oil products is geared up with international market.

Though China has become a big nation of energy production and consumption in the world, there are still some problems. The structure of energy varieties is irrational and supply of quality energy is insufficient. The proportion of coal in the structure of primary energy is too high and the gap between the supply and demand of oil at home is getting wider and wider with limited oil resources and with the output standing still. Since 1993, China has become a net petroleum import country from a net petroleum export country. The proportion of natural gas in the structure of energy is too low. The development of hydraulic power is also very low, accounting for only 18.5% and leaving the rich water energy resources in the western area not fully utilized.

During the "10th Five-Year Plan", the strategy for energy development in China is as follows. The first priority will be given to optimization of energy structure, striving to improve energy efficiency, protect ecological environment and speed up the development of the western area. The proportion of quality coal will be raised with coal as the fundamental energy. Attention will be given to both oil and natural gas, speeding up the exploration, development and utilization of natural gas, introducing foreign natural gas and increasing proportion of natural gas consumption. Efforts will be made to explore petroleum resources, developing petroleum resources in a rational way and making efforts to develop the offshore oil. Foreign resources will be used in an active way, setting up overseas bases to supply petroleum and natural gas and importing petroleum from different channels. Construction and transformation of grid in both urban and rural areas will be strengthened, constructing the three major channels in the north, center and south for transmission of electricity from the west to east regions and promoting the nationwide grid. The power structure will be further readjusted, making full use of existing power generation capacity, developing hydraulic power station and pit-mouth power plant with larger generating set and cutting down smaller thermal power plant in an active way, developing nuclear power plant appropriately and encouraging co-generation of power and power generation with comprehensive utilization. A number of large-scale waterpower stations and pit-mouth power plants will be started for construction. New energy and regenerable energy, such as wind energy, solar energy and geothermal energy, will be actively developed. The technology for economizing energy and comprehensive utilization of energy will be promoted.

The main target for energy development in the "10th Five-Year Plan" is that in 2005 the national output of primary energy is expected to reach 1.32 billion tons of standard coal, of which coal comprises 1.17 billion tons with an average increase of

3.23% annually, 165 million tons of petroleum keeping the same level as the year of 2000, fifty billion cubic meters of natural gas with an average increase of 13.19% annually, 355.8 billion KWh of water power with an average increase of 8.38% annually, and sixty billion KWh of nuclear power with an average increase of 29.67% annually.

In the respect of energy structure, the proportion of coal in the primary energy consumption in the year of 2005, compared with 2000, is expected to decrease 3.88 percentage points while the proportion of clean energy such as natural gas and water power to reach 17.88%, increasing around 5.6 percentage points.

INDUSTRIES AND MARKETS

ECONOMY IN GENERAL

Between 1979 and 2001, the average annual growth of the Chinese GDP was 9.3%, of which the average annual growth in 1990's was over 10%, and the average annual GDP growth per capita was 8.1%. In 2001, the Chinese GDP reached 9,593.3 billion yuan, ranking sixth in the world and the average GDP growth per capita was over USD 800, entering the rank of those countries with lower-medium incomes.

Since 1998, the Chinese GDP growth rate has maintained smoothly for four successive years around 7% to 8% with the average annual growth of 7.55%. Compared with 1990's, after the Chinese economic growth reached the peak of 14.1% in 1992, it tended to slide down gently for seven successive years between 1993 and 1999. And then with the promotion of the expansive financial policy, the downturn began to be reversed and the economic growth rose a bit in 2000. In 2001, under the situation of obvious retard of world economy, particularly in the general background with a few developed countries falling into economic recession and downturn in step with world economy, the Chinese economy still maintained a growth speed of 7.0%.

At present, the primary products and general industrial products manufactured in China rank first in the world, the proportion of agricultural laborers has come down from 70.5% at the initial stage of reform and opening-up to 50%, and the output value proportion of the secondary industry in the GDP is over 50%. All this shows that the process of Chinese industrialization has basically stridden the initial stage and entered the intermediate stage. Now China is promoting the upgrade of industrial structuring so as to bring about the quality of industrial growth and the improvement of international competitive power, to speed up transformation of traditional industries

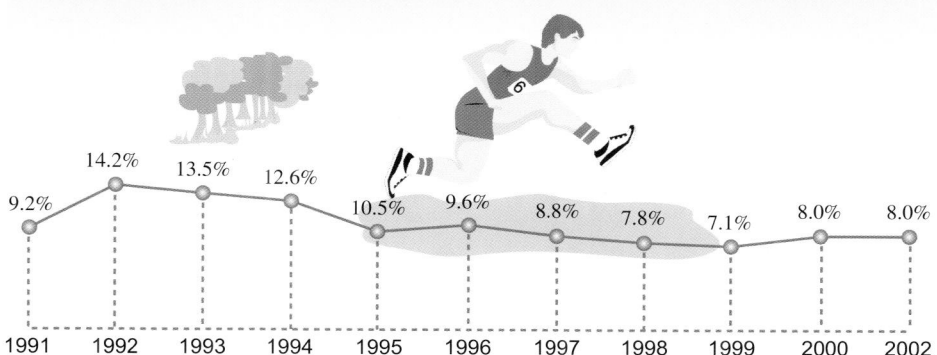

China's GDP Growth Rate between 1991 and 2002

9.2%   14.2%   13.5%   12.6%   10.5%   9.6%   8.8%   7.8%   7.1%   8.0%   8.0%

1991   1992   1993   1994   1995   1996   1997   1998   1999   2000   2002

and development of newly-developed industries, to promote coordinated development of marketization, urbanization and industrialization, to enhance proportion of
the output value of tertiary industry in the GDP, to promote transfer of surplus rural
laborers to non-agricultural industries, and to further promote the process of industrialization and transfer from a big industrial country to an industrial power.

In most of the years in the 20th century, the Chinese economy was basically operated in shortage of everything. After entering 1990's, the basic sectors of industry
like energy, communications and transport, postal service and telecom, important
raw materials, and infrastructures had a rapid development; the phenomenon of economic growth restricted by "bottleneck" industries was eased; seller's market was
being transferred to buyer's market for general industrial products; and the era of
commodities shortage went with the wind. Today, not only has a buyer's market
formed for the general industrial and agricultural products but also a buyer's market
has initially formed for the means of production. The factors that restricted economic development are primarily market demands; the way of development for enterprise is changed from scrambling for project, for investment and for expanding
production capacity to improving its nuclear competitive power; and the target of
government's macroeconomic policy lays emphasis on expanding the demands so as
to provide more employment opportunities and maintain social stability.

What must be pointed out here is that the status of supply of consumer goods and
means of production exceeding demand is only a relative surplus at a lower level.
The average income of the Chinese is still considerably low. In addition, due to the
fact that the supply structure cannot adapt itself to the changes of consuming structure,
there are large numbers of surplus low-level supplies but the supply of quite a number of products and services still cannot meet the demand.

Rolls-Royce on display

China practices an economic system with public ownership as the main body to develop diversified ownerships jointly. The economic composition can be divided into two categories. One is public economy, including state-owned economy and collective economy as well as the sections owned by the state and the collective in the mixed ownership. The other is non-public economy, including private economy, Hong Kong-Macao-Taiwan economy, and foreign-funded economy. With the breakup of the boundary between economies of different ownerships, a new form of owner-ship with cross holding of shares has emerged and the form of mixed ownership such as stock system, joint operation and enterprise group develops rapidly.

At present, state-owned economy, mixed economy and private economy take one-third of the GDP composition respectively, forming a pattern of tripod. The state-owned economy holds the absolute superiority in the infrastructure departments such as railway, civil aviation, postal service and telecom, and supply of water, elec-tricity and gas in urban areas as well as in the fields of scientific researches, education, national defense and banking.

Compared with the early 1990's, the output value of private business in 2001 increased 117 times and the total number of private enterprises increased 19.5 times in 2001. a large number of private enterprises have started to separate themselves from traditional industries such as retail, catering, service and repair, and aimed at the target of sectors with higher demands of knowledge, science and technology. Take the Zhongguancun High-Tech Park in Beijing for instance. Over 90% of the enterprises are private. Zhejiang, renowned as "a kingdom of small and medium enterprises (SMEs)", is the most developed province for SMEs in China, having over 600,000 various kinds of private SMEs, accounting for around 99% of the total number of enterprises in the whole province. After the unceasing development and capital accumulation, the size of development for more and more private enterprises is expanding with each passing day, and capital investment and grouping operation are also growing at a rapid pace.

At present, there are some major problems in the operation of national economy as follows. The deep-seated contradiction of economic structure and the issue of economic system are still rather prominent; the foundation for economic rise is still very unstable and the mechanism for continuous growth of social demand has not been completely formed yet; unemployment pressure is increasing, the growth of farmers' income is still fairly slow, and a part of masses is still leading a hard life; enterprises are not strong enough to make their own management decisions and new creations, neither to adapt themselves to the market, and the production and management of part of the enterprises are still very difficult; and the social economic order is to be further rectified.

The main targets for the development of national economy of the "10th Five-Year Plan" are as follows. The national economy will maintain a fairly rapid development speed with the expected average annual growth speed of around 7% and in 2005 the GDP calculated in accordance with the price of 2000 will reach 12,500 billion yuan and the GDP per capita 9,400 yuan on the average. New job opportunities in cities and towns and transfer of agricultural laborers will reach 40,000,000 people respectively and the registered unemployment rate in cities and towns will be controlled around 5%. Prices in general will be kept basically stable and international revenue and expenditure basically balanced.

INDUSTRIAL POLICIES

China classified economic activities into three industries and each industry includes several sectors: the primary industry is agriculture (including forestry, animal husbandry, fishery, etc.), the secondary industry is industry (including excavation industry, manufacturing industry, power supply, water supply, heat supply, etc.) and the tertiary industry includes all the other sectors not included in the primary and secondary industries, such as service sector and government organs.

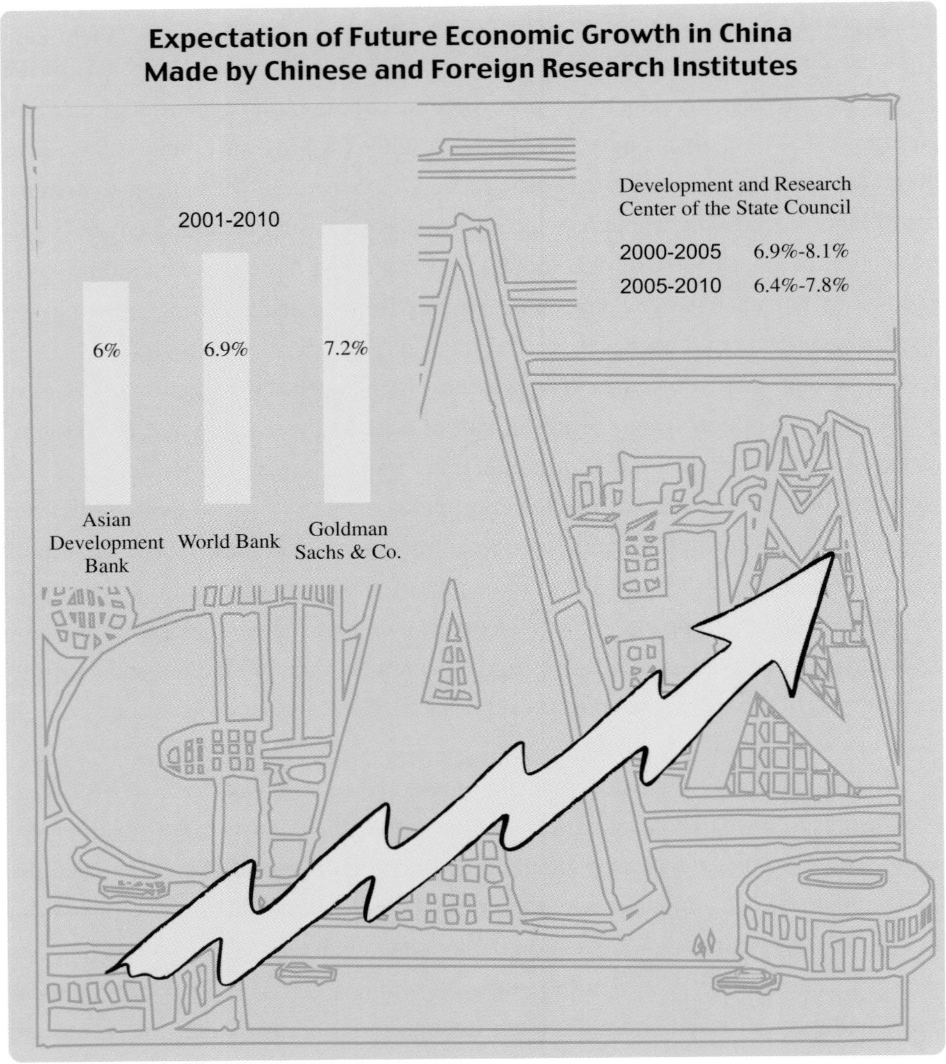

Expectation of Future Economic Growth in China Made by Chinese and Foreign Research Institutes

2001-2010

Development and Research Center of the State Council

2000-2005	6.9%-8.1%
2005-2010	6.4%-7.8%

6%

6.9%

7.2%

Asian Development Bank

World Bank

Goldman Sachs & Co.

Irrational industrial structure is one of the main issues facing the Chinese economic operation. That is why the "10th Five-Year Plan" has taken economic restructuring as the main line for economic and social development and industrial restructuring as the key to economic restructuring.

In 2001, the proportion of increased value of the three industries in the GDP was 15.9:50.9:33.2 and the rate of employment in the three industries was 52.9:23:24.1. Compared with world standard pattern, the output value proportion of the secondary industry was a little higher, the development of the tertiary industry lagged behind, the primary industry detained too much labor force, and urbanization was behind industrialization. The cause that led to the deviation of structure is mainly due to the economic development strategy of "giving priority to the development of heavy industry" long practiced before 1980's.

From a long-term point of view, the proportion of the output value of primary and secondary industries and the employment will be further decreased and the proportion of the tertiary industry will be continuously raised. Anyhow, the recent changes are mainly expressed in the mutual changeover between the output value of the primary and tertiary industries and the employment proportion, while the secondary industry will be kept at the present level. As China is situated at a time of rapid development for industrialization, the task for industrialization is far from completed. At this period of time, overwhelming majority of manufacturing industry will go on developing while part of the newly developed industry and the high-tech industry will undergo a rapid development.

The target of industrial restructuring for the "10th Five-Year Plan" is to consolidate and strengthen the fundamental position of agriculture, to speed up industrial reorganization and transformation and structural upgrading and optimization, to develop the service sector energetically, to speed up national economy and social informatization, and to go on with strengthening infrastructure construction. Mainly the following aspects will be made prominent:

1. At the same time to stabilize the grain production capacity, to optimize strains, improve quality and increase efficiency will be taken as the center for actively restructuring crop farming and speeding up the development of animal husbandry, forestry and aquatic products industry;

2. High-tech and appropriate advanced technologies will be used to transform and upgrade traditional industries, mainly expressed in technological transformation of key enterprises, in developing and manufacturing large-scale high-efficient and advanced technical equipment in complete sets, in developing large corporation and large enterprise group, and in transforming old industrial bases;

3. Those factories and mines turning out products with inferior quality, wasting resources, causing serious pollution, and with no safety in production will be continuously shut down in accordance with the law, backward production capacity will die out and surplus production capacity will be cut down;

4. High-tech industries will be developed and industrialization will be brought about by informatization, including the development of IT industry, biological engineering industry and new material industry, and giving full support to the development of broadband information network, key integrated circuit, new carrier rocket and software industry;

5. The construction of infrastructures like water conservancy, communication

and energy will be strengthened and special attention will be given to the issue of resource strategy;

6. The development of service sector will be sped up. Modern service sector will be actively developed and traditional service sector will be reformed.

In 2005, the increased value of the primary, secondary and tertiary industries will reach 13%, 51% and 36% respectively in the proportion of the GDP and the employed personnel will make up 44%, 23% and 33% respectively in the proportion of the employed personnel of the whole society.

At present, the Chinese Government is pushing forward and implementing the restructuring of five kinds of industrial policies.

1. Support-based industrial policy The state will make use of the measures of investing capital fund, financial discounting, issuing bonds, and debt-to-equity swap to support the development of the special industries, special enterprises and special products that play important roles in industrial upgrading;

2. Encouragement-based industrial policy During a certain period of time, the state will reduce or exempt from tax to encourage and develop the reform on traditional industries encouraged by the state, the growing strategic industries, and the growing strategic products;

3. Competition-based industrial policy Most sectors, most enterprises and most products belong to the sphere of competition-based industry with the exception of the sector related to the national security, the sector of natural monopoly, the sector providing important public goods and services, the pillar industries and the major key enterprises in the high-tech industries. The state will provide fair, just and transparent policy environments in the four aspects of fair investment tax policy, strict technical quality criterions, standardized the anti-monopoly laws and regulations, and rapid market information services so as to realize "survival of the fittest".

4. Limit-based industrial policy Limit-based industrial policy will be exercised to eliminate those industries that cause environmental pollution, that are backward in technology, and that produce much more products than needed.

5. Protection-based industrial policy Protection-based industrial policy will be applied to the two industries of agriculture and service sectors that are weak in international competition, particularly aiming at some infant industries, so that it will help to speed up the development of infant industries, agriculture and service sectors without going against the legal framework of the WTO but protecting the security of industries in an appropriate way.

In 2000, China revised and promulgated a "List of Industries, Products and Technologies Currently Encouraged by the State for Development" to encourage the development of 526 varieties of products, technology, part of the basic industries and service sectors in total, falling into 28 realms. These projects are in compliance with the following principles. 1. They are badly needed in the market at present and in a certain period of time in the future, having a vast range of prospects for development and beneficial to the exploration of the domestic market; 2. They contain considerable technological elements, beneficial to the promotion of upgrading enterprise equipment, to the progress of industrial technology, and to enhance the competitive power; 3. The technical foundation developing from R&D to the materialization of industrialization exists at home, beneficial to technological innovation and formation of new economic growing points; 4. They are in compliance with the strategy of sustainable development, beneficial to the economization of resources and improvement of ecological environments; and 5. The supplying ability lags comparatively behind but with the improvement of the supplying ability the rationalization of economic structure will be promoted and a continuous, rapid and healthy development of national economy will be kept on.

Now, on the one hand the supply of large numbers of products with low technology and low added value is beyond the demand in China but on the other quite a few high-tech achievements have not been commercialized or have been commercialized

The Amount of Investment for Basic Industries and Infrastructures between 1989–2001

The Amount of Investment for Capital Construction	6,251.6 billion yuan	Average Annual Growth (%)	25.4
The Sector of Agriculture, Forestry, Animal Husbandry, Fishery and Water Conservancy	495.5 billion yuan		27.5
Energy Industry	2,203.8 billion yuan		18.9
Raw Materials Industry	524.4 billion yuan		9.6
The Sector of Communication, Transportation, Postal Service and Telecom	2,299.8 billion yuan		27.9
The Sector of Urban Public Service	728.1 billion yuan		39.4

Data

The Seven Industrial Sectors To Be Developed

At present, the industrial sectors that are in the making and have great potentiality for development in China are newly-developed marine sector, environmental protection sector, relaxation sector, the sector of supporting the elderly, physical culture sector, the sector of agricultural science and technology, and the other sectors making the sector of agricultural science and technology complete.

Newly-developed Marine Sector   First of all, the explored offshore petroleum resources is less than 7% of the total volume of nationwide resources. Therefore, the development of petroleum exploration will be promoted from shallow sea to deep sea. Secondly, seashore tourism will be a fashion. Various resources for tourism have appeared along coastal cities and islands and islets. Thirdly, marine industries, such as marine pharmaceutics and health-care food, will be developed. Finally, because of a few cities are short of water resources, desalination of seawater and direct utilization of seawater have been listed by the Chinese government as key development projects for newly-developed marine sector.

Environmental Protection Sector   Experts predict that an investment of around 700 billion yuan is needed for environmental protection during the "10th Five-Year Plan". In accordance with the calculation that the annual income of environmental industry in 2000 was 1.6 times of the investment on environmental protection year on year, the total income from environmental industry in the "10th Five-Year Plan" will reach 1.1 trillion yuan, comprising approximately 1.8% of the year-on-year GNP.

Physical Culture Sector   Chinese people are paying more and more attention to sports activity but the development of sports economy has just started.

Relaxation Sector and the Sector of Supporting the Elderly   Chinese people are paying more and more attention to improving their quality of life and the proportion of expenditures on relaxation and health care are continuously rising. Simultaneously, China has entered an ageing population society and there is a very broad market for the sector of supporting the elderly.

Sector of Agricultural Science and Technology   The level of agricultural productivity in China is still not high enough and technological element is small. Therefore, it is an inevitable choice for the development of agriculture in China to raise agricultural labor productivity as well as the ratio of investment and production. The sector of science and technology related to agriculture is sure to become a new industry for development.

slowly. In 2001, the State Planning Commission and the Ministry of Science and Technology issued "A Guide to Key Fields of High-tech Industrialization for Preferential Development at Present" pointing out 141 key realms of high-tech industrialization for preferential development in China falling into ten major industries. They are information, biology and pharmaceutics, new materials, advanced manufacturing, advanced energy, advanced environmental protection and comprehensive utilization of resources, aviation and spaceflight, modern agriculture and modern communication.

According to the related planning, the proportion of the increased value of the Chinese high-tech industries in the GDP will be raised from 4% in 2000 to around 6% in 2005 and the proportion of the export volume of high-tech products in the export volume of industrial manufactured goods will be raised from 14.9% in 2000 to around 25% in 2005.

The working report of the central government of 2002 said that to further resolve the issues of the structural contradictions and system-based obstacles that had restricted the economic development was a fundamental measure to promote continuous growth in economy and improve economic quality and competitive power. First of all, for speeding up the optimization and upgrade of industrial structures, it is necessary to adopt high-tech and appropriate advanced technology to reform and upgrade the traditional industries. Supports should be given to key sectors and key enterprises as well as to the large manufacturing enterprises that have undertaken national key tasks for improving their ability of product development and technological innovation. The achievements made in washing out the backward production capacity in the sectors of textile, metallurgy and coal should be consolidated and expanded and the work to cut down the surplus and backward production capacity in the sectors of petrochemistry, building materials, machinery, pharmacy, sugar refinery, and tobacco should be continuously promoted. The energy structure should be continuously readjusted. Readjustment and transformation of old industrial bases should be sped up. Supports should be given to those cities and old mining areas with resource extraction as the main industry to develop continuous and replacement industries. Then, the development of high-tech industries such as information, biology and new materials should be sped up. Great attention should be continuously paid to the organization and implementation of the major projects in high-tech industrialization such as information networks, new electronic components and parts, integrated circuit, software, new materials and modernization of Chinese traditional medicine. A push should be given to national economy and social informatization. Finally, tertiary industry should be actively developed, particularly modern service sectors. The development of sectors such as banking, accounting, consultation and legal service should be expedited. The organization form and service form of chain management, logistic distribuiton, agency service and E-business should be gradually pursued. Major efforts should be made to develop tourism and cultural industry.

AGRICULTURE AND FARM PRODUCE MARKET

Resources

There are various kinds of land resources in China but there are more mountain areas than plains. Mountain areas, hilly areas and plateaus comprise 66% of the total land space in China. Besides, the proportion of semi-dry and dry areas is large, making up over 50% of the total land space. The farmland area of China is 127,000,000 hectares, approximately 7% of the farmland area in the world, mainly concentrated in plain and basin areas of monsoon regions in the east part. Crop farming is the most important department in agricultural production. The main cereal crops are paddy rice, wheat, corn and soybean while the main industrial crops are cotton, peanuts, rape, sugarcane and beet.

China is a country with less forest. The forest coverage in 2001 was 16.5%, doubled than that fifty years before. Natural forest concentrates and distributes in northeast and southwest areas. For environmental protection and economic construction, China, the largest country in the world with man-made forest area, has planted large numbers of wind-break forests, waterhead forests and forests for water and soil conservation. China is a "kingdom of bamboo". The area of bamboo groves, the volume of stored bamboo and the output of bamboo materials make up around one-third of the world's total volume respectively.

The grassland area of China is vast, comprising approximately one-fourth of the total area of China. The four major pastures are the Inner Mongolia Pasture, the Xinjiang Pasture, the Qinhai Pasture and the Tibetan Pasture. A number of animal husbandry bases scattered in the vast grassland extending over 3,000 kilometers from the northeast to the southwest can provide a large quantity of domestic animals, meat, milk and fur. In 2001, the proportion of the output value of animal husbandry made up as much as 30% of the total output value of agriculture. According to the "10th Five-Year Plan", the proportion is expected to reach around 33% in 2005.

The area of offshore waters in China is vast and the fishing ground at the shallow waters along the coast occupies 1,500,000 kilometers, making up one-fourth of the world's total fishing ground area at the shallow waters. The sea is extremely rich in aquatic products. Hairtail, large yellow croaker, little yellow croaker and cuttlefish are the four major economic fishes of China. Numerous rivers and lakes provide favorable conditions for developing the industry of freshwater aquatic products. Since 1990, the output of aquatic products of China has always been ranking first in the world, making up around one-sixth of the total aquatic products of the world.

Agricultural Development

In the history of China, agriculture was the base to build up the nation. But since 1950's China has started the construction of industrialization on a large scale. At the beginning of 1980's, agriculture made up around 32% of the GDP. Then the percentage gradually decreased, dropping to 15.2% in 2001. The proportion of agricultural laborers in the total employed dropped from 70.5% in 1978 to 50%, approximately 365,000,000 people.

In China, the land is owned by the state and the collective. During quite a long period of time after the founding of the PRC, under the strict system of planned economy, land, agricultural machinery and domestic animals were all managed by the collective and the state decided what the farmers should produce and how much they should produce; and farmers were not enthusiastic in production because of the distribution system that "all farmers get the same reward as everyone else regardless of one's performance in work". At the end of 1978, a reform started first in the rural areas. A kind of new management system was promoted on a nationwide scale, that

Countryside in Mountain Area

was a household contract responsibility system with remuneration linked to output. The so-called "remuneration linked to output" meant the payment of labor was mainly calculated on the basis of the quantity and quality of the laborer's end products and the "contract responsibility system" meant that the means of production or the management project owned by the collective was handed over to the household for management in accordance with a certain way of distribution laid down in the responsibility contract. By doing so, farmers' initiative for production was aroused. Later on, this system was gradually perfected, forming a system of unified management combined with independent management on the basis of the household contract responsibility system. Under such a system, the land is owned by the collective and the farmer household only has the right to use the land. On the basis of the household contract responsibility system with remuneration linked to output, a part of the land management is undertaken by the farmer household with independent management and a part is undertaken by the collective with unified management. That is why this kind of management form combined the unified management with independent management is called combination management system. The system features that what can be done by the household should be untaken to the best by the household itself while what cannot be done or cannot be done well can be managed by the collective. Generally speaking, in the comparatively developed area, the collective manages more content and more projects. Vice versa, the household manages more content and

Radio and TV Broadcasting Basically Popularized in Every Village in China

more projects. Today, some new economic forms and management forms, such as cooperation economy, stock cooperative system economy, unified economy and private economy, also have had a rather rapid development.

During the time of planned economy, the state carried out the policy of centralized procurement and centralized sale for farm products and sideline products, procuring the farm produce and sideline products at a low price and then supplying the urban residents in ration system also at a low price. In 1978, the agricultural produce under the management of centralized price by the state made up 94% of the total sum of the farm produce and sideline products sold by the farmers. Starting from 1980's, the state has carried a reform in the circulation system of agricultural produce and practiced a new policy of contracted procurement according to the national plan for a few major products such as grains and cotton. The produce not included in the contracted procurement can be sold freely or to the state according to agreement. Most of the other farm produce can be sold freely at the market and is no longer under the control of the state. The price fluctuates in response to the market conditions instead of being fixed by the state.

At the same time, the market of essential factors of production, such as rural area technologies, manpower, funds, information, etc. has also achieved a rapid development. The natural economy of self-sufficiency prevailing in the past few decades is fundamentally changed and a rather complete system for farm produce market has come into shape.

Since 1978, the annual growth rate of the gross output value of the Chinese agriculture has been 6.5% on the average, exceeding the average development level of the year-on-year world economy. Up to 1990's, shortage of agricultural products retarded the development of the Chinese agricultural economy. Affected by this shortage, the state paid more attention to the increase of total supplying volume than to the quality improvement of agricultural products when laying down the policy for agriculture. With a big increase in grains, animal husbandry, aquatic products, fruits and vegetables, urban residents' "vegetable basket" and "rice bag" are varied and abundant and the issue of adequate food and clothing is basically solved nationwide. The state has started to take active measures for agricultural restructuring with the market as the guidance to promote a diversified economy with great efforts under the prerequisite of ensuring stable growth of grain production. In the increased value of agriculture, the proportion of crop farming tends to decrease gradually and that of forestry, animal husbandry and fishery has increased a bit. In the recent two years, the state has turned its key point from the restructuring of agricultural economy to the improvement of the structure of agricultural products so as to meet people's demand for various kinds of agricultural products. Under the influence of readjustment and control of the national macro policy and market needs, farmers have also readjusted the varieties and quality of various crops of their own accords. Those products with inferior quality and bad market are gradually replaced by those with good quality and higher efficiency.

The issues of agriculture, rural areas and farmers are closely related to the issues of how China should develop and to what degree the development should be. The present agriculture of China still belongs to small-scale operation. Though labor cost is cheaper, productivity is low. Compared with big farms in developed countries, Chinese agriculture still lags far behind in the application of science and technology, marketing, business management, etc. In recent years, farmers' income grows slowly, directly affecting the consuming market. The transfer of surplus rural laborers, numbering over 100,000,000, needs to find a good way out with the help of the government.

The "10th Five-Year Plan" always puts agriculture at the first priority for the development of national economy so as to ensure agriculture to be developed continuously and steadily on the basis of enhancing the growth of over-all quality and efficiency and farmers' income in a rapid way. The main requirements of the "10th Five-Year Plan" for agricultural development are as follows: to keep steady the ability of grain production so as to ensure a basic balance between supply and demand of grains; to broaden the realm of increasing farmers' income; to readjust the structure of agriculture and rural area economy; to strengthen the infrastructure construction of agriculture and rural areas; to deepen the reforms in rural areas; and to provide assistance to poverty-stricken rural areas.

Major Agricultural Products

Since 1990's, the output of agricultural products in China such as cereals, meat, cotton, peanuts, rapeseed, fruit and tobacco has ranked first in the world; the output of tea and wool second in the world; that of soybean, sugarcane and jute third or fourth in the world but with less per capita possession on the average.

A report issued by the State Economic and Trade Commission states that in line with the calculation the total population of China in 2005 will be controlled within 1.33 billion and the annual growth rate of the Chinese economy during the "10th Five-Year Plan" is expected to be around 7% on the average. With the increase of residents' income, the consumption of farm produce will enter a stage of better-off life from a stage of adequate food and clothing, and the consumption in a few places will be entering a wealthy stage. Residents' nutrition level will be continuously improved.

It is expected that in 2005, Engel's coefficient will drop to 46%. In 2010, the average energy taken in daily per capita nationwide will be 2,300 kilocalories, 77 grams of protein (of which 30% coming from animal-based food) and 70 grams of fat.

Affected by the above-mentioned factors, the demand for agricultural products during the "10th Five-Year Plan" will maintain a steady growth and incessant structural optimization. The consumption of grain necessary for daily diet will decrease, while that for feed and processing will rise considerably. The demand for livestock products and aquatic products will grow. The consumption level of processed products with farm produce as raw materials will go up step by step and primary material products will develop towards products with higher added value, better packed and highly finished.

After China's WTO accession, the demand for agricultural products will be turned to both the domestic and world markets instead of primarily supplying to the domestic market. Other member countries of the WTO will enjoy the benefits from China's opening the market for agricultural products.

At present, the wheat price in China is higher than that of the world market but with the WTO accession China will import more grains. With the rapid development of animal husbandry, China's demand for feed grain such as corn will also grow. As the largest country in the world to produce and consume rice, China has its advantages in producing rice with its cost of production lower than some developed countries.

The average possession of eggs per capita in China is close to developed countries and higher than the average world level; that of meat is lower than the United States but higher than the average world level; and the consumption of dairy products is prominently lower than the world average consumption lever per capita. The animal husbandry of China (with the exception of milk and part of poultry) has certain competitive power in the world: on the one hand, the livestock products at home have considerable advantage in price but on the other there is a difference between the residents' consumption habit and the imported animal products. For instance, the Chinese residents prefer pork but the supply volume of pork in the world market is rather low. The Chinese are accustomed to eat farm chickens rather than the imported fast-grown broilers. Today in China, the production scale of dairy industry is not large, intensification is low and cost of production is comparatively high. But after China's entry into the WTO, more foreign dairy products (or brands) will enter the Chinese market.

Though China is rich in fruits, quality fruits only make up a small part and imported fruits have a strong competitive power in medium- and high-level consuming

markets. In addition, fruit processing in China is not very popular and foreign processed fruits such as fruit juice have a growing market. Anyhow when entering the
Chinese market, the fruit businessman must be aware of two facts. One is that the
price of the imported fruits is higher because of the higher cost of labor, cost of
freight, custom duty and cost of packing and that the consuming market for imported
fruits is limited because at present most of the consumers in China are not wealthy
enough. The other is that consumers have a preference for the differences between
the domestic and imported fruits. Take the oranges and tangerines for instance.
American oranges are tight-skinned, tasting sour rather than sweet, while the Chinese prefer loose-skinned tangerines, tasting sweeter.

In respect of vegetable oil, due to the pressure of total yield of grains, China
plants oil-bearing crops mainly with low-yielding land or in winter. As a result, the
per unit area yield is lower and the cost of production is higher. Besides, the processing technology is also limited. That is why the price of vegetable oil in the domestic
market at present is higher than the world market.

INDUSTRY AND THE MARKET FOR
INDUSTRIAL PRODUCTS

Between 1979-2001, the increased value of the Chinese industry developed at
the average speed of 1.5% annually. In 2001, the increase value of industry was
4,260.7 billion yuan for the whole year, accounting for 44.4% of the GDP. Though
industry took the leading role in the national economy of China but industrialization
was far from completed.

China has become a big power in the world in the field of manufacturing industry.
The output of quite a few industrial products, such as steel products, raw coal, crude
oil, cement, fertilizer, synthetic fiber and TV sets, has ranked either first or at the
forefront in the world. In the past twenty years or so, the economic growth of China
depended mainly on the growth of manufacturing industry. Though the proportion of
the increased value of manufacturing industry in the GDP influctuated, it basically
kept over 40%. A half of the national financial revenue came from manufacturing
industry. The manufacturing industry attracted almost fifty percent of the employed
population in the city and the surplus rural laborers. Since 1990's, the export of the
manufacturing industry has always kept over 80% and created around three-fourths
of foreign exchange income.

In recent years, the restructuring of the Chinese industry has had an active devel-

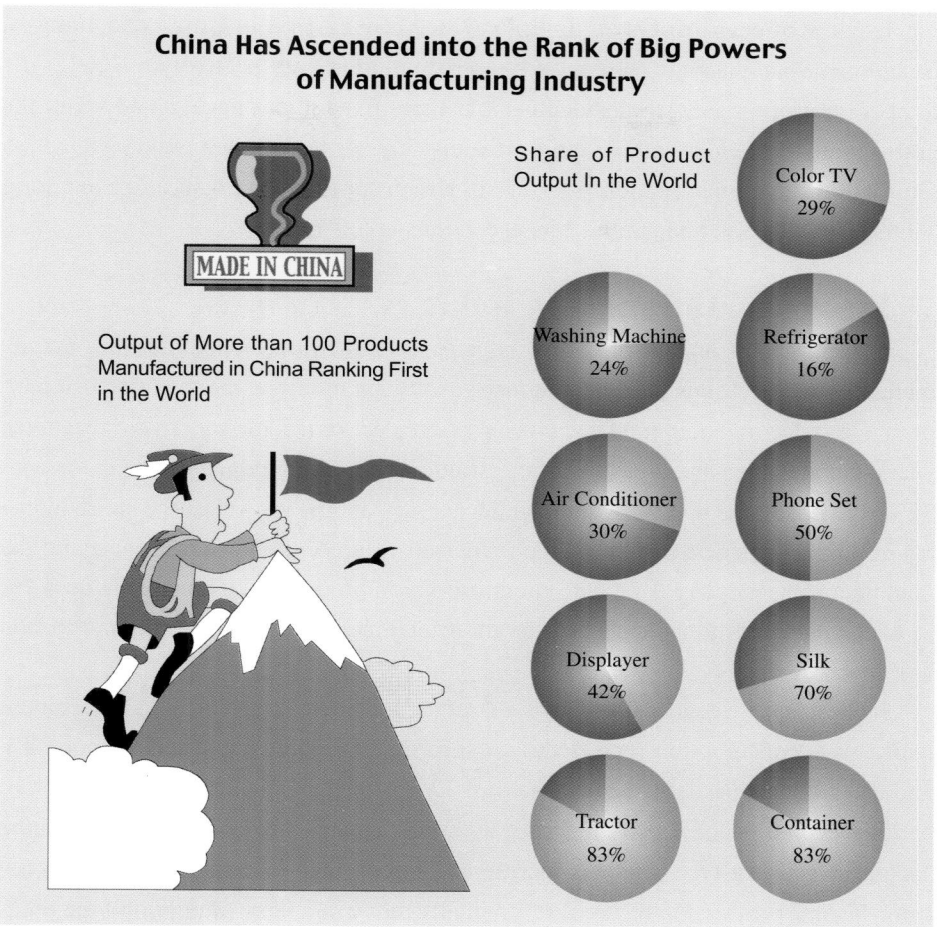

China Has Ascended into the Rank of Big Powers of Manufacturing Industry

MADE IN CHINA

Output of More than 100 Products Manufactured in China Ranking First in the World

Share of Product Output In the World

Color TV 29%

Washing Machine 24%

Refrigerator 16%

Air Conditioner 30%

Phone Set 50%

Displayer 42%

Silk 70%

Tractor 83%

Container 83%

opment and the high-tech products with higher technological element and higher added value have developed rapidly. In 2001, the output of electronic products and the products for telecom equipment such as the equipment for microwave telecom, the equipment for optical communication, the mobile phones and computers increased 28% ~ 87%, year on year.

In the forty major sectors of the Chinese industry in 2001, the manufacturing industry for electronic products and telecom equipment ranked first in the entire industrial sales in accordance with the order of materializing the gross sales and it had also been the sector with the largest sales for successively three years since 1999. The sales order ranking second to sixth was the electricity sector accounting for 8.2%; the manufacturing industry for communications and transportation equipment, 6.6%; the manufacturing industry for chemical raw materials and chemical products, 6.3%; the metallurgical sector, 6%; and the textile sector, 5.6%.

In view of regions, Guangdong Province ranked first in China and Jiangsu, Shandong, Shanghai and Zhejiang ranked second to fifth respectively in 2001. The total volume of the industrial added value in these five regions made up 48.5% of the entire industrial added value, approximately 50% of the whole country, of which Guangdong Province made up 13.2% of the proportion, Jiangsu and Shandong 10.8% respectively, Shanghai 7.1%, and Zhejiang 6.6%.

Electronic Information Industry

In China, electronic information industry is a newly-developed industry, mainly including the electronic computer industry, software industry, the manufacturing industry for telecom equipment and consumption electronic industry. In the recent ten years, the average annual growth of electronic information industry in China is over 32%, 18 percentage points higher than the average annual growth of the entire industry in the same period. In 2001, the increased value of the telecom sector and the manufacturing industry for electronic information products in China made up 4.2% in the GDP proportion. According to an official prediction, in 2005 the proportion will reach over 7%.

In 1980's, the leading product of electronic information products in the Chinese market was consumption-type electronic information product, particularly color TV and the products in assortment with color TV. After 1990's, with the promotion of national economy and social informatization, particularly the rapid growth of telecom sector, investment-type products represented by computer and telecom products became leading products in the market, gradually replacing the consumption-type products represented by color TV. In 2001, the production of investment-type products made up almost fifty percent of the whole sector.

The electronic information industry is the largest sector in China's foreign trade export, accounting for 28% of the total at present. The output of electronic products such as program-controlled telephone switchboard, mobile phone, color TV, laser disk player, and radio-cassette recorder ranks first in the world.

In recent years, the competition among the electronic information products in the Chinese market, including the competition of brand and price, is getting tougher and tougher. The supply of a part of the realm such as the consumption-type electronic information products is beyond the demand, resulting even tougher competition in the market. The development of electronic information industry tends to have a new trend.

China is becoming a manufacturing base for world IT products. The production and processing with PC, mobile telecom product, network products, and components and parts as the main body have formed a certain scale. After China's entry into the WTO, the huge market potentiality and excellent investment environments will further attract international capital, technology and talented people, making the production and processing base that has already started further developed.

Telecom products and network products are becoming new economic growing points. Viewed from the point of development, the gravity of the future market will be transferred gradually from providing a single product to providing a systematic plan for solution and systematic service, which will bring about a rapid development and production of telecom products and network products.

The trend of mutual merging and penetration between the traditional electrical household appliances and IT is more and more clear. With the promotion of national economic informatization and optimization and upgrading of traditional industries, electrical household products for information or various kinds of digital products will enter innumerable households on a large scale.

Software, system integration and service, various kinds of application software, data bank and embedded chip will be greatly developed. Information service enterprises represented by E-business will emerge in large numbers and its industrial scale will also expand rapidly.

In recent years, in the competition with foreign products and capitals, the market share of the Chinese products is incessantly growing and program-controlled telephone switchboard, computer, integrated circuit etc. have all reached a considerable scale and standard. But there is still quite a distance between China and developed countries. The overall scale and enterprise scale of the information technological industry of China are still quite small and the products and industrial structure are not rational enough. Though computer industry grows rapidly, the Chinese enterprise only has a certain advantages in the microcomputer with low added value and the basic

Rapid Growth for Demands of Chips by Chinese Industry

components and parts for the computer are still monopolized by foreign enterprises. Besides, the technical level of the industry is still not high enough, failing to supply many high-tech products badly needed in the market. The trend of importing these products has always been rising.

After the WTO accession, the import volume of foreign information technological products will be further growing with the dropping of custom duty. Due to the facts that China is in need of large volume of information technological products and rich in resources of talents and that the investment environments will be more and more loose with China's entry into the WTO, foreign funds will enter the information technological industry on an even larger scale. More and more foreign enterprises have set up R&D institutions in China, which means that the Chinese and foreign enterprises are not only directly facing the market competition but also the competition for the resource of talented people, particularly high-tech talents.

Computer Market

China has formed an industrial system with PC production as the main body and has the ability to make complete sets for large-scale production in the five categories of hardware products, namely, the main set, the peripheral apparatus, the application products, the network products, and the components, parts and consumption materials. A certain scale is available in the realm of certain computer products, such as displayer, hard disk, optical drive, printer, network terminal products, and information transmission equipment. China is becoming one of the important bases in the world to produce these computer products. For quite a few years, the market share of China's computer hardware products has made up around three-fourths of the entire market. Anyhow, the proportion of the hardware is decreasing with each passing year with the expansion of the market share of software and information service.

After 1990's, the computer market in China entered a stage of rapid development with the average growth of 56.9% between 1991-1997. In the following few years, the growth dropped to a certain extent but in the later 2000 it entered a rapid growth stage again with the growth rate reaching over 20%. At the same time, the speed of upgrading computer products is picking up swiftly. For instance, the rise of cost performance for notebook computer has made the notebook computer market grow faster than the desktop PC market and the LCD computer has started to move into ordinary households. The computer products pay attention not only to function improvement but to individualization, fashion and networking as well. In addition, health and environmental protection are also gradually becoming the consumption fashion.

Sales Volume of Main Computer Products in China in 2001

Product	Sales Volume (00,000 Sets)	Growth Compared with Previous Year (%)
PC Server	19.7	20.9
Desktop PC	750	21.0
Notebook Computer	58	38.4
Printer	376	22.2
Displayer	950	33.8
Scanner	110	33.7

Forecast of Domestic Sales Volume Of Main Computer Products in China in 2005

	1996-2000 Average Annual Growth (%)	Sales Volume in 2005 (00,000 Sets)	2001-2005 Average Annual Growth (%)
Desktop PC	41.9	1,800	23.8
Notebook Computer	42.2	160	30.7
IA Framework Service	23.5	60	29.8
Printer	32.5	1,100	29.0
Displayer	40.2	2,000	23.0
Scanner	81.3	360	34.3

A report submitted by the Electronic Information Industry Development Institute under the Ministry of Information Industry of China predicts that the computer market in China will grow at the annual rate of 25% on the average from 2002 to 2005. The scale of the entire computer market in China in 2001 reached 270 billion yuan but it will reach 650 billion yuan in 2005. The Institute also predicts the domestic sale of main computer products in 2005 in China. For the details, please see the following tables:

Software Market

The software industry of China is in an industrial mode with domestic need as a main factor. In 2001, the gross sale of software at home was approximately thirty billion yuan, of which the market for platform software was one-third, the Unix and Windows series still made up the overwhelming market share but the Linux technology and products were getting more and more matured. In the embedded operational system and high-grade professional application, the development of Linux cannot be

Mother's Consultation for Buying a Computer for Her Daughter

neglected.

The market for network security products has started in the recent couple of years and the volume of market demand in the future will be bigger and bigger. The bright spot of this market will be transformed from supplying a single product to supplying a complete solution plan and security service.

In 2001, application software made up around 60% of the software market share at home. Management software has become the market hotspot. The largest potential user's market for management software will be the 11,000,000 SMEs all over China. With the market expansion and tougher competition of products, solution plan and service facing different sectors will become key points of client's needs and competition focus of factories and companies. Besides, with the speeding-up steps of informatization in the sectors of finance, telecom, financial tax, transportation, energy and medical treatment, the market share of the application software for different sectors will expand gradually.

Since the development of the software industry in China, its gravity has began to tilt over to service, particularly large-scale application software, and the service level will directly affect the success or failure of product implementation. In line with the prediction made by the organization under the Ministry of Information Industry, the sales of the software and information service industries in China in 2005 will reach 300 billion yuan with an average annual growth rate of above 30%. The world software market share taken up by China will be raised from the present 1.2% to 3% and the domestic market share of the homemade software and the relevant information service industry will be raised from the present 33% to over 60%.

Market for Consumption Electronic Products

China is a big power for both manufacturing and marketing electronic products for consumption in the world. The market sales in 2001 were eighty-two billion yuan. As China is still a developing country, the consumption electronic products are still mainly the audio and video products related to broadcasting and TV. The competition of production and sales for this kind of products is fairly tough.

Color TV   In the industry of consumption electronic products, the development of color TV industry is the fastest and the scale is the largest. In 2000, China produced 37,420,000 color TV sets and sold 35,760,000 sets. In the domestic market, the possession of color TV in the city is over 100 sets for every one hundred households and the possession of color TV with homemade brands is about 80%. With the rapid development of digital technology and network technology, color TV in China is developing towards the direction of multimedia terminal for future home enjoyment and an important means for surfing the net. At present, color TV is at the stage of upgrading.

Laser Disc Player   The upgrading speed of this kind of products is very fast. In the three years between 1997-2000, the sales of DVD were raised from 50,000 sets to 4,000,000 sets. Now it is gradually becoming the mainstream product in the market.

Video Recorder and Camcorder   More and more camcorders are entering resident's home and growing at a rather rapid speed. The sales in 2000 were 864,000 sets and the sales of video recorder and camcorder are expected to increase at the speed of 10% in the next few years. In recent years, digital camcorder is growing rapidly and will become the mainstream product.

Machinery Industry

In general, the machinery industry of China is basically capable of providing the technical equipment for modernization of national economy. Since the reform and openness, the average growth speed of machinery industry in China has been higher than that of the year-on-year GDP and industrial gross value. The total economic volume of China is around 5% of the total volume of the world machinery industry, ranking fifth in the world. The increased value and sales income of machinery industry make up around one-fifth to one-fourth of the national industry. The output of some machinery industrial products, such as power generation equipment, machine tool, motorcycle and camera, ranks at the forefront in the world.

As a big power of machinery industry, China has great potentiality to export some advantageous machinery products. For instance, in Southeast Asia and Middle East area there is a good prospect for the product with high added value such as the complete set for thermal power generation with the capacity of 300,000 KW or below; in some European and American countries and medium-developed countries there is a rather big market for boats and ships, small and medium farm machinery, medium-power engineering machinery, small and medium equipment for heavy-duty mining, small and medium electrical machinery, power-operated tools, wires and cables, high and low tension electrical appliances, motorcycles, auto parts and components, ordinary machine tools, pumps, valves, medium-rank instruments for scientific testing, optical instrument, bearings, chains, standard fittings and electrical household appliances; in the developing countries and medium-developed countries technical export and construction of exterior-territorial factories can be done for some special products such as motorcycles, equipment for power transmission and transformation, farm machinery, KWh meters and water meters so as to materialize localized production.

Anyhow, the machinery industry of China also has some outstanding problems, such as big enterprises are not big and strong enough, small enterprises are not professional and specialized enough and concentration intensity of sector production is low. The technical level of products is quite low and the structure is irrational. The capacity of manufacturing low- and medium-grade machinery products and products for general use is much more than overproduced. The ability to develop and produce major technical equipment, high-tech products, special equipment and fundamental machinery fittings badly needed in the market is very low. The quality of products and after-sale services can't meet the users' demands. Large volume of machinery products has to be imported every year. Besides, the ability of technological innovation is not strong enough, restricting the technical progress and industrial upgrading.

According to the prediction made by the State Economic and Trade Commission in the "10th Five-Year Plan" for machinery industry, the market demands for machinery products will be ever increasing and higher requirements will be placed on major technical equipment because of industrial upgrading. In the field of power industry, the volume needed for large-scale, high-efficient and power generation equipment with environmental protection and new equipment for power transmission and transformation is much larger. In the field of metallurgical industry, the demand for automatic, large-scale, continuous, high-efficient and advanced equipment in complete set will grow rapidly. Petroleum, petrochemical and chemical industry will put forward even higher requirements for key products such as large-scale air separation equipment and compressors. The coal industry will raise the requirements for improving the automation of comprehensive mining equipment, security technological equipment and ore washing and dressing equipment and for developing large-scale installation for coal gasification and liquidation. The textile industry is in a bad need of getting rid of a number of backward technology and equipment, and upgrading and transformation the production process. The machinery products for light industry will develop towards large-scale, sophisticated and automatic direction. And the building material industry will transform a number of equipment in complete set to produce cement and wall material and the equipment for superfine grinding, and improve the successful rate of the products made with glass fiber reinforced plastic. In addition, during the promotion of restructuring and industrial upgrading, the industries and sectors such as nonferrous metal, electronics, tobacco, pharmacy, railway and communication will also

Audience Passing by a Poster of International Ocean Shipping Expo

raise their requirements for varieties, level, quality and performance of machinery products. The machinery products with the characteristics of high efficiency, energy saving, low pollution, intelligence, flexibility and completion will gradually become the mainstream of the market. In order to step up industrial upgrading and technological innovation, machinery and auto industries themselves are in need of large numbers of advanced processing equipment and instruments for testing.

The development of rural economy provides new market opportunity for agricultural equipment. The speeding-up of agricultural industrialization will not only raise new requirements for various kinds of advanced and appropriate farm machinery for ploughing, cultivating and harvesting but also new demands for the equipment used to process seeds before and after the production of crops, to improve varieties, to dry agricultural products and byproducts, store, transport and deep processing. With the continuous development of agricultural technology, facility agriculture, precision agriculture and green agriculture will grow rapidly in the economic-developed regions of China and the requirements for equipment will keep on rising. China is short of water resources so the potentiality of technical equipment for water-saving irrigation is very big. With the speeding-up of urban green coverage and the development of animal husbandry economy, the demand for garden machinery and animal-husbandry machinery will also grow. Besides, large numbers of equipment are necessary to convert the land for forestry, to return grain for green and lake as well as for basic construction of farmland.

Expansion of domestic demand and implementation of the western development strategy will bring about growth for demanding machinery products. With the implementation of the western development scheme, the project of "west-to-east power transmission" and the project "west-to east natural gas transportation" will spur the development of gas turbine generators, the equipment to transmit and transform 750,000 VAC and the equipment to transmit super-high DC voltage as well as to bring about the growth of a large number of universal machinery products, such as pumps, valves, pipes and containers. The construction of the infrastructure projects in the west, such as key highways, railways, buildings, water conservancy, power and airport, will provide new development opportunity for producing engineering construction machinery, medium- and heavy-duty trucks, light passenger cars and autos for special uses.

Generally speaking, the demand for machinery equipment in a quite long period from now on will grow steadily but the demand structure will incessantly be readjusted and changed. The demand for general products will drop but the demand for high-level products, the products with technology continuously improved and the products in the new realms will incessantly rise and the competition between the enterprises will be tougher and tougher,

After the WTO accession, due to the fact that the actual tariff rate for machinery products is already below 10% and viewed from the import tariff rate dropped to 10% for industrial products, many conventional mechanical products will not face serious impact from imported products. With the internationalization of domestic market with each passing day, the accession strategy of the world-renowned multinational corporations for the Chinese market of mechanical and electrical products is changed from mainly selling products in the past to an all-round market accession with various means such as products, capital, technology and service. The market competition for important machinery products (such as autos, power equipment, NC machine tools and automatic control equipment) embodying the national strength and technological level will become tougher. It is mainly shown in the serious compact to be faced by major equipment in complete set and high-tech products, such as some advanced and high-efficient power generation equipment, new metallurgical equipment, large-scale petrochemical equipment, large-scale agricultural machinery, heavy-duty engineering machinery, the fundamental machinery represented by medium- and high-grade NC machine tools, the industrial control system represented by digital instruments and meters, and new environmental protection machinery. At present, the contradiction between supply and demand for the above-listed products and equipment is very sharp at home and the supply mainly depends on import.

Auto Industry

The auto industry of China was born under the planned economic system with the purpose of meeting the needs of economic development, national defense and official duties at that time and developed with the government investment through the planned economy. After the reform and opening-up, the auto industry of China started to face the market and now the volume of auto output is among the first ten countries in the world; both the varieties and volume of trucks have basically met the demand of the domestic market and the outstanding issue of the contradiction between the demand and supply has been eased up. Due to the change of market conditions, the auto industry of China had a surge of new round for developing new products in 1998. The main auto manufacturers successively pushed out their respective new models, showing that the ability of developing the auto industry independently in China has been greatly improved.

In early 1980's, China began to establish auto-manufacturing enterprises on the basis of Sino-foreign joint venture. At present, the total number of three kinds of foreign-invested enterprises or ventures (Sino-foreign joint ventures, cooperative businesses and exclusively foreign-owned enterprises in China) have reached 600, the assets totaling twenty billion US dollars approximately 50% of the total asset of auto industry. The joint-venture auto enterprises have become the main body of the Chinese auto industry.

Forecast of Auto Possession Volume and Demand Volume in 2005

Unit: 00,000 Units

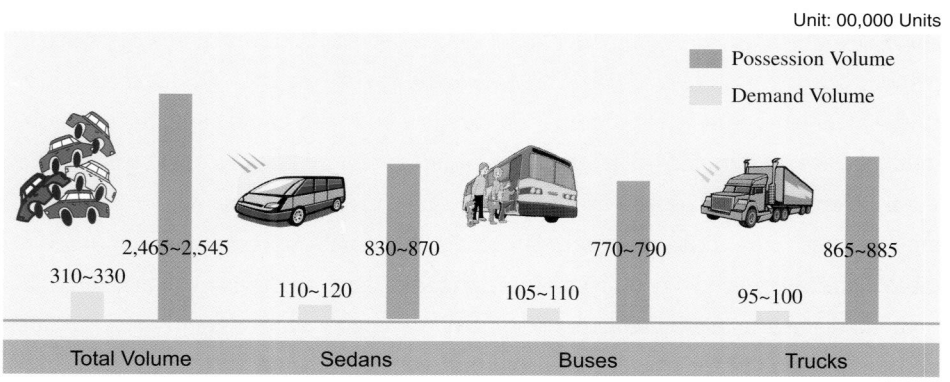

Possession Volume
Demand Volume

2,465~2,545   830~870   770~790   865~885
310~330   110~120   105~110   95~100

Total Volume   Sedans   Buses   Trucks

From 1990 to 2000, the proportion of the output of sedan, bus and truck was readjusted from the total output volume of 8.3%, 25.1% and 66.6% to 29.2%, 33.9% and 36.9% respectively. The personal possession of cars in China was raised from 816,000 in 1990 to 7,890,000 in 2001 growing at an annual rate of 20%-plus on the average. Since 1998, 50%-plus autos have been personally purchased.

Due to the small scale, insufficient strength and some other reasons, the enterprises of auto production in China have not formed their strong ability for development and there is a great disparity when compared with foreign manufacturers. They have not formed a high-level system to develop truck products, let alone the ability to develop cars independently.

After entering the WTO, the tariff for auto and components and parts will be cut to a large extent and the import license will be gradually cancelled. All this will exert impacts to different extents on the production of various kinds of autos and components and parts.

From the viewpoint of products, sedans, engines and driving bridges with higher technological content, and the key components and parts will suffer the most serious impact and the next will be high-quality heavy-duty trucks. Comparatively speaking, the impact on minicars, medium-sized trucks and medium and large buses will be less. Before canceling the quota license, the impact on import quota is larger than that on the tariff as China has already made the commitment to the outside world that starting from the year of the WTO accession, China will have considerable large quota for importing complete cars and components and parts. After canceling the quota license, due to the facts that the import volume is not limited and the tariff for sedans and components and parts is cut to a great extent, the volume of imported sedans and key components and parts will be increased and the impact will be more prominent.

After entering the WTO, China will open to the outside world the domestic market for selling autos and their components and parts, importing and exporting autos and distribution service, and the realm of auto services such as management transport company, auto installment plan and financing lease, and financing for auto production. With the openness of these realms, foreign products will enter the Chinese market unblocked. It will greatly affect the Chinese auto industry that has not yet established a sound service and trading system.

With the continuous and rapid development of national economy and the continuous enhancement of people's living standards, the auto market at home will keep on a rapid growth and the structure of product demand will also greatly change. The volume demanded for trucks will grow but the market share will correspondingly

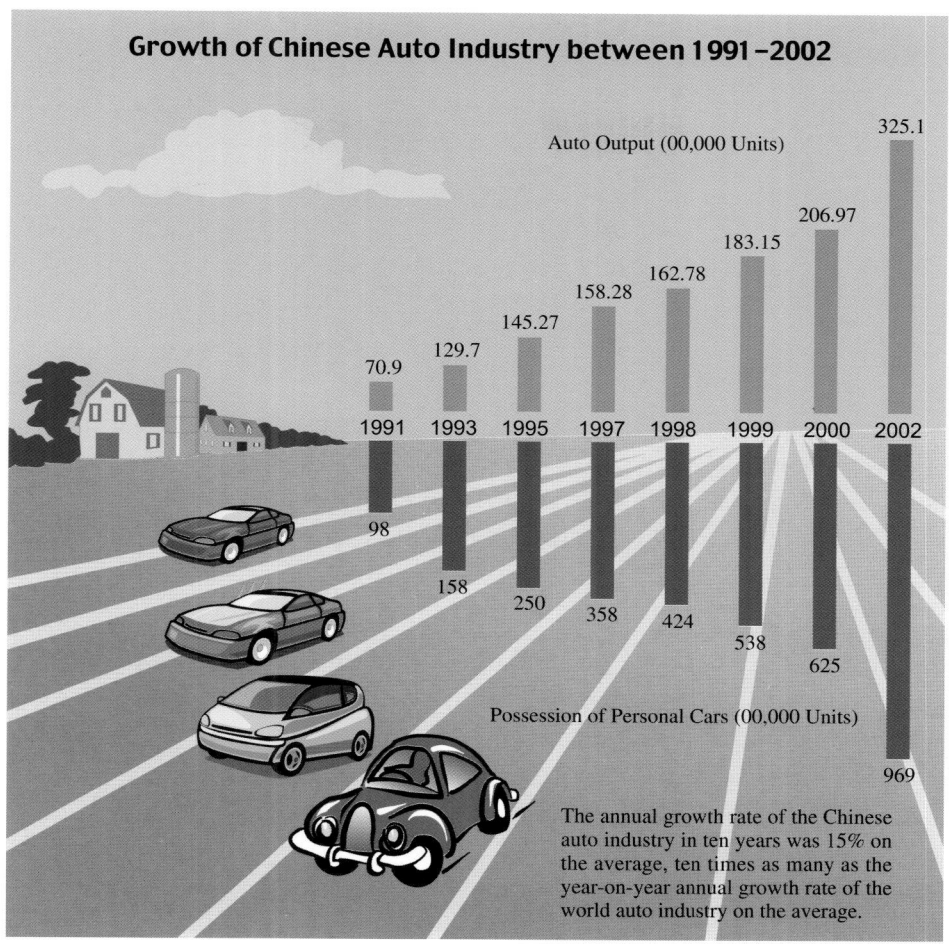

Growth of Chinese Auto Industry between 1991–2002

Auto Output (00,000 Units)

1991	1993	1995	1997	1998	1999	2000	2002
70.9	129.7	145.27	158.28	162.78	183.15	206.97	325.1

Possession of Personal Cars (00,000 Units)

98 — 158 — 250 — 358 — 424 — 538 — 625 — 969

The annual growth rate of the Chinese auto industry in ten years was 15% on the average, ten times as many as the year-on-year annual growth rate of the world auto industry on the average.

drop. The volume demanded for sedans and buses, minicars in particular, will grow considerably and their market share will be further increased. The "10th Five-Year Plan" for the auto industry issued by the State Economic and Trade Commission makes a prediction for auto consumption market in the next few years as follows:

Sedans The development trend of continuous speeding-up of the Chinese industrialization process and people's even more wealthy life will inevitably expand the group of sedan buyers. Sedans will become the main force of auto demand growth and the proportion of sedans in the auto demand volume will steadily rise. With the unveiling of the country's new policy to encourage people to buy cars for personal use, the proportion of buying personal cars is expected to grow rapidly with each passing year. The demand for medium- and high-grade sedans will keep on steadily growing but the market share will drop to a certain extent while ordinary sedans, economic sedans in particular, will be the leading products in the market with the

varieties tending to be diversified and personalized and their market share will rise continuously. The first level market to buy cars with public funds and for official duties will gradually shrink; the demand of the second consumption level

Advertisement for car purchase on loans appears at car exhibition

market to buy cars with company funds for business use will maintain relatively stable or drop a bit; and the trend of development of the third level market to buy cars for personal use will be excellent and will be the main body to absorb the volume of auto growth.

Trucks   The improvement of traffic conditions and change of consumption pattern will promote the change of truck demand structure and the trend for trucks to develop towards heavy-duty trucks, light trucks and mini trucks will be more prominent. With the rapid development of highways, freeways in particular, the continuous improvement of environmental protection requirements and the implementation of fuel tax, the demand for heavy-duty auto will notably grow, the total demand for medium-sized trucks will shrink to a certain extent, and the market demand for light trucks will grow steadily. With the rapid development of agricultural economy, light trucks and mini trucks will have a larger market demand. During the "10th Five-Year Plan", the state will embark the strategy of expanding the domestic needs and the western development, and strengthen the construction of highways and infrastructures in the west. All this will play an important role in spurring the auto market and the demand for heavy-duty and medium-duty trucks, various kinds of autos for special uses, trucks for mining use and medium and large buses will significantly rise.

Buses   The western development and rapid construction of high-grade highways will provide new market space for highway buses. Medium and large buses will maintain the main car models for intermediate distance and long distance passenger transport and the demand will grow step by step. With the development of holiday economy and tourism, the demand for medium- and high-grade buses will rise in a steady way. The speeding-up of urban construction and continuous extension of streets in the urban area will make public transport in the city busier and busier and the demand for buses, large, medium and small, in the city grow steadily. In addition, the implementation of urbanization strategy will promote the market demand for light buses and mini buses to further expansion, particularly mini buses.

Petroleum and Petrochemical Industries

In 1978, the output of petroleum in China broke 100,000,000 tons, striding into the rank of oil-producing big nations in the world. Since 1980's, due to the rapid growth of national economy and more strict requirements for environmental protection, the demand for petroleum and natural gas has been gradually rising. Since 1993, China has become a net petroleum import nation. In 2001, the output of crude oil nationwide hit 160,000,000 tons, ranking fifth in the world.

According to the information issued by the State Economic and Trade Commission, the geological deposit of the petroleum in China is ninety-four billion tons but in line with the analysis of present technical and economic conditions, the deposit of the final recoverable petroleum is around fourteen billion tons. The 140-years history of the development of the main oil-producing countries shows that when the known deposit reaches 40% ~ 60%, the storage and output volume will enter a relatively longer stable period. At present, the proven petroleum deposit of China is 42.4% and generally speaking, the storage and output volume has begun to enter a steady growing period.

The State Economic and Trade Commission predicts that in the next 15 years, the national economy of China will develop at the rate of around 7% and the demand for crude oil will grow at the rate of around 4%. The year-on-year growth rate of crude oil output at home will be only 2% or so, lower than the growing speed of the needs for crude oil. The gap between the supply and demand of petroleum at home will be ever expanding. It is expected that the demand for crude oil in 2005 will be around 245,000,000 tons.

In 2001, the output of natural gas nationwide was 30.3 billion cubic meters, ranking fifteenth in the world. The information released by the government shows that the total volume of the geological deposit of natural gas in China is 38 trillion cubic meters and the volume of the expected recoverable natural gas is about 10.5 trillion cubic meters. So far, the known deposit of natural gas for recovery in China is only 14% so the prospecting of natural gas is still at an early stage.

Now the proportion of natural gas in the structure of primary energy consumption in China is much lower than the average level of 24% in the world and 8.8% in Asia. There is great potentiality for development of natural gas market in China. The consumption demand of natural gas for power generation, industrial uses and urban fuel will grow rapidly. It is expected that the volume of natural gas demanded in 2005 will reach sixty to seventy billion cubic meters. Though the resource basis for the rapid development of natural gas in China is available, the market development mainly depends on the factors such as the price and consumption pattern of the natural gas. At present, the price of natural gas at home is higher and a lot of work has to be done for the market development.

Since the 1980's, China has sped up the exploration speed of oil and gas resources at home with various kinds of ways of cooperation and joint venture to introduce foreign capital, advanced technology and management experiences. Between 1982 and 2000, China cooperated successively with more than seventy oil companies in eighteen countries in the fields of petroleum exploration and development on the sea, directly making use of 6.45 billion US dollars of foreign funds to find nineteen oil-and-gas fields on the basis of cooperation drilling. As regard to the petroleum on land, around 170 regional blocks were opened to the outside world for exploration and development and one billion US dollars of foreign funds was introduced.

Based on the principle of "having complementary advantages and win-win mutual benefits", China is further perfecting the rules and regulations for foreign cooperation to explore and develop the petroleum resources on the land and on the sea so as to expand the sphere and realm of exploring and developing petroleum and natural gas with foreign cooperation. Foreign corporations are encouraged to make investment to explore oil and gas deposits in the areas with larger potentiality and greater risks, to make investment in developing the resources not developed yet and to improve the oilfield coverage, and to participate in the infrastructure construction for natural gas and promote upstream and downstream integrated development of natural gas.

The petrochemical industry of China, starting at the end of 1950's, has entered the rank of big petrochemical nations in the world with the production capacity of main petrochemical products ranking at the forefront of the world. In 2001, the primary processing ability of crude oil in China ranked third in the world and the capacity of three main oil products, gasoline, kerosene and diesel oil, could basically meet the market demand at home. The production capacity of ethylene ranked fifth in the world, meeting nearly 50% of the market demand at home. The production capacity of five kinds of synthetic raisin ranked fifth in the world, totaling almost a half of domestic market consumption. The production capacity of synthetic rubber ranked fourth in the world, the output accounting for a little more than 70% of domestic market consumption.

But from the viewpoint of enterprises, China is not a strong power in petrochemical industry yet mainly because the distribution of petrochemical enterprises is scattered, the scale is smaller and the technical level is lower. In oil products, the total output can basically meet the needs of domestic market but the quality and quantity of a part of the petroleum products still cannot meet the market demand, particularly lubrication oil and fuel oil. The quality criterion of gasoline and kerosene falls behind world advanced level, hardly able to meet more and more strict environmental requirements. For petrochemical products, the market share of the three major synthetic materials and organic petrochemical materials is only 50% and large volume has to be imported.

The State Economic and Trade Commission forecasts the average yearly growth of the consumption volume of gasoline, kerosene and diesel oil during the "10th Five-Year Plan" will be 3.4% ~ 4.6% and in 2005, the total demanded volume of gasoline, kerosene and diesel oil is expected to hit 136,000,000 ~ 138,000,000 tons. The equivalent demand for ethylene will rise at the speed of 8.5%, expected to hit 15,000,000 tons in 2005. The average annual growth of the five major kinds of synthetic raisin is expected to reach 7.0% ~ 8.0% and the volume needed will hit 25,000,000 ~ 27,000,000 tons in 2005. The growth speed of consumption for synthetic rubber will slow down with an expected annual growth rate of 4% on the average and the volume demanded in 2005 will be around 1,100,000 tons. The average annual growth rate of synthetic materials is 5.4% ~ 8.3% and the volume needed is expected to reach 10,800,000 ~ 12,600,000 tons in 2005.

After China's WTO accession, with the tariff cut and gradual cancel of non-tariff measures and with the foreign companies obtaining the right of trade and distribution, the market share of foreign products in the domestic market of petrochemical products will be further raised. Viewed from the interior situation of petrochemical industry, the most serious impact of oil-refining industry will result from the restoration of importing oil products and foreign distribution of oil products in China. The challenge to synthetic raisin will come from good prestige and service of foreign business. The import quota for most synthetic fibers will be cancelled, and facing with the import products with lower price and higher quality, the domestic synthetic fiber industry will be in an obvious inferior position.

Chemical Industry

The chemical industry includes the realms of extended chemical industry with petrochemical fundamental raw materials for processing object, coal chemical industry, salt chemical industry, biological chemical industry and sophisticated chemical industry. China has formed a chemical industry system with rather complete categories and with varieties basically in complete set that can in the main meet the domestic demands, including twelve major sectors, namely, chemical mine, chemical fertilizer, inorganic chemicals, soda ash, chlorine alkali, basic organic materials, agricultural chemicals, pigments, paints, sophisticated chemical industry in new realms, rubber processing and new materials.

In recent years, the priority of investment in chemical industry has been given to four series of agricultural chemical products, giving first priority to seven major engineering constructions such as chemical fertilizer and agricultural chemicals. The situation for the development of chemical industry is like this. First of all, the base of production capacity and output is large. The output of a dozen of major chemical industrial products ranks at the forefront in the world, of which synthetic ammonia, chemical fertilizer, calcium carbide and dyestuff rank first in the world, sulphuric acid, agricultural chemicals, soda ash and caustic soda rank second in the world, and pyrites, phosphorus mine, phosphate fertilizer, acetic acid, paints and tires also rank at the forefront. And then, the cost for production is relatively low. Due to the fact that the development cost of most chemical industrial products of China at the earlier stage was lower and the resources at home (including natural resources and labor resources) are relatively cheaper, the cost for production of some products is also relatively lower.

On the other hand, the

A Forecast of Demand for Major Chemical Industrial Products in 2005

(Unit: 00,000 Tons)

Description of Products	Consumption Vol. in 2000	Consumption Vol. In 2005
Synthetic Ammonia	3000	3600
Chemical Fertilizer	4100	4600
In which: Nitrogenous Fertilizer	2530	2740
Phosphate Fertilizer	900	1070
Potash Fertilizer	507	700
Pyrites	1570	1200
Phosphate Rock	2950	3800
Sulphuric Acid	2400	3000
Soda Ash	650	850
Caustic Soda	620	700
Methanol	300	380
Acetic Acid	85	140
Benzoic Anhydride	50	70
PVC	440	500
Agricultural Chemicals	32	42
Dyes	13	32
Paint	200	270
Tires (00,000)	7450	12200

production technology of Chinese chemical industry is generally backward, the production scale is small and scattered, the capital strength is insufficient, the scientific research ability for innovation is weak and the network of sales has not been completed established. The irrational structure of chemical industrial products is shown in lower percentage of petrochemical products, organic chemical products and high-grade new products but higher percentage of products with high consumption, rough processing and low added values, resulting more supply than demand in the total output and redundant production capacity on the one hand but large volume of some products for import on the other. For instance, in 2000, the new varieties of farm chemicals developed at home comprised only 20% of the total volume of farm chemicals, the proportion of energy-saving and low-pollution pigment only made up 15% ~ 20% (60% for developed countries), high-concentrated nitrogenous fertilizer made up only 60% of the total output of nitrogenous fertilizer, and high-concentrated phosphate fertilizer only 35.5% of the total.

After China's entry into the WTO, the market and the resources will be integrated. Foreign businesses in China can enjoy the national treatment and the domestic enterprises are to lose the advantage in the cost for production. In respect of quality of products, development of new products and competition in talented people, foreign enterprises have the competitive advantages. In addition, the market openness, reduction of tariff and lift of non-tariff measures will thoroughly change the existing system of sales network in China. Those sectors protected by state policy and depending too much on the state for funds and technology will face serious impacts.

Chemical industrial products have great potentiality in the market at home. During the "10th Five-Year Plan", China will pay more attention to making use of foreign funds and loose the limited conditions to make use of foreign funds for some high-tech products not affecting general national security and badly needed in China.

Competitive Power of Major Chemical Industrial Products

In 2001, the State Economic and Trade Commission issued the "10th Five-Year Plan" for the chemical sector and made an analysis of the competitive power of the major chemical industrial products of China as follows:

At present, the large-scale nitrogenous fertilizer enterprises with natural gas as raw material still have fairly strong competitive power under the condition of enjoying preferable price for raw materials within the plan. The large-scale nitrogenous fertilizer enterprises with light oil and heavy oil as raw materials and the newly-established large-scale nitrogenous fertilizer plants with natural gas as raw material and supplied with the market price, affected by the two factors of higher price for raw material and higher investment for the installations, have higher cost for production resulting in poor competition. The medium-sized installations for producing nitrogenous fertilizer, enjoying the advantages of lower price for raw materials and favorable price for electrical power, are sill competitive after the technical innovation of saving energy, cutting down the raw material consumption and increasing the production. Most of other small-sized nitrogenous fertilizer installations, particularly those located far away from the supply of raw materials, have higher cost for production and have no competitive power at all.

The large-scale phosphate fertilizer installations, after improving the rate of operation and solving the burden of debts, are competitive with the cost for production basically similar to imported product. Though the cost for production is higher for small- and medium-sized phosphate fertilizer installations, they are able to resist, to a certain extent, imported product because they can keep with the national conditions and have regional advantages.

The inorganic salts industry of China at present is still an extensive- and resource-type industry. But due to its lower investment in the production installation and low-priced localized resources, it still possesses a certain competitive advantage in the world market. After the WTO accession, the inorganic salts industry of China will face a severe challenge in case of entrance of huge foreign capital.

The production capacity and output of soda ash are both big enough in China and the production scale and technical installation level of synthetic alkali rank among the world advanced level. After entering the WTO, the soda ash sector is rather competitive.

Due to the fact that the chlorine alkali sector is small in scale and scattered and poor in technological equipment in addition to higher price of electricity than the main countries producing chlorine alkali in the world as well as irrational structure of chlorine products, the chlorine alkali industry is rather weak in competition.

With the exception of a few large-scaled installations constructed with introduced technology and equipment in recent years, most installations for producing organic materials in China are rather small in scale and backward in technological equipment. In addition, the technical route of raw materials is irrational and the combination with upper-stream raw materials is not close, this sector has no competitive power after the WTO accession.

Because of the low investment for the earlier stage development and production installations, the agricultural chemicals of China are rather competitive in the world market. After entering the WTO, the advantages of foreign business in the development of new products, technological equipment, product quality, production scale and market strategy can be fully developed so they will speed up their pace to enter the Chinese market.

The traditional vulcanized pigment, scattered pigment, reductive pigment, and lower- and medium-grade yellow, red and blue organic pigments of China are very competitive in both output and price. But in general, technological equipment is low in level and products are poor in quality, it is likely that medium- and high-grade products in active, direct and scattered pigments will have to be imported in large volume with the development of high-grade garment fabrics of the Chinese textile industry and the renovation of printing technology.

There is a strong desire for localization of paint products. Because of the strong ability in China to produce paints and earlier operation of marketization, no serious impact will affect the Chinese paint industry after the WTO accession. On the contrary, the entry will benefit improvement of raw materials used for paints and the quality of products.

China started sophisticated chemical industry in new realms fairly late. There is a large gap in most of the products compared with foreign countries in manufacturing technology, product variety and quality and, in addition, the development for application and technical service also lag behind. So most of the products in this industry will face a serious challenge with the entry of foreign high-quality but low-priced products and good service with the exception of a few products like phosphate, citric acid, lysine, vitamin E, vitamin A and iso-ascorbate which have already formed a considerable scale.

The technical level and product quality of tire sector have made considerable improvement, possessing the ability of technical development and raw materials and most of the equipment have been materialized. So this sector is quite competitive in the market. However, from the viewpoint of overall competitive power, the domestic enterprises still lag behind foreign big companies in the fields of technical development, product brand, production scale, varieties and volume.

The sector of new materials in the chemical industry of China is still at a starting stage. As new materials in chemical industry belong to high-tech products, China is rather weak in the ability of independent development. Besides, as it is rather difficult to introduce foreign advanced technology, the overall competitive power is still very weak.

Now, the contradiction between supply and demand at home market is turning from shortage of supply to relative surplus of supply. In accordance with the national economy and the development of the relevant sectors, the prediction made by the State Economic and Trade Commission for the demand of the market of chemical industrial products on the basis of consumption of chemical industrial products at home is that the demanding growth for staple chemical industrial products will be lower than the year-on-year GDP growth but the growth rate of sophisticated chemical industrial products will be a littler higher than the GDP growth speed.

Metallurgical Industry

After quite a few years of construction, the metallurgical industry of China has entered the stage of speeding up restructuring to improve competitive power. The output of main products in 2001 was 152,000,000 tons of steel, 145,00,000 tons of pig iron, 157,00,000 tons of steel products respectively. In 1996, with the output of steels over 100,000,000 tons, ranking first in the world and maintaining this position successively for six years, China has become a big power in the world to turn out steels.

In 1995, the domestic market share of the Chinese steel products was 86% and in 2001 reached 90%. A few steel products badly needed in the construction of various departments of national economy and national defense, such as heavy rail, light rail, ship plate, container plate, bridge plate and plate for making pipes, can all be supplied at home. At the same time, the overall level of manufacturing technological equipment and localization level have been improved. A few technological equipments for metallurgy mainly depended on import in the past, such as the continuous rolling mill for steel bar and high-speed rolling mill for wire rod, have been localized.

However, the iron and steel industry of China is not highly concentrated, the benefits of scale economy are not sufficient, and very few large-scaled enterprises have had their entire equipment reaching the advanced level in the world. In the respect of product structure, there is still a big gap between production and consumption of steel plates and strips. In 2000, the imported steel plates and strips reached 14,100,000 tons, accounting for 88% of the total volume of imported steel products. Part of key steel products with high added value still cannot meet the demand at home and has to be imported.

The iron and steel industry of China also has the problem of relatively insufficient resources. For instance, the resource of iron ore in China is limited and the grade not high enough. In addition, the iron mines are old, leading to the output drop of iron ore. In recent ten years of so, the output of iron ore in China cannot meet the need of the growth of iron and steel production and the volume of import is increasing with each passing year. In 2000, the iron ore imported reached 69,970,000 tons and the pig iron produced with the imported ore made up one-third of the total volume of the pig iron in China.

China has become one of the largest steel-consuming nations in the world. In recent years, the state has carried out proactive fiscal policy, made increasing investment in fixed assets and strengthened the infrastructure and urban construction, and the iron and steel industry is one of the industries that has

Informatization, the Only Way to Develop Chinese Industries

benefited from the expanded investment scale. According to the prediction of the State Economic and Trade Commission, the total consumption volume of steels in 2005 is expected to reach over 140,000,000 tons. The capacity of Chinese steel market is very large but there are still quite a few realms needed for further development, for instance, new-type steels needed by agriculture and construction sector; high-grade steels needed for upgrading in the sectors of auto manufacturing, machinery, electrical household appliances, power, petroleum and communication; the steel products needed for developing the west such as the piping steel used for the West-to-East Natural Gas Transportation Project and the high-strength and high corrosion-resisting steel pipes used for recovering oil-gas fields in the west; and the new varieties of steels needed in national defense construction and the production of war industry.

In recent years, China imports around 150,000,000 tons of steels per year on the average. But due to insufficient production capacity or poor quality that fails to meet users' requirements, 7,000,000 tons more have to be imported at present. The main varieties are hot-rolling sheet, cold-rolled sheet, stainless steel plates and strips, car plate, sheet for making electrical household appliances, galvanized plate, tinned plate, cold-rolled silicon steel sheet, superior high-carbon coil rod, petroleum pipe, superior alloy-steel lengthy material, etc. So far as ordinary iron and steel products are concerned, Chinese iron and steel enterprises have the advantage of cost and only small volume is needed for import.

After entering the WTO, the average tariff of importing iron and steel products will be further cut down but the average range will not be big enough. Compared with the imported steels, small-sized steels, wire rod and medium plate produced at home are competitive in both quality and cost of production. What will be seriously impacted in the steels is mainly some products with high added value. The impact of lifting non-tariff measures (such as import quota, and ratified operation of iron and steel products) will be greater than that of tariff reduction.

Nonferrous Metal Industry

Since the reform and opening-up, the nonferrous metal industry of China has had a rapid development. The total output of ten commonly used nonferrous metals such as copper, aluminum, lead and zinc has ranked second in the world for six successive years. From 1995 to 2000, the average annual growth rate of the output of these ten nonferrous metals reached 9.3%, changing the long-standing situation of supply shortage. At present, with the exception of importing copper because of limitation of resource, the supply and demand of aluminum is basically balanced; lead, zinc and magnesium are more than sufficient; the traditional export products like tungsten, tin, stibium, smithsonite, and rare-earth metal are still exported on a certain scale; and the smelted products of nonferrous metal have been changed from net import to net export.

Anyhow, the nonferrous metal industry of China is still faced with resource issue, mainly lower grade of copper mine and less large-scale copper mine, difficult to meet the needs to develop copper industry. The resource of lead, zinc, tungsten, tin, stibium and rare-earth metal is comparatively rich but most of the rich mines have been developed and utilized and the resource advantage is gradually decreasing. For instance, lead concentrate has to be imported in large volume, 310,000 tons in 2000.

So far as enterprises are concerned, production concentration is low and technological equipment is poor. The capacity for primary processing is more than enough while high-tech products and high-precision products cannot meet the market demand. For instance, high-precision aluminum plate and strip, high-grade aluminum foil, electrolytic copper foil, framework material for leading line, super-long copper condensation tube for power station, highly pure metal materials, large diameter monocrystalline silicon, aviation and space materials, etc. have to be imported. In calculation with value volume, these products make up 45% of the total volume of imported nonferrous metals.

The State Economic and Trade Commission forecasts that during the "10th Five-Year Plan" the industries that consume large volume of nonferrous metals such as information industry, communication, energy and construction will keep on developing rapidly and the demanding volume for nonferrous metals in China still tends to rise. In 2005, the demand for copper, aluminum, lead and zinc will be 2,000,000 tons, 3,800,000 tons, 600,000 tons and 1,200,000 tons respectively; the growth rate of average annual consumption of copper and aluminum 1.0% and 2.2% respectively; a slight growth of lead and zinc; the demanding volume for copper processing material 2,600,000 tons and for aluminum processing material 2,800,000 tons.

The main realms for copper consumption are electrical, electronic and light industries as well as communication and transportation, accounting for about 77% of the total volume of the consumption. The main realms for aluminum consumption are construction, machinery, packing and energy, accounting for about 78.3% of the total volume. The main realms for lead consumption are battery, glass, cable and manufacturing industry, taking up about 85.6% of the total volume. The main realms for zinc consumption are light industry, metallurgy, pigments and the zinc used for copper alloy material, accounting for about 84% of the total volume.

The nonferrous metal industry of China was geared with world market at a rather early time. China's WTO accession will be beneficial to those enterprises adopting foreign advanced technology and management in an even broader way, giving a full play to the advantage of comparison, and participating in international competition. But they will also face serious challenges. First of all, compared with foreign advanced level, the enterprises at home lag behind in equipment level, the ability to research and develop new products, the efficiency to make use of energy resource, management, sales and service. Secondly, with the reduction of tariff, the competitive power of the enterprises at home producing products with deep processing and high added value with nonferrous metals will suffer an impact. Finally, in the realms of high-tech and new materials, transnational corporations have more advantages in funds, technology, management and sale so the high-tech enterprises at home will face even bitter competition.

Building Material Industry

Building material industry is an important material industry of China. Building material products include three main categories, namely, building materials and products, nonmetal mines and their products, and inorganic nonmetal new materials.

Since the reform and opening-up, the building material industry of China has developed at a rapid pace. For quite a few years, the output of cement, glass, building ceramics and sanitary ceramics has ranked first in the world, basically meeting the needs for national economy and social development. At present, the main problem of this industry is that the enterprises are small in scale and low in production concentration. The traditional building material products produced with backward technology are excessive while part of superior and high-grade products is structurally insufficient. For instance, superior float glass and glass for processing, high-grade building ceramics and sanitary ceramics, glass fiber and glass fiber products, and part of deep processed products with nonmetal mine still have to be imported.

After entry into the WTO, when compared with foreign advanced level, the enterprises at home lag behind in the level of technological equipment, in R&D ability, and in the utilization efficiencies of energy and resource. The tariff reduction of part of commodities may result in the increase of import volume. With the internationalization of domestic market, multinational corporations will increase their investment in the building material realm of China by depending on their advantages in funds, technology and management, so that the building material enterprises at home will face an even tougher competition.

During the "10th Five-Year Plan", the average annual investment in fixed assets of the whole society is around four trillion yuan, calculated on the basis of 7% average annual growth of the GDP. The main factors that will spur the growth of the demand for building material products are as follows: With the speeding up of urbanization process, there will be a big increase in the investment scale for small and medium cities and towns. With the housing industrialization, enhancement of people's living standards and improvement of farmers' housing, the demand for green building material products with high quality and multi functions and the prefabricated housing products with systematic integration will grow at a rapid pace. The demand for building material products will also be further raised by the Yangtze River Three Gorges Project and other key water control projects, the

Forecast of Demanding Volume for Main Building Material Products at Home in 2005

Products	Unit	Demanded Volume
Cement	000,000,000 Tons	6
In Which: Super-quality Cement	000,000,000 Tons	2
Plate Glass	000,000,000 Weight Boxes	1.8~1.9
In Which: Super-quality Float Glass	000,000,000 Weight Boxes	0.6~0.65
Sanitary Ceramics	00,000 Pieces	5500
Building Ceramics	000,000,000 M²	15
Fiber Glass	00,000 Tons	38
Wall Body Material	000,000,000 Standard Bricks	7500

construction of a number of large-scale reservoirs and the south-to-north water diversion project, the infrastructure construction of hydropower station, railway, highway, etc. and the ongoing western development.

According to the forecast of the State Economic and Trade Commission, the total volume of the demand for traditional building materials will maintain relatively stable on the basis of improving the product quality. In 2000, the output of cement was 597,000,000 tons and plate glass 182,000,000 weight boxes. In 2005, the total demand for cement and plate glass will maintain the existing level but the demand for quality products will prominently grow. The trend of changes in the demand for building ceramics and sanitary ceramics is that the market for low-grade products will continuously shrink while that for medium- and high-grade products will grow moderately.

With the development of construction, war industry, automobile, information, petrochemical industry and the relevant industries, new building materials, inorganic nonmetal new materials and deep processed non-metal mineral products will grow considerably, particularly the new wall-body material, new thermal insulation material and new waterproof material in new building materials, the fiber glass and its products, compound material and glass fiber reinforced plastic in inorganic nonmetal materials, and super-fine material with the property modified in deep processed non-metal mineral products.

With the commercialization of residential houses, housing fitting-up and ornament are becoming popular in China and there will be a rapid growth. In addition, there will also be a rapid growth in demand for exterior wall coating, high-grade plate for exterior wall decoration, secure and environmental interior wall paint, high-grade hardware and chemical building material products like quality plastic-steel door and window and plastic pipe and fittings.

Light Industry

Light industry is the principal part of the Chinese consumer goods industry. China has become a big power to produce light industrial products in the world with the output of some main products ranking in the forefront of the world. For instance, the output of bicycle, clock, ceramics for daily use, shoes, electric fan, electric rice cooker, refrigerator, washing machine and plastic film for agricultural use has ranked first in the world; the output of salt, synthetic detergent and beer has ranked second in the world; and the output of watch, machine-made paper and cardboard, sugar and air-conditioner has ranked third in the world. Light industrial products have been developed from the past tens of thousands of varieties to the present over 300,000 varieties.

Product quality has been prominently improved and quite a few famous brands and world-known trademarks have been created.

With update and renovation, the production technology of a few sectors of traditional light industry has reached the world level of 1990's. Newly developed sectors have developed at a rapid speed and the proportion of output value is gradually increasing. Take the five major sectors, namely, electrical household appliances, plastic products, beverages, cosmetics, and packing and ornament, for instance. They account for 30% of the total output value of the light industry sector.

Compared with other sectors, the production of large-scaled enterprises and enterprise groups of light industry is highly concentrated. For example, the output of the first six foremost refrigerator enterprises has comprised 75% of the total nationwide output, the output of the first six foremost washing machine and air-conditioner enterprises has made up 74.6% and 68.5% respectively of the total nationwide output, and the output of the first ten foremost beer breweries has taken up 40% of the total nationwide output.

By 2000, the total import and export of light industrial products had hit around 92.5 billion US dollars, of which about 22.1 billion was for import and about 70.3 billion was for export. In the export products, the proportion of technical and fund-intensive products and products with high added value grew up rapidly. The light industry of China has made use of foreign funds of about forty billion US dollars, of which thirty-five billion US dollars were directly invested by foreign businesses.

Faced with the rapid process of marketization and the formation of buyer's market at home as well as the new situation of tougher international competition, the contradiction of light industry structure is becoming prominent with each passing day. For instance, as the structure of products could not adapt itself to the changes of market needs, the supply exceeds the demand and the transformation of industry lags behind the upgrade of consuming structure. Most enterprises of light industry are backward in technological equipment and not competitive in the world. The turnover of China's light industry only takes up 5% in the world light industrial products.

The consuming trend, viewed from the next couple of years, will be a continuous upgrade. In general, the consumption of Chinese residents will be transformed from meeting the needs for daily life to paying more attention to the quality of life and from going after material consumption to seeking intellectual consumption and service consumption. Besides, people's concept of consumption will also have a big change, paying more attention to the consumption of famous brand, and a common pursuit for the products of environmental protection, energy conservation and cultural and ideological progress will be a fashion for future consumption.

At present, there is a stage difference between the changes of rural consumption and urban consumption. The consumption hotspot with the feature of popularization of electrical household appliances in the city occurring in 1980's is now being formed in the rural areas. Therefore, the special feature that rural consumption lags behind urban consumption can provide an opportunity for light industry to be expanded in rural market.

With the continuous expansion of world economic trade and mutual cultural penetration of various countries, the internationalization trend of domestic consumption also begins to emerge. Generally speaking, the demanding trend for consumer goods is developing towards the pursuit of intelligent, convenient, individual and green products.

The State Economic and Trade Commission predicts that with the development of national economy and improvement of residents' consuming level, the consuming structure of the Chinese residents will change drastically in the fields of food, clothing, shelter, transportation and expanses.

Food Consumption   In 2005, the average GDP per capita in China will reach 9,400 yuan. This will be a critical period for a rapid change of people's consumption pattern, including food consumption. Though the Engel's coefficient will decrease gradually, the total volume of food consumption will continuously rise, the grade and structure of food consumption will also have great changes, and the proportion of home-cooking food consumption will drop gradually. At the same time, food consumption will become multi-level and the demand for some nourishing, convenient, leisure food and food with non-environmental pollution will have big potentiality for growth. In addition, the rural consumption tends to be urbanized and home-cooking consumption pattern will be further transformed towards commercial consumption pattern. All this will make the consumption of industrialized food grow rapidly. It is expected that the

At Present, Consumption Volume of Toys in China Almost Hitting 10 Billion Yuan

Market of Electrical Household Appliances

Engel's coefficient will drop from 39.2% in 2000 to 38% in 2005 for urban residents, from 49.1% in 2000 to 46% in 2005 for rural residents, and the proportion of expenses on food consumption in consumption expenses of nationwide residents will drop from 46% to 42%. Anyhow, food consumption will still be the largest proportion for residents.

Clothing Consumption   The proportion of clothing consumption for nationwide residents is expected to be maintained around 7% ~ 8%, lower than the world average standard. The proportion of clothing consumption for city and town residents will drop from 11.7% in 2000 to 10.4% in 2005 and rural residents will keep steadily around 6%. In urban clothing consumption, the trend for individuality and medium- and high-grade consumption will be more and more prominent and brand consumption will gradually become a tidal current. But in rural areas, general clothing consumption, economical and practical and cheap but good, will still be the dominant factor.

Consumption of Family Equipment Facilities   During the "10th Five-Year Plan", the trend for the consumption of family equipment facilities in urban areas and rural areas will be different from each other. From the viewpoint of consumption trend, it is expected that the proportion of consumption for family equipment facilities in cities and towns will drop from 7.0% in 2000 to 5.9% in 2005 and in rural areas will keep steadily around 5.5%. From the viewpoint of consumption pattern, the electrical household appliances purchased during 1980's by city and town families have entered the upgrading time. The durable consumer goods have entered the stage of continuous upgrading. The consumption volume of new electrical household appliances, communication equipment and computer for home use will grow rapidly. With the enhancement of people's quality of life, the demand for air conditioner, various kinds of new kitchenware for home use, sanitary wares, keeping-fit facilities, etc. will have a rapid growth too. In rural areas, general electrical household appliances have started to enter a period of rapid growth.

Consumption on Entertainment, Education, Culture and Services   When the living pattern of consumption is in the process of transforming from adequate food and clothing to moderate prosperity or even to a wealthy life, people's cultural and intellectual demands for entertainment, education, culture and services will continuously grow, tourism consumption will also grow continuously and residents' consumption realms will be incessantly expanded. The development of new economy and the speeding up of marketization process will make the competition in employment even tougher. Besides, the appearance of "holiday economy" will make the consumption proportion of entertainment, education, culture and tourism grow constantly in cities and towns. According to a prediction, the consumption proportion of urban and rural residents in entertainment, education and culture in 2005 will go up to 14.2%, rising to the second rank in various kinds of consumption proportion The consumption proportion of rural residents in entertainment, education, culture and services will go up to 13.9%.

Housing Consumption   Cities and towns in China have basically materialized the reform in housing distribution on monetary basis and commercialization of housing consumption. During the "10th Five-Year Plan", the proportion of housing consumption in cities and towns will increase in a steady way. The proportion of rural residents' consumption in housing will be basically steady. With the development of housing sector, the volume of people's demand for housing products and articles for interior decoration will grow endlessly.

In the '10th Five-Year Plan" of light industry sector, the State Economical and Trade Commission makes the following prediction for main light industrial products at home in the year of 2005:

Paper and Cardboard   According to the analysis of the paper and cardboard needed by press, publishing, printing, packing and other related departments, the total volume of paper and cardboard consumption in 2005 is expected to be 50,000,000 tons. Compared with the 36,000,000 tons in 2000, the average annual growth will be 6.8% with the consumption of 38,000 grams per capita, of which the paper for newspaper is 2,200,000 tons, the paper for printing and writing 11,400,000 tons, the paper for daily use 3,200,000 tons, the paper for packing 5,300,000 tons, white paperboard 5,300,000 tons, the cardboard for boxes 7,800,000 tons and the paper for corrugated boxes 9,300,000 tons.

Electrical Household Appliances   The production and consumption of electrical household appliances are developing towards the direction of high-efficiency, energy saving, environmental protection, noise-free, high quality, multiple functions

Data

Tips for Foreign Investors to Merge Share Ownership of SOE and Participate in Assets Reorganization of SOE

The following legal issues should be specially taken care of for foreign investors to merge the share ownership of SOE and to participate in the assets reorganization of SOE:

Industrial Policies It must be clarified whether the SOE to be merged or invested is an industry that is allowed by the Chinese government for foreign investors to make investment. In case of YES it should also be known what is the share percentage allowed to be held by foreign investors.

Organ of Examination and Approval and Its Limits of Authority Prior to merging the share ownership of the SOE or making investment in the SOE, foreign investors should be clearly aware of the procedure of examination and approval laid down by the Chinese law and the limits of authority of the organ of examination and approval so as to prevent government departments to exceed their authority for examination and approval or to go against the procedure simply for the benefits of the locality and departments. The invested project without being approved by the state regulations will have troubles in future financing and transfer of share ownership and will also likely be fined by the supervising department of the state.

Status of Property Right Surveys should be made for the status of property right of the SOE, clarifying the property ownership of the assets. Besides, investigations should also be made whether the assets of the SOE is involved in any mortgage, pledge, lien, guarantee, litigation, arbitration or other disputes.

Land-use Right When merging the share ownership of the SOE or making investment in the SOE, foreign investors should make arrangement in advance the land of the enterprise to be used by foreign investors. The common practice is that the charge paid by the Chinese party for the land-use right is fixed for investment. The alternative is that the foreign investors can pay directly to the government departments for the charge to obtain the land-use right.

Creditor's Rights and Debts Investigation should be made for creditor's rights and debts of the SOE. The related creditor's rights and debts should be standardized so as to ensure the legitimate right and effectiveness of the relationship related to creditors' rights and debts.

Making Investment in Foreign Countries In case the SOE happens to be not standardized or illegal in making investment in foreign countries, foreign investors should request the SOE to standardize the investment or make its investment in foreign countries legal before merger or investment so that unnecessary disputes can be avoided.

Business Contract It matters a lot to the normal management of an enterprise whether it can establish long-term and steady partnership with other enterprises with good reputation and credit.

Non-operational Assets Due to historical reasons, most of the SOEs have the issue of so-called "enterprise-run society", i.e. the SOEs own their own hospital, canteen, nursery and school. All this belongs to the SOE's non-operational assets. Prior to merging the share ownership of the SOE or making investment in the SOE, foreign investors should discuss in details the separation of the non-operational assets and rearrangement of the relevant personnel. When necessary, resort to the support of the local government or ask the local government to offer corresponding favorable policies.

and networking. The demand for main electrical household appliances in 2005 is 13,000,000 refrigerators, 18,000,000 washing machines, 20,000,000 air-conditioners, 9,000,000 microwave ovens, 4,000,000 dishwashers and 10,000,000 electric water heaters.

Plastic Products The demanding volume for plastic products in 2005 is expected to be 25,000,000 tons, of which 4,700,000 tons are plastic products for agricultural uses, accounting for 19.0% of the total demanding volume; 5,500,000 tons are plastic products for packing, 22.0% of the total demanding volume; 4,000,000 tons are for building, 16.0% of the total demand; 4,500,000 tons are for industrial uses, 18.0% of the total demand; 4,720,000 tons are plastic products for daily use and medical use, 18.7% of the total demand; 780,000 tons are for man-made leather and synthetic leather, 3.1% of the total demand; and 800,000 tons for other plastic products, 3.2% of the total demanding volume.

Cleansing Articles The average annual consumption of cleansing articles per capita of the present China is 3,000 grams, only one-fifth to one-fourth of European and American countries. In China, synthetic detergent, the main variety of cleansing articles, accounts for 85.7% of the total volume of cleansing articles with 26% as liquid detergent, and toilet soap makes up 30% of the total of toilet and laundry soaps. According to a prediction, with the enhancement of people's quality of life, the consumption proportion of synthetic detergent and liquid detergent will grow continuously. In 2005, the consumption of cleansing articles will hit 4,600,000 tons, 4,140,000 of which will be synthetic detergent, accounting for 90% of the proportion of the total

Boutiques Seen Everywhere in Urban Streets

volume of cleaning articles.

Salt   The total volume demanded for salt in 2005 will be 32,000,000 tons, of which 7,500,000 tons is for table salt, 23,300,000 tons for industrial use, 200,000 tons for agricultural and animal husbandry use, and 1,000,000 tons for export.

Sugar   The sugar consumption volume of the present China is 8,000,000 tons with an average annual per capita consumption of 6,200 grams. The average annual consumption in the world is 20,000 grams per capita while that of developed countries is 35,000 – 45,000 grams. So far, China is still one of the countries with lowest annual consumption of sugar on the average per capita in the world. From the viewpoint of regions, sugar consumption is mainly concentrated in the medium and big cities along the coast while the sugar consumption in mid-western areas and the extensive rural areas is still very low. From the long-term point of view, sugar consumption will grow considerably. According to the analysis of the recent trend of consumption growth and in consideration of the factors of production and consumption of chemical synthetic sweeteners like compressed gluside, the consumption for sugar is predicted to hit 10,000,000 tons in 2005.

Beer   The average annual consumption of beer in China is sixteen liters per capita while that in the world is twenty-three liters. With the enhancement of people's living standards and increase of farmers' income, beer consumption in China will maintain a considerable growth. People will prefer superior-quality beer, light beer, draught beer, famous brand beer and the beer with new packing in compliance with the consumption fashion. The beer consumption is expected to reach 25,000,000 tons in 2005.

Bicycle   The varieties, functions and quality of bicycle will have continuous new development with its function as a means of transportation for short distance instead of walking expanded to multi functions such as leisure, entertainment and fitness. The consumption demand for bicycle at home in 2005 is expected to be steadily maintained at 19,000,000.

Sewing Machine   Light and handy modern multi-functional sewing machine coordinated with furniture for home use is still at the stage of guidance and growth at home but it has great potentiality in the world market. Ordinary sewing machine for home use will be gradually replaced by multi-functional sewing machine. With the development of relevant industries, the market demand volume of the sewing machine for industrial use will keep on growing. It is predicted that in 2005, the demand of homemade industrial sewing machine will reach 3,100,000 sets and the growth of social demand for industrial sewing machine with electrical and mechanical integration will be particularly fast.

Watch and Clock   The demand for thin watch, fashion watch, sports watch and gift watch will tend to grow. Consumers' pursuit for famous brand will also further grow and the market share of famous-brand watches and clocks made at home will grow notably. In 2005, the demanding volume for watches at home is predicted to be 70,000,000 while for clocks 30,000,000.

As there are large numbers of sectors in light industry, different sectors and different products of a same sector will suffer different impacts after China's WTO accession. First, it will be beneficial to the sectors with higher degree of openness and the sectors using higher foreign funds such as electrical household appliances, chemical industry of everyday use, beer and beverages. Second , the world market for labor-intensive light industrial products can be further expanded, such as bicycle, sewing machine, toy, watch and clock, furniture, hardware products, ceramics, canned food, leather, suitcase and drawnwork products. Third, the impact will be negligible to those products that are not too much dependent on import for the domestic market or those foreign products that have a certain market share at home, such as electrical appliances for illumination, glass for everyday use, salt industry, articles for recreational and sports activities and pen-making but a certain barrier will be formed for upgrading products and technology. Fourth, the impact will be great to the sectors using agricultural products as raw material and facing mainly the domestic market, such as dairy products, grape wine and monosodium glutamate. Finally, the impact will also be considerable to the sectors having a wide gap with foreign advanced level in the aspects of technical equipment level and the economic scale of products, and to the sectors with higher cost of production incompatible in the market competition, such as papermaking, papermaking machinery and sugar refinery.

Textile Industry

The textile industry includes textile sector, garment sector, the manufacturer of chemical fiber and the manufacturer of special equipment for textile sector. The textile sector includes cotton spinning and weaving (printing and dyeing), wool spinning and weaving, linen spinning and weaving, silk spinning and weaving, and knitting; the garment sector includes garment, hat and shoes; and the sector of chemical fiber includes synthetic fiber and man-made fiber.

As China is abundant in manpower resources with comparatively low cost for labor, it has a resource advantage to develop labor-intensive industries like textile and garment. At present, China is the largest nation around the world to produce textile and garment. The output of yarn, cloth, wool fabric, textile, chemical fiber and garment has been steadily ranking first in the world for quite a few years. The position of the Chinese industry of textile and garment in foreign trade has become more prominent. Since 1980's, the textile and garment has been the number one commodity for export in China, making the proportion of one-fourth of the total volume of national commodity export. It was not until 1995 that the export volume of mechanical and electrical products exceeded that of textile and garment. The Chinese export of textile and garment in 2000 hit over fifty-two billion US dollars, accounting for 20% of the total volume of export commodities of China and around 13% of the turnover of world textile and garment. Since 1994, the interior of China has become the largest place to export textile and garment in the world, exceeding Hong Kong.

Anyhow, there still exist some problems in the Chinese sector of textile and garment, such as smaller production scale, poorer technological equipment and lower labor productivity. The development for some products with higher standard and newer technology is slow, unable to adapt itself to the market demand, neither at home nor abroad, but excessive competition occurs to part of low- and medium-grade products. In the products for export, medium-grade products are in the main and the proportion of products with high added value is very small. The garment for export is mainly in the form of processing trade. Most of the garments have no independent brands by themselves. The textile fabric, low in standard and few in varieties, can't meet the demand for garment production and the garment for export has to use imported fabric.

After the WTO accession, the common view is that the Chinese textile industry will face an even better environment for development. But because of smaller scale and higher material cost of the chemical fiber enterprise at home, there is quite a distance in varieties, quality and price compared with foreign enterprises. After entering the WTO, the prospect of the market for imported products with lower price and better quality is much brighter. With the reduction of import tariff for textile fabrics, the import of medium- and high-grade fabrics in general trade will increase considerably.

Environment of Domestic Market   During the "10th Five-Year Plan", the proportion of clothing consumption for urban and rural residents in the total consumption will drop fairly but the total consumption volume will grow.

Factor of Population Growth   At present, the per capita consumption of fiber in China is only 6,600 grams, lower than the average world level of 7,500 grams. In 2005, the per capita consumption of fiber in China will reach 7,400 grams. During the "10th Five-Year Plan", the average annual growth of population will be 12,000,000 people. If the consumption of the newly increased population is calculated on the average basis of 7,400 grams per capita, the net increase of the consumption volume of fiber will be 450,000 tons.

Changes of Consumption Pattern   With the initial formation of buyers' market, people will have more selections in consumption. With the enhancement of the living standards of the urban and rural people, the consumption pattern will have big changes: the proportion of food and clothing will drop but that of housing and transportation will rise. The proportion of clothing consumption in social consumption retail total will gradually drop but the actual expenditure will still grow. People have a higher demand for textiles both in quantity and quality and the urban consumption pays particular attention to individuality, comfortableness, superior quality (brand) and fashion.

Experts Warning Ready-Made Clothing Market in China to Pay Attention to Different Regions for Consumption

Textile Market in Rural Areas   At present, due to farmers' actual income, consumption pattern and other causes, the rural consumption still lags far behind the urban consumption and the consumption level of textiles and garment in the rural area is still not high enough. During the "10th Five-Year Plan", the consumption demand will be further spurred with the increase of farmers' income, the transfer of 40,000,000 rural laborers and the speeding-up of urbanization process. The consumption of textiles and garment in rural areas will have great potentiality. The key tone of the clothing consumption in the rural area is inexpensive but elegant textiles and the products appropriate to the needs of rural consumption will be developed, particularly chemical fiber textiles.

Changes of Textiles in Applied Realm   In the three major realms of clothing, ornament and industry of China's textiles, the proportion of fiber consumption in China differs greatly from the consumption pattern of developed countries, higher proportion in clothing but lower proportion in industry and ornament. With the improvement of housing conditions and the increasing needs for textiles in the sectors of agriculture, water conservancy, communications and building, particularly the application of new textile technology and the development of new materials, the application realm for textiles will be further expanded. During the "10th Five-Year Plan", the potentiality for fiber ornament consumption will be great and a trend of development for market expansion will emerge.

Medicine Sector

The main categories of medicine sector include medicine and preparations made with chemical materials, traditional Chinese medicine, prepared herbal medicine in small pieces ready for decoction, pharmacist-prepared traditional Chinese medicine, antibiotics, biological products, biochemical medicine, radioactive medicine, medical apparatus and instruments, hygienic materials, pharmaceutical machinery, medicine packing materials and pharmaceutical commerce.

Since the reform and openness, the medicine industry has been keeping a fairly fast pace in its development with the enhancement of people's living standards and the continuous growth for the demand of medical treatment and health care. Between 1978 and 2000, the output of medicine industry showed a yearly average increase of 16.6%, one of the sectors with the fastest development in the national economy.

China is a pharmaceutical big power in the world. Statistics show that China has the capacity of turning out 1,500 varieties of medicines with chemical materials with the total output of 430,000 tons, ranking second in the world and 4,000 varieties of chemical medicine preparations fallen into thirty-four preparation types. Some important varieties such as vitamin C and penicillin occupy a pivotal position in the world.

The medicine sector is one of the sectors that were open the earliest to the outside world

Experts Predicting China to be 5ᵗʰ Largest Pharmaceutical Market around the World

in China. Now, the first foremost twenty pharmaceutical companies in the world have made investment and set up factories in China.

The main issues existing in the Chinese medicine sector are as follows: Most of the medicine enterprises are small in scale and backward in manufacturing technology and the production concentration lags far behind advanced countries. The basis for creating new medicine is weak, the mechanism of medicine technical creation and rapid commercialization of scientific and technological achievements has not yet been completely formed and they are lack of new products with independent intellectual property. Most of the medical apparatus and instruments that can be manufactured at home are the conventional low- and medium-grade products with low added values while most of high-grade, high-precision and advanced medical apparatus and instruments and new practical medical equipments have to be dependent on import. Though China is a big power in producing medicines with chemical materials in the world, the varieties of preparation products are not compatible and very few have accessed the world market.

The imported medicine of China is mainly preparations. After the WTO accession, in spite of tariff reduction, there is still a big difference in price between the imported products and homemade products. This is an issue foreign factories and companies have to face squarely at. However, foreign factories and companies will benefit a lot from the tariff cut in the aspects of the medicines and medical apparatus and instruments unable to be produced in China because of low production technology.

Since 1993, China has practiced patent protection for medicines and administrative protection conditionally for the medicines that obtained patent in forty-plus countries such as the United States, the European Union and Japan between 1986 and 1992. After the entry of the WTO, the protection of intellectual property rights will be stricter and the patent medicines needed for clinical treatment in China will depend mainly on import.

Before the WTO accession, China always limited foreign funds to enter the realm of medicine circulation in China. But after entering the WTO, the medicine circulation enterprises at home, unable to compete with world transnational companies in the fields of management and capital quality and scale, will suffer a lot from the impact with the opening-up of distribution service of medicines.

At present, the per capita average consumption of medicine of the medium-developed nations in the world is forty to fifty US dollars but in China less than ten US dollars. With the enhancement of people's living standards and quality of life and updating of medicine consumption ideas, the growth of medicine market in China will soon be faster than the world medicine market.

During the "10th Five-Year Plan", the reform on basic medical insurance system for urban and rural workers and staff members will be unfolded in an all-round way. The basic principle of this system is "low level, wide coverage". Its implementation will expand the scope of people covered by medical insurance on the one hand, that is to say, to increase the number of insured people from the present 160,000,000 to 300,000,000. On the other, irrational medicine consumption will be readjusted by inhibiting the use of expensive medicines and large-scale medical equipments and promoting the use of ordinary medicines with lower price but curative effects.

The growth of total population and ageing population and the development of urbanization will increase the needs for medical products. Now, China has entered the society of the elderly. It is predicted that during the "10th Five-Year Plan", the aged will grow at a speed of 3% annually on the average. In 2005, the number of senior people will exceed 100,000,000 and the total population will reach 1,330,000,000. During the "10th Five-Year Plan", China will have an increase of 10,000,000 of urban population yearly on the average. At present, the ratio of per capita average medicine consumption in urban areas and that in rural areas is around 7:1. During the "10th Five-Year Plan", the demand for medicine consumption in rural areas will be an important growth for the medicine market.

Comprehensively, the growth rate of the Chinese medicine market during the "10th Five-Year Plan" is expected to be 12% annually on the average, faster than the world medicine market.

SERVICE SECTOR AND POLICY FOR ITS DEVELOPMENT

The Chinese industries are divided into three categories, the primary, the secondary and tertiary. The service sector is roughly equivalent to the tertiary industry defined by China, and the sector of construction and engineering service is classified as the secondary industry, which is regarded as a department of service sector by the WTO.

In the 30 years starting from the founding of the new China in 1949, the state laid all its emphasis on the primary and secondary industries, causing the development of tertiary industry drastically lagging behind. Since the reform and openness in 1978, the state has attached great importance to the development of tertiary industry. Since then, the tertiary industry has maintained a rather rapid growth. In 1980's and 1990's, its average annual growth reached 12.4% and 9.06% respectively. From the late 1980's up to the present day, the proportion of the added value of tertiary industry has been accounting for 30% ~ 34% of the total output value at home. The number of employees in tertiary industry also grows at a rapid pace, becoming the main way to resolve the employment issue in China. In 2001, the number of people employed in tertiary industry comprised 27.9% of the total number of the whole society

Interior Scene of a Shopping Center

employment.

Compared with the developed countries where the service sector takes up 70 ~ 80 % of the GDP, the service sector of China accounts less than 40% in the GDP proportion, much lower than the average level of developing countries. Its comparative advantage is mainly focused on labor force and natural resources but it lags behind in capital and development of the sector with intensive technical resources. From the viewpoint of structure, the proportion in the wholesale and retail sector, the catering sector, the sector of communication, transportation and storage, and the sector of telecom service is all over 20%. In China, the sectors of finance, insurance, consultation, telecom and other service sectors with technical intension and knowledge intension that make up the largest trade volume in the world are still at preliminary development stage. The degree of service marketization is rather low and the development is unbalanced in various regions. Generally speaking, the rural area lags behind the urban area and the hinterland lags behind the coastland. The service sector of China has long been under the status of scattered operation, lacking large enterprises with world competition power.

In 1980's, only the service sector of tourism and catering and a few other realms in the service sector were open to foreign funds. After entering 1990's, the service sector has been expanded for openness, becoming an important symbol of all-dimensional openness of China. The realm of commodity retail, tourism, real estate, bank, insurance, communication and transportation, information consultation, special services and others is gradually open to foreign investors.

With the WTO accession, the Chinese government makes the commitment of opening the service sector in an all-round way. In a study regarding the commitment made by various countries for service trade, the World Bank made a survey of the status of openness of China's service sector within one year after China's entry into the WTO and after the transitional period respectively. The study holds that the Chinese government, after the WTO accession, has kept its commitment in all departments, at least partially, in respect of consumption in foreign countries, commercial existence and flow of natural persons. In the field of cross-border supply, over 80% of the departments have kept the commitment. Compared with other state groups, China has made more commitments but in the field of commercial existence there are more restrictions. After the transitional period, the average number of the Chinese entire market accession commitment is 57.4%, higher than the commitment made by other state groups (including the state groups with higher income) in the Uruguay Round. China reaches 38% of the average proportion of the market accession commitment, a little higher than the 36% of those high-income states. The average number and average proportion of the commitment made by China in the field of national treatment is 57.4% and 45% respectively, higher than other state groups.

There remains much room for development in the realm of China's service sector. After the WTO accession, this industry is becoming a new hotspot for foreign investment. For adapting the service sector to the development trend in the important realm of world economic and trade development and competition, the Chinese

A corner of supermarket

government has clearly put forward in the "10th Five-Year Plan" that great efforts will be made to develop the service sector, providing policy-based guarantee for foreign investment. In accordance with WTO's related provisions, the service sector will become a realm with its range open the widest after China's WTO entry, which itself implies great business opportunities.

Wholesale and Retail Sector

Wholesale, retail, trade and catering are the main sectors of tertiary industry. In 2001, the sector accounted for 27% of the proportion of the increased value of tertiary industry.

China started a pilot project of Chinese-foreign joint venture in a commercial retail enterprise in 1992. At present, a few well-known transnational chain enterprises, such as Walmart, Metro, Auzhan and B&J, have made investment and run stores in China to enfold chained operation. In accordance with China's commitment to the WTO and the development plans to make use of foreign funds in the commercial realm, the department related is revising the "Interim Measures for the Administration of Foreign-Invested Commercial Enterprises". The new provisions are planned to turn the pilot project of foreign investment in commercial realm into normal opening-up and to further soften the terms for foreign investment access.

After the WTO accession, foreign large-scale transnational retail groups will have far better advantages in the fields of commodity, service and price than most of the Chinese retail enterprises. In addition, they also have better advantages in the fields of mechanism, size, financing, technological equipment, operation and sales, ways of settling accounts, brand, channel for supply of goods and commodity composition. After their access into China, the domestic enterprises will be forced to give up a part of shares in the retail market and the existence of small and medium retail sector will be faced with rather great pressure. Anyhow, the status of the openness of the Chinese retail market is already above the commitment of the initial stage of market openness specified in the agreement. The competition of the domestic retail market has been comparatively rather tough. Part of the retail enterprises at home has already grown up in the competition and a few large enterprises have become already rather strong in the competition. In the competition with foreign commercial retail enterprises, Chinese enterprises have the advantages in selection of the location for stores, in sharing common resources, etc.

Logistic and Transportation Sector

The statistics issued by the State Economic and Trade Commission shows that the present total value of the Chinese logistic market is around 200 billion yuan, accounting for only one-fifth of the GNP, and the total value of the third party logistic market will hit ten billion yuan from four billion yuan in the next few years. "Logistic distribution" has already been listed in the "10th Five-Year Plan" as a service sector for key development.

In accordance with the protocol to enter the WTO, land freight transport, storage sector, freight agent and other auxiliary services will be open to the outside world step by step within three years. It will provide favorable conditions for world logistic enterprises to enter China.

In July 2002, China started to launch pilot projects for foreign business to make investment in logistic sector in the three provinces of Guangdong, Jiangsu and Zhejiang and the four municipalities directly under the Central Government, namely, Beijing, Tianjin, Chongqing and Shanghai. Foreign investors were allowed to set up logistic enterprises either in the form of Chinese-foreign joint venture or Chinese-foreign cooperation in the above-mentioned areas; and foreign investors were also allowed to make investment and run international interflow of goods and materials business or third-party logistic business either in the form of Chinese-foreign joint venture or Chinese-foreign cooperation.

According to the government scheme, China will establish one hundred logistic centers and seven major transaction centers in China within ten years. These major transaction centers are the Northeast area with Shenyang as the center, the North China area with Beijing as the center, the Northwest area with Lanzhou (or Xi'an) as the center, the East China area with Shanghai as the center, the Central China area with Wuhan as the center, the Southwest area with Chongqing as the center, and the South China area with Guangzhou as the center. Beijing will establish a central processing system and a management and decision-making system for the national logistic transaction centers.

The land transportation sector of China was officially open to the outside world in 1988 but at present the foreign-funded enterprise is still at a stage of initial development. The coastal cities and economically developed areas are the key areas for foreign investment. So far as the investment realm is concerned, land passenger transport is mainly to run freeway passenger transport and tourism transport while land cargo transport is mainly to run container transport and through cargo transport in and out of Hong Kong. With the development of logistic sector in recent years, more and more investment is made in the realms of logistics and storage.

Between 2001 and 2002, the relevant departments of the state successively promulgated the "Provisions Concerning the Administration of Foreign-Invested Land Transport Sector", the "Regulations of the People's Republic of China for Ocean Shipping", the "Interim Provisions on Foreign-Invested Civil Aviation Sector" and the "Provisions Concerning the Administration of

Sector of Interflow of Goods and Materials, an Important Domain for Development of Postal Service

Foreign-Invested International Freight Agency Section" and worked out respective provisions on the relevant foreign-invested realms.

Compared with large logistic and transport enterprises in the world, Chinese enterprises are strong in domestic network and wide in distribution but weak in network conformity ability. They are also strong in assets, domestic logistic experiences, lower cost in labor and great potentiality for development and the privately-run logistic transport enterprises at home also have the special feature of flexible operation. International logistic transport enterprises are weak in the domestic network and lack of domestic experiences, have comparatively higher operational cost, and know little about humane environment. Anyhow, they are strong in global transportation, information network and operation, and have advantages in the fields of talented people, management, technology and service consciousness. They are well experienced in international business, particularly international logistic projects, and have rich experiences in IT, management experiences in the supply chain as well as the experiences in planning, management and control of logistic projects. Therefore, the domestic enterprises will face serious challenges in the fields of network reform and conformity, logistic project experiences, service consciousness, management system, technology and talents, and fund support.

Telecom Sector

In recent years, the telecom market in China has constantly been in a status of rapid development. Though the mobile telecom market got a serious start only seven to eight years ago, it has been developed to first in the world. The Internet has been developed to second in a short period of four years, only next to the United States.

What is more important is that the telecom market in China still has a huge room for development. Take telephone subscribers for instance. The total number is over 300,000,000, but its national popularization is only 30% while the mobile phone only 15%. Take netizens for another instance. The national popularization is less than 4%. In line with the plan of the Ministry of Information Industry, at the end of 2005, the increased value of the Chinese telecom operation sector and the manufacturer of electronic information products will exceed 7% and the total size of the information industry will be over three trillion yuan, of which the total volume of telecom business will reach 1.2 trillion yuan and the market size will double that of the present.

Before the WTO accession, the telecom operation business was a forbidden realm for foreign investment. But after the WTO accession, in accordance with the commitment made by China, the telecom business will open to foreign investors step by step with some restrictions and within five years after the WTO accession, the restrictions on regions, foreign-funded proportion and business scope will be gradually lifted. In December 2001, the "Provisions Concerning the Management of Foreign-Invested Telecom Enterprises" was promulgated, defining clearly the conditions and procedures for foreign-invested telecom enterprises. In the "Guidance Catalog for Foreign-Invested Industries" revised in April 2002, the ban for foreign investment in telecom operation was lifted. In March 2002, the first telecom operational enterprise founded on the basis of Sino-US joint venture was officially open for business in Shanghai.

China, the Largest Mobile Phone Market in the World

Comparatively speaking, the operation and management of the domestic telecom enterprise at present is basically in an extensive form and the foreign-invested enterprise has competitive advantages in management mechanism, market operation, funds, talents and technology. In accordance with the related protocols to enter the WTO, China has to open the telecom market at different times, different regions and different realms after the WTO accession.

In China, there are thousands of enterprises related to IT industry of Internet but there is still not any leading enterprise yet. According to the agreement to enter the WTO, foreign funds can get in at once. Experts predict that a few domestic enterprises weak in strength will be eliminated while the IT enterprises on the basis of Sino-foreign joint venture will take up the dominant position.

The market potentiality for the realm of mobile telecom is great and technical updating is fast. It is comparatively easy to access the network construction and market so there will be more foreign-invested enterprises to make applications for setting up IT enterprises of Sino-foreign joint venture.

In the realms of fundamental network and fixed business, China has already established a key net for fundamental network of optic cable transmission with its size only next to the United States, the total assets reaching over 400 billion yuan. The foreign business trying to get into the fundamental telecom business in China can do nothing but form joint venture with the domestic enterprise that has already obtained the access of fundamental telecom business. In addition, they must be approved by the government in accordance with the "Provisions Concerning the Administration of Foreign-Funded Telecom Enterprises" for operation.

Banking Sector

In the domestic market, China's commercial bank takes the absolute share. The four exclusively state-owned major commercial banks, the main body of the Chinese banks, are under step-by-step reform into modern financial enterprises to manage currency. The other small and medium commercial banks are seeking for association with merger, reorganization and business cooperation. More and more commercial banks are trying to expand their respective business in the form of financial holding companies to get ready for transferring into all-round banks in the future.

China started the pilot item of absorbing foreign investment in the banking realm in 1982. Now foreign banking institutions are allowed to run operational banking institutions in all cities in China. The investment forms include foreign-funded branch bank, wholly-owned or joint-venture bank, wholly-owned or joint-venture financial company, and joint-venture investment bank. In 2002, there were over 200 opera-

"Newly Emerged World Market Bank in 2000" Published in a Magazine
Entitled "European Currencies", Ranking Bank of China First

tional foreign-invested banking institutions within the territory of China with total assets of over thirty-eight billion US dollars, making China one of the developing countries with high degree of openness in banking sector. At the end of 2001, the State Council promulgated the newly revised "Provisions Concerning the Management of Foreign-Invested Banking Institutions in the People's Republic of China" and the details for implementation. The main revised content is as follows: to allow foreign-funded bank to enfold foreign exchange business in an all-round way with no restriction of regions and service objects; to eliminate the requirement of business size and volume set up for foreign-funded financial institutions to enter the RMB business market; to require no more the Chinese partner of the joint-venture bank or financial company to be a financial institution; and to open up RMB business step by step in accordance with the commitment of time and regions made at the time of WTO accession until all restrictions on regions and service objects are lifted within five years.

Though the domestic banks have localized advantage and enjoy a certain period of time for protection, the competitions from foreign-funded banks and domestic non-banking institutions are becoming stronger and stronger. These competitions feature the competition in business, flow of employers, creation of new products, and reform on financial operation system. At present, the business of setting export accounts handled by foreign-invested banks in China accounts for over 40% of the interior market share, and the intermediate business and on-line business are becoming the focus for competition between Chinese and foreign-funded banks. In terms of capital strength, operational management and service, foreign-funded banks have more advantages.

Insurance Sector

Since the reform and opening up, insurance sector has had a rapid development. Since 1990's, the operation pattern monopolized exclusively by the Chinese People's Insurance Company has been broken, and a new pattern of mutual competition and development between Chinese and foreign insurance companies is formed. At the end of 2001, there were fifty-two insurance companies in China, of which five were exclusively state-owned companies, fifteen were Chinese stock system companies, twenty were Sino-foreign joint ventures, and thirteen were branch companies of foreign insurance companies.

In recent years, people's insurance consciousness has been greatly enhanced and the insurance market grows at a rapid pace. Since 1990's, the yearly growth of insurance is around 25%. In 2001, the total insurance income was 210.9 billion yuan, in which

Growth of Insurance Business in China from 1991 to 2001

Year	Insurance Income (000,000,000 Yuan)	Growth Rate (%)	GDP Growth Rate (%)	Insurance Depth (%)	Insurance Density (Yuan/Per Capita)
1991	239	33.0	22.0	0.9	22.02
1993	406	29.0	13.4	0.98	42.0
1995	615.7	23.6	10.2	1.06	50.83
1997	1087.4	43.5	8.8	1.45	87.66
1999	1393.2	10.2	7.1	1.7	110.6
2000	1595.9	14.5	8.0	1.8	127.7
2001	2109.4	32.2	7.3	2.2	168.8

32.5% was from property insurance and 67.5% from life insurance. However, the insurance sector of China is still at an initial stage of development and the overall level is quite low. To compare with developed countries and world average level, an obvious difference exits so the potentiality of insurance market is very great.

In 1992, China started to open the insurance market with conditions. Restricted by operational scope and regions, foreign-funded insurance institutions possessed only a small market share. After the WTO entry, the insurance sector is further opened. The competitive power of foreign-invested insurance company can be clearly felt and Chinese insurance company is faced with the challenge in the respects of talents, price, the capital operation ability of insurance enterprise and the ability of assets management. At the end of 2001, the State Council inaugurated the "Regulations for the Management of Foreign-Invested Insurance Companies", defining clearly qualification conditions, setting-up procedures, business scope and legal obligations for foreign investors to make investment in insurance sector.

Tourism Sector

For over 20 years, China has changed from a big power with tourism resources to a big power for tourism in Asia. Entrance reception and earning foreign exchange through tourism have maintained a two-digit growth. In 2001, the gross income from tourism sector in China was 499.5 billion yuan, an equivalent to 5.2% of the GDP., the income of foreign exchange through tourism sector hit 17.8 billion US dollars, up 9.7% compared with the previous year and leaping to fifth place in the world, and the income from domestic tourism hit 352.2 billion yuan, up 10.9% compared with the previous year. The exit number of Chinese citizens reached 12,130,000 people/times, up 15.9% compared with the previous year, in which the exit number for private affairs was 6,945,400 people/times, up 23.3% compared with the previous year.

In recent years, China has been encouraging the people to increase consumption activities such as tourism and rest for leisure and relaxation. With increased income and longer holidays, more and more people go abroad for touring. China has become a newly developed tourist export nation with rapid growth in Asian area. According to the prediction of world tourism organization, China will become the first largest country for tourism destination and fourth tourist-source export nation in the world in 2020. At that time, the number of Chinese tourists going abroad will exceed 100,000,000 people/times. Based on this prospect, more and more countries have expressed their hope to the Chinese government that they can be approved as early as possible as destination countries for Chinese citizens to visit at their own expenses. Traveling companies in many countries, attracted by his huge market, have come to China to set up traveling agency or sent people to take care of tourism or cooperation, making great efforts to win over tourist resources for traveling from the country with the largest population in the world.

The reason why the tourism market of China is particularly worth the attention is first of all because of its tremendous potentiality. The increase of residents' income level will give an impetus to the rapid growth of tourism needs at home. Simultaneously, with the further rise of world economy and trade, international tour-

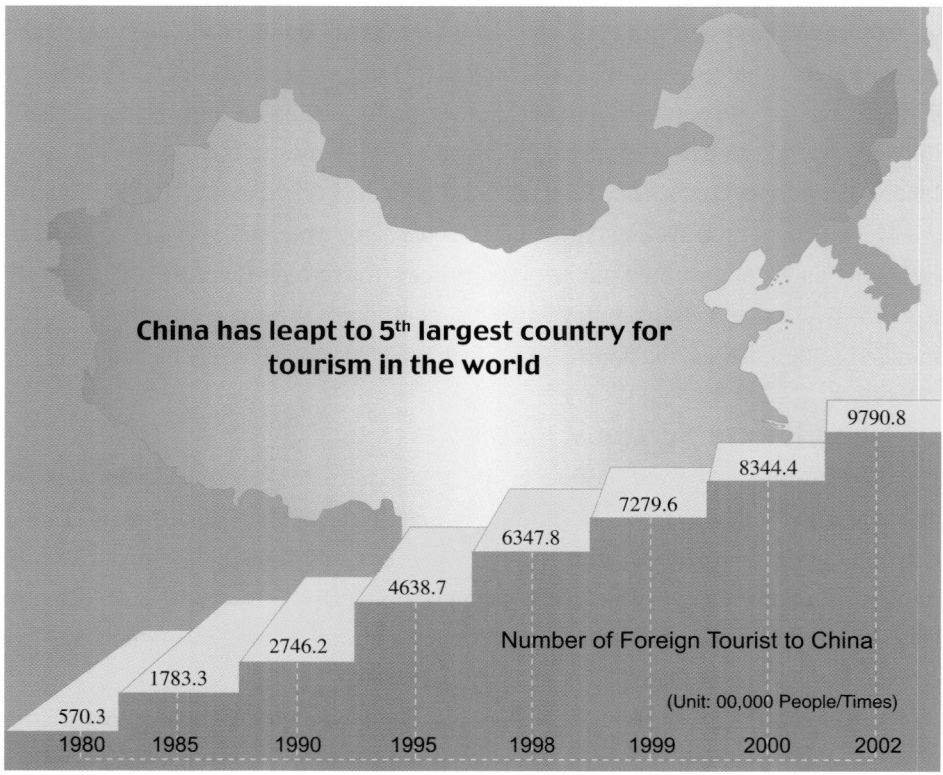

China has leapt to 5th largest country for tourism in the world

9790.8

8344.4

7279.6

6347.8

4638.7

2746.2

Number of Foreign Tourist to China

1783.3

570.3

(Unit: 00,000 People/Times)

| 1980 | 1985 | 1990 | 1995 | 1998 | 1999 | 2000 | 2002 |

ist source will also further rise. Besides, there is great potentiality for development of tourism resources in China, particularly a number of unique and monopolistic tourism resources in the world located at the under-developed western areas will be rapidly transformed into industrious advantages with the implementation of the western development strategy. Furthermore, tourism and its relevant industries will speed up its step to gear with the world after the WTO accession and the environments for development will be further optimized, which will promote the growth of world business and tourism. Tourism sector has won great attraction of the central government and the local governments at different levels. The policy environment to promote the development of tourism sector is being formed. After the WTO entry, foreign-funded traveling agency can do business publicly, the restrictions on business scope and region for foreign-funded tourism enterprises will be both lifted, and the conformity among tourism enterprises will get tougher and tougher.

Before 1998, traveling agency with Sino-foreign joint venture was only allowed to be set up in state-class traveling areas and resorts. Then the area of openness was gradually expanded. The "Regulations on the Management of Traveling Agencies" promulgated by the State Council in January 2002 further lowered the standard of registered capital for joint-venture traveling agencies (the minimum registered capital for foreign-invested traveling agency was 4,000,000 yuan) and eliminated the regulation that foreign investor could only set up one traveling agency. The related Chinese and foreign parties can make application for setting up joint-venture traveling agency and run entrance traveling business and domestic traveling business so long as they are in compliance with the conditions laid down in the "Regulations on the Management of Traveling Agencies". At the same time, the Ministry of Foreign Economy and Trade worked out relevant policies for foreign funds to set up wholly foreign-invested traveling agency as a pilot item in advance in some areas. By the middle of 2002, China had approved ten foreign-invested traveling agencies.

Rear Estate Sector

The housing of the urban residents of China used to be based mainly on welfare-oriented distribution system. In recent years, with the deepening of the reform on housing system, relevant housing policy, tax policy and financial policy are being implemented in succession and the concept of housing commercialization is being accepted by more and more residents. Purchase of housing by individuals has become the main body of housing consumption market.

At present, the urban living space per capita on average in China is only a little more than ten square meters. In accordance with the forecast of experts, housing construction of China in the next few years will be maintained at an annual average growth rate of 15% so as to meet residents' housing demand. Housing construction on a large scale needs huge volume of funds, including foreign funds. In 2005, at least 1.5 billion square meters of housing will be built in cities and towns, 3.5 billion square meters in rural areas and 2.9 billion square meters of existing old buildings will be remolded. All this will undoubtedly provide a huge market for foreign business to make investment in the real estate sector of China.

Cities: People and Housing

The introduction of housing reform policy in China makes further restructuring of real estate sector. Ordinary housing construction is becoming the mainstream of rear estate development and real estate development tends to be more and more rationalized and standardized. China has worked out a series of preferential policies for foreign business to make investment in real estate sector, including exemption of investor's regulation tax, financing of the funds needed through related channels, and transfer of investor's profits from China without any limit after paying the tax in line with the rules.

At present, there are around 1,200 foreign enterprises and 3,800 enterprises from Hong Kong, Macao and Taiwan making investment in China's real estate sector, totaling over 5,000 enterprises and accounting for 29% of the total number of nationwide enterprises for real estate development.

Construction Sector

In accordance with the data issued by the relevant departments, the total sum of

Construction Sites Seen Everywhere in China Today

engineering value of the present construction market in China amounts to 200 billion US dollars, and the share taken by foreign construction companies is around 2%. At present, out of the 225 largest world engineering contracting companies around the world, 140 are involved in China. China has approved 120 construction engineering designing offices based on Sino-foreign joint venture or cooperation. There are 100,000 domestic enterprises engaged in construction sector, employing 34,000,000 people, with obvious excess of production capacity and irrational organizational structures.

In September 2002, the "Provisions Concerning the Management of Foreign-Invested Construction Enterprises" and the "Provisions Concerning the Management of Foreign-Invested Construction Engineering Designing Enterprises" were promulgated. They define the provisions for application of being engaged in foreign-invested construction sector and the qualifications of foreign-invested construction engineering designing enterprises, their scope of engineering contracting, monitoring and management, etc. In accordance with the TWO protocol, the Chinese government will permit foreign business to set up wholly-owned enterprises within three years, and joint-venture and cooperation enterprises can start to enjoy the national treatment of China within three years.

Medical Treatment Service

Hospitals and medical treatment establishments at different levels are spread out all over China and a fairly perfect public health service network in cities and towns has been initially established. A medical insurance system with the combination of social overall planning and personal account for workers and staff members in cities and towns is being gradually expanded. The expected average lifespan of the Chinese people, the infant mortality, the mortality of pregnant woman and lying-in woman and other health targets all rank among the forefront in the developing countries and some health targets have approached the level of developed countries. At the end of 2001, all over China there were 4,500,000 medical technicians, of which 2,100,000 were doctors and 1,280,000 were nursing staff and nurses, on the average 1.69 doctors for every thousand people.

At present, the annual expenditures on medical treatment and health care for urban and rural residents in China are as high as 100 billion yuan, of which around one billion yuan is on insurance expenditure for child birth, and the speed of expenditures on medical treatment and health care is at a rapidly growing pace. On the average, the medical cost for each outpatient/time was 86 yuan and inpatient/time 3,048 yuan in 2000, an increase of seven times and six times respectively compared with that in 1990. With the enhancement of people's living standards and paying more attention to health, the medical treatment sector will become a fast developing sector.

China is undergoing three items of reform in medical treatment service, i.e. the basic medical insurance system, the medical and health system and the medicine production and circulation system and a series of new policies to support the reform have been unveiled. Medical establishments can be divided into two kinds: profit seeking and non-profit seeking; and medical charges can be divided into three kinds: to be taken care of by the state fundamental medical insurance, by the supplementary insurance of enterprises and by the individual. Within the scope of the state policy, both private funds and foreign funds can be invested in medical establishments. The medical treatment and medicine of state-owned hospitals will be separately calculated while medicine will be procured through public bidding. With the WTO accession and introduction of competition mechanism, medical treatment will no longer be a sector depending on state financial support and subsidy.

Since 1989, China has allowed foreign funds to access the medical service market of China in the forms of commercial existence (medical service mechanism) and natural person circulation (medical technicians). In 2000, the "Interim Measures for the Management of Sino-Foreign Joint Venture or Sino-Foreign Medical Cooperation" was formulated.

Education

Education used to be operated dependently on the state or local financial allocations but in recent years the government puts forward that the initiatives of the various aspects in the society to run schools will be brought into full play, the allocations for education will mainly be used for popularizing compulsory education and taking care of most of the funds needed for regular higher education, and during the period of non-compulsory education, the proportion of tuition fee will be properly increased for the cultivation costs. Starting from 1997, all the enrolled new students of colleges and universities have to pay tuition fee by themselves. At present, the standard of the charged tuition fee comprises about 15% ~ 20% of the costs to cultivate college and university students. In the changes of family consumption pattern of recent years, the expenditure on education consumption has become one of the items with the fastest growth.

In recent years, foreign educational establishments come to China one after another to struggle for the educational market and to cooperate with domestic counterparts to run economic management education and vocational training. At the same time, the private capital at home is more and more attracted by the good prospect of this investment market. The policy adopted by the state for running schools by non-governmental sectors is "active encouragement, energetic support, correct guidance

In Recent Years, Foreign Colleges and Universities
Coming to China One by One to Develop Market

and better management".

Accounting Service

For promoting gradual establishment and healthy development of registered accountant system in China and for minimizing the distance between the domestic accounting and auditing sector with the world counterparts, China started in 1992 to allow world-renowned accounting companies to set up accountant offices on the basis of cooperation with Chinese accountants conditionally. By 2002, China had approved nine Sino-foreign cooperated accountant offices. These accountant offices are allowed to provide corresponding services within the regulated business scope for the enterprises both at home and abroad. According to the news issued by the Ministry of Foreign Trade and Economic Cooperation, the relevant departments are considering to permit foreign accountants acquired qualifications of registered practicing accountants in China to set up accountant offices on the basis of partnership system with Chinese registered practicing accountants, and are ready to formulate related provisions concerning foreign-invested accountant offices and to define the form and procedure of examination and approval for foreign-invested accountant offices so as to standardize foreign investment in this realm.

Legal Services

So far, China has not permitted any foreign business to set up lawyers' office in China. Anyhow, lawyers' office in foreign countries or in Hong Kong Special Administrative Region can set up their respective representative office, if approved, to handle the relevant business not included in Chinese legal affairs. Now 110 representative offices of this kind have been set up in the Chinese mainland. After the WTO entry, the State Council promulgated the "Regulations for the Management of Representative Organs in China Set Up by Foreign Lawyers' Offices" in 2001, lifting the original regional restriction and quantity restriction for setting up representative offices and permitting foreign lawyers' office to set up more than one representative organ within the boundary of China in line with the commitment made for entering the WTO.

Policies for Speeding Up Development of Service Sector

For speeding up the development of service sector, the State Planning Commission has worked out the "Proposals on some Policy Measures to Speed Up the Development of Service Sector during '10th Five-Year Plan'" as follows:

1. To Optimize Structure of Service Sector

It is necessary to intensify reorganization and reformation in the sectors of communication and transportation, commercial and trading circulation, catering, public utilities, agricultural service, etc. and to give an impetus to the development of organizational form and service ways of chain operation, franchise operation, agent system, various ways of through transport, e-business, etc.; to develop vigorously the sectors with great demanding potentiality such as real estate, property management, tourism, community service, education and training, culture, physical training, etc.; and to develop energetically the intermediate service sectors such as information, finance, insurance, accounting, consultation, legal service, scientific and technical services, etc.

2. To Expend Employment Size of Service Sector

It is required to support energetically the various sectors in service industry to expand service realm and to expand new channels for employment; to actively encourage the development of sectors with great employment potentiality; to encourage laid-off workers, post-changed cadres in villages and towns, and demobilized servicemen and armymen transferred to civilian work to run community service enterprises and agricultural service enterprises; to actively guide labor force to get cross-region employment on mobile basis and eliminate various kinds of policies for and regulations on rational flow of labor force; and to encourage service sector to practice party-time employment, temporary employment, elastic working time employment, and other flexible and diversified forms of employment.

3. To Speed up Enterprise Reform and Reorganization

It is advisable to lift gradually the access restriction for non-state-owned economy to enter the sectors with higher state-owned economic proportion and to expand openness to the outside world such sectors as foreign trade, public utilities, tourism, culture, telecom, finance and insurance; to step up standardized company system reform for medium and large enterprises (MLEs) of state-owned service sector; to give more authority to and invigorate the SMEs of state-owned service sector; and to embark the reform on property order and operational mechanism with various kinds of forms.

4. To Relax Market Access to Service Sector

It is sensible to actively encourage non-state-owned economy to participate in the service sector development in an even broader realm; to speed up the reform on management system in railway, civil aviation, telecom, public utilities and other sectors and to relax the qualification conditions for market access in foreign trade, education, culture, intermediate service and other sectors. All realms that foreign funds are encouraged for access should also be encouraged for domestic investors' access. The relevant departments of the State Council should work out and promulgate, as soon as possible, the realms for conditional access, the access conditions, the procedures of examination, approval and confirmation, and ways of management and supervision.

5. To Expand the Opening-up to the Outside World Step by Step

Tourism promotion from overseas

It is suitable to further open the realms of banking, insurance, securities, telecom, foreign trade, commerce, culture, tourism, medicare, accounting, auditing, assets appraisal, and international freight agency; to encourage enterprises with necessary conditions available to develop transnational companies in service sector and to give encouragement to carrying out design consultation, foreign engineering project and technological contracting and labor cooperation. Related departments must provide necessary conditions for enterprises to expand the world market.

6. To Give an Impetus to Industrialization of Part of Service Realms

The relevant departments of the State Council and the governments in the localities at different levels should complete as soon as possible the transformation of the realms appropriate to industrialization from "running by the government" to "running by the society". The governments at different levels should accomplish the fundamental public services of the related realms, and the realms beyond the fundamental public services should exercise industrialized operation. The system of all profit-seeking public institutions should be restructured into enterprises or practice enterprise management while non-profit seeking institutions should also use competition mechanism and face the market and provide services.

7. To Spur Socialization of Logistic Services

The service facilities of schools, hospitals and enterprises, public institutions and rear-service organizations with conditions available should all face the society. The profit-seeking rear-service organizations of schools, hospitals and enterprises, public institutions and Party and government organizations should all be restructured into independent legal person enterprises. The newly established administrative public institutions with state financial allocations, in principle, should not set up rear-service organizations any more.

8. "To Shrink Secondary Industry And Develop Tertiary Industry" in Key Cities

It is essential to restructure the land use in city proper by cutting down the proportion of land use for industries and enterprises and raising up the proportion of land use for service sector, and to promote the measures of "shrinking secondary industry and developing tertiary industry" effective in some cities to other cities. Key cities should move out or close down the industrial enterprises in city proper that cause serious pollution or occupy large areas improperly for urban functional positioning in accordance with the overall plan of the city. The land returned by the industrial enterprises should be used for service sector as the first priority.

9. To Speed Up Training of Talents for Service Sector

It is necessary to speed up training of various kinds of talented people needed by service sector, particularly the talents urgently needed by the society; to train in a planned way at the existing colleges and universities and secondary vocational schools the specialties badly needed in service sector; to expand the channel for training talents and attract and employ in an energetic way overseas senior talents; to intensify the training of post occupations and improve the level of the employed in service sector; and to promote in an all-round way the system of occupational qualification certificate and to set up the system of occupational qualification criterion in service sector.

10. To Increase Investment in Service Sector from Various Channels

Both the central government and the governments in the localities at different levels are advised to arrange properly a certain amount of investment as the guiding capital to speed up the development of service sector. Banks should actively issue loans on the basis of independent loan examination to service sector enterprises and their construction projects that are in compliance with the loan conditions. The service sector enterprises with conditions available should be encouraged to enter capital market for financing.

11. To Expand Service Consumption of Urban and Rural Residents

It is necessary to improve the environments for service consumption, perfect consumption policies and work out social surroundings beneficial to the expansion of service consumption; to establish personal credit system, perfect the ways of consuming credit service and raise credit service level; to strengthen various kinds of infrastructure constructions, giving particular attention to the expansion of coverage of infrastructure in rural areas, and spur farmers to increase their service consumption; to promote urbanization in an active and steady way and expand the group of service consumption in urban areas; and to embark yearly paid leave system for workers and staff members. The departments related should work out as soon as possible detailed measures for implementation.

12. To Strengthen Organization and Leadership of Service Sector

The governments at different levels should create excellent conditions for speeding up the development of service sector. The planning department should be responsible for working out the overall planning and authorized size, laying down the policies, and dovetailing and balancing the work related to service sector; the supervision department of the relevant sector should also work out the overall planning and authorized size of the relevant sector, lay down the policies and organize the implementation work; and the various regions and various departments should work out and implement detailed policy measures to speed up the development of service sector in line with the proposals raised here.

MARKET FOR CONSUMER GOODS

Twenty years ago, "modernization" meant to most of the Chinese "upstairs and downstairs, electric light and telephone". Color TV, refrigerator and washing machine were regarded as major consumer goods in 1980's and 1990's but now they are replaced by computer, automobile and housing. For quite a long time, most part of resident's income was mainly spent on food and there were very few other expanses. In recent years, fundamental changes have taken place. The family consumption struc-

Per Capita Income of Urban and Rural Residents' Family on Average

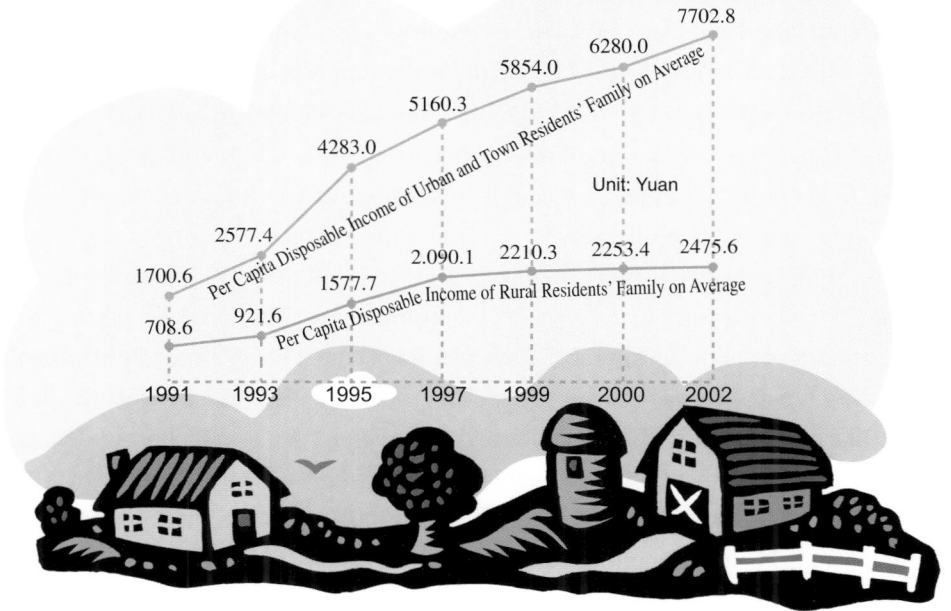

Motorola achieved the biggest turnover in 2001, coming first
among the top 500 overseas businesses in China

ture of most urban residents has been transformed from the past "adequate food and
clothing" to the present "development" and "enjoyment".

Consumption Status

In 2001, the Engel's Coefficient of the urban residents' family in China was
37.9%. At the same time with the growth of consumption of meat, edible oil, eggs
and milk, the proportion of grain consumption was considerably reduced. The growth
of purchasing volume of various kinds of finished products and semi-finished products in food consumption has reduced the residents' burden of household drudgery.
In clothing consumption, the growth is a little slower. The trend of fashion, famous
brand and individuality is more obviously and the trend of ready-made clothes has
become the mainstream. In the respect of consumer goods for daily use, particularly
in the respect of purchasing durable consumer items, the trend of expenditure growth
is slowing down with each passing year. The supply of electrical household appliances like color TV, refrigerator and washing machine used to fall short of demand
but now seller's market is changed into buyer's market.

Though the growth speed of farmers' income is lower than that of urban residents' income, the consumption is also being continuously restructured. In 2001, the
Engel's Coefficient of the rural residents' family in China was 47.7% and food con-

sumption was still the main expenditure with rather rapid growth. The expenditure on clothing, housing, household equipment and articles of everyday use, and services is still fairly slow. Various kinds of new consumption like medicare, healthcare and non-food items have shown a trend of steady and even rapid growth.

The change from the consumption of paying attention to articles of everyday use to the consumption of paying attention to health, knowledge, efficiency and leisure shows that the consumption ideas of the Chinese people have been changed from pursuing modernized material life to chasing a kind of modernized way of lfe.

As a whole, the living standards of the Chinese residents are universally enhanced. Nevertheless, the difference of income varies greatly with different regions, different occupations and different people in urban area and rural area. In accordance with the sample survey, between 1994 and 1999, the people with medium and above medium income made up 28% while those with medium and below medium income 64%. Those who have enriched first possess spacious house and personal car but quite a number of people with low income still have to squeeze themselves in limited space. The statistics also show that there is a great difference of income between those with lower educational level or lower social position and those with higher educational level or higher social position.

At the same time, there are still quite a number of poverty-stricken people in China. According to the white paper "China's Poverty Alleviation and Development in Rural Areas" issued by the Information Office under the State Council in 2001, there were still 30,000,000 poverty-stricken people in rural areas. In recent years, with the establishment of market-oriented economy system the issues of layoff and unemployment are become more and more serious and there are more and more poverty-stricken people in urban areas. The special study of Asian Development Bank showed that in 2001 there were 14,800,000 poverty-stricken people in the urban areas of China. After obtaining government aid and social support, these poverty-stricken families can only maintain basic existence and cannot be easily satisfied with healthcare, education, social intercourse and many other fundamental needs. The poverty-stricken strata in urban and rural residents mainly include laid-off workers and staff members, the unemployed, the retired ahead of the due time or the retired decided by the working unit itself, the workers and staff members of the closed or semi-closed enterprises, and those insured by the minimum standard of living because of illness or old age.

In recent years, the Chinese market for consumer goods has a pattern of "supply exceeding demand". The information issued by the State Economic and Trade Commission shows that about 100 out of 600-odd main commodities supply is basically

balanced with demand, the other 500 exceed the demand, and that there are no commodities with supply falling short of demand. In the respect of agricultural products, the supply and demand of agriculture products and by-products are basically balanced except that the supply and demand of grains is basically balanced but a little tight on the supply side. In the respect of industrial products, the supply of clothing exceeding demand is a little improved; the supply of articles of daily use prominently exceeds demand; and the demand for stationary is increasing but the supply and demand relationship is improved.

According to statistics, the growth speed of savings deposit of the rural and urban residents in China has always exceeded the GDP growth. At the end of 2001, the savings deposit hit eight trillion yuan, an equivalent to 76% of the GDP. If the stock, bonds and insurance funds were added, the total savings deposits were estimated to hit ten to eleven trillion yuan. Though China has a population of 1.3 billion, the consumption market in China, for quite a long period, is not very active.

First of all, the expected psychological changes lead to the trend of consumption decrease. During the process of speeding up the re-tracking of economic system, the guarantees provided by the government and SOEs to urban residents such as employment, housing, medical treatment, retirement and children's education are being successively transformed for residents themselves to take care all or part of the costs. This exerts an impact on the increase of uncertain factors for resident's future life. Simultaneously, with the increase of employment opportunities slowing down, the increasing number of layoff and unemployed workers and the establishment of social guarantee system lagging behind, the growth of residents' income slows down and people have no favorable expectations for increase of income. Residents have increased their risk consciousness and self-insurance consciousness. To increase savings and put off current consumption have become the first choice for most residents.

Insufficient consumption demand of rural residents is the most prominent issue. In 2001, the income of city and town residents was 2.89 times higher than rural residents and the average consumption expenditure of rural residents was only 33.41% of urban residents. Though in some developed rural areas, every household lives in a separate house with all electrical household appliances available but the living standards of most farmers are still very low. So far as durable consumer goods such as electrical household appliances are concerned, the popularization rate in rural areas lags behind urban areas for ten to fifteen years. This also shows that the present overstock of electrical household appliances is relative and the consumption potentiality in rural areas is very large. In recent years, the government has tried various kinds of policies to increase farmers' income. In 2001, after a decrease of growth

Average Distribution of Financial Assets Owned by Urban Residents' Family

Assets Items	Average Sum Owned by Each Household (Yuan)	Composition (%)
Total Yuan Assets	73706	100.00
Savings Deposit	51156	69.41
Stock (Small Shareholder)	7374	10.00
Treasury Bond	3210	4.36
Insurance	3094	4.20
Surplus of housing provident fund	3036	4.12
Cash in Balance	2730	3.70
Loan	2512	3.41
Other Negotiable Securities	359	0.49
Others	235	0.32

79800

30982

7809

1338

Growth Trend of Financial Assets (Yuan)

1984   1990   1995   June 2002

speed for several successive years, farmers' income had an increase at a large range for the first time.

Besides, there is a wide difference among residents' income. Though the balance of savings deposit of the Chinese urban and rural residents is rather high, there is an obvious difference of income between the residents in urban areas and rural areas, between different sectors, and between different regions. So far as cities and towns are concerned, the 20% families with the maximum financial assets own around 55% possession of the total urban residents while the 20% families with the minimum financial assets own only around 1.5% possession. Therefore, what the Chinese consumption market faces is that the consumption trend of those with high income is rather low. They are already satisfied with general commodities and have transformed their surplus purchasing power into savings and financial assets. As a group of main power for consumption, the army of middle class is not large enough. The consumption of the strata with medium income is very flexible. Their durable commodities for daily use are basically saturated, but the expected pressure for future expenditure such as old age, medicare, housing and children's education is increasing. Some consumption targets like housing and personal car are either too difficult to be materialized or they simply wait and see with the money available. The low-income stratum is the largest consumption group. They do have great consumption demand but cannot afford it or dare not to consume too much.

Since 1999, for expanding domestic needs and boosting the continuous and steady growth of economy, the state has put out a serious of policies with the purpose to expand consumption demands. These policies mainly include (1) to raise the income of urban and rural residents, such as to raise the salary of the city and town residents and lower farmers' burdens; (2) to expand consumption realms, such as consuming

Annual Consumption Expenditure Per Capita Of Urban Residents On Average

Unit: Yuan

Items	2000	2001	2002
Consumption Expenditure	4998.0	5309.0	6029.9
Food	1958.3	2014.0	2271.8
Clothing	500.5	533.7	590.9
Family Equipment, Articles for Use and Services	374.5	438.9	388.7
Medicare and Healthcare	318.1	343.3	430.1
Communication	162.2	175.5	267.2
Telecom	232.8	281.5	358.8
Durable Consumer Goods for Entertainment	217.8	211.6	245.2
Education	363.8	428.3	495.2
Housing	500.5	548.0	624.4
Miscellaneous Goods and Services	258.5	284.1	195.8

Annual Consumption Expenditure Per Capita Of Rural Residents on Average

Unit: Yuan

Items	2000	2001	2002
Total Expenditure Per Capita on Average	2652.42	2779.96	2923.6
Expenditure on Family Operational Costs	654.27	695.97	731.0
Expenditure on Living Consumption	1670.13	1741.09	1834.3
Food	820.51	830.72	848.4
Clothing	95.95	98.68	105.0
Housing	258.34	279.06	300.2
Family Equipment, Articles for Use and Services	75.45	76.98	80.4
Medicare and Healthcare	87.57	96.61	103.9
Communication and Transportation	93.13	109.98	128.5
Goods for Culture, Education, Entertainment and Services	186.71	192.64	210.3
Other Commodities and Services	52.46	56.42	57.7

credit service, reforming holiday system for expanding holiday consumption, and reforming housing system; (3) to raise consumption level, such as levying income tax on savings interest and lowering several times the interest rate of bank savings; and (4) to improve consumption environments, such as expanding the construction and transformation of infrastructure like electrical grid in rural areas, and checking up and improving market order.

Since implementation, these policies have played an active role to start and expand domestic consumption demands. Between 2000 and 2001, the growth speed of the total retail of consumer goods of the whole society exceeded the GDP growth for successively two years and the development of the market for consumer goods showed a trend of stabilization with prosperity. When the consumption of food, clothing and expenditure is basically met, new consumption hotspots are being formed. The consumption of telecom, car, housing, entertainment and culture is growing at a rapid pace. More and more people start to accept credit consumption. With the construction of social insurance system like medicare and old age, people's confidence in current consumption is gradually restored and strengthened. These new consumption hotspots include the following:

Housing Consumption　As national housing reform is basically completed, housing consumption is transiting from group to individual. Therefore, the gross sales of commercial residential buildings and individual commercial residential buildings nationwide have had a continuous big increase since 1999. At present, the average building space for per-capita housing in the city has just reached twenty square meters in China. In the days to come, housing demand will be rather prosperous.

Auto Consumption　According to statistics, the proportion of personal car purchase in China, starting from 1998, is over 50%. At present, this proportion exceeds 70% in some large and medium cities. In 2001, the increase of auto sales volume was almost 20%.

Consumption of Telecom and Electronic Products　This is the hotspot with the fastest development. In recent years, the telecom sector in China is growing at the speed of over 20% and the development speed ranks first in the world.

Cultural and Educational Consumption　In 2001, the expenditure of educational consumption was immediately after the telecom. At the same time, cultural consumption such as concert, movie, library, etc. is also increasing.

Holiday Consumption and Tourism Consumption　Other consumption caused by holiday and tourism consumption such as communications, catering and shopping have made many places to play the tourism card to a great extent.

Experts' analysis points out that the consumption of Chinese residents will step

Satisfaction Degree of Interviewees
to Commodity Supply at Different Regions (2001)

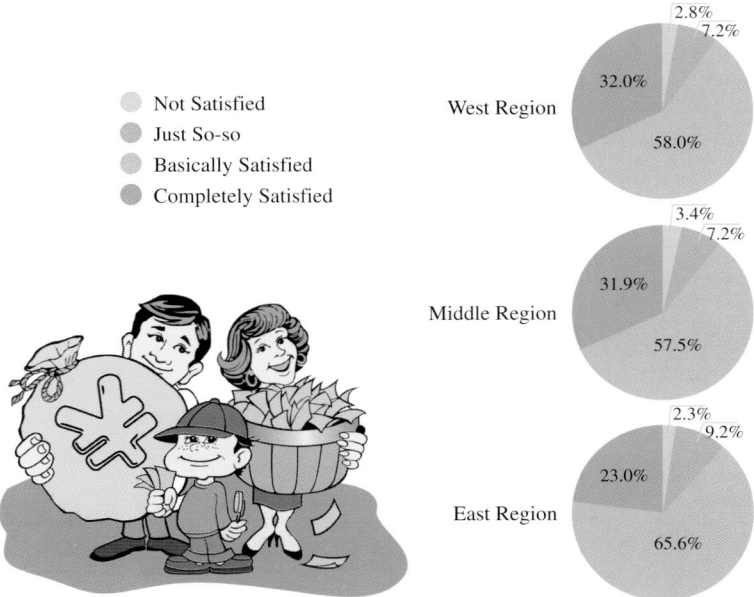

Not Satisfied
Just So-so
Basically Satisfied
Completely Satisfied

West Region

2.8%
7.2%
32.0%
58.0%

Middle Region

3.4%
7.2%
31.9%
57.5%

East Region

2.3%
9.2%
23.0%
65.6%

by step enter a new round of consumption cycle, with the main symbol of popularization of electrical household appliances in rural areas, and housing, sedan and PC in
urban families. The consumption of rural residents is developing from hundred-yuan
class to thousand-yuan class or even to tens-of-thousand-yuan class while the residents in cities and towns from thousand-yuan class to tens-of-thousand-yuan class or
even to hundreds-of-thousand-yuan class.

In accordance with the "10th Five-Year Plan", the state will incessantly increase
the income of urban and rural residents, particularly farmers and those with low income in cities and towns. It is expected that the average disposable income of urban
residents per capita and the average net income of rural residents per capita will grow
around 5% annually. Simultaneously, residents' consumption environments will be
improved and the consumption pattern will be optimized. In the respect of expanding the consumption realms, they are mainly as follows:

On the basis of improving the fundamental consumption level of residents in
food and clothing, attention will be given to improving housing and traveling
conditions. The system of housing provident fund will be perfected, housing construction will be more emphasized on economically affordable buildings, and a system of ensuring low-rent housing will be established. Public transportation in urban
and rural areas will be actively developed and personal cars will be encouraged. In-

formation service prices will be cut down so as to stimulate residents' information consumption. Computer will be popularized, over 4% in 2005. Paid holiday system for workers and staff members will be practiced, residents' working time and leisure time will be rationally readjusted and services and supplies will be expanded so as to encourage residents' service consumption. The infrastructure construction of water supply, power supply, gas supply, heat supply, information and environments will be strengthened and the coverage of the infrastructure in rural areas will be enlarged so that better conditions can be created for improving the life quality of urban and rural residents. Personal credit system will be established and the scale of consumer credit service will be expanded.

The Consumption Feature and Its Trend

The main difficulty to appraise the Chinese market is that the market is ever changing. Business people are advised to keep an eye on customers' realistic demands and predict the changes of their demands.

For consumer goods there are various purchasing strata and large demands in the Chinese market. With the growth of China's economy, a part of people has become wealthy ahead of others. The difference of income among different social strata is gradually enlarged and the difference of consumption level between coastal areas and hinterland cannot be eliminated within a short period of time and as a result it will cause more and more consumption levels. Anyhow, due to the large population of 1.3 billions, the size of the demand of detailed market for each stratum with different incomes is still very huge.

The feature of consumer goods market in China is quick upgrading. The process of expansion of foreign and domestic new products in China is always in the form of leaping. For instance, just as beeper started to become popular, mobile phone stepped into the Chinese market. Another example, before a war on VCD price came to an end, DVD took over the market. At present, the sales structure of the market for consumer goods in China is being readjusted towards the direction of housing, communications and telecom, culture and education, and tourism and leisure.

The structure of the main body of consumer goods market is undergoing changes. Since1980's, the family structure of China has tended to be smaller. On the average, the present family is about 3.44 people in cities and towns and 3.65 people in rural areas. Traditional big families are less and less. The core family established by young people makes the demand for consumer goods smaller in size. Anyhow, the Chinese people still respect traditional family concept very much. When they do shopping, particularly making decision to buy durable consumer goods, the decision

Children's Market, a Ready Market to Business People

is always made jointly by the whole family. In addition, as the family relations based on blood relations and marriage relations are still so close that you can see, wherever you go, business people make a big fuss about "love" and "propriety".

Rational consumption plays a leading role. Compared with a few years ago, the consumption ideas and consumption behaviors of the Chinese people are getting matured slowly but surely. Consumer's first priority of choosing a commodity is whether it is really needed, whether both the quality and service are good enough, and whether it is worth the price. Although consumers are still greatly interested in transnational products, very few people will be proud of purchasing "imported goods" as they used to. What they pay more attention to is the ratio between cost and quality.

Consumer credit is a new upsurge. The traditional consumption concept of the Chinese people is "to keep expenditures below income". Generally speaking, the consumption expenditure of a family will not go above the income. On the contrary, they will set aside a certain proportion of their income every month for savings. This kind of phenomenon is still quite common, particularly among the old and middle-aged people. Anyhow, the younger generation takes a new attitude. At the end of 1997, the size of national consumer credit was only 17.2 billion yuan but at the end of 2001, it hit 699 billion yuan, an increase of forty times. From the viewpoint of consumption realm, consumer credit has been developed from the loan to buy housing to buy car, durable consumer goods, home decoration, tuition fee and other realms. Credit consumption will have an even broader development with the establishment of personal credit service system, further transformation of consumption conception, and improvement of financial service level.

Personality consumption is on the rise. The Chinese people's way of life is already diversified. After experiencing the consumption time of quantity and quality, the personality consumption conception with perceptual color is on the rise. Those consumers with high income and high academic credentials are chasing psychological enjoyment. They are expecting manufacturers to develop commodities with personality. From the special order of refrigerator, mobile and even car, it can be easily seen that the time to show personality has come into being.

Detailed division of market is more obvious. Take the market for only child for an example. The family planning policy started in 1980's shows no sign of relaxation so far. Parents pay great attention to children's cultivation. Material living conditions, education and entertainment are by no means a small expenditure. Take the market for the aged for another example. China has entered a senior citizens' society. The population over sixty-five is over 88,000,000. The traditional way of looking after the parents by children in their old age is being transformed to a new mode of taking care of them by the society. It is a very promising new industry to offer services of medicare and healthcare, culture and entertainment, and nursing of daily life to aged people. Still another instance is the while-collar market. At present, educational factor plays a more and more important role in consumers' purchasing mode and purchasing power. The white-collar stratum with good educational background is a stratum with very high income in the Chinese society, and plays a leading role in the consumption trend. The last example cited here is the market for professional woman. As the target of consumption pursued by professional woman is to lay stress on the realization of their own value, the demand for consumer goods like cosmetics is ever increasing. In addition, the market in the mid-west part and rural areas is also worth attention. Anyhow, due to the comparatively lower purchasing power there, business people have not paid enough attention to them yet.

Social consciousness is even much stronger. As consumers care more about purchasing products with environmental protection and beneficial to health, renewable products, regenerable system, and those products and byproducts that can reduce or eliminate harmful residuals in the environments are particularly favored.

Channels of Market Sale

Compared with other sectors, the marketization of commodity distribution sector

of China started rather early and has achieved a rather high level. The direct administration intervention of the state over the market of consumer goods has been greatly
weakened. All is open with the exception of keeping some policy restriction in the
sale of medicine and tobacco and the price of energy, communications and telecom
services. Free trading and equal competition in the Chinese market of consumer
goods have reached a fairly high level, particularly in the market for articles of everyday use. The flexibility of trading ways and operation of competition means can be
compared with the market-oriented economy in foreign countries.

In recent years, the state-owned enterprises of commodity circulation sector have
completed the transformation of operational system and basically established a modern enterprise system. A large number of enterprises of commodity circulation sector
with different ownership, such as collective-owned, private-owned, stock-cooper-
ated and foreign-invested, have been set up and are taking up larger and larger market
share. Their ways of operation are diversified, such as wholesale market, large-scale
market, supermarket, chain operation, distribution agency, lease, auction, selling on
credit, installment and e-business. The competition among domestic circulations
enterprises is very tough and the development of various kinds of competition means
and ways is very rapid in the realms of traditional sector of department store and
newly-developed specialized stores like the retail sector of electrical household
appliances. Simultaneously, world commercial magnates are speeding up their steps
to march into the Chinese market one after another.

Though the domestic industrial and commercial enterprises are actively striving
for reorganization and expansion, the enterprises, in general, are still small in size. In
many cities, it often occurs that a few big shopping centers reign over their respective
domains. Though chain operation has had a rapid development, a well-organized
sales network has not yet been formed in a large area. There is still big room for
improvement of enterprise operation and management in the commodity circulation
sector. Facing buyer's market, many enterprises in the commodity circulation sector
are still limited by their traditional marketing means like price reduction. Besides,
the enterprises of commodity circulation in China are concentrated in medium and
large cities but more and better networks for commodity circulation sector are still
lacking in small cities and towns and the extensive rural areas with large population.
As a matter of fact, the potentiality of consumption in these areas is very large.

According to statistics, on the average every 20,000 people own a commodity
transaction market and every 100 people own a market stall in China. In view of
regional distribution, the progress of marketization in the east coastal areas and in the
areas with rapid economic development is fairly fast and their market radiation func-

tion is stronger and denser than other areas. In view of the operational mode of commodity market, most of the markets open all year round, mainly for retails, and have good operational environments. Comprehensive market takes up around 70% of commodity market and overwhelming majority of the specialized market sell textiles, clothes, shoes and hats. Most of these markets were newly built in the recent decade. Generally speaking, they have a higher starting point with quite complete facilities and functions available, and fairly strong market radiation functions.

Since 1992, over forty foreign-invested commercial enterprises have been set up in China with the approval of the State Council, actually absorbing over three billion US dollars, and over a half of the fifty largest retail companies in the world have entered China. In accordance with the related rules of the WTO, China will allow foreign funds to completely hold the stocks of the Chinese distribution and retail sectors after China's entry into the WTO for three years.

The data available show that in 2001 the ten largest cities in China took up 20% of the total of the national retail market and the foremost twenty-four cities comprised 34% of the national retail total. These cities will obviously be the first choice for transnational retail businesses to enter the Chinese market. New commercial pattern will come together with these transnational chain stores. People will have more choices in commodity quality, grade, price and service ways. With the appearance of a new market pattern, the commercial setups of a number of cities will have significant changes. The traditional market is faced with readjustment of setups and upgrade of functions. The wholesale market for farm produce with backward facilities and unsound management will be gradually readjusted or rescinded.

Boutiques Selling Famous Brand, a Resort for the White-Collar

Stationery Promotion for New Semester

In 2001, the news released by the State Economic and Trade Commission showed the state would unveil a series of measures to expand the scale of utilization of foreign funds in commercial realm and to improve the quality of using foreign funds. These measures include:

On the basis of the existing "Pilot Measures for Foreign-Invested Commercial Enterprises" and in accordance with the commitment made by China to enter the WTO, the "Interim Measures for the Administration of Foreign-Invested Commercial Enterprises" will be worked out and great efforts will be made to end the experiment and switch it to formal openness as soon as possible. Chain operation and interflow and distribution of goods and materials will be taken as the key link to expand the sphere of openness, to encourage introduction into China advanced foreign management experiences and technology in interflow and distribution of goods and materials, to encourage the transformation of traditional commerce with foreign funds, and to speed up the establishment of modern circulation system.

The structure of foreign-invested sector will be optimized. In recent years, the main realms for the Chinese commerce to utilize foreign funds are large-scale comprehensive supermarket, warehouse market and department store. In the days to come, the state will promote these sectors to get developed in the mid-western areas with an even broader market. Simultaneously, the state will also pay special attention to and introduce those sectors that are comparatively insufficient in China such as large-scale shopping center, convenient store, medium-scale supermarket and special store. As a result, the structure of foreign-invested sector can be continuously optimized and more convenient, fast, secure, and attentive and satisfactory services can be provided to consumers.

In accordance with international common practice, the scheme for commercial development in the city and the plan to utilize foreign funds in commerce will be quickly worked out to guide foreign investment. Efforts will be made to avoid for-

Data

Views on Huge Consumption

Color TV with the value of over one hundred thousand yuan, refrigerator with the price of tens of thousand yuan, spacious housing, expensive educational training, etc. are an extension of the wealthy life of those with higher income. There rises quietly a trend of huge consumption in Chinese metropolis. As regard to these relevant issues, in 2002 the China Economic Situation Monitoring Center made a survey of over 700 consumers in Beijing, Shanghai and Guangzhou.

When inquired about the causes of the huge consumption, 4.9% of the interviewees thought it was because people expected a better life in the future; 24.7% held it was because people's living standards were enhanced and they could afford it in economy; 56.4% regarded it a blind consumption influenced by social atmosphere after becoming abruptly wealthy; and 13.1% felt that it was affected by citing the cases of others in support to one's own claim, a kind of vanity psychology to chase wealth.

44.9% of the interviewees thought huge consumption should be classified as consumerism, a luxurious consumption. 50% thought they belonged to pragmatism in consumption. 14.6% admitted that they had already entered consumerism and 34.3% regarded themselves situated between consumerism and pragmatism. Compared with the same survey for this group of data made two and a half years before, pragmatism dropped 7.5 percentage points, consumerism basically remained the same and the in-between rose 6.4 percentage points. 51.5% of the interviewees are against huge consumption. The main reasons are as follows. 1. China is still a developing country. Social wealth should be used to develop national economy. What should be proposed is personal investment rather than personal consumption. 2. As China has a large population, the general and specific policies laid down should avoid excessive consumption and be advantageous to sustainable development. 3. At present, the regional development is uneven and it is an obvious mistake to go on expanding the difference between the rich and the poor. 4. Environmental pollution is serious in quite a number of places. With the ever-increasing urban burdens, huge consumption is not practical. 5. People hold that high quality of life does not mean waste. However, 13.6% of the interviewees are for huge consumption. The reasons are as follows. 1. Huge consumption could give a boost to updating people's economic conception, advantageous to opening-up and development. 2. As huge consumption matches with the living standard, there is no need to restrain it. 32.3% of the interviewees adopt an attitude of indifference because any economic phenomenon will appear and disappear with the time.

The Foremost Ten Cities with Highest Income for Urban Residents in 2001

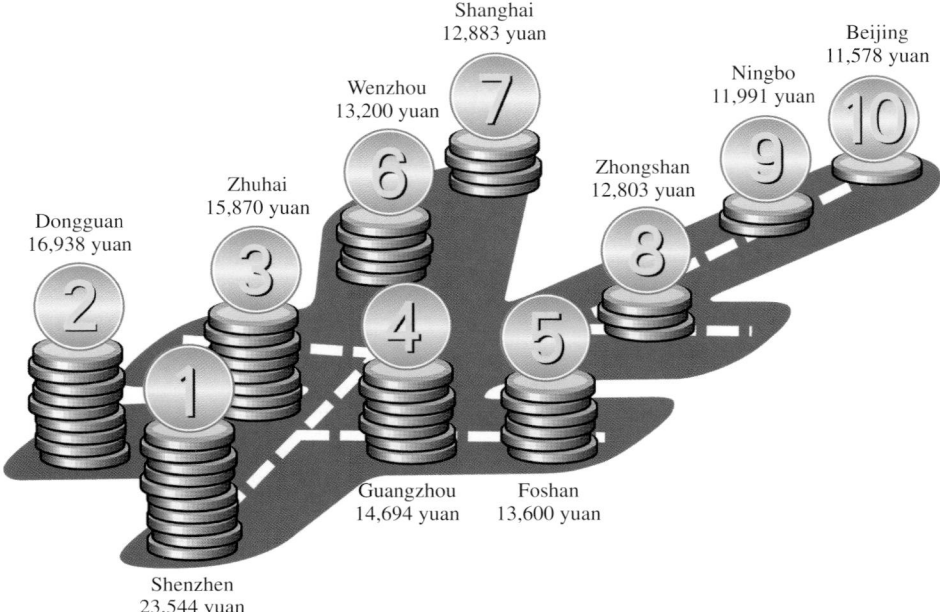

Shanghai
12,883 yuan

Beijing
11,578 yuan

Wenzhou
13,200 yuan

Ningbo
11,991 yuan

Zhuhai
15,870 yuan

Zhongshan
12,803 yuan

Dongguan
16,938 yuan

Guangzhou
14,694 yuan

Foshan
13,600 yuan

Shenzhen
23,544 yuan

eign business making blind investment in certain areas as well as excessive competition to cause unnecessary waste of resources. Attention will be paid to distribution in the mid-western areas, particularly the western areas, and support and encouragement will be given to foreign businesses to make investment in the western areas so that the development of modern circulation sector in the mid-western areas can be spurred.

At the same time when foreign investment is introduced in large volume, more attention will be given to introducing advanced technology, management and talented people and enterprises will be encouraged to do so. With the incessant introduction, digestion, absorption and development, the modernization level of the circulation sector in China can be raised at a rapid pace.

List of Industries, Products and Technologies Currently Encouraged by the State for Development

(Revised in 2000)

I. Agriculture

1. Breeding of quality varieties of animals and plants
2. Key pest control
3. Genetic engineering and construction of gene pools of crops and poultry
4. Development of seed and seedling disinfection technologies
5. Soilless culture of vegetables, flowers and plants
6. Breeding of good strains of perennial cash crops such as fruit, tea and mulberry and development of fine quality products
7. Breeding, storage, processing and inspection of seeds seedling. of crops
8. Fine-quality, high-yield, high-efficiency and model culture and breeding
9. Development and popularization of advanced agricultural technologies
10. Storage, preservation, processing and comprehensive utilization of agricultural products
11. Comprehensive harnessing of medium and low-yield fields
12. Construction of agricultural product bases of commodity grain, cotton, oil, sugar, meat and wool
13. Construction of dry-land farming, water-saving farming and ecological farming
14. Plantation of natural rubber
15. Grass-grow straw industry
16. Ecological breeding of aquatic products
17. Cattle breeding with straw ammoniation
18. Milk industry
19. Factory-production of embryo of cattle and sheep
20. Development of agricultural clone technologies
21. Development of technologies to raise soil fertility

II. Forestry and Ecological Environment

1. Protective projects for natural resources such as wildwood
2. Tree-planting and grass-growing projects
3. Soil and water conservation technologies and projects
4. Fine-quality seed and seedling projects
5. Breeding and storage of fine-quality varieties of economic-forest trees, flowers and plants, and Chinese medicinal crops

 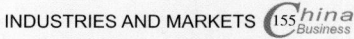

6. Prevention and control of forest fires

7. Development of soil-fixing and forestation technologies for regions with special difficulties and weak ecological environment

8. Ecological demonstration projects

9. Quick-growing and high-yield forestation projects

10. Construction of bamboo forest bases

11. Construction of projects for famous, special, fine-quality and new economic forest

12. Projects of shelter forest

13. Projects of returning the grain plots to forestry and recovering of forest resources

14. Prevention and control of desertification

15. Paper making with wood pulp of the supplementary raw material forest bases

16. Deep-processing of planted forest, radial timber, bamboo forest and forest residuals and development of serial products

17. Improvement of the functionality of the timber

18. Production of bamboo engineering materials and vegetable fibre engineering materials

19. Deep-processing of products of forest chemical industry

20. Development of extraction technologies of physiological and active substances of trees

21. Production of new materials for sand-fixing, water-retaining and soil-improving

22. Middle and young-growth tending projects

23. Protection and development of varieties of trees of the natural economic forest

24. Construction of gardens for protection of rare and endangered animals and plants and forest gardens

25. Construction of gene pools of wild animals and plants

26. Projects for comprehensive harnessing of the ecological environment and small watersheds

27. Projects for recovering of mining vegetation

III. Water Conservancy

1. Harnessing of large rivers and lakes, and trunk and tributary control projects

2. Cross-watershed water diversion projects

3. Water source projects for regions with a shortage of water resources

4. Drinking water and water-improving projects for people in arid regions

5. Safety constructions in flood storage and detention areas

6. Coastal embankment protection, maintenance and construction

7. Dredging works for rivers, lakes and reservoirs

8. Danger-eliminating and reinforcing works for defected and endangered reservoirs and dykes

9. Flood control works for cities

10. Dredging works for ports to the sea

11. Comprehensive utilization of key water control projects

12. Development and utilization of brackish water, inferior water and seawater, and seawater desalting projects

13. Protection and development of hydro-energy resources

14. Development and manufacturing of geo-technical synthetic materials for water conservancy projects

15. Reconstruction of large- and medium-sized irrigated areas and construction of supporting facilities

16. High-efficiency water delivery and distribution, water-saving irrigation technologies and equipment manufacturing

17. Manufacturing of high-efficiency, abrasion-resistant, low-lift and high-flow pumps

18. Development of water regimen automatic forecasting and warning and flood control and dispatch automation systems

19. Development of series of software for hydraulic engineering survey and design CAD.

20. Manufacturing of hydrological data acquisition instrument and equipment

IV. Meteorology

1. Development of automatic meteorological station system technologies and equipment manufacturing

2. Manufacturing of special meteorological observation and analysis equipment

V. Coal

1. Coal field geological and geophysical exploration

2. Reconstruction and expansion of high-yield and high-efficiency mines including open-pit. with an annual output above 1.2 million tons

3. Construction of large- and medium-sized high-efficiency coal preparation plants

4. Prevention and control of gas, coal-dust, mine water and underground fires

5. Production of industrial and domestic environmental protection coal

6. Development of water-coal pulp technologies

 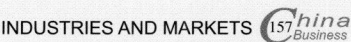

7. Coal gasification and liquefaction of coal

8. Exploration, development and utilization of the coal bed

9. Development and utilization of low heat value fuel and coal mine associated resources

10. Pipeline coal transporting

11. Development of clean fire coal technologies

VI. Electric Power

1. Hydro-electric generation

2. Construction of large-sized electric power stations near the coal mines and key pivotal power stations

3. Co-generation of heat and electric power.

4. Solar energy, geothermal energy, marine energy, bio-mass energy and wind power generation

5. Gas combined cycle power generation

6. Clean coal-fired power generation

7. Power generation with coal gangue or inferior coal

8. Remote extra-high voltage transmission and transformation

9. Reconstruction and construction of rural and urban electric network

10. Development of relay protection technologies

11. Development of transformer station automation technologies

12. Development of trans-regional electric network internetworking and engineering technologies

13. Development of electric network commercialized operation technologies

VII. Nuclear Energy

1. Construction of MKW-grade pressurized water reactor nuclear energy power station

2. Low-temperature feed reactor, fast neutron reactor, fusion reactor and advanced research reactor

3. Uranium mine geological prospecting and advanced uranium mining and refining

4. Manufacturing of high-performance nuclear fuel components

5. Post-treatment of exhaust fuel

6. Manufacturing of nuclear analysis and nuclear detection instrument and meters

7. Development of isotope and irradiation application technologies

8. Advanced uranium isotope separation technologies

9. Manufacturing of nuke rubbish pollution monitoring and observation equipment

VIII. Petroleum and Natural Gas
1. Prospecting, development and utilization of petroleum and natural gas
2. Construction of crude oil and finished oil pipeline transportation and network of pipe lines
3. Natural gas pipeline transporting
4. Petroleum and natural gas storage technologies and facility construction
5. Comprehensive utilization of oil-gas associated resources
6. Development of technologies to improve the oil field recovery ratio

IX. Railway
1. Construction of railway arterial grid
2. Speed acceleration and capacity expansion of existing railways
3. Development of rapid transit railway system technologies and construction
4. Development of 25-ton axle load freight heavy-duty technologies
5. Development of railway driving safety technological safeguarding systems
6. Manufacturing of heavy-duty high-quality rails and new-type sleepers
7. Manufacturing of marshalling station automation, loading and unloading operation mechanization, and freight yard equipment
8. Manufacturing of railway passenger and freight transportation equipment
9. Development of railway passenger and freight transportation information systems
10. Railway container transportation

X. Highway
1. Construction of the national road trunk network
2. Development of intelligent highway transportation system technologies
3. Development of high-speed highway passenger and freight transportation systems
4. Development of highway administration information systems
5. Development and production of new materials for highway engineering
6. Design and manufacturing of new-type highway machinery and equipment
7. Highway container transportation
8. Development of super-huge trans-radial bridge construction technologies
9. Development of large and lengthy tunnel construction technologies

XI. Water Transport

1. Construction of key pivotal ports along the coast

2. Construction of inland trunk cruise-ways and docks

3. Large-sized port loading and unloading automation projects

4. Development of ocean carriage electronic data exchange systems

5. Development of water transport safety control system and equipment manufacturing

6. Design and manufacturing of new-type harbor machinery and equipment

7. Water container transportation

8. Combined container transportation in multiple forms

9. High-speed over-water passenger transport

10. Development of coastal ship oil spilling monitoring and emergency elimination systems

11. Water roll-on-roll-off multi-modal transport

XII. Air Transport

1. Reconstruction of trunk line airports

2. Development and manufacturing of high-performance airport safety detection equipment

3. Manufacturing of special aviation vehicle

4. Development of aviation computer management and network systems

5. Manufacturing of aviation cargo loading and unloading equipment, freight yard equipment, warehousing equipment, container an auxiliary equipment

6. Manufacturing of aviation cargo detection equipment

7. Development of airport communication and navigation systems

8. Manufacturing of high-performance airport fire-fighting equipment

XIII. Information Industry

1. Construction of photo-timing transmission systems at 2.5 Gb/s and above

2. Construction of digital microwave synchronous transmission systems at 155Mb/s and above

3. Construction of satellite communication earth stations

4. Construction of communications supporting networks such as network management and monitoring, No.7 signaling, clock synchronization and toll

5. Construction of data communication networks

6. Construction of new services networks such as intelligent network

7. Construction of wide-band asynchronous transfer mode networks

8. Construction of digital cellular mobile communication networks

9. Construction of IP services networks

10. Construction of communication link real-time scheduling systems cross connection.

11. Construction of postal financial networks

12. Construction of postal integrated services networks

13. Mail handling automation projects

14. Manufacturing of optical fiber wave division multiplex transmission system equipment

15. Manufacturing of digital synchronous serial fiber-optical communication system equipment at 2.5 Gb/s and above

16. Manufacturing of digital cross connection equipment

17. Development of new technologies for supporting communication networks and equipment manufacturing

18. Manufacturing of satellite communication system including satellite mobile communications. and earth station equipment

19. Manufacturing of intelligent network equipment

20. Manufacturing of high-speed wide-band digital program controlled switches

21. Manufacturing of data communication network system equipment

22. Development of key technologies for isothermal layer communication system and equipment manufacturing

23. Manufacturing of digital synchronous serial microwave communication system equipment at 155Mb/s and above

24. Manufacturing of digital mobile communication GSM, CDMA, DCS1800, etc. handsets, base stations and switching equipment subject to the approval of the State Planning Commission.

25. Manufacturing of cable and wireless subscriber access network system equipment

26. Manufacturing of digital clustering communication system equipment

27. Manufacturing of network equipment such as router, hub, gateway and network card

28. Manufacturing of workstations and high-performance servers

29. Manufacturing of large- and medium-scale computers

30. Manufacturing of high-performance micro-computers

31. Design and manufacturing of large-scale integrated circuits with a line width of 1.2μm and below

32. Manufacturing of new-type electronic power devices and systems

 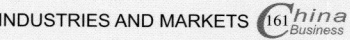

33. Manufacturing of new-type surface pasted components

34. Manufacturing of opto-electronic devices, sensitive elements, and sensing devices

35. Manufacturing of special electronic materials, electronic-function ceramic materials

36. Development and production of software

37. Development and manufacturing of computer aided design CAD. , computer aided test CAT. , computer aided manufacturing CAM. and computer aided engineering CAE. systems

38. Manufacturing of special electronic equipment, instrument, tools and moulds

39. Manufacturing of mass storage optical and magnetic disk drives and their components and parts

40. Development and manufacturing of new-type display devices such as liquid crystal display devices, plasma display PDP. devices

41. Development and manufacturing of large-screen color projection television and its key devices

42. Manufacturing of laser printers and ink jet printers

43. Manufacturing of mono-mode optical fiber and fiber-optical prefabricated rod

44. Manufacturing of digital audio-video broadcasting system equipment

45. Core, optical head and special chip of DVD series of digital video disk products

46. Manufacturing of discs for high-density digital video disk players DVD. designated by the state.

47. Development of digital video playing and recording technologies

48. Manufacturing of digital television products including transmission equipment, digital color television sets.

49. Manufacturing of normal paper facsimile machines

50. Manufacturing of new-type security machines

51. Manufacturing of multi-media terminals

52. Manufacturing of high-speed wireless paging system equipment

53. Manufacturing of multi-function telephone sets

54. Manufacturing of new-type frequency devices

55. Manufacturing of mercuryless alkaline-manganese secondary cells, nickel-hydrogen cells, lithium cells and solar cells

56. Manufacturing of radio-frequency cables for mobile communications

57. Manufacturing of hybrid integrated circuits

58. Manufacturing of monocrystalline silicon, polycrystalline silicon and chip

59. Production of ink for ink jet printers

60. Manufacturing of digital camera

61. Doppler radar technologies and equipment manufacturing

62. Development and manufacturing of air traffic control systems

63. Manufacturing of automobile electronic products

64. Manufacturing of medical electronic products

XIV. Iron and Steel

1. High-efficiency mining and transportation

2. High-efficiency dressing and comprehensive utilization of mineral resources

3. Production of oxidized ball

4. Development of coking coal humidifying, matched coal coke making, tamping coke making and dry-method coke quenching technologies

5. Development of technologies for long-life high-temperature hot-blast furnace

6. Development of blast-furnace oxygen-enriched coal powder injection technologies

7. Development of comprehensive technologies for long-life and high-efficiency blast furnace

8. Direct reduction

9. Fused reduction

10. Recovery and comprehensive utilization of blast-furnace and converter gas

11. Pre-treatment of hot-metal

12. External refining of molten steel

13. Development of converter splash-protection technologies

14. Development of high-efficiency continuous casting technologies

15. Development of continuous casting billet hot-pack and hot-feed technologies

16. Near-end-type continuous casting and rolling of sheet billet and tape billet

17. Development of comprehensive technologies for automation of metallurgic process

18. Development of controlled rolling and controlled cooling systems

19. Development of plate-mould control systems

20. Surface zinc-plating zinc and aluminium. , tin-plating, color coating and composition

21. Smelting of micro alloyed steel

22. New technologies for smelting of large- and medium-sized stainless steel

23. Production of cold rolled silicon steel

 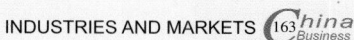

24. Production of high-strength mechanical steel

25. Production of hot and cold rolled stainless steel

26. Production of high-speed railway steel

27. Production of oil well pipelines and long-distance oil and gas pipelines

28. Exploitation of high-alumina bauxite and hard paste and clinker production

29. Development of smelting furnace and kiln and energy-saving technologies

30. Production of high-performance precision alloy sheet and band

XV. Nonferrous Metals

1. Exploitation of deep and hard-to-exploit mineral deposit

2. Comprehensive utilization of polymetallic and paragenous mineral deposit

3. Comprehensive recovery of hard-to-process gold deposit and gold-containing tailings resources

4. Development of technologies for utilization of low-grade and hard-to-process copper deposit

5. Development and comprehensive utilization of rare and dissipated metals

6. Adoption of new roasting technologies, hot-press preliminary oxidizing and cyaniding gold-extracting technologies, and bacterial oxidizing and cyaniding gold-extracting technologies to develop and utilize hard-to-process gold ore

7. Development of technologies for pollution-free strengthening smelting of metallic sulfide minerals

8. High-efficiency energy-saving dressing and electrochemical controlled floatation

9. Development of high-efficiency beneficiation reagents

10. Aluminium oxide production and new technology development

11. Development of prebaked cell electrolytic aluminum technologies

12. Wet-smelting of nonferrous metals

13. Development of supercritical extraction technologies

14. Development of aluminum and aluminum alloy high-speed casting and rolling technologies and equipment manufacturing

15. Manufacturing of amorphous alloy tape

16. Rare-earth application

17. Manufacturing of nonferrous metal composite and new-type alloy materials

18. Manufacturing of high-performance, high-precision hard metal, tin compound, antimony compound and ceramic materials

19. Manufacturing of high-performance magnetic materials

20. Manufacturing of super-fine materials, electronic size and their products

21. Manufacturing of new-type brake materials

22. Manufacturing of high-performance metal materials for metro

XVI. Chemical Industry

1. Construction of large- and medium-scale chemical mines

2. New construction of large-scale nitrogenous fertilizer production facilities and energy-saving and capacity expansion reconstruction of existing nitrogenous fertilizer enterprises

3. Production of high-concentration phosphate compound fertilizer, potash fertilizer and various special compound and mixed fertilizer

4. Development and utilization of various new-type fertilizers

5. Development and production of high-efficiency J-poison, new-brand safety pesticides

6. Production of recoverable and degradable agricultural films

7. New construction and reconstruction of existing inorganic chemical productions with new-type energy-saving and environmental protection technologies

8. Production of new-type fine inorganic chemical products

9. Production of new-type coating materials

10. Production of new-brand dyes

11. Production of feed additives, food additives, water treatment chemicals, electronic chemicals, oil-field chemicals, papermaking chemicals, leather chemicals and adhesive chemicals

12. Production of new-type biochemical products

13. Production of new-type information chemicals

14. Production of new-type high-efficiency catalytic agents

15. High-performance production of engineering plastics and general-purpose plastics

16. Production of organosilicon products

17. Production of organofluorine products

18. Production of new-type membrane materials and products

19. Production of inorganic nanometre materials

20. Manufacturing of high-grade radial tire and special complementary materials and special critical equipment

21. Disposal of waste gas, water and industrial residue of chemical production and comprehensive utilization of resources

22. Production of bioactive feed and fertilizers

 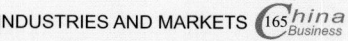

XVII. Petrochemical Industry

1. Reconstruction of oil refining and deep-processing of heavy oil that adapts to the readjustment of crude oil structure and variety structure of petroleum products and the improvement of the quality of petroleum products

2. Large-scale ethylene and post-processing

3. Reconstruction and expansion of ethylene

4. Large-scale synthetic resin and new synthetic resin technologies and new product manufacturing

5. Large-scale synthetic rubber and advanced rubber-plastic elastic body technologies and new product manufacturing

6. Manufacturing of large-scale synthetic fibre monomer and polymer

7. Production of engineering plastics and new-type plastic alloy

8. Production of basic organic industrial chemicals that comply with the economic scale

9. Development of technologies that can improve the differential ratio of the synthetic fibre and manufacturing of new varieties of differential synthetic fibre

10. Polyvinyl chloride produced with the method of vinyl oxidization and chloridization

11. Production of raw materials for geotechnical synthetic materials

12. Comprehensive utilization of by-products from refinery gas and chemicals industry

13. Control and comprehensive utilization of waste gas, water and industrial residue

XVIII. Building Materials

1. Cement production with new-type dry-method clinker with a daily output of 4,000 tons and above

2. Production of new-type walling materials, new-type heat insulating materials, new-type water-proof materials and new-type building sealing materials

3. Production of conservation building materials

4. Development of 10,000-ton-and-above alkali-free glass fibre direct melting technologies and equipment manufacturing

5. Fine-quality plastic composite door and window and plastic pipe production lines with an annual output above 10,000 tons

6. Development of deep-processing technologies for plate glass

7. Construction of high-grade sanitary and clean fixture production lines with an annual output above 75,000 pieces and hardware production lines with an annual

output above 300,000 pieces

8. Development of super-fine and modified deep-processing technologies for non-metal ore and equipment manufacturing

9. Development of hi-tech ceramic technologies

XIX. Medicine

1. Production of new domestic, Category-1, Category-2 and Category-3 pharmaceuticals

2. Production of products with high added value and export advantages

3. Development of new medicinal bioengineering technologies

4. Production of radiopharmaceuticals

5. Production of therapeutical medicines for AIDS

6. Production of new-type pharmaceutical preparations and adjuncts

7. Production of pharmaceutical intermediates in short supply

8. Production of new-type diagnostic reagents

9. Production of new-type medicinal packing materials

10. Production of new-type sanitary materials and adjuncts

11. Production of new pharmaceuticals and appliances for family planning

12. Development of new pharmaceutical screening technologies and screening models

13. Development of new bacterial culture technologies

14. Development of antibiotic extracting and purifying technologies

15. Automatic fermentation process control

16. Large-scale pharmaceutical polypeptide composition and purification

17. Large-scale pharmaceutical nucleic acid composition and purification

18. Production of high-yield genetic engineering bacteria

19. Production of natural medicine and marine medicine

20. Development of technologies for extracting, purifying and analyzing of the active principle of traditional Chinese medicine

21. Development of membrane technologies, crystallizing technologies, supercritical extracting technologies, chirality technologies and separating technologies in the course of production of pharmaceuticals

22. Development of large-scale animal and plant cell culture technologies in the course of production of pharmaceuticals

23. Development of enzyme technologies

24. Development of transfusion soft-packing technologies

25. Development of medicinal butyl latex production technologies

 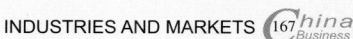

26. Development of technologies for fine-quality, high-yield and pure medicinal materials and technologies to turn wild varieties into domestic varieties

27. Development of immersion preparing technologies for medicine materical crude slices

28. Development of medical image information gathering technologies

29. Development of new-type medical apparatus and instrument manufacturing technologies

30. Manufacturing of apparatus and instruments for involvement treatment

31. Production of new-type medical materials that are implanted into or enter the human body

32. Manufacturing of high-efficiency and energy-saving pharmaceutical machinery

33. Development of disposal technologies for waste of medicine production

34. Production of pharmaceuticals that fill in the domestic gaps

XX. Machinery

1. Development of precision forming technologies and equipment manufacturing

2. Development of high-speed five-axis-above linkage precision numerical control machine, numerical control system, and A.C. servo-gear and straight-line electric machine

3. Development of advanced computer software and hardware for development of mechanical products and equipment manufacturing

4. Development of advanced testing and detecting technologies for development of mechanical products and equipment manufacturing

5. Manufacturing of key parts and components for numerical control machine high-speed shaft, tool magazine, dynamic adapter socket.

6. Manufacturing of new-type sensing elements

7. Car bearings, railway vehicle bearings, precision bearings and high-speed bearings

8. Manufacturing of combined flow and axial flow hydroelectric units with a rotor diameter of 8.5 meters and above and their key auxiliaries

9. Manufacturing of large-sized tubular and pump-storage hydroelectric units and their key auxiliaries

10. Manufacturing of supercritical thermal power generation units

11. Manufacturing of large-sized air-cooling units at 600,000 KW and above

12. Manufacturing of re-circulating fluidized bed boilers at 100,000 KW and above

13. Manufacturing of combined gas-steam recycle units at 36,000 KW and above

14. Manufacturing of large-sized wind power generation units

15. Manufacturing of nuclear power generation units and their key auxiliaries

16. Manufacturing of super-pressure A.C.-D.C. transmission and transformer equipment at 500,000 KV and above

17. Large current breaking capacity testing and abrupt transformer short-circuit testing equipment

18. Development of desulfurization technologies and devices

19. Manufacturing of new-type insulating materials

20. Development of key manufacturing technologies for large-scale fertilizer and ethylene devices and equipment manufacturing

21. Development of decentralized control systems for key technical equipment

22. Development of automatic on-line testing technologies and systems

23. Manufacturing of large-sized precision instruments

24. Manufacturing of new-type hydraulic, sealed and pneumatic components

25. Manufacturing of intelligent low-voltage electrical apparatus

26. Manufacturing of high-strength irregularly shaped fasteners

27. Manufacturing of resin sand casting equipment at 20 t/h and above

28. Development of advanced die design and manufacturing technologies and equipment manufacturing

29. Development of large-scale vacuum electron beam welding technologies and equipment manufacturing

30. Development of controllable atmosphere and vacuum heat treatment technologies and equipment manufacturing

31. Development of new technologies for safety-production and environmental protection detection instruments and equipment manufacturing

32. Development of new straw decomposition and utilization technologies and key equipment manufacturing

33. Development of urban garbage disposal technologies and equipment manufacturing

34. Development of large-scale sewage disposal technologies and equipment manufacturing

35. Manufacturing of flue gas desulfurization and denitration equipment

36. Development of key natural calamity monitoring technologies and equipment manufacturing

37. Manufacturing of complete equipment for smoke prevention and dust control

38. Manufacturing of environmental monitoring instruments and testing instruments

 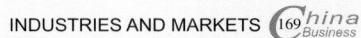

39. Manufacturing of complete equipment for gangue power generation units

40. Manufacturing of complete equipment for flyash storage, transportation and brick-making

41. Manufacturing of waste and old plastic recovery and utilization equipment

42. Development of sea water desalination technologies and equipment manufacturing

43. Development and manufacturing of industrial robots

44. Manufacturing of complete equipment for underground trackless mining, loading and transporting with an annual output of 5 million tons and above

45. Manufacturing of complete equipment for large-scale open-pit mines at 20 million tons and above

46. Manufacturing of tunnel borers

47. Manufacturing of subway dark excavation equipment

48. Development of 2-meter-and-above large-scale combined hot and cold continuous rolling and process control technologies and equipment manufacturing

49. Manufacturing of air separation plants at 30,000 cubic meters an hour

50. Manufacturing of mechanical three-dimensional garages

51. Manufacturing of natural gas centralized transportation equipment

52. Manufacturing of large-sized supporting turbocompressors for petrochemical devices

53. Manufacturing of key equipment for flexible plate printing

54. Manufacturing of full-automatic high-speed multiple-color printing equipment

55. Manufacturing of advanced and applicable agricultural machinery

56. Manufacturing of equipment for deep-processing and resource comprehensive utilization of farming, fishing, husbanding, cane sugar products

57. Manufacturing of equipment for ecological agriculture

58. Manufacturing of harvesting machinery for crops such as cotton, rice, corn, bean and green-feed . and agricultural farm implements

59. Development of manufacturing technologies for forestry machinery

60. Development of vacuum refining and casting technologies and equipment manufacturing

61. Manufacturing of new-type instrument elements and materials

62. Manufacturing of large-sized engineering construction machinery

63. Manufacturing of advanced internal combustion engines and key components

64. Manufacturing of central heating heat measuring system equipment

65. Manufacturing of urban water-supply, sewage treatment instruments and apparatus and centralized control equipment

66. Manufacturing of subway varying-voltage and variable-frequency VVVF. equipment

67. Urban track communications equipment localization projects

68. Manufacturing of oil and natural gas prospecting and well drilling equipment

69. Manufacturing of high-performance dredging equipment

70. Development of urban green-type sod industrialized production technologies and equipment manufacturing

71. Manufacturing of tourist emergency system and equipment

XXI. Automobiles

1. Development and manufacturing of auto body and body accessories

2. Manufacturing of new-type engines for automobiles and motorcars

3. Development and manufacturing of key auto components

4. Precision press forging, black casting, non-ferrous casting and blank manufacturing of key parts for automobiles

5. Development and manufacturing of auto moulds

6. Manufacturing of new materials for light-duty automobiles

7. Development and manufacturing of assembly, engines, components and development of systems for automobiles and motorcars

8. Development and manufacturing of automobile tail-gas emission control systems such as engine management systems and three-dimensional catalytic converters

9. Development of authentication and testing systems of the state-level testing center for models and styles of automobiles and motorcars

10. Development and manufacturing of key gas-fired automobile components and parts such as gas conversion systems

XXII. Shipping

1. Design and manufacturing of hi-tech, high-performance and special vessels and large vessels above 60,000 tons

2. Manufacturing of passenger roll-on-roll-off ships and passenger box ships at 10,000 tons and above

3. Manufacturing of liquefied petroleum gas LPG. and liquefied natural gas LNG. ships at 5,000 cubic meters and above

4. Manufacturing of main engines of ships

5. Manufacturing of ship electric power plants

 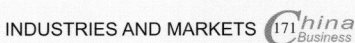

6. Manufacturing of marine crankshafts, special auxiliaries and electronic instruments

7. Manufacturing of offshore drilling ships, drilling platforms

8. Manufacturing of container ships with 3,000 TEU and above

XXIII. Aerospace

1. Development and manufacturing of civil aircraft and components and parts

2. Development and manufacturing of aircraft engines

3. Development and manufacturing of comprehensive aviation electronic systems and construction of modern warehousing facilities

4. Development and manufacturing of airborne equipment and systems

5. Development and manufacturing of helicopter overall, rotor systems, and driving systems

6. New-type aeronautical materials and technologies and applications

7. Manufacturing of gas turbine engines

8. Manufacturing of satellites, carrier rockets and components and parts

9. Satellite applications

10. Applications of aviation and space technologies

11. Development and manufacturing of aircraft ground analog training systems

12. Development and manufacturing of aircraft ground maintenance, repair and testing equipment

XXIV. Light Industry and Textile

1. Design, processing and manufacturing of non-metal product dies

2. Production of paper pulp, paper and paper products that conforms to the standards of the economic scale

3. Manufacturing of agricultural plastic water-saving apparatus

4. Production of new-type high-speed 9-layer-above corrugated paper

5. Post finishing and processing of leather

6. Manufacturing of hi-tech ceramics and high-grade export-oriented domestic ceramics

7. Manufacturing of special industrial sewing machines

8. Enzyme production

9. Production of synthetic perfume and mono-isolate

10. Development of floride-free refrigeration technologies

11. Production of xanthic glue food-grade.

12. Production of new-type packing materials

13. Manufacturing of new-type composite materials

14. Development of digital printing technologies and high-definition platemaking systems

15. High-grade fabric printing and dyeing and hi-tech post finishing and processing

16. Single-series polyester production with a daily output of 400 tons and above

17. Production of highly artificial chemical fibre lining

18. Production of textile oiling agents, auxiliaries and dyeing materials

19. Production of carbon fibre, new-type cellulose fibre, and multi-function and differentiation chemical fibre

20. Processing of special natural fibre

21. Manufacturing of industrial special textiles

22. Development of hi-tech light industry and textile machinery, and key technologies and manufacturing of components and parts

23. Production of direct-spinning polyester short staple with an annual single-thread output of 30,000 tons and above

24. Production of direct-spinning polyester filament yarn with an annual single-thread output of 10,000 tons and above

25. Production of continuous-spinning viscose filament yarn that conforms to the economic scale

XXV. Construction

1. Construction engineering computer-aided design

2. Building machinery computer-aided design and manufacturing

3. Development of key construction energy-saving technologies

4. Manufacturing of high-rise building and space-filling equipment

5. Manufacturing of key construction equipment

6. Manufacturing of high-performance housing peripheral building enclosure materials and components

7. Development of new-type building structure systems

8. Manufacturing of building shock isolating and absorbing materials

9. Development of underground engineering shield construction technologies and equipment manufacturing

10. Manufacturing of municipal infrastructure composite pipelines

11. Development of walling noise-absorbing technologies and materials

XXVI. Urban infrastructure and Real Estate

1. Construction of urban subway, light railway proportion of equipment localiza-

tion of 70% and above. and public transit

2. Construction of urban roads

3. Manufacturing of urban traffic control systems and equipment

4. Urban water-supply source, city water, drainage and sewage treatment projects

5. Innocuity, resource realization and decrement treatment and comprehensive utilization of urban garbage and other solid wastes

6. Urban gas projects

7. Urban central heating projects

8. Manufacturing of energy-saving and low-pollution heating installations

9. Construction of urban landscape-style, green-type and ecological housing estate

10. Construction of urban three-dimensional parking areas

11. Generally affordable and functional housing construction

12. Urban automobile gas reconstruction projects

XXVII. Environmental Protection and Comprehensive Utilization of Resources

1. Ecological and environmental harnessing projects

2. Bio-diversity conservation technologies and projects

3. Comprehensive development and utilization of forest resources

4. Comprehensive utilization of wastes and residues

5. Marine development and marine environmental protection

6. Development of consumption ozonosphere substitutions

7. Radioactive waste processing and disposal

8. Development of agricultural film recovery and innocuous decomposition technologies

XXVIII. Services

1. Construction of modern distribution centers, processing centers, and factoring support facilities and chain-store operation

2. Construction of modern warehousing facilities for key commodities such as grain, cotton, sugar, edible oil, fertilizer and oil

3. Integrated operation of agriculture, industry and trade, integration of production with sale for agricultural products, and circulation facility construction

4. Idle equipment regulate markets

5. Establishment of a socialized service system for agriculture

6. Construction of infrastructure including tourist and communications

7. Construction of key tourist and holiday-making projects and special-purpose

tourist projects

8. Construction of large-scale comprehensive development projects for tourist resources

9. Development of tourist information service systems

10. Credit cards and their network services

11. Leasing services

12. Construction of cultural, art, broadcasting, film, television, and sports-for-all facilities

13. Preservation of cultural relics

14. Higher education, vocational-technical education and special education

15. Construction of remote education systems

16. Construction of information networks

17. Construction of urban community service centers and service networks

18. Construction of old-age services facilities such as homes for old-ages, old-age apartments, and old-age nursing centers

19. Constructions of services facilities for the disabled

20. Construction of basic medical services facilities

21. Construction of preventive and health care services facilities

22. Construction of blood centers above the prefecture level

23. Construction of the state engineering technical. center, the state key lab, the high and new technological pioneering services center, the new product development and design center, the scientific research and testing bases, experiment bases

24. Scientific and technological services in areas such as technology popularization, scientific and technological exchanges, technical consulting, meteorology, environmental protection, surveying and mapping, earthquake, marine, patent, technical supervision

25. Economic, scientific and technological, engineering, management, accounting, auditing, employment, legal, and environmental protection consulting services

26. High and new technology advertisement producing, economic and scientific and technological exhibitions, scientific popularization

27. Precision instrument and equipment maintenance and services

28. Cooperation and sharing services for pillar scientific research factors such as scientific instruments, experimental animals, chemical reagents, and documentation information

FOREIGN TRADE

AN OVERVIEW

Today, products bearing the words "made in China" can be seen everywhere across the world. Statistics indicate that there are already more than a hundred kinds of manufactured products coming first in quantity in the world. Over 50 per cent of cameras, 30 per cent of air conditioners and television sets, 25 per cent of washing machines and nearly 20 per cent of refrigerators sold worldwide are made in China.

According to statistics from the Customs, China has been for years on end the country exporting the largest quantity of labor-intensive products including textiles, garments, shoes, clocks and watches, bikes, sewing machines, etc. In recent years, the export volume of mechanical and electrical products such as mobile phones, CD players, displays, air conditioners, containers, optical components, motor-driven tools, small electrical household appliances, etc. has also risen to the first place while color TV and motorcycles rank second in export volume in the world.

Since 1978, China's import and export have been increasing at an average annual rate of 15 per cent, which is not only higher than the growth rate of China's national economy, but exceeds the average annual growth rate of world trade by over 8 percentage points. In 1978, China ranked 32nd in the world's import and export trade. But in 2001, China's import volume, export volume, and total import and export volume each ranked sixth in the world, with an import and export turnover reached 509.8 billion US dollars.

China's low-cost and high labor quality superiority has brought substantial benefits to the consumers the world over. Thanks to China's large quantity of inexpensive but elegant products, the price of some staple commodities on world market that has kept on the high side for many years has dropped. The 1994 analytical report of the World Bank pointed out that if importing commodities from other countries than China, the American consumers would have to pay 14 billion US dollars more per year. Now as China-US trade volume has doubly increased, American consumers must have saved much more on expenditure, and such is also the case with consumers in other countries and regions.

By the end of the 1980s, China completed the shift from exporting primary products to finished industrial products. After that, China started the second shift, that is, from exporting roughly processed, low value-added products to deep processed, high value-added products. In 2001, among the total export commodities, primary products accounted for only 9.1 per cent while finished industrial products accounted for 90.1 per cent. From 1995 up to now, high value-added mechanical and electrical products have for eight consecutive years taken the place of textiles and garments and become the largest category of export commodities. In recent years, high-tech products have become a new aspect of export growth. In 2001, the export of mechanical and electrical products and high-tech products accounted for 45 per cent and 17.5 per cent respectively of the total export volume. Traditional staple labor-intensive products such as garments, shoes, toys, etc., though still keep increase in absolute value, appear slow in growth rate. In the total volume of import products, primary products account for 18.8 per cent whereas finished industrial products account for 81.2 per cent. The import of advanced technology, key equipment and raw and processed materials in short supply that are urgently needed, keeps a relatively rapid growth rate. Of the total import and export volume, mechanical and electrical

1991–2002 China's Foreign Trade Turnover

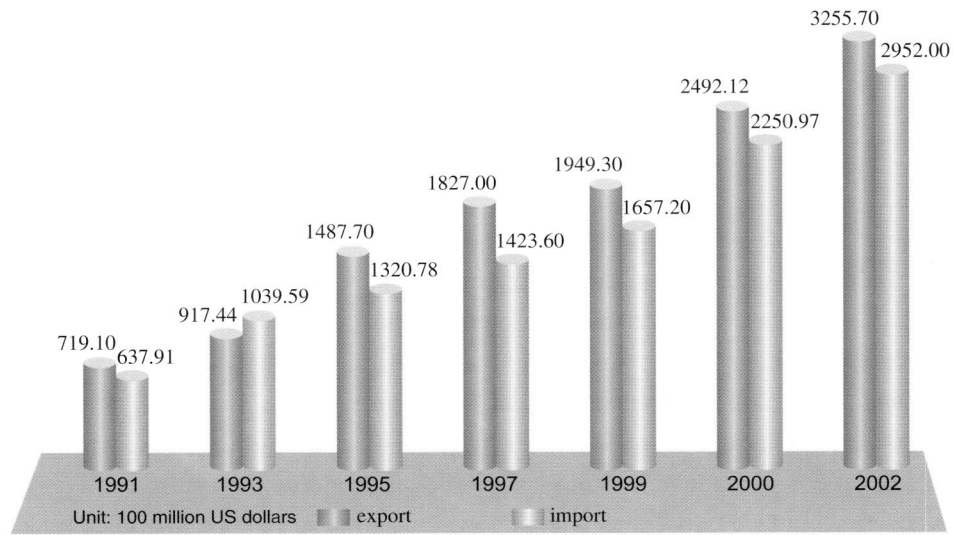

Unit: 100 million US dollars   export   import

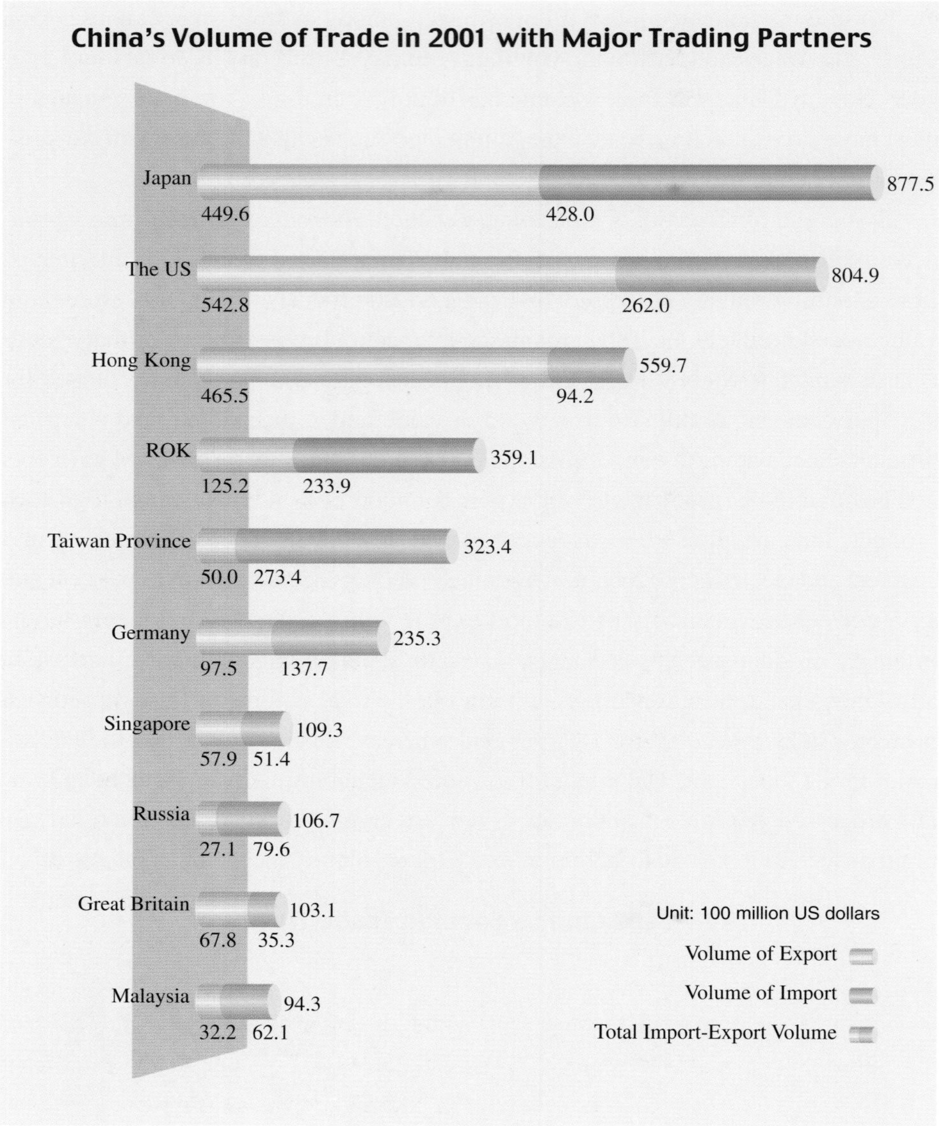

China's Volume of Trade in 2001 with Major Trading Partners

Partner	Volume of Export	Volume of Import	Total Import-Export Volume
Japan	449.6	428.0	877.5
The US	542.8	262.0	804.9
Hong Kong	465.5	94.2	559.7
ROK	125.2	233.9	359.1
Taiwan Province	50.0	273.4	323.4
Germany	97.5	137.7	235.3
Singapore	57.9	51.4	109.3
Russia	27.1	79.6	106.7
Great Britain	67.8	35.3	103.1
Malaysia	32.2	62.1	94.3

Unit: 100 million US dollars

Volume of Export

Volume of Import

Total Import-Export Volume

products account for over 40 per cent.

There are over 220 countries and regions that have trade contacts with China. In 2001, China's key trade partners included Japan, the US, China's Hong Kong, ROK, China's Taiwan, Germany, Singapore, Russia, Great Britain, Malaysia, Australia, Holland, France, Italy, Canada, Thailand, and Indonesia.

China conducts various modes of trade such as processing with customer's materials, processing with customer's samples, assembling with customer's parts, compensation trade, processing with imported materials in addition to general trade.

Other trade forms such as consignment sale, marketing on commission, exclusive sales, sole agency, leasing trade, auction, public bidding, futures trading are also adopted in specific businesses. In import and export of technology, various forms such as providing technology licensing, consultation, technical service, and cooperative production are adopted. Since 1979 China has started counter trade with some developing countries. From the 1980s onwards, border trade has been widely established. In the 1990s as enterprises in China experienced a rapid growth, business people started to develop processing trade in developing countries using mature technology, equipment and raw and processed materials. Later on the development of information technology has brought along electronic commerce, that is, conducting import and export trade on the Internet. Starting from 1996, China has started to promote its own E-commerce. By establishing China international E-business center, opening up online "China Commodities Trading Market" and "China Technical Commodities Trading Market," this new trading form is gradually extended.

Among various newly developed trading forms, processing trade is more prominent than all the others. Firstly emerged with the import of foreign capital, it has become a leading trading form in China after 20 years' development. In 2001, its total import-export amount reached 241.43 billion US dollars, accounting for 50.9 per cent of the total foreign trade turnover.

Currently the key issue confronting China's foreign trade is that the export commodities remains at a lower structural level and that the export competitiveness needs to be raised. The technical content and added value of China's export commodities are still not high. Some labor-intensive products that have been energetically developed since the 1980s have already acquired a considerable share on international market, leaving not much room for further development.

China conducts a unified foreign trade management. Its foreign trade administration legal system, centered on the Foreign Trade Law of the People's Republic of China, consists of laws and regulations with respect to the Customs, foreign exchanges, tax revenue, commodity inspection, anti-dumping and anti-subsidy, import-export of commodities, import-export operation rights, etc.

The Law, which came into force on July 1, 1994, is China's basic law governing foreign trade. It mainly specifies China's basic foreign trade system and norms of foreign trade relationship, and defines the basic principle in handling the import-export of technology and commodities and the international service trade. The basic system referred to includes primarily the following:

(1)Foreign trade operation license system. (2) Stipulations for prohibition and restriction of some specific items with regard to the import and export of commodi-

ties and technology while the principle of free import-export is established. The quota and licensing are adopted as specified in the Foreign Trade Law for commodities and technology the import-export of which is restricted. (3) With respect to the most favored nation treatment, national treatment, and market access for international service trade, the Foreign Trade Law provides that China shall, in line with the international treaties and agreements it has concluded or participated, gradually open service trade market in China and grant market access opportunities and national treatment to other participants of the international treaties and agreements. (4) Anti-dumping and anti-subsidy investigation and safeguard measures to maintain a fair market order. (5) Measures to promote foreign trade such as establishing import-export banks, allocating foreign trade development funds and risks funds, carrying out the policy of export tax-refund, encouraging the development of foreign trade consultation services.

In addition to the Foreign Trade Law, China has promulgated one after another a large number of foreign related economic laws and regulations such as the Arbitration Law, Customs Law, Contract Law, Foreign Exchanges Administration Regulations, Import-Export Commodities Inspection Regulations, Regulations on Management of Technology Import Contract, Patent Law, Trade Mark Law, etc.

China has concluded and entered into bilateral agreements or treaties with more than 100 countries and regions in the world. It has also joined a number of interna-

Traditional garment market still has great potentialities

tional conventions concerning economic and trade, recognized and adopted quite a few universally accepted customs and practice such as the United Nations Convention on International Goods Marketing Contract, the Pact for Recognition and Implementation of Foreign Arbitration Award, Paris Convention on the Protection of Industrial Property and Convention for Resolution of Investment Disputes Between a Country and the Nationals of Another Country.

The Ministry of Commerce has opened on its website (www.moftec.gov.cn) a special column entitled Laws and Regulations Governing Foreign Economic and Trade where matters concerning laws, regulations, stipulations of government departments, and matters about clearing up in foreign trade can be consulted.

RIGHT OF IMPORT-EXPORT MANAGEMENT

China adopts the registration and approval system for import-export management qualification. The right of import-export management is divided basically into two categories as per registered or approved scope of business: one is the right of foreign trade circulation management, that is, the import-export of commodities and technology and the other is the right of production enterprises conducting import-export on their own, that is, exporting their own products or importing machinery, equipment, spare parts, raw and auxiliary materials needed for their own use.

To apply for the right of foreign trade circulation management, an enterprise needs to have registered capital of no less than 5 million yuan (or 3 million yuan in the central and western regions) and other related conditions; to apply for the right of import-export on its own, a production enterprise (including wholly owned private enterprise, partnership enterprise) needs to have registered capital of no less than 3 million yuan (or 2 million yuan in the central and western regions and ethnic minorities regions); a scientific research institution, a hi-tech enterprise or a machinery and electrical products manufacturing enterprise needs to have registered capital of 1 million yuan and other conditions. Applications shall be submitted to local foreign economic and trade administrations authorized by the Ministry of Commerce which, within 10 working days on receipt of the application, must make decision as to whether approve or reject the registration application.

All sorts of import-export enterprises shall engage in the operation of relevant commodities or technology as per approved scope of business, exclusive of the commodities the import-export of which is prohibited or is to be operated by state designated enterprises.

Foreign-invested enterprises enjoy the right to import machinery, equipment, raw and processed materials needed for their own use and the right to export their own products, but shall not engage in import-export agency service unless the investment corporations and joint ventures have been approved to conduct such service.

The Chinese government stipulates that foreign business people may set up trading enterprises in the bonded areas approved by the State Council, engage in entrepot trade in the bonded area, import as agent raw and processed materials used for production by enterprises in the area and export their products.

In 1996, the former Ministry of Foreign Trade and Economic Cooperation promulgated the Interim Measures for Setting Up Pilot China-Foreign Joint Invested Foreign Trade Corporations, which provides that China-foreign joint invested foreign trade corporations are permitted to be established in the special economic zones in Pudong Shanghai and Shenzhen to engage in commodities and technology import-export business except for some specific commodities the export of which is unitarily managed and organized by the state and the commodities the import of which is designated to specific corporations by the state. Thus started the experiments in attracting foreign investment in China's foreign trade sphere.

Currently, foreign invested enterprises, which are authorized to engage in import-export business and some other foreign trade, primarily include the following types:

Foreign invested foreign trade companies   By the middle of 2002, there were altogether 5 authorized joint venture foreign trade companies in China. Currently the Ministry of Commerce is revising the experimental measures for setting up foreign invested foreign trade companies. It plans to relax the requirements, call off restrictions on regions and the number of companies to be experimented.

Foreign investment companies   According to the Interim Provisions on the Establishment of Investment Companies by Foreign Investors issued in 1995 by the former Ministry of Foreign Trade and Economic Cooperation and the two supplements issued in 1999 and 2001 respectively, an investment company established within China's territory by foreign business people is entitled to sell the products of the invested company in the form of agency or marketing, and to export the commodities it has purchased within the nation's territory that involve neither export quotas nor export license management. An investment company is permitted to sell at home or abroad the products it has purchased from the enterprise it has invested after systematically integrating the products. If the products manufactured by the invested enterprise fail to meet the needs of system integration, the investment company may purchase at home or abroad auxiliary products needed for system integration on condition that the cost of the auxiliary products shall not exceed 50 per cent of the cost of

Quantity and Amount of Primary Customs Imported Commodities

Description	Unit of Quantity	2001		2002	
		Quantity	Amount (10,000 USD)	Quantity	Amount (10,000 USD)
Grain and grain powder	10,000 tons	344	63,426	285	49,350
Edible vegetable oil	10,000 tons	165	47,756	319	130,965
Natural rubber	10,000 tons	98	59,195	96	69,375
Synthetic rubber	10,000 tons	75	79,425	92	93,944
Log	10,000 m³	1,686	169,398	2,433	213,841
Paper pulp	10,000 tons	490	207,612	526	216,767
Sawed timber	M³	4,016,052	98,669	5,395,957	115,907
Raw cotton	10,000 tons	6	7,104	18	18,644
Wool & sliver	Ton	309,141	104,917	237,264	103,777
Synthetic fiber for spinning and weaving	10,000 tons	92	96,295	104	106,281
TV kinescope	10,000 pieces	805	57,620	1,349	77,138
Soya bean	10,000 tons	1,394	280,952	1,132	248,298
Crude oil	10,000 tons	6,026	1,166,645	6,941	1,275,734
Product oil	10,000 tons	2,145	376,940	2,034	379,900
Primary shaped plastic	10,000 tons	1,426	1,172,537	1,584	1,333,085
Steel products	10,000 tons	1,722	896,359	2,449	1,236,585
Unforged copper and copper products	Ton	1,694,792	350,690	2,247,873	443,688
Automatic data processing equipment and parts	Set	68,168,810	498,150	114,790,306	673,328
Spares of automatic data processing equipment	Ton	145,890	662,661	183,634	919,437
Spares and accessories of audio-visual & radio signal equipment	Ton	45,682	358,010	47,348	411,488
Integrated circuits & microelectronic components	10,000 pieces	2,618,586	1,659,233	3,444,396	2,564,787
Car & chassis	–	72,047	174,810	127,393	317,465
Car spares	–	–	252,774	–	300,119
Aircraft	–	233	365,637	170	284,231
Ships	–	1,308	48,834	1,136	36,364
Copying machines	Set	97,674	5,890	112,871	6,251

the total products needed for system integration. At the same time, before the invested enterprise or any of its new products puts into production, for the purpose of market exploration, an invested company, upon approval, may import from its parent company a small quantity of non-import quota products that is identical or similar to

Quantity and Amount of Customs Exported Major Commodities

Description	Unit of Quantity	2001		2002	
		Quantity	Amount (10,000 USD)	Quantity	Amount (10,000 USD)
Grain & powder	10,000 tons	876	109,825	1,482	171,745
Raw cotton	Ton	52,366	8,002	149,538	16,959
Crude oil	10,000 tons	755	138,537	721	123,249
Medicines & chemical reagents	Ton	220,356	197,845	261,309	232,404
Plate glass	10,000 m²	6,133	15,031	11,359	24,990
TV sets	10,000 sets	2,103	159,153	3,165	239,642
Triode & similar semi-conductor device	10,000 pieces	6,123,513	95,992	8,848,950	133,867
Cars & chassis	–	24,839	20,822	43,490	26,115
Motor & generator	10,000 sets	245,617	184,188	302,837	218,427
Ships	–	68,034	188,866	63,223	189,405
Yarn, fabrics & products	–	–	1,684,204	–	2,058,330
Automatic data processing equipment and components	10,000 sets	54,393	1,309,625	67,962	2,013,483
Spares of automatic data processing equipment	Ton	716,525	798,234	915,832	1,312,008
Hand or car radiophone	Set	39,627,201	411,994	63,147,302	528,024
Spares and accessories of audio-visual and radio signal equipment	Ton	133,189	311,999	171,733	435,839
Furniture	–	–	395,863	–	536,055
Chests, bags and articles for traveling use	–	–	387,656	–	435,762
Garments & clothing accessories	–	–	3,656,150	–	4,119,009
Shoes	–	–	1,009,646	–	1,109,053
Plastic products	Ton	3,782,144	509,622	4,598,770	605,276
Toys	–	–	516,489	–	557,463

the products manufactured by the invested enterprise and sell on home market on a trial basis.

Foreign invested production enterprises with an annual export turnover exceeding 10 million US dollars In July 2001, China extended the scope of trading right granted to foreign invested production enterprises, mainly in the following aspects:

1. Extend the scope of foreign invested production enterprises' export right. Those up to the requirements listed below are permitted to purchase and export non-franchised goods and goods not under quota license management and may take part

in bidding for export quotas for self-manufactured products: (1) Foreign invested production enterprises with annual turnover exceeding 10 million US dollars; (2) For two consecutive years prior to application, no records for breaking the law or rules with respect to tax, foreign exchange and import and export; (3) Having a staff of professionals specialized in international business.

2. Extend the scope of import right of foreign investment companies whose parent companies belong to a production-based group. Matters concerning foreign investment companies importing system integration auxiliary products or goods on trial sale shall be dealt with in light of related regulations stipulated by the Ministry of Foreign Trade and Economic Cooperation.

3. Permit foreign invested research centers to import hi-tech products manufactured by their parent companies for the purpose of carrying out market tests of the product they have developed and to sell a small quantity of the said products. The quantity of the products imported must be appropriate for the need for market test.

According to statistics, there are over 2,000 foreign invested enterprises in China each with annual export turnover exceeding 10 million US dollars.

ADMINISTRATION OF IMPORTED AND EXPORTED COMMODITIES

Administration of imported commodities

China permits free import-export of goods and technology, except for those otherwise stipulated in laws and regulations. For commodities the importation of which is restricted, import quota and import license management shall be administered.

In 2002, there were in China 12 commodities under import license management.

Commodities subject to import quota permit management include: petroleum products, natural rubber, car tires, cars and related parts, motorcycles and related parts, cameras and camera bodies, watches, car jacks and chassis, eight kinds in all.

Commodities subject to import license management include: CD production equipment, controlled chemicals, chemicals that can be easily used in producing narcotics, and materials depleting ozonosphere, four kinds in all.

Imported mechanical and electrical products not included in import-quota management lists (machinery equipment, electronic products, components and their parts etc.) are subject to non-quota management. Among them, those in need of rapid development at home but still at an initial stage of industrial production are listed in the catalogue of special products, which are purchased mainly through international bid-

Data

Export to China

To export to China is an easy as well as a traditional way of entering Chinese market. Of course, the competition can be intense because the future of the Chinese market looks promising.

To export goods to China, direct or indirect method can be adopted. The main difference lies in whether the export enterprise itself engages in marketing or not. If an enterprise with only a small export volume is not powerful enough, or it does not fully understand Chinese market situation, it may contract out the export of its goods to an export middleman. Such is indirect export.

The most simple and convenient way for an enterprise outside China's territory to export its products directly to China is through an agent. The enterprise may seek a wholesale agent or a retail agent according to the quantity of the products. However, the agent it seeks must have a business license specifying the forms of operation and scope of business in which the products are included. The agency can be full power or regional, can be run jointly or can be one engaging in special marketing.

Overseas enterprises may adopt self-marketing form and set up local offices. When there is market demand, products can be imported through large Chinese import-export companies and then sell the goods by its staff to the market or to other distributors. Besides, there are other direct forms such as attending order-placing meetings or commodities fairs, etc.

ding invitation. Others are subject to voluntary registration management in which each importing unit gets and fills up related registration forms. The Ministry of Commerce is in charge of this matter.

With a view to enhancing macro control over the import of a few staple raw and processed materials and sensitive commodities, China administers voluntary registration management of a dozen or so specific commodities including foodstuffs, crude oil and steel products. The State Development Planning Commission is responsible for the guidance and management in this regard.

The very few staple raw and processed materials that are of importance to the national economy and the people's livelihood, that are highly monopolized on international market and are price sensitive are operated and managed by authorized companies. The Ministry of Commerce is responsible for the ratification of such companies and shall make known the result to the public.

Importing waste materials from abroad and dumping, stacking or disposing them within China's territory is prohibited in China. Importing waste materials that can be used as raw material is restricted. In case it is necessary to import waste materials listed in the Catalogue of Waste Materials that can be Used as Raw Material the Importation of Which is Under State Restriction, the importing unit or utilizing unit must apply to local environmental protection authorities or to the State Environmental Protection Administration and report to the State Environmental Protection Administration for examination and approval.

The State Environmental Protection Administration exercises unified management and environmental supervision of chemicals imported for the first time and the import-export of toxic chemicals. It is responsible for the issuance of the list of toxic chemicals that are prohibited or strictly limited in China. Foreign business people or their agents who export to China any chemicals that have not been registered in China (not including pesticide), must apply to the State Environmental Protection Administration for environmental management registration for chemicals imported for the first time and provide samples for experiments free of charge.

No enterprise is permitted to engage in entrepot trade in waste materials.

Management of Exported Commodities

In 2002, China exercised export license management of 54 commodities in the forms of export quota license, export quota bidding invitation, export quota paid use, export quota free use by bidding and export license management in light of specific conditions.

China exercises quota management of a part of export commodities under two circumstances: one is that the importing country has quantity limit and through negotiation China is required to control its own export quantity through allocating quota, which is called passive quota, primarily textile quota and the other is export quantity limit enforced on the state's own initiative with a view to maintaining the market order of China's export commodities, protecting domestic resources and bio-environment, which is called active quota, mainly applying to staple farm produce and industrial products, non-regenerable resources and traditional large quantity export commodities.

The export license management is exercised of major famous, high-class and special export products that are in large amount and easy to get confused in operation, and a few commodities that actually need to be managed. The annual export volume of such commodities is basically not limited provided that market supply and demand are normal.

The government department in charge exercises dynamic management of the above-mentioned commodities, making adjustment usually at the turning of the year.

In the allocation of export quotas, bidding invitation is practiced for commodities that are suitable for bidding, such as some commodities in need of active export quotas and some textiles in short supply that are in need of passive export quotas. The import and export enterprises (including foreign invested enterprises), having gone through preliminary examination of their bidding qualification and registered at the corresponding bidding office, can obtain a bidding qualification credential if they are up to the requirements.

A measure combining paid use and regularized allocation is adopted for a part of commodities on which the government charges a certain amount of quota use fee as a means to regulate export enterprises' protective profit brought by the use of quotas. It is an economic measure to adjust gains and losses between enterprises.

Apart from the above two categories, quota allocation for other commodities is regularized. That is to adopt an allocation system of multi-quantified indices cover-

---

Data

Exposition and Exhibition

In China, there are a series of expositions and exhibitions held every year to attract people seeking business opportunity on this huge market of China. They are sure to find an opportunity in a corresponding expo whether they intend to buy Chinese commodities, to market their products or services, or to take part in exchange activities.

In recent years, there are nearly 500 large-scaled expositions and exhibitions held annually in China with the number ever increasing, of which a considerable are held in great metropolises such as Beijing, Shanghai, Guangzhou, etc.

It is not possible for us to introduce each of so many trade expos as regards the scope, size, cycle, duration, venue and sponsors, which may change sometimes. Nevertheless we have attached in this book a chapter titled Organizations and Websites, which records the websites of major expositions and exhibitions from which you can get more detailed and precise information.

Each year, a book titled "Expositions and Exhibitions in China" is published by "China Council for the Promotion of International Trade", introducing the expositions and exhibitions to be held in China the following year. Moreover, they can also obtain the latest information related from some specialized websites of exhibitions.

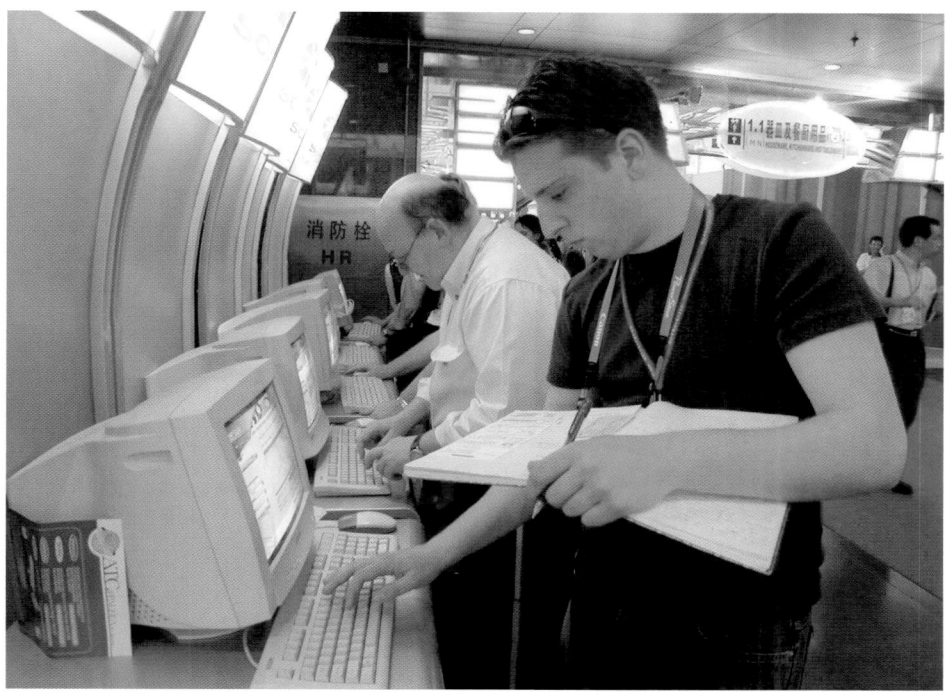

Clients inquiring about information on line at an economic and trade fair

ing actual export results, export price, quota use ratio, etc. In this way, the administrator's subjective casualness and the enterprises' thoughtlessness in applying for quotas can both be avoided.

All sorts of export enterprises (foreign invested enterprises included) may apply to local foreign trade and economic authorities for quotas that are distributed in a regularized way or in a regularized way combined with paid use.

Enterprises are not permitted to export such commodities as:

1. Endangering the state security;

2. Cultural relics, animals or plants on the brink of extinction, products made in reform-through-labor units prohibited by laws and regulations;

3. In violation of international obligation committed by the People's Republic of China;

4. Musk, natural bezoar, flagelliform nostoc, platinum, etc. that are particularly in short supply at home.

The catalogue of commodities under import-export quota or license management is published annually by the Ministry of Commerce, which will be adjusted in the light of the state policy, the development of foreign trade and economy and changes on world and domestic markets. Relevant information is available on the official website of foreign trade and economic authorities.

POLICIES ON CUSTOMS DUTY

China's policies on customs duty are based on the idea of further extending opening up and reducing customs duty level step by step. The principle of determining tariff rate is to encourage earning foreign exchanges through exports and step up the import of domestic necessities to boost the development of national economy.

China collects ad valorem duties for import-export tariff. The import duty is calculated as per the CIF rate of the shipment, which includes the regular wholesale price at the purchasing place plus all expenses in transportation including packing charge, freight, insurance premium, handling charges, etc. If it is not possible to determine the wholesale price at the overseas purchasing place, it can be calculated as per the regular wholesale price of the commodities of the same kind at the imported place at home minus expenses in the import links as well as regular domestic warehousing and transport charges after importing. The export duty is levied as per the FOB rate.

Since 1992, to adapt to the need of economic development and to merge at a quicker pace into the world economic current, Chinese government has reduced tariff rate 5 times of its own accord. The arithmetic average tariff rate was reduced from 43.2 per cent in1992 to 12 per cent in 2002, by a margin of 60.6 per cent; the weighted average tariff rate from 32.37 per cent in 1992 to 13.3 per cent in 2002, by a margin of 59.3 per cent.

POLICIES ON PROCESSING TRADE

Processing trade refers to the total or a part of raw and auxiliary materials, spares and parts, component, packing material imported from overseas (hereinafter called imported materials and articles) and kept in bonded warehouses which, after processing or assembling by domestic enterprises, are exported again. Processing trade is classified into two categories: processing with customer's materials and processing with imported materials. The former refers to that the materials imported are provided by foreign business people, and that there is no need to pay foreign exchanges for the import. The processed products are delivered to foreign business people for exporting who pay processing charges to the enterprise conducting the processing; the latter refers to that the materials imported are paid for by the operating enterprise that exports on its own the products processed.

To encourage the development of processing trade, the government has implemented a series of preferential policies on processing trade. The first is to exempt from customs duty and import link value-added tax on imported equipment provided by foreign business people for processing trade except a few imported commodities that are not exempted from duties as stipulated by the state; the second is that the bonded policy is exercised on materials and articles imported for processing trade; and the third is that no quantity limit is set to materials and articles imported for processing trade except a very few sensitive commodities.

With a view to ensure the sound and orderly development of processing trade, the government executes the following measures:

Individual examination and approval of processing trade projects   An enterprise, before starting processing trade, must report to foreign trade and economic authorities for examination and approval, which is conducted at different levels. The Ministry of Commerce is in charge of the examination and approval at the state level while the provincial, prefectural and municipal foreign trade and economics authorities are in charge of the examination and approval at each local level respectively. The major points for examination and approval are the processing capability of the enterprise and the processing agreement. Strict precautions must be taken

China inland province economic and trade exchange meeting

against smuggling.

Classified management of commodities Materials and articles imported for processing trade are classified in terms of commodities into categories of prohibition, restriction and permission. The prohibition category refers to commodities prohibited from importing as specified in the Foreign Trade Law of the People's Republic of China as well as commodities that are beyond the customs' bonded supervision. The restriction category refers to imported materials and articles which are sensitive commodities with great price difference between home and overseas markets and are hard for customs to supervise. Enterprises importing commodities under such category, except Class A enterprises, shall pay export earnest money to the customs, which is effected by actual transfer from the bank margin account. The category of permission refers to the majority of commodities not included in the categories of prohibition and restriction for the importing of which no earnest money is needed.

Classified management of enterprises The customs have set up four different management categories for enterprises engaging in processing trade: classes A, B, C and D. By means of inspecting and assessing the law-abiding degree of the enterprises in their processing trade and import-export business, appropriate management category for each enterprise is determined. However, such management is conducted in a flexible way, meaning that the category for each enterprise will be adjusted at appropriate time.

Class A enterprises refer to bonded factories which are supervised by customs officials stationed at the factory as approved by the General Administration of Customs or networked with the customs in charge, and which engage in processing trade in accordance with the law without smuggling or illegal activities, and processing enterprises with a considerable import-export volume engaging in aircraft or ship processing. Materials and articles imported by class A enterprises are under the customs' bonded supervision to which no bank margin account system is applied. Besides, the bank margin account system shall not be exercised for processing trade conducted by enterprises in the bonded area. Instead, the Measures for the Customs Supervision in Bonded Areas shall be exercised.

Class B enterprises refer to those conducting processing trade in accordance with the law without violating regulations or smuggling behavior. The customs make a levy on the commodities of dutiable tariff as per the on-file contract amount and a sum of earnest money at the rate of 50 per cent of import link value-added tax payment. For commodities imported under the category of permission, the bank margin account "void transfer" system is exercised in which no earnest money is collected.

Class C enterprises refer to those having violated related regulations enacted by the Ministry of Commerce and the General Administration of Customs as confirmed by the customs. For such enterprises the bank margin account "actual transfer" system is exercised. The customs make a levy on the materials and articles imported for processing trade of dutiable import tariff and earnest money equivalent to the import link value-add tax payment.

Class D enterprises refer to those having violated regulations or having smuggling behavior for three times or over as confirmed by the customs. For such enterprises, while the customs deal with their malpractice in accordance with the law, the foreign trade department in charge may call off their processing trade right. For such foreign invested enterprises, the foreign trade department in charge may notify the customs to suspend their import-export business for a year.

The name lists of class A, class C and class D are determined by the General Administration of Customs together with the Ministry of Commerce and published by the Ministry of Commerce. The lists of enterprise classification are managed flexibly and regulated at the right moment. Enterprises under class B shall not be specifically listed.

Bank margin account "actual transfer" management   The customs levy on commodities under restriction imported by class B enterprises earnest money at the rate of 50 per cent and levy on the total materials and articles imported by class C enterprises full earnest money, and deposit it in the customs' designated account with the Bank of China. When the enterprises have exported the processed commodities on stipulated schedule and handled the procedures of cancellation after verification, the customs shall advice the Bank of China to return the earnest money with interest to the enterprises. If the enterprises fail to export on stipulated schedule or sell their processed commodities on domestic market without approval, the earnest money and interest shall be turned to the enterprises' dutiable tax payment and interest for delayed taxation or the enterprises shall be punished in accordance with specific conditions.

Management of processing trade conducted at other places   Processing at places within another customs region shall be managed by means of on-file contract registration. For processing trade conducted in the form of processing deal for export, the trading unit must conclude with the processing enterprise a standard outside processing contract. The trading unit shall not sell the imported materials and articles in bond to the processing enterprise. A trading unit consigns processing to a class C enterprise shall handle on-file contract registration after paying corresponding earnest money to the customs. Trading units shall not consign processing to class D enterprises.

Management of transferred deep processing

Processing trade enterprises conducting deep processing for export with carry-over products in bonded area shall be supervised in light of stipulations for commodity classified management. Commodities under restriction and class C enterprises in need of deep processing transferred to other factories shall be supervised by the customs by means of customs transference or computer network management. Those

Economic and trade cooperation – the most frequent Sino-foreign activities

fail to meet the requirements for customs transferred transport or computer network management shall be levied an earnest money by the customs equivalent to the taxation of bonded goods transferred to other factories for deep processing.

Management of processed commodities sold on domestic market   According to regulations, products after processing shall be exported again and not be held up on the home market. If, under some specific conditions, the goods need to be sold on home market or used for producing commodities for the home market, tariff shall be levied on materials and articles imported with taxation interest added. If the materials and articled imported are in the category under the import license or registration management, the trading unit must produce to the customs import license or registration certificate for selling materials or articles imported on home market or using for producing goods for the home market. If it fails to produce the documents within specified period of time for verification and cancellation, the customs, apart from levying tariff and interest, shall impose a fine at a rate above 30 per cent but lower than the equivalent value of the materials and articles imported.

Management of processing trade cancellation after verification　　The materials and articles imported shall be examined, approved, supervised and cancelled after verification in accordance with the national unified standard of per unit consumption quota for imported commodities to process.

FOREIGN INVESTMENT

CURRENT SITUATION OF FOREIGN INVESTMENT

Starting from 1993, China maintained to be a developing country using the second largest amount of foreign investment for nine consecutive years, next only to the United States. By the end of December 2001, China had 202,300 foreign-invested enterprises among which 96,222 were Sino-foreign joint ventures, 23,420 Sino-foreign cooperative enterprises, 82,381 wholly foreign owned enterprises and 283 Sino-foreign joint-stock enterprises. The total number of employees in foreign-invested enterprises topped 23 millions, accounting for 10 per cent of the urban employees of the whole nation.

In recent years, the number of foreign-invested enterprises in China, including some internationally renowned businesses, keeps on the increase. Of the 500 top transnational corporations in the world, nearly 400 have made investment in China. Others are making studies of Chinese market in preparation for investment here. Big projects continuously grow in number and investment in average individual project shows a gradual increase. As regards the target of investment, foreign investments mainly focus on manufacturing industry, in particular in electronic and communication equipment manufacturing. Basic industry and infrastructure have become hot spots to entice foreign investment. Scientific researches and comprehensive technical services are rapidly developing. Regionally the eastern part of the country has been attracting the largest amount of foreign investment at an ever-increasing pace, whereas the central and western regions are becoming more and more appealing to foreign investors. Judging from the rate of growth, exclusively foreign-owned enterprises rank first, Sino-foreign joint ventures are developing smoothly, Sino-foreign cooperative enterprises lag behind and Sino-foreign joint-stock enterprises are pro-

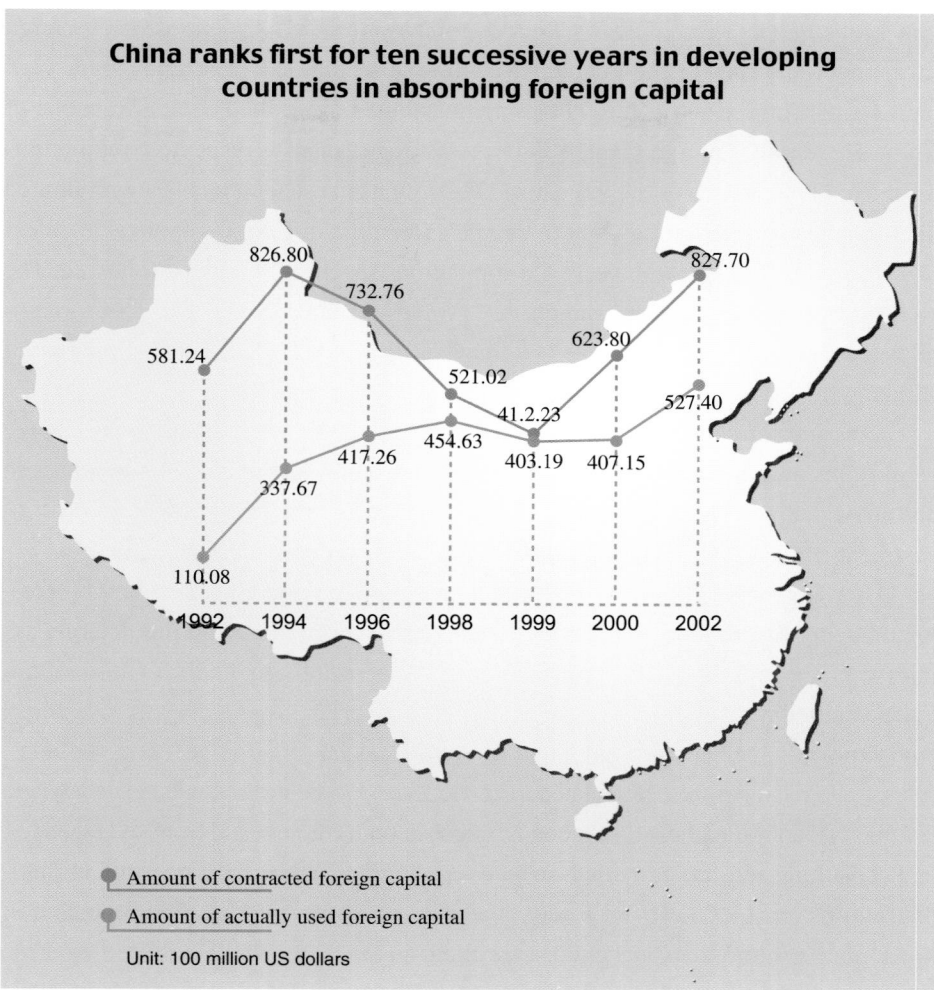

China ranks first for ten successive years in developing countries in absorbing foreign capital

826.80

732.76

827.70

581.24

623.80

521.02

41.2.23

527.40

417.26

454.63

403.19 407.15

337.67

110.08

1992   1994   1996   1998   1999   2000   2002

● Amount of contracted foreign capital

● Amount of actually used foreign capital

Unit: 100 million US dollars

gressing at a relatively fast pace.

In the past 20 years since reform and opening-up, in order to lure more investors China has improved infrastructure facilities involving airport, seaport, communication, water, power and gas supplies, in particular in some state-level economic and technical development areas where such facilities can be compared favorably with developed countries. Meanwhile, local governments at all levels are working for a better 'soft' investment environment such as a sound legal environment, a steady and transparent policy environment, an open and fair market environment and a clean and efficient executive environment for foreign investment.

From 1979 onwards, a comparatively complete set of laws, statutes, regulations and measures has been enacted as regards the establishment, operation, termination and liquidation of foreign-invested businesses, which include three basic laws: the

Law of the People's Republic of China on Joint Ventures Using Chinese and Foreign Investment, the Law of the People's Republic of China on Cooperative Joint Ventures Using Chinese and Foreign Investment and the Law of the People's Republic of China on Wholly Foreign Owned Enterprises, together with respective regulations for the implementation of the three laws. To foreign-invested companies with limited liability, the Corporation Law of the People's Republic of China is applicable unless otherwise stipulated in which case the stipulations specified should be followed. The contract concluded for establishing foreign-invested enterprise is a kind of foreign-related economic contract bounded by the Contract Law of the People's Republic of China.

To assure foreign investors of the security of their investment and to protect the legal rights and interests of foreign-invested corporations, the Chinese government has arrived at agreements with regard to encouraging and protecting reciprocal investment and agreements regarding averting dual taxation with many countries.

After China's accession WTO, legal and policy environment for foreign investors is being further improved, with policies more transparent and predictable, administrative examination and approval procedures simplified, and formation of domestic unified market. In many places stipulations for improving the soft investment environment have been promulgated. Many provincial governments have policies, rules, systems, measures, etc. related to economy and trade promulgated except where commercial confiolentiality is concerned, some in both Chinese and English languages, and consulting services provided. In an overwhelming majority of investment fields restrictions on stock ratio are lifted or relaxed, requirements for the proportion of homemade goods and export goods cancelled, technical transfer conducted between foreign and Chinese business people in cooperative enterprises and joint ventures are not longer interfered by government departments so that foreign-invested enterprises can have more decision-making power. All the above measures aim at reducing transaction cost and structural risks in introducing foreign capital. Politically stable and economically burgeoning, China with vast domestic market together with ever-improving soft investment environment will enter a new growing stage in using foreign capital. Home experts hold that during the Tenth Five-Year Plan period China will absorb foreign capital at an annual rate of no less than USD50 billions.

FORMS OF FOREIGN INVESTMENT

China mainly adopts three forms in using foreign capital: direct investment, loan capital, and other investment. Direct investment includes China-foreign joint ventures,

China-foreign cooperative joint ventures, foreign-funded enterprises (wholly foreign owned enterprises), foreign-invested shareholding enterprises and China-foreign co-operative exploitation. Loan capital includes loans from foreign governments, loans from international financial organizations, commercial bank loans, export credit and issuance of external debenture. Other ways of foreign investment include issuance of foreign stocks, international lease, compensation trade, processing and assembly. Here we will focus on introducing specific forms of foreign direct investment.

China-foreign joint ventures

China-foreign joint venture, also known as stock ownership joint venture, is a corporation established in China by a foreign corporation or business or other economic entity or individual, together with a Chinese corporation or business or other economic entity or individual in accordance with Chinese laws. The basic feature of this kind of venture is that each party concerned shares in investment, in operation, in risks and in profits or losses. Funds can be contributed in the form of currency, buildings, machinery and equipment, right of site use, industrial property right, or technical know-how. The investment ratio is calculated in the same currency no matter in what form the funds are contributed. The investment ratio of foreign investors shall not be lower than 25 per cent of registered capital. A China-foreign joint venture shall be a corporation with limited liability whose supreme power is exercised by its

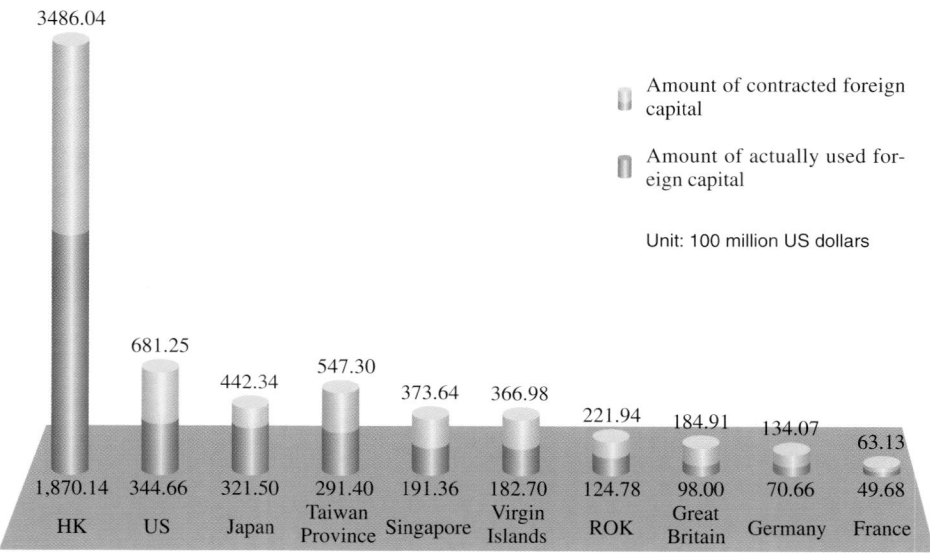

**First 10 Countries and Regions Invested in China
Up to the End of 2001**

Amount of contracted foreign capital

Amount of actually used foreign capital

Unit: 100 million US dollars

	HK	US	Japan	Taiwan Province	Singapore	Virgin Islands	ROK	Great Britain	Germany	France
Contracted	3486.04	681.25	442.34	547.30	373.64	366.98	221.94	184.91	134.07	63.13
Actually used	1,870.14	344.66	321.50	291.40	191.36	182.70	124.78	98.00	70.66	49.68

China has for the first time become the most attractive investment target country

In September 2002, AT. Kearney, a world-known management advisory firm, published the Foreign Direct Investment (FDI) Confidence Index in which China replaced for the first time the United States as the most attractive investment target country.

Result of such an authoritative global survey indicates that China mainland's foreign direct investment confidence index (numerical value range: 0 – 3) in 2002 was 1.99, the highest among the first 25 countries.

The index shows that in 2002, investment attraction was declining in almost all countries except China whose market was appealing to more and more investors who held an optimistic attitude towards China's economic prospect in the coming 1 –3 years.

The Kearney FDI confidence index is based on interviews with senior executives such as CEO, chief financial inspector, etc. of the 1,000 large enterprises in the world. With reference to the three factors investigated: "market scope of the nation (region)", "situation of market growth" and "degree of political stability", China not only takes the lead in market scope, but also maintains a rapid economic growth. In addition, China is consistent in its foreign investment policy.

board of directors.

China-foreign joint ventures are less restricted fields by laws and regulations with regard to investment fields. The term of operation can even be free of restriction for projects encouraged or permitted by the state.

China-foreign cooperative joint venture

China-foreign cooperative joint venture, also called contracted joint venture, refers to a corporation established in accordance with Chinese laws by foreign corporation, business, other economic organization or individual together with Chinese corporation, business or other economic organization jointly invested or cooperated between Chinese and foreign parties. China-foreign cooperative joint venture differs from China-foreign joint venture in that the investment made by either party is not evaluated in terms of money by which investment ratio is calculated; neither are the profits distributed as per the funds provided. The rights and duties of each party, including capital invested, cooperative conditions contributed, distribution of profits or products, risks and losses undertaken, mode of management and ownership of property at the termination of the contract, shall be specified in the contract concluded and signed by the parties concerned.

A cooperative joint venture can be an entity in the capacity of a legal person, i.e. a corporation with limited liability, or an economic entity without the capacity of a legal person in which each cooperative party provides funds or cooperative conditions, manages the entity in accordance with the terms and conditions of the contract concluded and share unlimited joint liability for the debts of the entity. Funds or cooperative conditions provided by each cooperative party in the non-legal person entity may be owned by each party or shared by all the parties involved and used and managed by the cooperative entity. None of the parties shall act unilaterally. For entity in the capacity of a legal person, a board of directors and administrative organization shall be set up. The board of directors is the supreme organ of power to determine all the important matters of the entity. For cooperative entity without the capacity of a legal person, a joint management commission shall be set up consisting of representatives from each of the cooperative parties to jointly manage the entity. Moreover, when a cooperative joint venture is established, it can be entrusted to the management of a contracting party or a third party if agreed unanimously by the board of directors or the joint administrative commission and approved by the original examination and approval authorities. If it is specified in the contract that all property of the entity shall belong to the Chinese side at the termination of the contract, the foreign side may recover the funds contributed within the cooperation period.

In a China-foreign cooperative joint venture the funds or cooperative conditions contributed can be in cash, material objects, right for land use, industrial property rights, non-patent techniques or other property rights. Usually techniques and equipment and total or greater part of funds are contributed by the foreign partner whereas land, factory building and usable resources and sometimes a part of funds are contributed by the Chinese partner. China-foreign cooperative joint venture has the advantage of flexibility in form and simple procedures in establishment.

Foreign-invested enterprises

Foreign-invested enterprise, also known as wholly foreign owned enterprise, refers to an enterprise established in accordance with Chinese laws and regulations within the territory of China by overseas corporations, enterprises or other economic organizations or individuals who contribute the total funds and operate independently all on their own. The funds contributed can be freely convertible cash, machines, equipment, industrial property rights or technical know-how. Foreign-invested enter-

Structure of the forms of foreign direct investment
up to the end of 2001

Unit: 100 million US dollars

Investment form	actually used foreign capital	proportion (%)
Total	3,952.23	100
Joint venture	1,765.15	44.66
Cooperative venture	777.25	19.67
Wholly foreign owned corporation	1,338.91	33.88
Co-operative development	70.92	1.79

prises in general are corporations with limited liability, but can also be other forms of liability if ratified. The foreign investors who own the total capital of the enterprise are entitled to determine for themselves everything concerning the enterprise, including financing, staff and workers, equipment and materials, marketing, rules and regulations, and routine management.

Foreign-invested enterprises in China are subsidiaries of foreign corporations, enterprises, other economic organizations or individuals conducting business accounting independently and assuming sole responsibility for profits or losses. As economic entities bearing independently civil liabilities, they are different from subdivisions of foreign enterprises or other economic organizations set up in China such as branch company or permanent representative offices, which are not independent economically or legally.

The establishment of foreign-invested enterprises must be beneficial to the development of China's national economy. The state encourages foreign business people to launch export-oriented or technically advanced foreign-invested enterprises. In recent years this form of investment has occupied the first place in foreign direct investment in China.

China-foreign co-operative exploitation

China-foreign co-operative exploitation refers to the exploration and exploitation of petroleum resources by foreign corporations together with Chinese corporations in accordance with Chinese laws. Cooperative exploitation is a widely adopted mode of economic cooperation in the world in the field of natural resources. Its most marked feature is high-risks, high-input and high-profits. In the sphere of petroleum exploitation, China usually takes this form of cooperation with foreign countries.

China issued the Ordinances of the People's Republic of China on the Exploitation of Offshore Petroleum Resources Cooperated with Foreign Businesses, and the Ordinances of the People's Republic of China on the Exploitation of Land Petroleum Resources Cooperated with Foreign Businesses in 1982 and 1993 respectively, specifying explicitly that under the prerequisite of maintaining national sovereignty and economic interests, foreign corporations are permitted to join in the exploitation of Chinese petroleum resources. Usually the mode of international tendering is adopted for China-foreign cooperative exploitation. Foreign corporations may bid alone or join hands with other corporations to form a group. The winner of the bid enters into a contract with the Chinese party for jointly exploring and exploiting petroleum in which the rights and duties of each party are specified. The term of the contract is usually no more than 30 years. The contract shall become effective as of the date of approval by competent authorities in charge of foreign trade and economic affairs. The whole exploitation period consists three phases: exploration, exploitation and production. At the exploration phase all expenses and risks shall be borne by the foreign party. If no oil or gas field worthy of exploitation is discovered within the area specified in the contract, the contract is terminated with no liability for compensation on the Chinese side. If oil and gas field is discovered, the exploitation phase shall start at which the Chinese side can join in the work with foreign side in the form of joint stock (generally its stock does not exceed 51per cent of the total), each party contributing capital in agreed proportion of investment. When the oil field has entered the regular production phase, related taxes and exploiting area use fee shall be paid as specified by law. Chinese and foreign sides can recover the capital invested and distribute profits in the form of material object according to the proportion specified in the contract. The risk of losses shall be borne by both parties.

The Chinese government has the permanent ownership of the natural resources jointly exploited by Chinese and foreign corporations. The state authorizes China National Offshore Oil Corporation to take charge of the business concerning China-foreign cooperative exploitation of offshore oil resources, and China Oil and Natural Gas Group Company and China Petrochemical Group Company to take charge of China-foreign cooperative exploitation of land oil resources. Generally the two parties take the form of non-legal person contracted co-operation without forming into an enterprise in the true sense. Chinese and foreign corporations are still two independent legal persons who have entered into a contract on the basis of equality and mutual benefit and shall act in accordance with the rights and duties specified in the contract. China-foreign cooperative exploitation of oil resources mainly adopts the combining form of risk contract and joint operation, but rarely takes the mode of leasing, products sharing contract or operation on contracting basis.

Foreign-invested limited company

Foreign-invested limited company, also called foreign-invested shareholding enterprise, refers to a legal entity established in accordance with the Corporation Law of the PRC and other related laws and regulations. The total capital of the entity is composed of equal amount shares. The shareholders bear responsibility for the company with the shares they subscribe and the company bears responsibility for the total debt of the company with its total assets. Chinese and foreign shareholders hold together the shares of the company in which foreign shareholder(s) purchases and holds shares accounting for more than 25 per cent of the company's registered capital.

Foreign-invested limited company is a new form of using foreign direct investment appeared in recent years against a background of continuous expansion of China's securities market and ever deepening reform of the enterprise shareholding system. Foreign-invested limited company is in common with China-foreign joint venture, China-foreign cooperative joint venture and wholly foreign owned enterprise in that they are all enterprises of limited liability and an effective form for China to use foreign direct investment, but they are different in many ways such as the form of establishment, the minimum registered capital required, stock ownership transfer and requirements for making public.

China-foreign joint venture, China-foreign cooperative joint venture and wholly foreign owned enterprise already established, if applying for transfer into a foreign-invested limited company, must have a record of gaining profits for recent three consecutive years. It should be initiated by the investors of the original foreign-invested enterprise (or together with other initiators) who enter into and sign agreements regarding the establishment of a new company and apply to the authorities at the place the original enterprise is located for preliminary approval and, when the preliminary approval is granted, submit the application for approval to the Ministry of Commerce. Other shareholding enterprises in conformity with related demands and stipulations, if absorbing foreign capital accounting for more than 25 per cent of the total capital stock, can also apply for transferring into foreign-invested limited company which, when approved, can effect the transference by issuance of B-share, which is a special share with a par value in RMB but subscribed and traded in US dollars in the Shanghai Stock Exchange, or in Hong Kong dollars in the Shenzhen Stock Exchange, or

Industries using foreign direct investment and trade structure up to the end of 2001

Unit: 100 million US dollars

Industry and trade	Contracted foreign capital	Proportion (%)
Total	7,452.91	100
First industry: agriculture, forestry, animal husbandry, fishery	140.71	1.89
Second industry: manufacture, production	4,631.60	62.14
Tertiary industry	2,680.60	35.97
1. Building industry	215.14	2.89
2. Communication, transportation, warehousing, post, telecommunication	172.70	2.32
3. Wholesale and retail trade, catering	247.94	3.33
4. Real estate, public utilities	1,688.76	22.66
5. Health, sports, social welfare	49.06	0.66
6. Education, culture, art, radio, film, TV	21.95	0.29
7. Scientific research, technical service	27.79	0.37
8. Others	257.26	3.45

otherwise by issuance of H-share, N-share or other shares registered in China and listed in the stock market of Hong Kong or overseas for investors from Hong Kong, Macao and Taiwan and overseas to subscribe and trade.

BOT Investment

BOT is an acronym from Build-Operate-Transfer, which refers to a contract concluded between the Chinese government and the project company of a private organization (in China it means a foreign-invested enterprise). The project company shall be responsible for financing, building, operation, maintenance and transfer of an infrastructure facility or a public project. During a period of time agreed upon (generally 15 – 20 years), the project company shall exercise the operation right so as to recover the investment, pay debts of the project and make profits. On the expiration of the contract the project company shall transfer the project gratis to the host country.

BOT is a newly emerged form of investment in China. In view of that infrastructure construction can not keep pace with the rapid growth of Chinese economy, introducing foreign capital using BOT form is an effective way of financing for the funds needed. The BOT form of investment has wide prospects in China. In recent years, in order to standardize the operation of BOT, Chinese government departments involved have issued a series of stipulations including primarily the Notice on Matters Concerning Absorbing Foreign Investment Using BOT Form issued in 1994 by the former Ministry of Foreign Trade and Economic Cooperation; the Notice on Matters Concerning Examination and Approval of Pilot BOT Projects jointly issued in 1995 by the State Development Planning Commission, the former Ministry of Electric Power and Ministry of Communication; and the Interim Provisions on BOT Projects issued by the State Development Planning Commission. In this way China has enacted a basic law framework for financing using BOT form, which is based on the state policy of making experiments first, spreading gradually, guiding macroscopically and developing in a standardized way.

BASIC POLICY ON FOREIGN INVESTMENT

Industrial policy

In order to make foreign investment tally more with the orientation of China's industrial development and to better guard the legitimate interests of investors, the Chinese government has issued the Provisions on Guiding the Orientation of Foreign Investment (called Provisions for short) and the Catalogue for the Guidance of Foreign Investment Industries (catalogue for short), which are made known to the public China's industrial policies on absorbing foreign investment. The industrial guidance catalogue is an auxiliary policy on investment direction, which classifies foreign investment projects into four categories: encouraged, permitted, restricted and prohibited. Investment projects launched by investors from overseas, Hong Kong Special Administrative Region, Macao Special Administrative Region and Taiwan shall operate on the basis of the above documents.

Since China's entry into the WTO, the original regulations and catalogue have been revised in the light of economic development and put into effect on April 1, 2002. The new catalogue has the following characteristics:

1. To persist in the expansion of reform and opening-up; encourage foreign investment in China. Articles included in the category encouraging foreign investment have increased from 186 to 262 and those restricting foreign investment have re-

duced from 112 to 75. Restriction in stock ratio has been slackened such as removal of the demand that Chinese side must be the holding party of the shareholder of docks commonly used by Chinese and foreign parties. Urban pipeline and network of telecommunication, gas, thermal power, water supply and drainage are open to foreign investors for the first time.

2. To implement China's commitment to WTO, services and trade fields involving banking, insurance, commerce, foreign trade, tourism, telecommunication, transportation, accounting, auditing and law are further opened according to the time table, region, quantity, business scope, stock ratio as committed. At the same time, a table of committed items is appended to the catalogue.

Distribution of Foreign-Invested Industries and Trade in 2001

Line of Business	Number of Enterprise	Proportion (%)
Manufacturing	141,668	70.03
Social services	16,169	7.99
Whole sale, retail, trade and catering	12,249	6.05
Real estate	11,925	5.89
Building sector	5,139	2.54
Agriculture, forestry, animal husbandry and fishery	4,752	2.35
Transportation, warehousing, post, telecommunication and communication	3,499	1.73
Production and supply of power, gas and water	1,268	
Excavation	1,047	
Scientific research and comprehensive technical services	1.851	
Education, culture, art, radio, film and TV	530	
Health, sports and social services	469	
Geological prospecting	128	
Finance and insurance	74	

3. To encourage foreign business people to invest in China's vast western region where trade restrictions and limits to the stock ratio of foreign investment are relaxed.

4. To bring into play the function of market competition mechanism. Ordinary industrial products are listed in the category of permission with a view to upgrade the structure of industries and products through competition.

According to the new catalogue, in a certain period of time in the future, foreign business people are encouraged to invest in the following fields of business: (1) traditional agriculture reform, modern agriculture development and agricultural industrialization; (2) infrastructure and fundamental industries such as transportation, energy, raw and processed materials; (3) high-tech industries such as electronic information, bioengineering, new material, space and aviation; the establishment of research and development center also encouraged; (4) updating and upgrading traditional industries such as machinery, light industries and textiles using advanced technology; (5) comprehensive utilization of resources, resources regeneration, environmental protection projects and municipal engineering; (6) dominant industries in the western region; (7) projects of exclusively export products in the category of permission.

Starting from the day the new catalogue is put into effect, foreign investment projects under the catalogue of encouragement can enjoy the preferential treatment of exemption from customs duties on imported equipment and import link value-added tax.

To adapt to the new situation after China gained WTO membership, the system of examination and approval governing foreign investment projects in China has to be reformed. Since foreign investment is a kind of foreign fixed assets, the reform of the above-said system shall be carried out together with the reform of investment and financing management. Currently nothing is mentioned in the new regulations in this regard so that the examination and approval procedures for foreign-invested projects shall remain the same at the moment.

Regional policy

With respect to regions opening to foreign investors, the Chinese government attracts foreign investment mainly through setting up special economic zones, economic and technological development zones and opening up coastal cities. Within these regions, examination and approval power over foreign-invested projects shall be transferred to local authorities where special policies and measures shall be adopted regarding application, examination and approval procedures, customs management, taxation, exchange management, business management, land use, and labor management so that foreign resources can be easily centralized in these regions. China's opening up to the outside world started from the eastern coastal region from where the opening area will be extended to hinterland by stages and by levels. As the investment environment in the eastern region is more favorable, where more preferential treatment is granted and a greater part of reform measures are conducted, the majority of foreign funded enterprises are located in this region.

In recent years, as the strategic focus of China's economic development is gradually shifting westwards, the Chinese government has enacted corresponding policies in support of the central and western regions. As a result, investment there is greatly increased and the construction of infrastructure accelerated such as water conservancy, transportation and communication. While the eastern region continues to take advantages of using foreign capital, the central government shall help it in developing its capital- and technology-intensive industries and export-oriented industries. Meanwhile, foreign business people are encouraged and guided to invest in the central and western regions.

For this purpose, the Chinese government has formulated the Catalog of Dominant Industries with Foreign Investment of the Mid-west Region in which industries and products having notable advantages or potentialities in environment, resources, manpower, production, technology and market in the 20 provinces (regions or cities) in the central and western regions are included. In the meantime, the state shall adjust and revise the catalogue at the right moment as per the needs in economic development and changes in the market environment, home and abroad.

At present, policies encouraging foreign investment in the central and western regions primarily include:

Foreign-invested construction projects listed in the Catalog of Dominant Industries with Foreign Investment of the Mid-west Region shall enjoy various preferencial policies indicated in the encouragement category of the Interim Provisions on Guiding the Orientation of Foreign Investment and other related preferential policies. Requirements for setting up projects in the restriction category and projects restricting foreign investors' stock ownership proportion, and the scope of opening up for such projects, can be properly relaxed as compared with the eastern region.

Appropriately increase domestic auxiliary capital as loans to the central and western regions in absorbing foreign investment. Loans from foreign governments and preferential loans from international banking institutions are chiefly used in important infrastructure and environmental protection projects in these regions.

Foreign-invested projects listed in the category of encouragement in central and western regions shall be levied enterprise income tax at reduced rate of 15 per cent for three years after the expiration of the period for tax exemption and reduction.

To encourage foreign business people who have already invested in the eastern region to invest again in the central and western regions, projects with foreign investment exceeding 25 per cent in proportion shall enjoy the same treatment as enjoyed by wholly foreign-owned enterprise.

Foreign-invested enterprises in coastal areas are permitted to contract for the management of wholly foreign-owned enterprises and domestic invested enterprises in central and western regions.

Provinces, autonomous regions and municipalities directly under the central government in the central and western regions are permitted to apply for setting up a state-level economic and technological development zone inside a development zone already established in their respective capital cities.

The state shall preferentially arrange a number of projects in central and western regions seeking foreign investment in the fields of agriculture, water conservancy, transportation, energy, raw and processed materials and environmental protection. The state shall take coordinated measures and grant funds to help in such projects.

Financial support for foreign-invested enterprises

Funds needed for production and management in foreign-invested enterprises can be obtained by applying for loans to banks within national boundary in accordance with China's laws and regulations. The term, interest rate and service charges of the loans are the same as those granted to domestic invested enterprises. Foreign-invested enterprises can also borrow money directly from a bank outside national boundary after going through formalities of foreign debt registration according to regulations. The foreign exchange thus borrowed shall be put on file at the department of foreign exchange

China — Intel's second largest market in the world

control.

Chinese-invested commercial banks are permitted to accept a guaranty provided by a foreign shareholder for a foreign-invested enterprise raising funds within the territory of the People's Republic of China. A foreign-invested enterprise is permitted to apply for loans in RMB to a designated Chinese invested foreign exchange bank within China's territory in the mode of pledge in foreign exchanges. All funds in foreign exchanges owned by a foreign-invested enterprise can be used for pledge. Banking institutions outside China's territory or foreign-invested banking institutions within national boundary may provide a credit guaranty for loans in RMB under foreign exchange guaranty. Registration procedures for foreign exchange pledge and foreign exchange guaranty have been repealed and special restrictions on credit rating for foreign-invested banks providing foreign exchange guaranty lifted. Guaranty provided by foreign shareholders and loans in RMB guaranteed in foreign exchanges shall be in accordance with the industrial policy. Such loans may be used to meet the need for fixed assets investment or circulating funds, but not for purchase of foreign exchanges.

Special industrial investment foundation has been set up to help the Chinese side to alleviate insufficiency of share capital in case additional funds for a foreign-invested enterprise are needed. At the same time, Chinese invested banks within the national boundary are permitted to provide loans in a certain proportion to the Chinese shareholder as share capital under the prerequisite that the additional share capital on the part of foreign shareholders in a China-foreign joint venture or a China-foreign cooperative joint venture has been in place.

A foreign-invested enterprise within national boundary is permitted to provide mortgage using overseas assets to an overseas branch of a Chinese invested bank for a loan, which shall be granted by either an overseas branch or a domestic branch of a Chinese invested commercial bank.

A foreign-invested enterprise up to requirements may apply for issuance of A- or B-shares.

Foreign business people invested in the fields specially encouraged by the state such as energy, transportation, etc. shall be provided with insurance against political risks, performance insurance, margin insurance, etc. in line with the principle of security and reliability.

Program for using foreign investment during the Tenth Five-Year Plan period

During the Tenth Five-Year-Plan period, the strategy of introducing foreign capi-

tal to China will be shifted to introducing advanced technology, modern management and talented people. The fields where foreign capital is used will be extended from processing industry to service sector. The mode of using foreign capital will be expanded from absorbing foreign direct investment to verified means of introducing foreign capital. The governmental management will be shifted from administrative examination and approval towards giving guidance, supervising and normalizing practices in accordance with the law.

Main tasks of using foreign capital during the Tenth Five-Year Plan period

In the first place, focus on absorbing foreign direct investment and promote the development of using foreign capital. Make efforts to expand the scope of using foreign capital, enhance the quality of using foreign capital and improve distinctly the structure of using foreign capital in the light of national economic development, supply and demand of funds at home and abroad, and domestic capacity for absorption and assimilation of foreign capital. Strive to have more foreign capital used in the central and western regions in industries encouraged by the state. Launch more projects introducing advanced foreign technology and management.

Secondly, guide enthusiastically foreign business people in investment direction. Adjust domestic industrial structure and facilitate industrial optimization and upgrading. Revise and promulgate the Provisions on Guiding the Orientation of Foreign Investment and Catalogue for the Guidance of Foreign Investment Industries to conform to the trend of economic globalization and world industrial restructuring. Adopt effective measures to optimize the structure of foreign-invested industries; devote major efforts to introducing advanced overseas technology, key equipment and management; actively lead foreign business people to invest in the fields encouraged by the state such as agriculture, high-tech industries, basic industries, infrastructure and environmental protection construction; step up reformation and technical upgrading of traditional industries; energetically attract overseas fund-intensive and technique-intensive industries; and strive to form a number of production bases with world market oriented products so as to enhance structural adjustment, optimization and upgrading of domestic industries.

Thirdly, carry forward step by step the policy of opening up in the service sector including banking, insurance, trade, telecommunication and tourism so as to adapt to the new situation after entering the WTO. Develop various kinds of foreign-invested intermediary agencies and services. Actively attract foreign investment to education and health care fields. Focus on introducing advanced overseas mode of operation, experience in management and qualified personnel to promote the overall quality level of home service sector.

Economic and Technological Development
Zone – an ad inviting investment

Fourthly, introduce investment from overseas multinational corporations and else-where to boost strategic restructure and reformation of state-owned enterprises. According to the overall planning of national reform and opening up and the need for industrial restructuring, sell as planned to foreign investors a part of stocks of a number of state-owned enterprises in particular some large-scaled ones that have completed or are in the process of incorporation. Foreign investors are permitted to gain control of the company's business by holding a certain amount of the shares except for key enterprises concerning national safety or economic lifelines, which have to be controlled by Chinese sides. A number of deliberately chosen large-scaled key enterprises up to requirements will be listed on overseas stock markets in batches and by stages. Encourage multinational companies to form joint venture or cooperative joint venture with domestic enterprises with a view to increase the proportion of investment from multinational companies.

Fifthly, expand the use of foreign capital in the central and western regions to foster coordinated regional development. Priority shall be given to provincial capital cities, large and medium sized cities with favorable conditions, state-level economic development zones and high-tech development zones in the light of regional advantages and actual situation in the use of foreign capital to improve the soft and hard investment environment and form an advantageous investment microclimate. And then concentrate funds, qualified personnel and technical force to develop a number of foreign-invested enterprises that are capable of leading the way for others to follow so as to achieve new breakthrough in absorbing foreign capital.

Take full advantage of eastern coastal region's funds, talents, technology and location to absorb more foreign capital, develop fund- and technology-intensive industries, export-oriented and high-tech enterprises, raise the technical grade of foreign-invested projects and enhance their added value, create new superiority and further play the roles of demonstration, radiation and leadership.

Sixthly, make rational use of overseas loans to improve quality and increase beneficial results. Continue to get loans on a certain scale from world banking institutions or from foreign governments, which shall be used in projects for the development of infrastructure together with projects for ecological environment, poverty alleviation and social development instead of laying special emphasis on infrastructure alone as before. International commercial loans shall be strictly restricted and the use of which limited to introducing advanced technology and key equipment. Long-term and favorable export credits shall be used rationally. Raising foreign loans or using other overseas commercial loans for other purpose shall be strictly restricted.

Seventhly, intensify full-scale management of foreign loans and improve the mechanism for raising, using and paying loans. Continue to control the total amount of China's foreign loans. Take care to keep a reasonable term structure, currency structure and debtor structure so that the main indices of foreign loans can be controlled within the internationally recognized safety line. Supervise strictly the changes in each of the indices of foreign loans and handle in time problems that may arise.

Policies and measures for the use of foreign funds in the Tenth Five-Year Plan period

1. Improve foreign-related laws and regulations and enhance investment environment. Put in order relevant laws, regulations, regional policies and stipulations in the light of the rules of the World Trade Organizations and China's commitment. Formulate relevant laws and regulations that are adaptive to the new situation. The administrative departments of governments at all levels shall take high-quality services as a starting point for shifting the government function. Give guidance relying on policy and information to investment behavior, reduce on a large scale the number of items that are subject to the examination and approval of government administrations, and simplify procedures in handling affairs.

2. Enhance guidance to foreign investors and implement normalized policies on using foreign funds. Adopt encouraging policies and measures to attract foreign investment in the light of national industrial policies, market situation and economic development. Grant preferential treatment to investment projects such as extending the scope of business in infrastructure, farming, forestry, water-conservancy and ecological environment protection. Grant national treatment to foreign-invested enterprises on a step-by-step basis in line with China's commitment to WTO and create a

fair play environment for Chinese-invested and foreign-invested enterprises. Implement various policies and measures on the development of the western regions to which substantial policy-related support shall be given in luring foreign investment.

3. Improve management of foreign loans and strengthen supervision and control of external debt. Enhance management of overseas preferential loans; simplify procedures in the examination, approval and use of the loans. Rationally use international commercial loans on a moderate degree. Study and determine a scientific method of affirming the qualification of loan-granting institutions. Find a way to conduct assets and liabilities proportional management of overseas loans raised by various banking institutions within national boundary under the circumstances that foreign banking institutions are gradually granted national treatment in China.

4. Enhance the supervisory system of law enforcement; improve macro-control mechanism adaptive to an open economy. The competent authorities in charge of various industries and trades including in particular banking, insurance, securities, telecommunication, commerce and tourism shall formulate a sound supervisory system for law enforcement, and strengthen executive supervision on foreign-invested enterprises. Study and put forward a new concept of capital project management under open economy circumstances so as to better promote international revenue-and-expenditure balance.

SPECIAL ECONOMIC ZONE AND DEVELOPMENT ZONE

With a view to introducing overseas capital, advanced technology and management experience, China started to set up special economic zones in 1980 and conducted market-oriented reforms on a tentative basis.

Fourteen East China's port cities from north to south were designated as coastal open cities in 1984 where foreign investors were granted preferential treatment only next in degree to that granted to special economic zones. On this basis economic and technological development zones, which were granted policy-related support similar to that given to special economic zones, were established to attract foreign investment in industries. In the following several years, the opening zones were extended from individual cities to a vast coastal open region.

In 1990, Shanghai Municipality, approved by the central government, started to develop Pudong new open area, which became a symbol of China's opening up in the 1990s.

Since 1992, China's opening region has been expanding in a broader range in the following manner: 1. With Shanghai in the lead, a number of cities along the Yangtze River are opened to form a Yangtze opening zone in which a coastal open city policy is carried out; 2. Thirteen inland border cities are opened in which fourteen border economic cooperative zones have been set up to foster economic and trade cooperation with surrounding countries; 3. All inland provincial capital cities are opened; 4. Fifteen bonded areas have been set up to carry out extrepot trade, warehousing and export processing business. Later on more inland cities are gradually opened. Thus, from the coastal region to inland area, an all-dimensional opening up framework has been initially formed.

In 2000, China started to execute the strategy of overall development of the western region. Foreign business people invested in that region are granted preferential treatment similar to that given to the special economic zones. Moreover, fifteen export processing areas were established in different places of the country.

In November 2001, China entered the WTO. The fields and regions for foreign investment are further expanded.

Since then, the preferential policy practiced in some regions in the past has gradually lost its superiority. The development in different places relies essentially on regional competitiveness involving market environment, industrial development level, talented personnel, technical innovation, government quality and executive efficiency. Currently each region is endeavoring to further create a favorable investment environment to attract foreign investors.

The following involves mainly the opening regions. For preferential treatment on taxation please see the section "Taxation policy for foreign-invested enterprises" under this chapter.

Special economic zone

Currently there are five special economic zones in China including Shenzhen, Zhuhai and Shantou in Guangdong Province, Xiamen in Fujian Province and Hainan Province. The former four, all located in southeast China's coastal region, were established in 1980. The Hainan Special Economic Zone was established in 1988, which is an island off the south coast of China, facing Guangdong Province across the sea.

The local government of special economic zone holds power over major economic affairs. Apart from special policies stipulated by the state, it also offers some preferential treatment for investors.

The period from 1980 to 1985 was the initial phase of the special economic zone when large-scaled infrastructure was constructed and favorable investment environ-

Special Economic Zone

Name	Foreign Economic and Trade Institution	Website
Shenzhe Special Economic Zone	Shenzhen Foreign Trade and Economic Cooperation Bureau	http://www.szboftec.gov.cn
Zhuhai Special Economic Zone	Zhuhai Foreign Trade and Economic Cooperation Bureau	http://www.zhuhai-trade.gov.cn
Shantou Special Economic Zone	Shantou Foreign Trade and Economic Cooperation Bureau	http://www.stfet.gov.cn
Xiamen Special Economic Zone	Xiamen Development Commission Xiamen Foreign Investment Bureau	http://www.xmtdc.gov.cn http://www.chinainvestguide.org
Hainan Special Economic Zone	Hainan Province Foreign Trade and Economic Cooperation Agency	http://doftec.hainan.gov.cn

ment created. The period from 1986 to 1995 was the growing phase when the export-oriented economy centered on export processing was developed. From 1996 onwards is the improvement phase when industries are undergoing a restructuring with the focal point shifted from traditional labor-intensive processing industries to high-tech and high value-added industries and high-level tertiary industry.

The special economic zone as an experimental and demonstrative base for China's economic restructuring, is the first to carry out multiple reform measures in which enterprises have flexible operational mechanism, the government has a high administration level, land, funds, personnel and technology are highly market-based.

As a result of construction and development over two decades, the five special economic zones have created favorable investment environment where the largest number of foreign investors in China assemble. However, with the deepening of reform and opening up, the advantages the special economic zones hold by offering preferential treatment have become less conspicuous than before. Now it has entered a new stage when the special economic zones have to create and give play to the superiority of their own.

Economic and technological development zone

An economic and technological development zone is an area designated in an open city for the construction of excellent infrastructure facilities to upgrade the investment environment with a view to attract foreign capital, advanced technology and expertise and thus push forward international economic and technical cooperation in the city and its surrounding regions. To date 54 state-level economic and technological development zones, approved by the Chinese government, have been established which are distributed in the major industrial cities from the coastal regions to hinterland area. They are among the regions attracting most domestic and overseas

State-Level Economic and Technological Development Zones

Name	Location (province, city, region)	Website
Beijing Economic and Technological Development zone	Beijing Municipality	http://www.bda.gov.cn
Dalian Economic and Technological Development Zone	Liaoning Province	http://www.ddz.gov.cn
Shenyang Economic and Technological Development Zone	Liaoning Province	http://www.sydz.gov.cn
Yingkou Economic and Technological Development Zone	Liaoning Province	http://www.ykdz.gov.cn
Qinhuangdao Economic and Technological Development Zone	Hebei Province	http://www.qetdz.com.cn
Tianjin Economic and Technological Development Zone	Tianjin Municipality	http://www.teda.gov.cn
Yantai Economic and Technological Development Zone	Shandong Province	http://www.yeda.gov.cn
Qingdao Economic and Technological Development Zone	Shandong Province	http://www.bestinvest.org.
Weihai Economic and Technological Development Zone	Shangdong Province	http://www.e-weihai.gov.cn
Nantong Economic and Technological Development Zone	Jiangsu Province	http://www.netda.com
Lianyungang Economic and Technological Development Zone	Jiangsu Province	http://www.lygetdz.gov.cn
Kunshan Economic and Technological Development Zone	Jiangsu Province	http://www.ketd.gov.cn
Nanjing Economic and Technological Development Zone	Jiangxu Province	http://www.njxg.com
Suzhou Industrial Park	Jiangsu Province	http://www.sipac.gov.cn
Shanghai Minhang Economic and Technological Development Zone	Shanghai Municipality	http://www.smudc.com
Shanghai Hongqiao Economic And Technological Development Zone	Shanghai Municipality	http://www.shudc.com
Shanghai Caohejing Economic And Technological Development Zone	Shanghai Municipality	http://www.e-caohejing.com
Shanghai Jinqiao Export Processing Zone	Shanghai Municipality	http://www.goldenbridge.sh.cn
Ningbo Economic and Technological Development Zone	Zhejiang Province	http://www.netd.com.cn
Wenzhou Economic and Technological Development Zone	Zhejiang Province	http://www.wetdz.gov.cn
Hangzhou Economic and Technological Development Zone	Zhejiang Province	http://www.hetz.gov.cn
Xiaoshan Economic and Technological Development Zone	Zhejiang Province	http://www.xetdz.com
Ningbo Daxie Economic and Technological Development Zone	Zhejiang Province	http://www.citic-daxie.com

Fuzhou Economic and Technological Development Zone	Fujian Province	http://www.fdz.com.cn
Fuqing Rongqiao Economic and Technological Development Zone	Fujian Province	http://www.fqrq.doe2e.com
Dongshan Economic and Technological Development Zone	Fujian Province	http://www.detdz.com
Xiamen Haicang Taiwan Business People Investment Zone	Fujian Province	http://www.haicang.com
Guangzhou Economic and Technological Development Zone	Guangdong Province	http://www.getdd.com.cn
Zhanjiang Economic and Technological Development Zone	Guangdong Province	http://www.zetdz.gov.cn
Guangzhou Nansha Economic and Technological Development Zone	Guangdong Province	http://www.nansha.gov.cn
Dayawan Economic and Technological Development Zone	Guangdong Province	
Harbin Economic and Technological Development Zone	Heilongjiang Province	http://www.kaifaqu.com.cn
Changchun Economic and Technological Development Zone	Jilin Province	http://www.cetdz.com.cn
Wuhan Economic and Technological Development Zone	Hubei Province	http://www.wedz.com.cn
Chongqing Economic and Technological Development Zone	Chongqing Municipality	http://www.cqedtz.gov.cn
Wuhu Economic and Technological Development Zone	Anhui Province	http://www.weda.gov.cn
Hefei Economic and Technological Development Zone	Anhui Province	http://www.hetac.com
Zhengzhou Economic and Technological Development Zone	Henan Province	http://www.zz-economy.gov.cn
Xi'an Economic and Technological Development Zone	Shaanxi Province	http://www.xetdz.com.cn
Chengdu Economic and Technological Development Zone	Sichuan Province	http://www.cdetdz.com
Kunming Economic and Technologic Development Zone	Yunnan Province	http://www.ketdz.gov.cn
Changsha Economic and Technological Development Zone	Hunan Province	
Guiyang Economic and Technological Development Zone	Guizhou Province	http://www.geta.net.cn
Nanchang Economic and Technological Development Zone	Jiangxi Province	http://www.nc-tdz.com
Shihezi Economic and Technological Development Zone	Xinjiang Uygur Autonomous Region	http://www.kfq.xjshz.com.cn
Urumchi Economic and Technological Development Zone	Xinjiang Uygur Autonomous Region	
Hohhot Economic and Technological Development Zone	Inner Mongolia Autonomous Region	http://www.hetdz.com.cn
Yinchuan Economic and Technological Development Zone	Ningxia Hui Autonomous Region	http://www.ycda.gov.cn

Hainan Yangpu Economic and Technological Development Zone	Hainan Province	http://www.yangpu.hainan.gov.cn
Xining Economic and Technological Development Zone	Qinghai Province	http://www.xnkfq.com
Nanning Economic and Technological Development Zone	Guangxi Zhuangzu Autonomous Region	http://neda.gxi.gov.cn
Lhasa Economic and Technological Development Zone	Tibet Autonomous Region	
Taiyuan Economic and Technological Development Zone	Shanxi Province	
Lanzhou Economic and Technological Development Zone	Gansu Province	

investment while achieving the fastest economic growth. In addition, there are also some provincial-level economic and technological development zones established.

The state-level economic and technological development zone is specially supported by the Chinese government and enjoys a series of preferential treatment enacted by the government. The State Council Special Zone Office is a governmental institution in charge of the management and guidance of the economic and technological development zones.

Economic and technological development zones are usually located in provincial capitals, regional economic center cities or transportation hubs where economics is flourishing and industrial foundation solid. The zones boast well-constructed infrastructure facilities, high-level and law-cost public utilities such as water, power, gas, heat supply, communication facilities and transportation. There are also convenient Internet and information services, high-quality technical personnel and skilled workers.

The development zone holds administrative power over economic affairs as stipulated by the state where there are easy, simple and convenient procedures adaptive to international customs and practice in examining and approving foreign-invested projects. With a view to provide favorable conditions for foreign-invested enterprises engaging in construction, production and management, service centers for foreign-invested enterprises and foreign business people complaint centers are usually set up in the zone.

In some cities about 30 ~ 40 per cent of foreign direct investment is concentrated in the development zone. In most development zones, high-tech enterprises and foreign-exchange earning export enterprises account for a sizable proportion. Such enterprises enjoy preferential treatment stipulated by the state.

Bonded area

A bonded area is an economic area established with the approval of Chinese

Bonded Areas

Name	Location (province, city, region)	Website
Shanghai Waigaoqiao Bonded Area	Shanghai Municipality	http://www.china-ftz.com
Tianjin Port Bonded Area	Tianjin Municipality	http://www.tjftz.gov.cn
Dalian Bonded Area	Liaoning Province	http://www.dlftz.gov.cn
Shenzhen Futian Bonded Area	Guangdong Province	http://www.szftz.gov.cn
Shenzhen Shatoujiao Bonded Area	Guangdong Province	http://www.szftz.gov.cn
Shenzhen Yantiangang Bonded Area	Guangdong Province	http://www.szftz.gov.cn
Guangzhou Bonded Area	Guangdong Province	http://www.getdd.com.cn
Zhuhai Bonded Area	Guangdong Province	http://www.zhfreetradezone.org
Zhangjiagang Bonded Area	Jiangsu Province	http://www.zjgftz.gov.cn
Haikou Bonded Area	Hainan Province	http://www.hkftz.gov.cn
Xiamen Xiangyu Bonded Area	Fujian Province	http://www.xmftz.xm.fj.cn
Fuzhou Bonded Area	Fujian Province	http://www.fzftz.gov.cn
Shantou Bonded Area	Fujian Province	http://www.ftftz.gov.cn
Ningbo Bonded Area	Zhejiang Province	http://www.nftz.gov.cn
Qingdao Bonded Area	Shandong Province	http://www.qdftz.com

government and supervised by the Customs to conduct international trade and bonded business in conformity to international practice. It is similar to the free trade zone in the world where foreign investors are permitted to engage in international trade, bonded warehousing, export processing and entrepot trade with special treatment granted to them such as "document-free, duty-free and keeping goods in bond". Enjoying free trade, free foreign exchange, free entry-exit of goods and personnel and other freedoms except for what is prohibited by the state, the bonded area is one of the open areas in China the highest degree in opening, most flexible in operative mechanism and most favorable in policies granted. Currently there are 15 bonded areas in China.

High-tech industrial development zone

A high-tech industrial development zone is a zone backed by intensive brainpower and opening environment, relying primarily on domestic technical and economic strength, absorbing fully overseas technical resources and funds and drawing on the experience of overseas administrative measures. By offering preferential treatment to high-tech industries and adopting various reform measures, partial optimization of soft and hard environment can be realized and technical achievements can be turned into productivity to the maximum. To date the State Council has approved the construction of 53 state-level high-tech industrial development zones.

State–Level High–Tech Industrial Development Zones

Name	Location (Province, City, Region)	Website
Zhongguancun Technological Park	Beijing Municipality	http://www.zgc.gov.cn
Shenzhen High-Tech Industrial Park	Guangdong Province	http://www.shipgov.net
Huizhou Zhongkai High-Tech Industrial Development Zone	Guangdong Province	http://www.hzzk.org
Zhuhai High-Tech Industrial Development Zone	Guangdong Province	http://www.zhuhai-hitech.com
Foshan High-Tech Industrial Development Zone	Guangdong Province	http://www.fs-hitech.gov.cn
Guangzhou High-Tech Industrial Development Zone	Guangdong Province	http://www.getdd.com.cn
Zhongshan Torch High-Tech Industrial Development Zone	Guangdong Province	http://www.zstorch.gov.cn
Guilin High-Tech Industrial Development Zone	Guangxi Zhuang Nationality Autonomous Region	http://www.guilin-ctp.net.cn
Nanning High-Tech Industrial Development Zone	Guangxi Zhuang Nationality Autonomous Region	http://www.nnhitech.gov.cn
Chengdu High-Tech Industrial Development Zone	Sichuan Province	http://www.cdht.gov.cn
Mienyang High-Tech Industrial Development Zone	Sichuan Province	
Kunming High-Tech Industrial Development Zone	Yunnan Province	http://www.kmhnz.gov.cn
Urumchi High-Tech Industrial Development Zone	Xinjiang Uygur Autonomous Region	http://www.khtz.gov.cn
Jilin High-Tech Industrial Development Zone	Jilin Province	http://www.jlhitech.com
Changchun High-Tech Industrial Development Zone	Jilin Province	http://www.chida.gov.cn
Anshan High-Tech Industrial Development Zone	Liaoning Province	http://www.asht-zone.gov.cn
Dalian High-Tech Industrial Development Zone	Liaoning Province	http://www.ddport.com
Shenyang High-Tech Industrial Development Zone	Liaoning Province	
Shijiazhuang High-Tech Industrial Development Zone	Hebei Province	http://www.shidz.com
Baoding High-Tech Industrial Development Zone	Hebei Province	http://www.bd-ctp.net.cn
Jinan High-Tech Industrial Development Zone	Shandong Province	http://www.jctp.gov.cn
Zibo High-Tech Industrial Development Zone	Shandong Province	http://www.china-zibo.com
Weihai High-Tech Industrial Development Zone	Shandong Province	http://www.whtdz.com.cn

Qingdao High-Tech Industrial Park	Shandong Province	http://www.hi-tech.chinaqingdao.net
Weifang High-Tech Industrial Development Zone	Shandong Province	http://www.wfgx.gov.cn
Luoyang High-Tech Industrial Development Zone	Henan Province	http://www.lhdz.gov.cn
Wuhan Donghu High-Tech Park	Hubei Province	http://www.elht.com
Xiangfan High-Tech Industrial Development Zone	Hubei Province	http://www.xfhdz.org.cn
Nanjing High-Tech Industrial Development Zone	Jiangsu Province	http://www.njnhz.com.cn
Changzhou High-Tech Industrial Development Zoen	Jiangsu Province	http://www.czxx.org.cn
Suzhou New Zone	Jiangsu Province	http://www.cs-snd.com.cn
Wuxi New Zone	Jiangsu Province	http://www.wnd.gov.cn
Fuzhou Technological Park	Fujian Province	
Xiamen Torch High-Tech Industrial Development Zone	Fujian Province	http://www.xmtorch.gov.cn
Haikou High-Tech Industrial Development Zone	Hainan Province	
Zhangjiang High-Tech Park	Shanghai Municipality	http://www.zjpark.com
Xi'an High-Tech Industrial Development Zone	Shaanxi Province	http://www.xdz.com.cn
Yangling Agricultural High-Tech Zone	Shaanxi Province	http://www.ylagri.gov.cn
Baoji High-Tech Industrial Development Zone	Shaanxi Province	http://www.bj-hightech.com
Chongqing High-Tech Industrial Development Zone	Chongqing Municipality	http://www.hnzcq.com.cn
Zhuzhou High-Tech Industrial Development Zone	Hunan Province	
Changsha High-Tech Industrial Development Zone	Hunan Province	http://www.cshtz.gov.cn
Baotou High-Tech Industrial Development Zone	Inner Mongolia Autonomous Region	http://www.re-zone.gov.cn
Hangzhou High-Tech Industrial Development Zone	Zhejiang Province	http://www.hhtz.com
Guiyang High-Tech Industrial Development Zone	Guizhou Province	http://www.guz.cei.gov.cn/kfc
Lanzhou High-Tech Industrial Development Zone	Gansu Province	
Harbin High-Tech Industrial Development Zone	Heilongjiang Province	http://www.hbhtz.com
Daqing High-Tech Industrial Development Zone	Heilongjiang Province	http://www.dhp.gov.cn

Tianjin High-Tech Industrial Development Zone	Tianjin Municipality	http://www.tjuda.com
Taiyuan High-Tech Industrial Development Zone	Shanxi Province	
Zhengzhou High-Tech Industrial Development Zone	Henan Province	http://www.zzgx.gov.cn
Hefei High-Tech Industrial Development Zone	Anhui Province	
Nanchang High-Tech Industrial Development Zone	Jiangxi Province	http://www.nchdz.net

Border Economic Cooperative Zones

Name	Location (Province, City, Region)
Heihe Border Economic Cooperative Zone	Heilongjiang Province
Suifenhe Border Economic Cooperative Zone	Heilongjiang Province
Dandong Border Economic Cooperative Zone	Liaoning Province
Bole Border Economic Cooperative Zone	Xinjiang Uygur Autonomous Region
Yi'ning Border Economic Cooperative Zone	Xinjiang Uygur Autonomous Region
Tacheng Border Economic Cooperative Zone	Xinjiang Uygur Autonomous Region
Ruili Border Economic Cooperative Zone	Yunnan Province
Wanting Border Economic Cooperative Zone	Yunnan Province
Hekou Border Economic Cooperative Zone	Yunnan Province
Erlianhaote Border Economic Cooperative Zone	Inner Mongolia Autonomous Region
Manzhouli Border Economic Cooperative Zone	Inner Mongolia Autonomous Region
Huichun Border Economic Cooperative Zone	Jilin Province
Pingxiang Border Economic Cooperative Zone	Guangxi Zhuang Nationality Autonomous Region
Dongxing Border Economic Cooperative Zone	Guangxi Zhuang Nationality Autonomous Region

Border economic cooperative zone

It is a zone in an opening border city established to develop frontier trade and export processing. The border region is a significant part in the opening up of the central and western regions. Since 1992, fourteen border economic cooperative zones have been set up with the approval of the State Council.

Export processing zone

In April 2000, with a view to boost the development of export processing, standardize management of processing trade, shift the management of processing trade from decentralized mode to comparatively centralized mode, create an easier operation environment for enterprises and encourage exportation, the State Council officially approved the establishment of export processing zones. For the convenience of

Export Processing Zones

Name	Location (Province, city, Region)	Website
Dalian Export Processing Zone	Liaoning Province	http://www.dlftz.gov.cn
Yantai Export Processing Zone	Shandong Province	http://www.yantaiepz.gov.cn
Weihai Export Processing Zone	Shandong Province	http://whckjgq.51.net
Suzhou Industrial Park Export Processing Zone	Jiangsu Province	
Kunshan Export Processing Zone	Jiangsu Province	
Xiamen Export Processing Zone	Fujian Province	http://www.xmckjgq.com
Chengdu Export Processing Zone	Sichuan Province	http://www.scepz.gov.cn
Tianjin Export Processing Zone	Tianjin Municipality	
Shanghai Songjiang Export Processing Zone	Shanghai Municipality	http://www.sjepz.com
Guangzhou Export Processing Zone	Guangdong Province	
Shenzhen Export Processing Zone	Guangdng Province	http://www.szgiz.gov.cn/epz
Beijing Tianzhu Export Processing Zone	Beijing Municipality	http://www.chinabaiz.com/ckjgq
Hangzhou Export Processing Zone	Zhejiang Province	
Wuhan Export Processing Zone	Hubei Province	
Huichun Export Processing Zone	Jilin Province	http://www.hcexport.com

operation, the export processing zones are located inside the already established development zones among which some are chosen for experiment. Fifteen export processing zones are included in the first batch approved by the State Council.

Export processing enterprises, warehousing enterprises specially serving the production of export processing enterprises, and transport services specially engaging in carrying goods in and out of the zone that have been approved by the Customs can be set up in the processing zone. The tax policy relating to export processing zones is enacted basically by consulting and following the existing policies adopted in the bonded area. For commodities in the export processing zone coming into and going out of the national boundary, the Customs conduct "putting on file" management, and the "through mode" or "Customs transference mode" of supervision in which no import-export quota or license management is exercised except for the passive export quota management.

ESTABLISHMENT OF FOREIGN-INVESTED ENTERPRISES

Forms of establishment of foreign-invested enterprises

Foreign-invested enterprises are largely divided into two categories: jointly invested enterprises, which include joint ventures and cooperative joint ventures, and wholly invested enterprises.

Joint venture

The qualification and investment form of the participants should be noticed when setting up a joint venture.

As is stipulated, the Chinese participant should be an economic entity with independent assets, practicing independent accounting, established with official approval, holding business license, and capable of bearing independently civil liabilities. The foreign participant should satisfy the following two requirements: 1. to hold an official certificate stating the status of a legal person issued by related authorities outside China's territory; 2. to have funds needed for executing the contract.

Each party to a joint venture may contribute cash, buildings, premises, equipment or other materials, industrial property rights, know-how, right to the use of a site etc., as investment, the value of which shall be ascertained.

The machinery, equipment and other materials contributed as investment by the foreign participant shall comply with the conditions that they are indispensable to the production of the joint venture and that the price fixed shall not be higher than the current international market price for similar equipment or materials.

The industrial property rights or know-how contributed by the foreign participant as investment shall conform to one of the following conditions:

1. Capable of improving markedly the property and quality of existing products, and raising productivity;

2. Capable of notably saving raw materials, fuel or power.

The site-use right as investment refers to the Chinese participant contributing its right to the use of a site as investment. Land in China is owned by the state or owned collectively. The Chinese participant can only contribute the right of land-use as investment. When the Chinese participant intends to contribute land-use right as investment, the joint venture shall file an application with the local municipal (county)

government and obtain the right to use a site only after securing approval and signing a contract.

Industries involved in joint ventures are classified into categories of encouragement, permission, restriction and prohibition as stipulated in the Provisions on Guiding the Orientation of Foreign Investment and Catalogue for the Guidance of Foreign Investment Industries.

The term of a joint venture shall be agreed on among all parties to the joint venture according to actual conditions of the particular lines of business. In some lines of business, the joint venture may or may not agree on the term. However, the term shall be agreed on for the following lines of business or conditions: service industry involving restaurants, apartments, office buildings, recreation, catering, taxi, color film enlargement, developing and printing, maintenance, consulting; land exploitation and real estate operation; resources exploration and exploitation; investment projects restricted by the state; others in which the term should be agreed on as stipulated by laws and regulations.

A joint venture enjoys the power of making its own management decision during its operational period. The government shall not take over the joint venture nor convert it to national ownership. If under special situation the joint venture shall be taken over for the need of public interest, the procedures should be conducted in accordance with the laws and regulations and appropriate compensation should be granted to the venture.

For foreign investors, advantages of joint venture include: 1. It is possible for the foreign and Chinese assets to complement and benefit each other; 2. It is possible to have adequate supply of necessities through the Chinese side, to facilitate contacts with government departments and social agencies, to reduce transaction cost and enjoy more preferential treatment; 3. It is possible to remove obstacles in examination, approval and access to markets.

Disadvantages for foreign investors include: 1. Owing to conflicts in operational and managerial concepts resulted from cultural divergence, inefficient management may occur, resulting in greater organizing cost of the venture; 2. The transferred technology may disseminate; 3. Scramble for the power to control may lead to "joint investment without joint hands."

Sole foreign-invested enterprises

For a long period of time, there were fewer sole foreign-invested enterprises than joint ventures. Later on sole foreign-invested enterprises started to surpass joint ventures, in the number of newly approved projects since 1997, in amount of investment agreed upon since 1998 and in actually amount of inflow since 2000.

The form of foreign capital entering Chinese market shifted into sole investment is caused in the first place by the change of environment. The new Catalogue for the Guidance of Foreign Investment Industries going into effect from April 1, 2002 has relaxed restrictions on the stock proportion of foreign investment, extended the scope of market access. Chinese market will be gradually opened as committed by China to the WTO. The situation at the initial stage when foreign capital had to enter a joint venture for market access has changed.

Secondly, it is the result of changes in investment environment. As China's domestic investment environment is becoming increasingly in line with international ones, foreign companies have acquainted themselves more and more with China's home situation. They are now able to control their own business, plan their business according to their strategy and expand their area and scope of business. At the same time they can also conduct marketing and sales on their own.

For foreign investors, sole invested enterprises have the following benefits: 1. To have the right to make their own management decisions, which helps to avert conflicts in joint ventures; 2. To ensure that technical know-how will not disseminate, which helps to make use of technical resources in acquiring earnings; 3. To be beneficial to large multinational companies in carrying out their global operational strategy.

The disadvantages are that there are more restrictions on market access and categories of business. With respect to production enterprises, sole foreign-invested enterprises have not much difference with joint ventures and cooperative joint ventures. But in projects in the fields of energy, transportation, public utilities, real estate, trust and investment, lease, etc., there are more rigid restrictions. In service field such as press, publication, radio, television, film, domestic commerce, sole foreign-invested enterprises are prohibited.

Procedures for the establishment of foreign-invested enterprises

Procedures for the establishment of China-foreign joint ventures and China-foreign joint cooperative ventures

According to the existing national laws and regulations, the establishment of a foreign-invested enterprise is subject to examination and approval by related competent authorities. The main procedures include: submitting report of feasibility study; submitting contract, regulations; applying for enterprise code; applying for the certificate of approval; applying for business license. For details see the following table.

Procedures for the establishment of sole foreign-invested enterprises

A sole foreign-invested enterprise shall entrust a qualified consulting agency with

1. Prepare and submit feasibility study report	The Chinese or foreign participant may choose through various ways partners to the joint venture or cooperative joint venture. Both parties shall conduct together feasibility study in respect to affairs involving business projects such as market, funds, technology, equipment, raw material (spare parts), selection of location, environment protection, labor safety, fire prevention, auxiliary infrastructure facilities, sales, economic returns, foreign exchange balance, and on the basis of which prepare a feasibility report. Difficulties encountered can be submitted to the examination and approval department for coordination and solution.
2. Submit contract and articles of association	The Chinese and foreign participants, at the same time of preparing the feasibility study report, may draw up the contract and articles of association and submit them for examination and approval.
3. Secure enterprise code	Apply for enterprise code by producing certificate of approval for the contract and articles of association
4. Apply for enterprise certificate of approval	After approval of feasibility study, contract and articles of association, it is up to the Chinese participant to apply to the examination and approval agency for enterprise certificate of approval.
5. Apply for business license	After receiving the enterprise certificate, the Chinese and foreign participants shall register at the industrial and commercial administrative department and get business license. The issuing date of the business license is the date of establishment of the joint (cooperative) venture. Finally, register at the departments of taxation affairs, foreign exchanges, labor, the Customs, finance and statistics.

the formalities of application and securing approval. The procedures shall be followed in the light of those for joint ventures and joint cooperative ventures.

Procedures for examination and approval

Application for the establishment of a foreign-invested enterprise shall be examined and approved by government authorities, including examination and approval of the feasibility study report, contract and articles of association. The feasibility study report is usually examined and approved by the department in charge of planning (technological transformation projects are approved and examined by the department in charge of economy and trade) together with other departments involved; the contract and articles of association of an enterprise are examined and approved by the department in charge of economy and trade.

China practices graded administration. The State Council is the highest administrative authority. The Ministry of Commerce (MOFCOM) is the competent authorities in charge of foreign investment, mainly responsible for enacting corresponding laws and regulations, granting approval for the establishment of foreign-invested enterprises, etc. The planning of key industries and experimental industries are made by respective departments in charge, which also exercise the right of examination and approval.

Provinces, municipalities, autonomous regions and cities separately listed on the state plan are entitled to examine and approve projects with gross investment not exceeding 30 million US dollars. Local governments can within this limit of authority examine and approve the establishment of unrestricted projects by themselves. Restricted and above-norm projects are subject to the examination and approval by the Ministry of Commerce.

Projects in which foreign investment is restricted, construction and production conditions need to be comprehensively balanced by the state, export of products involves quotas and license management, or the examination and approval goes beyond authority of local governments, shall be examined and approved by department in charge under the State Council. Service and trade projects under restriction such as airport construction, restaurants, hotels, retail business, leasing, freight transport, finance, insurance and the establishment of investment companies and stock companies, shall be examined and approved by related departments under the State Council.

Projects below-norm not included in the above-mentioned categories shall be examined and approved by respective government and its authorized organization of each province, autonomous region and municipality directly under the Central Government. A local government's authority of examination and approval is limited to projects whose gross investment is within 30 million US dollars. The local government, after granting approval for the establishment of an enterprise, shall submit related documents as stipulated to the department in charge under the State Council for the record. In order to simplify the procedures and save the time of examination and approval, some provinces, autonomous regions and municipalities have further transferred to lower levels the power of examination and approval within their limits of authorities.

Establishment of permanent representative agencies

Foreign enterprises that need to set up permanent representative offices in China shall submit application for approval and then register before an office can be established.

Application for the establishment of permanent office submitted by foreign enterprises shall be examined and approved respectively according to lines of business by the following authorities:

1. Trade, manufacture and freight agency shall be approved by the Ministry of Commerce;

2. Finance and insurance shall be approved by the People's Bank of China;

3. Ocean shipping and ocean-shipping agency shall be approved by the Ministry of Communication;

4. Air transportation shall be approved by the Civil Aviation Administration of China (CAAC);

5. Other lines of business shall be approved by respective authorities.

The foreign enterprise, after obtaining ap-

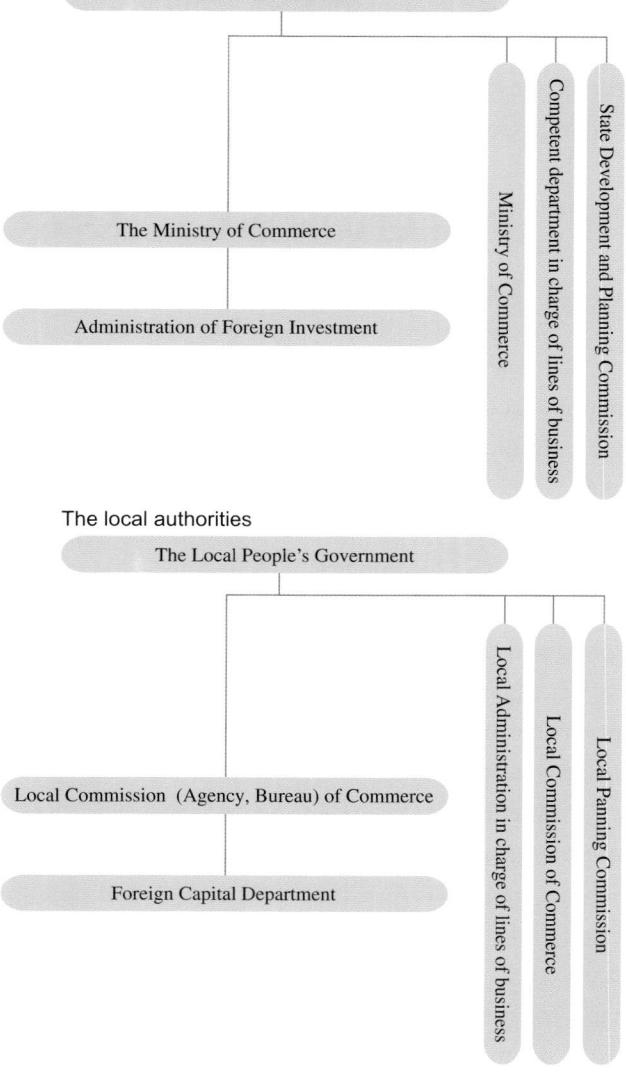

Administrative Authorities in Charge of Foreign Investment

The central authorities

The state Council

The Ministry of Commerce

Administration of Foreign Investment

Ministry of Commerce

Competent department in charge of lines of business

State Development and Planning Commission

The local authorities

The Local People's Government

Local Commission (Agency, Bureau) of Commerce

Foreign Capital Department

Local Administration in charge of lines of business

Local Commission of Commerce

Local Panning Commission

proval for setting up a permanent office shall, in addition to registration with the administrative bureau for industry and commerce, prepare official seal, apply for code certificate, open bank spot-exchange account and go through the formalities of taxation registration. Aliens shall have to secure a health certificate, employment certificate, work permit and long-term residence permit. Personal cars, things for office use and daily necessities, if imported, shall be registered and reported with the Customs.

A permanent representative office of a foreign enterprise established in China shall not engage in direct business activities. It can only import things for office or daily use and vehicles for transport, which are not exempted from tax as currently stipulated. It can employ Chinese staff and workers, but should in principle be by way of external services or other departments designated by the government. For details see Rules of the Ministry of Commerce for the Implementation of in Approval and Management of Permanent Representative Offices of Foreign Enterprises.

TAXATION POLICIES GOVERNING FOREIGN-INVESTED ENTERPRISES

Currently tax categories concerning foreign-invested enterprises (including compatriots from HK, Macao and Taiwan) include enterprise income tax, value-added tax, consumption tax, business tax and housing tax. Customs duty and import link tax shall be levied on import and export goods in line with the Customs' regulations for customs duty. Below is a brief introduction:

Enterprise income tax   The income tax on foreign enterprise is levied at a rate of 33 per cent for payable income including 3 per cent of local income tax. As regards foreign companies, enterprises and other economic entities that have no agencies or offices established in China, the income tax shall be levied in advance at a rate of 20 per cent on proceeds they have obtained from within China's territory such as dividend, interest, rent, royalties, and others.

Value-added tax   Units or individuals who import commodities, or sell goods, or provide processing service or labor service such as making repairs and supplying replacements within China's territory, shall pay value-added tax according to regulations. The value-add tax is levied at a rate of 17 per cent basically, but at a reduced rate of 13 per cent on a few commodities such as grain, edible vegetable oil, tap water, feed, chemical fertilizer, pesticide, and farm machinery.

Consumption tax   Consumption tax shall be levied on 11 varieties of consumer goods produced, entrusted to process within China's territory or imported, including cigarettes, alcoholic drinks and alcohol, cosmetics, face cream and hair conditioner, precious jewelry and gems, firecrackers and fireworks, gasoline, diesel oil, car tires, motor cycles, and cars. The consumption tax is levied in two ways: one is based on quantity (0.2 yuan on each liter of gasoline) and the other is based on price (a rate of 8 per cent on cars with cylinder capacity less than 2,200 ml.)

Business tax　Entities and individuals engaging in businesses such as communication and transportation, post and telecommunications, finance and insurance, architecture, culture and sports, recreation and services or transfer intangible assets or sell real estates within China's territory shall pay business tax at a rate of 3 or 5 per cent except for recreational business, which shall pay at the rate of 10 or 15 per cent.

Personal income tax　Expatriates working with Chinese-foreign joint ventures, Chinese-foreign cooperative joint ventures, wholly foreign-owned enterprises established within China's territory, aliens working in foreign companies, enterprises or offices of other foreign economic entities stationed in China, and other aliens working in China shall pay personal income tax on wages and salaries they have earned at half rate according to regulations stipulated in the Income Tax Law of the People's Republic of China.

The Chinese government has enacted a wealth of preferential policies on tax towards foreign-invested enterprises with respect to different industries, different places, term of operation, export condition of products, etc. For industries and projects in which foreign investment is encouraged, governments at provincial level have formulated preferential treatment to reduce or exempt from local personal income tax. Foreign investors who wish to enjoy fully preferential treatment better consult an accountant who knows well China's tax law at the beginning of investment.

Note: The term 'production enterprise' appeared on the table "Excerpts of preferential treatment to foreign-invested enterprise regarding income tax" refers to enterprises involved in such fields as machinery manufacturing, electronics industry, energy industry (exclusive of petroleum recovering and gas extracting), metallurgical industry, chemical industry, building materials industry, light industry, textiles, packing industry, medical apparatus and instruments, pharmaceutical industry, agriculture, forestry, animal husbandry, fishery and water conservancy, building industry, communications (exclusive of passenger transport), science and technology development that directly serves production, reconnaissance survey, industrial information and consultation, maintenance of production equipment and precision instruments, and other industries determined by department in charge of taxation affairs under the State Council.

Excerpts of Preferential Treatment to Foreign-Invested Enterprises Regarding Income Tax

	Policy Content	Nationwide Stipulations	Special economic zones	State-level development zones				Open cities and regions (including coastal, inland, border areas) and provincial economic development zones
				Economic and technological development zones	High-tech industrial development zones	Bonded areas	Border economic cooperation zones	
Rate of enterprise income tax	Production enterprises	30%	15%	15%	15%	5%	15%	24%
	Non-production enterprises	30%	15%	30%	30%	30%	30%	30%
	Knowledge-intensive and technical-intensive projects, projects with foreign investment exceeding 30 million US dollars which need a long period of time for recovery	30%	15%	15%	15%	15%	* (15%)	15%
	Export product enterprises whose annual export turnover tops 70% of the gross output value after the expiration of the period for tax exemption and reduction	15%	10%	10%	10%	10%	12%	12%
	Banking firms with foreign-invested operational funds exceeding 10 million US dollars and operation period exceeding 10 years	30%	15%	15% as specially approved by the State Council				
	Energy, communication, port projects or projects specially approved and encouraged by the state.	15%						

*Note: ( ) figure inside refers to figure based on policy consulting and following opening areas

	Policy Content	
Duration for enterprise income tax exemption and reduction (operation period exceeding 10 years, counting starts from the profit-making year)	Production enterprises and confirmed high-tech enterprises and technical research centers	Exemption for the 1-2 years, half-exemption for the 3-5 years;
	Newly started enterprises engaging in communication, power, water conservancy, post, radio, television in central and western areas	Exemption for the 1-2 years, half-exemption for the 3-5 years;
	Non-production enterprises	(In special economic zones, service-based enterprises with foreign investment exceeding 5 million US dollars and operation period exceeding 10 years; in special economic zones and other regions specially approved by the State Council, banking firms with foreign investment exceeding 10 million US dollars and operation period exceeding 10 years) exemption for the 1-2 years, half exemption for the 3-5 years;
	Technically advanced enterprises	After the expiration of the period for tax exemption and reduction, enterprises remain to be technically advanced shall be allowed a half reduced rate of income tax for another 3 years;
	The central and western regions	Foreign-invested enterprises encouraged by the state shall be allowed an income tax rate of 15% for another 3 years after expiration of the period for tax exemption and reduction in accordance with current stipulations;
	Enterprises engaging in port and wharf construction with operation period exceeding 10 years	Exemption from income tax for the 1-5 years, half exemption for the 6-10 years;
	Enterprises engaging in farming, forestry, animal husbandry and enterprises in underdeveloped border areas	After expiration of the period for tax exemption and reduction in accordance with provisions, enterprise income tax shall be allowed a reduction of 15-30 per cent for another 10 years subject to approval by the government department in charge; income from special farming products produced to protect ecological environment in the central and western regions shall be exempted from special farming products tax for 10 years.
	Tax refund for re-investment	Foreign investors who reinvest with assets or profits earned in the original enterprises or other foreign-invested enterprises newly launched with foreign investment exceeding 25 per cent of the total capital and operation period not less than 5 years shall be refunded 40 per cent of the tax payment for reinvestment after approval by the tax authorities. Tax payment for reinvestment in export-oriented enterprises or technical-advanced enterprises shall be refunded in full.

LAND, LABOR AND FOREIGN EXCHANGE MANAGEMENT

Land use

Public ownership of land is practiced in China, which includes state ownership and collective ownership. The land in urban districts is owned by the state, and land in rural area and suburbs is owned collectively except for the part owned by the state as stipulated in laws and regulations.

Foreign-invested enterprises can obtain the right to the use of state-owned land chiefly in the following manner:

1. Paid land use   The state may in the capacity of landowner transfer the right to the use of land for a fixed number of years to a foreign-invested enterprise, which makes a lump-sum payment for the land use. A foreign-invested enterprise may receive land use right by means of entering a bid, auction or agreement and, after concluding a contract for land-use transfer with land administration and making full payment in accordance with the terms and conditions specified in the contract, go through the formalities of land register and get land-use permit. The right of land use obtained in this manner can be transferred, let or mortgaged.

2. Government allocation   A foreign-invested enterprise enters into a contract for land use with the land administration, goes through registration formalities and gets the land use permit. The land user pays a one-time land development fee and then pays annually land use fee.

3. The Chinese participant may take land use right as a requirement for joint investment and cooperation. The Chinese enterprise may use the monetary equivalent of its premises, equipment together with the right to the use of land as part of its investment or as requirements for cooperation with the foreign participant.

4. House and site leasing   A foreign-invested enterprise may rent premises and sites directly from state-owned, urban collectively owned or township enterprises and pays rental. It is noteworthy that when a Chinese enterprise lets a house it lets at the same time the right to the use of the land. If the land the Chinese enterprise lets was originally obtained through purchase, the leasing is a legal transaction; but if it was obtained from government allocation, it is necessary to complete missing purchase procedures and make the payment. Otherwise the deal will be regarded as illegal.

5. Form of transfer   A foreign-invested enterprise may obtain the right to the use of land from another land user for a fixed number of years in accordance with specified form of transfer. The number of land use years is calculated by subtracting the

number of years already used from the number of years purchased.

A foreign-invested enterprise can obtain the right to the use of collectively owned land in the following manner:

1. The state, by taking over collectively owned land, turns it into state-owned land and then sells it to a foreign-invested enterprise. The collectively owned land is not permitted to sell or to rent directly.

2. When a rural collective economic organization or township enterprise uses the monetary equivalent of collectively owned land as its investment or as a requirement for cooperation in starting a joint venture or a cooperative joint venture, such project has to be approved by the county government.

The Constitution of the PRC and related laws governing land management have specified definitely a fundamental principle: any unit or individual shall not seize, sell or buy, or illegally transfer land in other forms. The right to the use of land may be transferred according to the law. In the use of the land, the following situations should be noted:

Any investment project, which involves taking farmland for construction use, shall be subject to approval by the central government, no matter how large the land is or whether it should be taken over for public use.

Any investment project, which involves taking over collectively owned land, shall be subject to approval by the central or provincial government.

Any investment project, which occupies for use a large area of land or land used for line-shaped projects such as the construction of roads or railways, shall be approved by the central government. Unitary development of land as a part of city planning shall be approved by the central government.

Local governments under provincial level are not entitled to grant approval to the use of farmland for other purpose or take over land for public use.

Environmental protection

Environmental protection is a basic policy of the state. China has formulated and put into effect a series of laws and regulations on environmental and resource protection and air, water and ocean pollution prevention. Foreign-invested enterprises while drafting enterprise feasibility study report on a project, must submit to the environmental protection authorities an environmental influence report. The state shall not approve any foreign-invested project that may cause pollution. The enterprise, upon completion of the project, must report to the environment protection authorities that have examined and approved the project for checking and acceptance of its environment protection facilities. If the facilities are not up to the standard, the project shall

Color TV market, where competition is most fierce in China

not be put into production or use. Foreign-invested enterprises must accept the supervision of the environmental protection authorities in its daily production

Labor force

A general survey

The rich resources of labor force in China top the world. By the end of 2001, China had an employed population of 712 millions.

China was a large agricultural country in history with the employed in the first industry forming a large proportion. In 1980, employees in the first industry accounted for 68.7 per cent of the country's total. In 2000, the number already reduced to 50 per cent while employment in the second and in particular the tertiary industry had been continuously increasing. At the same time, owing to labor surplus in the countryside, more and more rural labors flew into cities, resulting in a drastic change in China's urban labor market

Currently urban labor force in China has the following features: 1. Generally speaking, the supply of gross labor force exceeds demand. Employment pressure in the eastern part is less immense than the central and western part while job opportunities are more spacious in the east coastal cities as compared with the average eastern region. 2. Young and early middle-aged laborers take up a considerable proportion of the labor force. According to the statistics in the labor markets of 81 cities in 2002, job seekers aged between 16-34 accounted for 72 per cent of the total. 3. Females take up a fairly large proportion of labor force. According to the statistics mentioned above, women accounted for 47 per cent of the total job seekers. 4. The educational and skill level of job seekers are improving at a rapid pace. According to the statistics of the Fifth National Census conducted in 2000, there were in China 45.71 million people who received higher education and 141.09 million people who received secondary education. According to the statistics in 2002, labor force with secondary level of education already became the main body of job seekers, accounting for 44.3 per cent whereas labor force with higher level of education accounted for 29.4 per cent of the total. Moreover, there were 52.2 per cent of job seekers who held technical-grade certificates. With the development of basic education and vocational education, the overall quality of labor force in China will be further improved to adapt to the transfer of Chinese economy from manufacturing industry centered towards service industry and high-tech industry based.

At present, primary-level and long-line professionals are excessive while senior management personnel and professionals in high-tech fields are relatively in short supply. After China's entry into the WTO, more and more foreign-invested enterprises and firms have come to China whose need for high-level personnel has attracted the attention of Chinese government and the educational field. The guidelines on higher education have become more in favor of the actual need of the society. Now the number of college graduates has reached a million every year which, together with ever increasing number of returned overseas students, has made it much easier for foreign-invested enterprises to recruit staff and workers in China. Besides the government has implemented various policies in favor of talented people.

Employment of labor force

Foreign-invested enterprises have fully decision-making power in recruitment in which no department, unit or individual shall interfere. At the same time, the Chinese government has enacted laws and regulations governing protection of laborers' lawful rights and interest such as the Labor Law of the People's Republic of China and the Decisions Made by the State Council with Respect to Working Hours of Staff and Workers.

Enterprises are entitled to recruit workers on their own while laborers seeking a job shall not be discriminated because of nationality, race, sex or religion. Women enjoy the same rights as men. Employers shall not reject job application or raise employment standard on account of sex. Minors under 16 shall not be employed, nor women laborers be assigned to jobs prohibited by the state.

Generally foreign-invested enterprises are not permitted to employ staff and workers from outside China's territory, including Hong Kong, Macao and Taiwan except specially skilled personnel, senior technicians and senior executives that the enterprise are in need of but not available within the nation's territory. The employment of such persons from outside the nation's territory shall be subject to approval from labor authorities and go through the procedures of employment and residence in China in accordance with laws and regulations.

Foreign-invested enterprises recruiting staff and workers shall conclude and enter into labor contract with the employees in which employment, dismissal, salary, fringe benefits and other matters shall be specified.

It is an enterprise's legal right to discharge employees in accordance with the law, but to guard against discharging workers at random, the state has stipulated some restrictions including that employees under medical treatment for injury suffered while on duty and women employees during pregnancy, puerperium or lactation period shall not be discharged.

Enterprises shall be responsible for the welfare, insurance and safety production of the employees in accordance with relevant stipulations.

In recent years, China has started to carry out forcibly the professional qualification access system. In addition to the professions such as lawyers and physicians in which qualification certification is conventionally needed, in some other lines of business professional qualification is also required such as accounting, secretary, marketing, estate management, electronic commerce, psychological consultation, software engineering, etc. In employment, now more importance is attached to professional capability.

In China, it is convenient to recruit workers. The main forms include: putting on an advertisement in a media, holding special activities to invite applications, recruiting employees through talent intermediary agencies and online recruiting. Labor markets and talent markets have been commonly set up in various locations. The Ministry of Labor and Social Security and the Ministry of Personnel have set up nationwide online labor markets and talent markets on which millions of laborers every year shift jobs. Now with foreign talent agencies entering China, talent service level will be improved. As is stipulated, employment in wholly foreign-owned enterprises has to be conducted by local foreign enterprise services.

Working hours, wages and welfare

As is stipulated in the Labor Law of the People's Republic of China, working hours of workers shall not exceed 8 hours per working day, 44 hours per week, at least a day off per week, which should be guaranteed by the employing unit. January

1, the first through third day of the Spring Festival, May 1-3, Oct.1-3 are official holidays. Moreover, employees also enjoy home leave, marriage leave, mourning leave, and maternity leave for women employees.

The employing unit, out of the need for production, can prolong work hours after negotiation with the trade union and the employees themselves, for no more than one more hour a day. On special occasions the working hours can be prolonged for 3 more hours a day at the maximum and no more than 36 extra working hours in a month. But as it happens such stipulation often fails to be exactly followed in specific

Wage Level in Labor Market in 44 Large and Medium–Sized Cities in China

Total	Number of persons surveyed	Average wage in 1999 (yuan)	Average wage in 2000 (yuan)	Year-on-year increase (%)
	792,996	8,967	10,070	12.30
Classified according to registration				
1. Domestic funded enterprise	661,921	8.794	9,860	12.12
(1) State-owned enterprises	455,115	9,308	10,536	13.19
(2) Collectively owned enterprises	80,051	7,058	7.642	8.27
(3) Stock cooperative enterprises	29,050	7,384	7,748	4.94
(4) Joint operated enterprises	2,256	10,599	11,359	7.17
(5) Limited-liability companies	87,591	8,256	9,159	10.93
(6) Private enterprises	4,752	6,479	7,443	14.88
(7) Other enterprises	3,106	8,805	10,072	14.39
2. HK, Macao and Taiwan invested enterprises	17,463	11,607	12,547	8.10
3. Foreign-invested enterprises	24,965	13,350	15,037	12.64
Classified according to lines of business				
1. Farm, forestry, animal husbandry, fishery	10,204	6,929	7,650	10.40
2. Mining	11,703	7,561	8,282	9.54
3. Manufacturing	440,977	8,938	10,130	13.34
4. Production and supply of power, gas, and water	30,310	10,906	12,477	14.40
5. Building	46,966	9,528	10,345	8.57
6. Communication, transportation, warehousing,post, telecommunication	72,794	9,071	10,026	10.53
7. Wholesale, retail, catering	112,796	8,313	9,049	8.84
8. Banking, insurance	12,544	14,344	16,033	11.77
9. Real estate	9,318	13,578	14,946	10.08
10. Social services	26,264	9,142	10,147	10.98
11. Others	13,768	8,564	9,395	9.70

Statistics of Provinces, Autonomous Regions and Municipalities directly under the Central Government (an excerpt)

Area	2001 GDP (yuan/per capita)	2001 GDP year-on-year increase	2000 consumption level	2001 gross population (10 thousand)	Density of population (number of persons /sq. km)
Beijing	25,300	11.0	7,326	1,383	823
Tienjin	19,986	12.0	6,117	1,004	886
Hebei	8,337	8.7	2,543	6,699	359
Shanxi	5,444	8.3	2,037	3,272	211
Inner Mongolia	6,458	9.6	2,425	2,377	20
Liaoning	12,070	9.0	4,490	4,194	290
Jilin	7,640	9.3	3,381	2,691	146
Heilongjiang	9,349	9.3	3,669	3,811	81
Shanghai	37,382	10.2	11,546	1,614	2,657
Jiangsu	12,925	10.2	3,862	7,355	725
Zhejiang	14,550	10.5	4,366	4,613	459
Anhui	5,221	8.6	2,588	6,328	429
Fujian	12,375	9.0	4,428	3,440	286
Jiangxi	5,217	8.8	2,396	4,186	248
Shangdong	10,465	10.1	3,467	9,041	579
Henan	5,929	9.1	2,208	9,555	554
Hubei	7,813	9.1	2,857	5,975	324
Hunan	6,054	9.0	2,723	6,596	304
Guangdong	13,612	9.5	5,007	7,783	486
Guangxi	4,697	8.2	2,147	4,788	190
Hainan	7,110	8.9	2,904	796	232
Chongqing	5,655	9.0	2,466	3,097	375
Sichuan	5,250	9,2	2,456	8,640	172
Guizhou	2,865	8.8	1,608	3,799	200
Yunnan	4,872	6.5	2,530	4,287	109
Tibet	5,302	12.6	1,823	263	2.1
Shaanxi	5,015	9.1	2,035	3,659	175
Gansu	4,173	9.4	1,734	2,575	56
Qinghai	5,732	12.0	2,255	523	7.2
Ningxia	5,338	10.1	2,290	563	108
Xinjiang	7,898	8.0	3,207	1,876	12

situations.

Employees working extra hours shall be paid wages at no less than 150 per cent of the original wage rate. Employees required to work on days off without taking deferred ones shall be paid at no less than 200 per cent of the original wage rate, and no less than 300 per cent of the original wage rate for working on statutory holidays.

The wage level for workers at different places or in different lines of business is different. The differences can be several times as large. Since 1988, the Ministry of Labor and Social Security has started to practice the system of indicative wage level for different lines of business so as to normalize and carry out macro control on the labor market. However, it is hard to say to what degree such guideline will be followed by the employing units, in particular the foreign-invested enterprises and private enterprises because in the last analysis wages are determined by the labor market. In China, the minimum wage security system has been implemented, according to which the specific minimum wage standard shall be determined by the government of respective provinces, autonomous regions and municipalities. The employing units shall not pay wages below the local minimum wage standard.

With respect to welfare, the state has set apart social security funds to offer help or compensation for laborers suffering from old age, sickness, injury on the job, employment, etc. Enterprises must insure for social security in accordance with related regulations against old age, unemployment, illness, injury on the job, childbirth, etc. and pay adequate social security fees to the social security organization according to the standard stipulated by the local government. Moreover, the state encourages the employing units to offer additional insurance for employees and foster their welfare in the light of actual conditions of the units.

In recent years, the average annual wages in China have increased by 7~10 per cent or above. It is mainly for two reasons: 1. China's GDP keeps on an increase of 7~8 per cent, which means it is quite natural for wages to increase correspondingly; 2. The government has raised the income of low-paid employees; raised civil servants' salary; and increased by 30 per cent

Source of Foreign-Invested Enterprises in 2001

State (region)	Number of Enterprises	Percentage (%)
Hong Kong	926,000	45.78
Taiwan	25,000	12.37
The United States	18,800	9.3
Japan	15,200	7.5
ROK	11,000	5.45
Singapore	6,362	3.14
Virgin Islands of the UK	4,171	2.06
Macao	3,565	1.76
Canada	2,862	1.41
Australia	2,547	1.26
Great Britain	2,315	1.14

Note: Each of other countries accounts for less than 1%. Thailand, Germany, Malaysia and France each had more than 1,000 enterprises in China by the end of 2001.

urban residents' basic living allowance and unemployment allowance. Though this adds up to higher cost of labor and more public expenditure, it does not affect foreign investors. Statistics indicate that the labor cost in China such as in the manufacturing industry, is only 10 per cent of the labor cost in Hong Kong and 5 per cent in the US. There are 150 million surplus labors in China of whom 80 per cent of the newly employed have received regular training. The labor price in coastal regions is on the rise. However, wages of laborers from the central and western regions are rather on the low side. China has a vast area of territory with different degrees of development in different areas. When the cost of labor in the eastern coastal regions arises, enterprises there can move to hinterland for low-cost labor. For a comparatively long period of time, China shall maintain its labor advantages.

As is indicated by statistics, the annual income of China's urban employees in 2001 averages 10,870 yuan, a 16 per cent increase compared with the previous year, or an actual increase of 15.2 per cent after deducting the price factor. Among the income of employees, those from state-owned units earn an average of 11,178 yuan, from collectively owned units, 6,867 yuan and from other units, 12,140 yuan. Currently medium and high-level executives and specialized professions are in short supply and are paid much higher. The gap in payment between high-level talents and general labors is also a sign denoting that China's labor market has become mature.

Foreign Exchange Control

When the participants of foreign-invested enterprises contribute cash as investment, the foreign participant shall contribute convertible foreign exchanges as investment apart from its profits and other legal earnings in RMB obtained from foreign-invested enterprise in China that have been confirmed by foreign exchange authorities. The Chinese participant can contribute either cash in RMB or foreign exchanges as investment.

After receipt of business license, a foreign-invested enterprise shall handle foreign exchange business registration with the local foreign exchange administration, and then with the certificate of registration opens a foreign exchange account at a bank within the nation's territory. As is stipulated, except otherwise approved by the state, all the revenue and expenditure of foreign exchanges in a foreign-invested enterprise shall be released through the foreign exchange account with a bank within the nation's territory.

The conversion rate of foreign exchanges used as investment, profits, and non-trade flowing in a foreign-invested enterprise shall be based on the benchmark exchange rate issued by the People's Bank of China on the operating day.

To simplify the formalities for foreign-invested enterprises in handling affairs and facilitate their operation of invested funds, starting from July 1, 2002, China has conducted nationwide reform on the management of capital funds conversion under foreign investment, which shall be checked and handled directly by designated banks that are up to the standard. The banks shall perform the responsibility of checking, statistical monitoring, reporting and recording. The foreign exchange administration will not examine and approve one by one the foreign exchange conversion business under foreign investment but shift its function from enterprise management to bank monitor.

Provisions on Guiding the Orientation of Foreign Investment

the State Council

February 11, 2002

Article 1 In order to guide the orientation of foreign investment, to keep the orientation of foreign investment in line with the national economy and social development planning of China, and to protect the lawful rights and interests of investors, these Provisions have been formulated according to the laws and provision on foreign investment and the requirements of industrial policies of the State.

Article 2 These Provisions shall be applicable to the projects of investment and establishment of Chinese-foreign joint ventures, Chinese-foreign cooperative joint ventures and foreign-invested enterprises (hereinafter referred to as enterprises with foreign investment), and projects with foreign investment in other forms (hereinafter referred to as projects with foreign investment) within the territory of China.

Article 3 The Guidance Catalog of Industry with Foreign Investment and the Catalog of Dominant Industries with Foreign Investment of the Mid-west Region shall be formulated by the State Development Planning Commission, the State Economic and Trade Commission, the Ministry of Foreign Trade and Economic Cooperation jointly with other relevant departments under the State Council, and shall be promulgated upon the approval of the State Council; when it is needed to partly adjust the Guidance Catalog of Industry with Foreign Investment and the Catalog of Dominant Industries with Foreign Investment of the Mid-west Region in light of the actual situation, the State Economic and Trade Commission, the State Development Planning Commission, the Ministry of Foreign Trade and Economic Cooperation jointly with the relevant departments under the State Council shall make the revision and promulgation timely. The Guidance Catalog of Industry with Foreign Investment and the Catalog of Dominant Industries with Foreign Investment of the Mid-west Region shall be the basis of the application of relevant policies in directing and examining and approving projects with foreign investment and enterprises with foreign investment.

Article 4 Projects with foreign investment fall into 4 categories, namely encouraged, permitted, restricted and prohibited. The Projects with foreign investment that are encouraged, restricted and prohibited shall be listed in the Guidance Catalog of Industry with Foreign Investment. And the projects with foreign investment that do not fall into encouraged, restricted or prohibited categories shall be the permitted projects with foreign investment. The permitted projects with foreign investment shall not be listed in the Guidance Catalog of Industry with Foreign Investment.

Article 5 A project in any of the following situations shall be listed as encouraged projects with foreign investment:

1) Being of new agriculture technologies, agriculture comprehensive development, or energy, transportation and important raw material industries;

2) Being of high and new technologies or advanced application technologies that can improve the product performance and increase technological and economic efficiency of the enterprises or those that can produce new equipments and new materials not available at home;

3) meeting the market needs and being able to improve the product level, develop new markets or increase the international competitiveness of the products;

4) Being of new technologies and new equipments that can save energy and raw material, comprehensively utilize resources and regenerate resources, and prevent environment pollutions;

5) Being capable of bring the advantages of human power and resources of the mid-west region into full play and being in conformity to the industrial policies of the State;

6) Other situations as provided by laws and administrative regulations.

Article 6 A project in any of the following situations shall be a restricted project with foreign investment:

1) Backward in technology;

2) Unfavorable for saving resources or improving environment;

3) Engaged in the prospecting and exploitation of the specific type of mineral resources of which the State conducts protective exploitation;

4) Belonging in the industries that the State opens step by step;

5) other situations as provided by laws and administrative regulations.

Article 7 A project in any of the following situations shall be a prohibited project with foreign investment:

1) Harming the State safety or impairing public interests;

2) Polluting environment, damaging natural resources or harming human health;

3) Occupying a large area of farmland and being adverse to the protection and development of land resources;

4) Harming the safety and usage of military facilities;

5) Using China's specific techniques or technologies to produce products;

6) Other situations as provided by laws and administrative regulations.

Article 8 The Guidance Catalog of Industry with Foreign Investment may provide that an enterprise with foreign investment is "limited to joint venture, cooperative joint venture", "with Chinese party at the holding position" or "with Chinese party at the relatively holding position". By "limited to joint venture and cooperative joint venture" it refers to that only Chinese-foreign joint ventures and Chinese-foreign cooperative joint ventures are allowed. By "with the Chinese parties at the holding position" it refers to that the total investment proportion of the Chinese parties in the project with foreign investment shall be 51% or more. By "with Chinese parties at the relatively holding position" it refers to that the total investment proportion of the Chinese parties in the project with foreign investment shall be higher than the investment proportion of any foreign party.

Article 9 Apart from enjoying the preferential treatments according to the provisions of the relevant laws and administrative regulations, the encouraged projects with foreign investment that engage in the construction and operation of energy, transportation, municipal infrastructure (coal, oil, natural gas, electric power, railways, highways, ports, airports, city roads, sewage disposition, and garbage disposition, etc.) that needs large amount of investment and long term for recovery may expand their relevant business scope upon approval.

Article 10 The permitted projects with foreign investment of which the products are all directly exported shall be regarded as the encouraged project with foreign investment; the restricted projects with foreign investment of which the export sales accounts for more than 70% of their total amount of sales may be regarded as the permitted projects with foreign investment upon the approval of respective governments of provinces, autonomous regions, municipalities directly under the Central Government and municipalities separately listed on the State plan or the competent department under the State Council.

Article 11 The conditions may be eased for the permitted and restricted projects with foreign investment that really can bring the advantages of the mid-west region into full play; among which, those listed in the Guidance Catalog of Industry with Foreign Investment may enjoy the preferential policies for the encouraged projects with foreign investment.

Article 12 Projects with foreign investment shall be examined and approved, and put on record respectively by the departments of development planning and the economic and trade departments within the limit of authority for examination and approval; the contracts and articles of association of enterprises with foreign investment shall be examined and approved, and put on record by the departments of foreign trade and economic cooperation. Among which, the projects with foreign investment under the limit for restricted projects with foreign investment shall be subject to the examination and approval of the corresponding competent departments of respective governments of the provinces, autonomous regions, municipalities directly under the Central Government and municipalities separately listed on the State plan, and shall be reported to the competent departments at the higher level and the competent industrial departments, the power for examination and approval of this kind of projects may not be granted to the authorities at lower levels. The projects with foreign investment in the service area that are opened to the outside world step by step shall be subject to the examination and approval according to the relevant provisions of the State. The projects with foreign investment involving quotas and licenses must apply to the departments for quotas and licenses first. Where there are otherwise provisions of laws and administrative regulations on the procedures and measures for the examination and approval of projects with foreign investment, those provisions shall be observed.

Article 13 With respect to projects with foreign investment examined and approved in violation of the present provisions, the organ of examination and approval at the next higher level shall cancel it within 30 workdays from the day of receiving the documents for record of that project, its contract and articles of association shall be void, the department of enterprise registration shall not register it and the Customs shall not handle the procedures for import and export.

Article 14 Where the applicant of a project with foreign investment manages to obtain the approval for the project by deceiving or other illicit means, his legal liabilities shall be investigated for according to law in light of the seriousness of the circumstances; the organ of examination and approval shall cancel the approval for that project and the relevant competent organs shall deal with it correspondingly according to law.

Article 15 Where any staff member of the organ of examination and approval abuses his power or neglects his duties, criminal responsibilities shall be investigated for according to the provisions of the criminal law on the crime of abusing powers or the crime of neglecting duties; where the circumstances are not serious enough for criminal punishment, administrative punishment of recording a special demerit or more severe punishment shall be given.

Article 16 With respect to the investment projects established by overseas Chinese and the investors from the Hong Kong Special Administration Region, Macao Special Administrative Region or Taiwan Area, these Provisions shall be based for reference.

Article 17 These Provisions shall enter into force on April 1, 2002. The Interim Provisions on the Guidance of Foreign Investment Directions approved by the State Council on June 7, 1995 and promulgated by the State Planning Commission, the State Economic and Trade Commission and the Ministry of Foreign Trade and Economic Cooperation on June 20, 1995 shall be nullified simultaneously.

Promulgated by the State Council on 2002-2-11

Catalogue for the Guidance of Foreign Investment Industries

Catalogue of Encouraged Foreign Investment Industries

I. Farming, Forestry, Animal Husbandry and Fishery Industries

1. Transforming low- and medium-yielding farmland.

2. Planting technology, without environmental hazard, of vegetables (including edible fungus and melons), fruits, teas and serial development and production of these products.

3. Development and production of new breed varieties (excluding gene-modified varieties) of fine quality, high-yielding crops such as sugar-yielding crops, fruit trees, flowers and plants, forage grass and related new techniques.

4. Production of flowers and plants, and construction and operation of nursery of young plants.

5. Reusing in fields and comprehensive utilization of straws and stalks of crop, development and production of resources of organic fertilizers

6. Cultivation of traditional Chinese medicines (for joint ventures or cooperative joint ventures only.)

7. Planting of forest trees (including bamboo) and cultivation of fine strains of forest trees

8. Planting of natural rubber, sisals and coffees

9. Breeding of quality varieties of breeding stock, breeding birds and aquatic offspring (excluding precious quality varieties peculiar to China)

10. Breeding of famous, special and fine aquatic products, as well as cage culture in deep water

11. Construction and operation of ecological environment protection projects preventing and treating desertification and soil erosion such as planting trees and grasses, etc.

II. Mining and Quarrying Industries

*1. Risk prospecting and tapping of petroleum, natural gas.

*2. Exploiting of low-osmotic oil and gas deposits (fields).

*3. Developing of new technologies that help to increase the output of crude oil.

*4. Development and application of new technologies for prospecting and exploitation of petroleum, such as geophysical prospecting, well drilling, well logging and operation under the pit, etc.

5. Prospecting and exploitation of coal and associated resources

6. Prospecting and exploitation of coal-bed gas

7. Extracting and beneficiation of gold mines with low quality or difficult to beneficiate (for joint ventures or cooperative joint ventures only. Wholly foreign-owned enterprises are permitted in western regions)

8. Prospecting and extracting of iron ores and manganese ores.

9. Prospecting and exploitation of copper ores, lead ores and zinc ores (for joint ventures or cooperative joint ventures only. Wholly foreign-owned enterprises are permitted in west regions)

10. Prospecting and mining of aluminum ores (joint ventures or cooperative joint ventures only. Wholly foreign-owned enterprises are permitted in west regions)

11. Tapping of chemical deposits including sulfur ores, phosphate ores, potassium ores, etc.

III. Manufacturing Industries

1. Food Processing Industry

1.1 Storage and processing of food, vegetables, fruits, fowl and livestock products

1.2 Aquatic products processing, seashell products cleansing and processing, and development of function food made from seaweed

1.3 Development and production of drinks of fruits, vegetables, albumen, teas and coffees

1.4 Development and production of fond for babies and agedness, as well as function food

1.5 Production of dairy products

1.6 Development and production of biology feeds and albumen feeds

2. Tobacco Processing Industry

2.1 Production of secondary cellulose acetate and processing of tows

2.2 Production of tobacco slices in the way of paper making

3. Textile Industry

3.1 Production of special textiles for engineering use

3.2 Weaving and dyeing as well as post dressing of high-grade surface material

4. Leather, Coat Products Industry

4.1 Processing of wet blue skin of pig, cow and sheep with new technology

4.2 Post ornament and processing of bather with new technology

5. Lumber Processing Industry and Bamboo, Rattan, Palm, Grass Products Industry

5.1 Development and production of new technology and products for the comprehensive utilization of 'sub-quality, small wood and fuel wood' and bamboo in the forest area

6. Paper Making and Paper Products Industry

6.1 Construction and operation of integrated engineering of raw material base with an annual production capacity of over 300 thousand tons of chemical wood pulp or an annual production capacity of over 100 thousand tons of chemical mechanical wood pulp (CTMP, BCTMP, APMP) (joint ventures or cooperative joint ventures only)

6.2 Production of high-quality paper and cardboard (excluding newsprint)

7. Petroleum Refining and Coking Industry

7.1 Deep processing of needle coke and coal tar

7.2 Production of hard coke and dry coke quenching

7.3 Production of heavy traffic road asphalt

8. Chemical Raw Material and Products Manufacturing Industry

8.1 Production of alkene through catalyzing and cracking of heavy oil

8.2 Production of ethylene with an annual production capacity of 600 thousand tons or over (the Chinese partners shall hold relative majority of shares)

8.3 Comprehensive utilization of ethylene side-products such as C5 C9

8.4 Mass production of corvic (in the way of ethylene)

8.5 Production of organochlorine serial chemical industrial products (excluding high-residual organochlorine products)

8.6 Comprehensive utilization of basic organic chemical industrial raw materials: the derivatives of benzene, methylbenzenc, (para-, ortho-, or meta-) dimethylobenzene

8.7 Production of supporting raw materials for synthesized materials (bisphenol-A, 4.4' diphenylmethane, diiso-cyan ester, and vulcabond toluene)

8.8 Production of synthetic fiber raw materials: precision terephthalic acid, vinyl cyanide, caprolactam and nylon 66 salt

8.9 Production of synthetic rubber (liquid butadiene styrene rubber by butadiene method, butyl rubber, isoamyl rubber, butadiene neoprene rubber, butadiene rubber, acrylic rubber, chlorophydrin rubber)

8.10 Production of engineering plastics and plastic alloys

8.11 Fine chemistry industry: new products and technology for catalytic agent, auxiliary and pigment; processing technology for the commercialization of dye (pigment); production of high-tech chemicals for electronics and paper-making, food additives, feed additives, leather chemical products, oil-well auxiliaries, surface active agent, water treatment agent, adhesivcs, inorganic fiber, inorganic powder stuffing and equipment

8.12 Production of auxiliary agent, preparation agent, and dye-stuff for textile and chemical fiber ladder

8.13 Production of depurant of automobile tail gas, catalyzer and other assistant agents

8.14 Production of nature spices, synthetic spices and single ion spices

8.15 Production of high capability dope

8.16 Production of chloridized titanium white

8.17 Production of chlorofluorocarbon substitution

8.18 Production of mass coal chemical industrial products

8.19 Development and production of new technology and products for the forestry chemicals

8.20 Production of ion film for caustic soda

8.21 Production of biologic fertilizers, high-density fertilizers (potash fertilizer, phosphate fertilizer) and compound fertilizers

8.22 Development and production of new varieties of effective, low poison and low residual agriculture chemicals and pesticides

8.23 Development and production of biology agriculture chemicals and pesticides

8.24 Development and production of inorganic, organic and biologic films for environment protection

8.25 Comprehensive utilization and disposal of exhaust gas, waste liquid, waste residue

9. Medicine Industry

9.1 Production of material medicines under patent and administrative protection in our country or chemical material medicines which we need to import

9.2 Vitamins: production of niacin

9.3 Amino acid: production of serine, tryptophan, histidine, etc.

9.4 Production of analgesic-antipyretic medicines with new technique and new equipment

9.5 Production of new variety of anticarcinogen medicines, as well as cardiovascular and cerebrovascular medicines

9.6 Production of new, effective and economical contraceptive medicines and devices

9.7 Production of new variety of medicines which are produced by means of biological engineering technology

9.8 Production of vaccine through genie engineering technology (vaccine against AIDS, vaccine against type-C hepatitis, contraceptive vaccine, etc.)

9.9 Development and production of medicines made from allopelagics

9.10 Production of diagnostic reagent for AIDS and radioimmunity diseases

9.11 Medicines and pharmaceutics: production of new products and new dosage forms adopting new techniques such as slow release, control release, target preparation and absorbed through skins

9.12 Development and applications of new variety of adjuvant medicines

9.13 Processing and production of traditional Chinese herb medicines, products which distill from traditional Chinese herb medicines and Chinese patent medicines (excluding preparing technique of traditional Chinese medicines in small pieces ready for decoction)

9.14 Production of biological medical materials and products

9.15 Production of antibiotic material medicines used for animals (including antibiotics ami chemical synthesis medicines)

9.16 Development and production of new products and new dosage forms of antibiotic medical, anthelmintic, insecticide, anti-coccidiosis medicines used for animals

10. Chemical Fiber Manufacturing Industry

10.1 Production of differential chemical fiber and high, new technological fiber such as aromatic synthetic fiber, ammo synthetic fiber and carbon fiber

10.2 Production of chemical fiber of environmental protection variety such as direct viscose and asepsis spinning, etc.

10.3 Production of polyester used for fiber and non-fiber with a daily production capacity of 400 tons or over

11. Plastic Industry.

11.1 Production of polyimide clingfilm.

11.2 Development and production of new products and new technologies for agricultural films (photolysis film, multifunctional film and the raw materials, etc.)

11.3 Reutilization and counteraction of waste and old plastic

12. Non-metal Mineral Products Processing Industry

12.1 Production of fine-quality floating glass with a daily melting capacity of 500 tons or over (only in mid-west region of China)

12.2 Production of new type dry process cement of clinker with a daily output capacity of 2,000 tons or over (only in the mid-west region of China)

12.3 Production of glass fiber (product line with technology of wire drawing in tank furnace) and glass fiber reinforced plastic products with an annual capacity of 10,000 tons or more

12.4 Production of high level sanitation porcelain with an annual production of 500,000 pieces or over

12.5 Standardization refine of ceramic material and production of high-level decorative materials used for ceramics

12.6 Production of high-level refractory material used in furnaces for glass, ceramics and glass fiber

12.7 Production of inorganic, non-metal materials and products (artificial crystal, high-capability complex materials, special kind of glass, special kind of ceramics, special kind of airproof materials and special kinds of cementation materials)

12.8 Production of new type of building materials (lightweight high-intensity and multi-function materials for wall, high-level environment protecting decorating and finishing materials, high quality water-proof and airproof materials, and effective thermal insulation materials)

12.9 Deep processing of non-metal mineral products (super-fine comminution, high level pure, refined production, modification)

13. Ferrous Metallurgical Smelting and Rolling Processing Industry

13.1 Production of broad and thick armor plate

13.2 Production of galvanized and corrosion-proof aluminium-zincum alloy plates and clad plates.

13.3 Production of direct and fusion reduced iron

13.4 Processing of steel scrap

14. Non-Ferrous Metallurgical Smelting and Rolling Processing Industry

14.1 Production of alumina with an annual production of 300,000 tons or more

14.2 Smelting of gold mines with low quality or difficult to beneficiate (joint ventures or cooperative joint ventures only, wholly foreign-owned enterprises are permitted in west regions)

14.3 Production of hard alloy, tin compound and antimony compound

14.4 Production of non-ferrous composite materials, new type of alloy materials

14.5 Utilization of rare-earth

15. Metal Products Industry

15.1 Design and manufacturing of non-metal products molds

15.2 Design and manufacturing of car and motorcycle molds (including plunger die, injection mold, moldingdie, etc.) and chucking appliances (chucking appliances for welding, inspection jig, etc.)

15.3 Development and production of high-grade hardware for construction, hot-water heating equipment and hardware parts

16. General Machine-building Industry

16.1 Manufacturing of numerically controlled machine tools, digital control system and servomechanism installations which exceed triaxiality linkage

16.2 Manufacturing of high performance welding robot and effective welding and assembling production equipment

16.3 Production of high temperature resistant and insulation material (with F, H insulation class), as well as insulation shaped parts

16.4 Production with techniques of proportional, servo-hydraulic pressure, low-power pneumatic control valve and stuffing static seal

16.5 Production of precision plunger dies, precision cavity molds and standard components of molds

16.6 Manufacturing of precision hearings and all kinds of bearings used specially for principal machines

16.7 Manufacturing of casting and forging blanks for cars and motorcycles

17. Special-purpose Equipment Manufacturing

17.1 Development and manufacturing of new technology and equipment for the storage, preservation, classifying, packing, drying, transporting and processing of food, cotton, oil, vegetables, fruits, flowers, forage grass, meat and aqua-products

17.2 Manufacturing of facility agriculture equipment

17.3 Manufacturing of new technical agriculture and forestry equipment

17.4 Design and manufacturing of engines for tractors, combine harvesters, etc.

17.5 Manufacturing of equipment for reusing in fields and comprehensive utilization of straws and stalks of crop

17.6 Manufacturing of equipment for comprehensive utilization of waste agriculture products and waste fowl and livestock products which are bred in scale

17.7 Manufacturing of water-saving irrigation equipment with new technique

17.8 Manufacturing of earthwork for wet land and desilting machines

17.9 Technology of hydrophily ecological system for protecting environment and equipment manufacturing

17.10 Manufacturing of equipment for scheduling system which is used in long-distance transmitting water engineering

17.11 Manufacturing of special machines and equipment for flood prevention and emergency rescue

17.12 Manufacturing of key equipment in food industry such as high-speed asepsis canning equipment and brander equipment, etc.

17.13 Production technology and key equipment manufacturing of aminophenol, zymin, food additive

17.14 Manufacturing of complete set equipment with a hourly feed processing capacity of 10 tons or more and key spare parts

17.15 Manufacturing of multi-color offset press for web and folio of paper or larger size

17.16 Manufacturing of equipment with new technique for post ornament and processing of leather

17.17 Manufacturing of high-tech involved special industrial sewing machines

17.18 Manufacturing of complete set of equipment of new type of knitting machines, new type of paper (including pulp) making machines

17.19 Design and manufacturing of new type of mechanical equipment for highways and ports

17.20 Manufacturing of equipment for highways and bridges maintenance, automatic detection

17.21 Manufacturing of equipment for operation supervisory control, ventilation, disaster prevention and rescue system of highway and tunnels

17.22 Design and manufacturing of large equipment for railway construction and maintenance

17.23 Manufacturing of equipment for garden machines and tools with new technique

17.24 Manufacturing of special equipment for cities' environmental sanitation

17.25 Manufacturing of machines for road milling and overhauling

17.26 Manufacturing of tunneling diggers, equipment of covered digging for city metro

17.27 Manufacturing of city sewage-disposal equipment with capacity of 80,000 tons/day or more, industrial sewage film treatment equipment, up-flow anaerobic fluidized bed equipment, and other biological sewage disposal equipment, recycling equipment for waste plastics, desulphurization and denitration equipment for industrial boiler, large high-temperature resistant, acid resistant bag dust remover, incinerating equipment for rubbish treatment

17.28 Manufacturing of turbine compressors and combined comminutors of the complete set equipment with an annual production capacity of 300,000 tons or over of synthetic ammonia, 480,000 tons or over of urea, 450,000 tons or over ethylene

17.29 Technique for desulfurization of thermal power station and equipment manufacturing

17.30 Manufacturing of sheet conticasters

17.31 Deep processing technique and equipment manufacturing of plate glass

17.32 Manufacturing of equipment for underpit trackless mining, loading and transporting, mechanical power-driven dump trucks for mining of 100 tons or over, mobile crushers, 3,000 m3 /h or over bucket excavator, 5 m3 or larger mining loader, full-section tunneling machines

17.33 Design and manufacturing of new instruments and equipment for prospecting and exploitation of petroleum

17.34 Manufacturing of cleaning equipment for electromechanical wells and production of medical

17.35 Manufacturing of electronic endoscopes

17.36 Manufacturing of medical X-ray machines set with high-frequency technique, direct digital imagery processing technique and low radiation (80kw or over)

17.37 Manufacturing of equipment for high magnetic field intensity and super-conductivity (MRI)

17.38 Manufacturing of special purpose machines for collecting blood plasma

17.39 Manufacturing of equipment for auto elisa immuno system (including the functions of application of sample, elisa photo meter, wash plate, incubation, data, post treatment, etc.)

17.40 New techniques of quality control of medicine products and new equipment manufacturing

17.41 New analytical techniques and extraction technologies, and equipment development and manufacturing for the effective parts of traditional Chinese medicines

17.42 Producing and manufacturing of new packing materials, new containers for medicine, and advanced medicine producing equipment

18. Communication and Transportation Equipment Industries

*18.1 Manufacture of complete automobiles and complete motorcycles

18.2 Manufacture of engines for automobiles and motorcycles

18.3 Manufacture of key spare parts for automobiles: complete brakes, complete driving rods, gearboxes, steering knuckles, fuel pumps of diesel engine, fillers (3 filtering), even speed cardan joints, shock absorber, compound meters, car fastener

18.4 Production of electron-controlled fuel-oil injecting systems, electronic controlled brake and locking-prevention systems, safety aerocysts and other electronic equipment

18.5 Manufacture of key spare pans for motorcycles: carburetors, magnetors, starting motors, disc brakes

18.6 Manufacture of vehicles for special-purpose in petroleum industry: vehicles for deserts, etc.

18.7 Technology and equipment for railway transportation: design and production of locomotives and main parts, design and production of equipment for railways and bridges, related technology and equipment production for rapid transit railway, production of equipment for communicational signals and transportation safety monitoring, production of electric railway equipment and instrument

18.8 Equipment for urban rapid transit track transportation: design and manufacture of powered car and main parts for metro, city light rail

18.9 Design and manufacture of civil planes (the Chinese party shall hold a certain amount of shares to gain control of business)

18.10 Production of spares parts for civil planes

18.11 Design and manufacture of civil helicopters (the Chinese party shall hold the larger amount of shares)

18.12 Design and manufacture of aeroplane engines (the Chinese party shall hold the larger part of shares)

18.13 Design and manufacture of civil air-borne equipment (the Chinese party shall hold the larger part of shares)

18.14 Manufacture of light gas-turbine engine

18.15 Design and manufacture of crankshafts of low-speed diesel engine for vessel

18.16 Repairing, design and manufacture of special vessels, high-performance vessels (the Chinese party shall hold the relatively larger amount of shares)

18.17 Design and manufacture of the equipment and accessories of high-speed diesel engines, auxiliary engines, radio communication and navigation for vessels (the Chinese party shall hold the relatively larger amount of shares)

18.18 Manufacture of fishing boats and yachts made of glass fiber reinforced plastic

19. Electric Machinery and Equipment Industries

19.1 Thermal power plant equipment: manufacture of super critical units of 600,000kw or over, large gas-turbine, gas-steam combined cycle power equipment, coal gasification combined cyclic (TGCC) technique and equipment, pressure boost fluidized bed (PFBC), large air-cooling power units of600,000kw or over (for joint ventures or cooperative joint ventures only)

19.2 Hydropower plant equipment: manufacture of large pump-storage power units of 150,000kw and over, large tubular turbine units of 150,000kw or over (joint ventures or cooperative joint ventures only)

19.3 Nuclear-power plant equipment: manufacture of power units of 600,000kw or over (joint ventures or cooperative joint ventures only)

19.4 Power transmitting and transforming equipment: manufacture of super high-voltage DC power transmitting and transforming equipment of 500 kilovolts or over (joint ventures or cooperative joint ventures only)

20. Electronic and Telecommunications Industries

20.1 Manufacture of digital television, digital video camera, digital record player, digital sound-playing equipment

20.2 Manufacture of new type plate displays, medium and high resolution color kinescope and glass shielding

20.3 Manufacture of digital audio and visual coding or decoding equipment, digital broadcasting TV studio equipment, digital cable TV system equipment, digital audio broadcast transmission equipment

20.4 Design of integrated circuit and production of large scale integrated circuit with a line width of 0.35 micron or smaller

20.5 Manufacture of medium- and large-sized computers, portable microcomputers, high-grade server

20.6 Development and manufacture of drivers of high capacity compact disk and disk and related parts

20.7 Manufacture of 3-dimension CAD, CAT, CAM, CAE and other computer application system

20.8 Development and manufacture of software

20.9 Development and production of materials specific for semi-conductor and components

20.10 Manufacture of electronic equipment, testing equipment, tools and moulds

20.11 Manufacture of new type electronic components and parts (slice components, sensitive components, sensors, frequency monitoring and selecting components, hybrid integrated circuit, electrical and electronic components, photoelectric components, new type components for machinery and electronics)

20.12 Manufacture of hi-tech green batteries: non-mercury alkali-manganese batteries, powered nickel-hydrogen batteries, lithium-ion batteries, high-capacity wholly sealed maintenance-proof lead-acid accumulators, fuel batteries, pillar-shaped zinc-air batteries

20.13 Development and manufacture of key components for high-density digital compact disk driver

20.14 Manufacture of recordable compact disk (CD-R, CD-RW, DVD-R, DVD-ARM)

20.15 Design and manufacture of civil satellites (the Chinese party shall hold the large proportion of shares)

20.16 Manufacture of civil satellites effective payload (the Chinese party shall hold the larger proportion of shares)

20.17 Manufacture of spare parts for civil satellites

20.18 Design and manufacture of civil carrier rockets (the Chinese party shall hold the larger proportion of shares)

20.19 Manufacture of telecommunication system equipment for satellites

20.20 Manufacture of receiving equipment of satellite navigation and key components (joint ventures or cooperative joint ventures only)

20.21 Manufacture of optical fiber perform rod

20.22 Manufacture of serial transmission equipment of digital microwave synchronization of 622 MB/S

20.23 Manufacture of serial transmission equipment of phototiming synchronization of 10 GR/S

20.24 Manufacture of equipment for cut-in communication network with broad bond

20.25 Manufacture of optical cross-linking equipment (OXC)

20.26 Manufacture of ATM and IP data communication system

20.27 Manufacture of mobile communication systems (GSM, CDMA, DCS1800,

 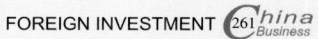

PHS, DECT, IMT2000): mobile telephone, base station, switching equipment and digital colonization system equipment

20.28 Development and manufacture of high-end router, network switchboard of gigabit per second or over

20.29 Manufacture of equipment for air traffic control system (joint ventures or cooperative joint ventures only)

21. Machinery Industries for Instrument and Meter, Culture and Office

21.1 Development and production of digital cameras and key components

21.2 Development and manufacture of precision on-line measuring instrument

21.3 Manufacture of new technical equipment for safe production and environment protection detecting instrument

21.4 Manufacture of new-tech equipment of water quality and fume on-line detecting instrument

21.5 Manufacture of instrument and equipment for hydrological data collecting, processing, transmitting and flood warning

21.6 Production of spare parts and materials for new type meters (mainly new switches and function materials for meters such as intelligent sensors, socket connector, flexible circuit board, photoelectric switches and proximity switches.)

21.7 Manufacture of new type printing devices (laser printers, ink-jet printers)

21.8 Maintenance of precision instrument and equipment, post-sale services

22. Other Manufacture Industries

22.1 Development and utilization of clean-coal technical product (coal gasification, coal liquefaction, water-coal, industrial lump-coal)

22.2 Coal ore dressing by washing and comprehensive utilization of powered coal (including desulphurized plaster), coal gangue

IV. Producing and Supplying of Power, Gas and Water

1. Construction and management of thermal-power plants with a single unit installed capacity of 300,000kw or above

2. Construction and management of power plants with the technology of clean coal burning

3. Construction and management of heat power plants

4. Construction and management of natural gas power stations

5. Construction and management of hydropower stations with the main purpose of power generating

6. Construction and management of nuclear power stations (the Chinese party shall hold the larger proportion of shares.)

7. Construction and management of new energy power plants (solar energy, wind energy, magnetic energy, geothermal energy, tide energy and biological mass energy, etc.)

8. Construction and management of urban water plants

V. Water Resources Management Industry

1. Construction and management of key water control projects for comprehensive utilization (the Chinese party shall hold the relatively larger proportion of shares)

VI. Communications and Transportation, Warehousing, Post and Telecommunications Services

1. Construction and management of grid of national trunk railways (the Chinese party shall hold the larger proportion of shares)

2. Construction and management of feeder railways, local railways and related bridges, tunnels and ferry facilities (joint ventures or cooperative joint ventures only)

3. Construction and management of highways, bridges and tunnels.

4. Construction and management of public dock facilities of ports

5. Construction and management of civil airports (the Chinese party shall hold the relatively larger proportion of shares.)

6. Air transportation companies (the Chinese party shall hold the larger proportion of shares)

7. Airline companies catering for agriculture, forest and fishery (for joint ventures or cooperative joint ventures only.)

*8. Liner and tramp international maritime transportation services

*9. International multi-modal container transport

*10. Road freight transportation companies

11. Construction and management of oil (gas) pipelines, oil (gas) depots and petroleum wharf

12. Construction and management of the facilities of coal pipeline delivery

13. Construction and management of storage facilities relating to transportation services

VII. Wholesale and Retail Trade

*1. Wholesale, retail and logistic distribution of commodities in general

VIII. Real Estate
1. Development and construction of ordinary residential houses

IX. Social Services
1. Public Facility Service Industries

1.1 Construction and management of urban access-controlled roads

1.2 Construction and management of metro and city light rail (The Chinese party shall hold the larger proportion of shares)

1.3 Construction and management of treatment plants for sewage, garbage, the dangerous wastes (incineration and landfill), and the facilities of environment pollution treatment

2. Information, Consultation Service Industries

2.1 Information consulting agencies of international economy, science and technology, environmental protection

*2.2 Accounting and auditing

X. Public Health, Sports and Social Welfare Industries
1. Services for the elderly and the handicapped.

XI. Education, Culture and Arts, Broadcasting, Film and TV Industries
1. Higher education institutes (joint ventures or cooperative joint ventures only)

XII. Scientific Research and Poly-technology Service Industries
1. Biological engineering technology and bio-medical engineering technology

2. Isotope, irradiation and laser technology

3. Ocean exploitation and ocean energy development technology

4. Seawater desalting and seawater utilization technology

5. Oceanic monitoring technology

6. Technology of energy saving

7. Technology of resource recycling and comprehensive utilization

8. Technology of environmental pollution treatment and control

9. Desertification prevention and sand control technology

10. Technology applied to civil satellites

11. Centers for research and development

12. Centers for hi-tech, new products developing, and incubation of enterprises

XIII. Permitted foreign invested projects whose products are to be wholly exported directly

Catalogue of Restricted Foreign Investment Industries

I. Farming, Forestry, Animal Husbandry and Fishery Industries

1. Development and production of grains (including potatoes), cotton and oil-seed (The Chinese party shall hold the larger proportion of shares)

2. Processing of the logs of precious varieties of trees (joint ventures or cooperative joint ventures only)

II. Mining and Quarrying Industries

1. Exploring and extracting of minerals including wolfram, tin, antimony, molybdenum, barite, and fluorite (joint ventures or cooperative joint ventures only.)

2. Exploring and mining of precious metals (gold, silver, platinum families.)

3. Exploring and mining of precious non-metals such as diamond.

4. Exploring and mining of special and rare kinds of coal (The Chinese party shall hold the larger proportion of shares.)

5. Mining of szaibelyite and szaibelyite iron ores.

6. Mining of celestine.

III. Manufacturing Industries

1. Food Processing Industry

1.1 Production of millet wine and spirits of famous brands

1.2 Production of soda beverage of foreign brand

1.3 Production of synthetic sweet agent such as saccharin

1.4 Processing of fat or oil

2. Tobacco Processing Industry

2.1 Production of cigarettes and filter tips

3. Textile Industry

3.1 Wool spinning, cotton spinning

3.2 Silk reeling

4. Printing and Record Medium Reproduction Industry.

 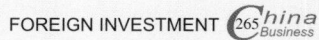

4.1 Printing of publications (The Chinese party shall hold the larger proportion of shares except printing of package decoration.)

5. Petroleum Processing and Coking Industries.
5.1 Construction and management of refineries.

6. Chemical Raw Material and Products Manufacturing Industry
6.1 Production of ionic membrane caustic soda
6.2 Production of sensitive materials
6.3 Production of benzidine
6.4 Production of chemical products from which narcotics are easily made (ephedrine, 3, 4-idene dihydro phenyl-2-acctonc, phenylacetic acid, 1-phenyl-2-acetone, heliotropin, safrole, isosafrole, acetic oxide)
6.5 Production of sulphuric acid basic titanium white
6.6 Processing of baron, magnesium, iron ores
6.7 Barium salt production

7. Medical and Pharmaceutical Products Industry
7.1 Production of chloramphenicol, penicillin G, lincomycin, gentamicin, dihydrostreptomycin, amikacin, tetracycline hydrochloride, oxytetracycline, medemycin, kitasamycin, ilotyin, ciprofloxacin and offoxacin
7.2 Production of analgin, paracetamol, Vitamin B1, Vitamin B2, Vitamin C, Vitamin E
7.3 Production of immunity vaccines, bacterins, antitoxins and anatoxin (BCG vaccine, poliomyelitis, DPT vaccine, measles vaccine, Type-B encephalitis, epidemic cerebrospinal meningitis vaccine) which included in the State's Plan
7.4 Production of material medicines for addiction narcotic and psychoactivc drug (The Chinese party shall hold the larger proportion of shares)
7.5 Production of blood products
7.6 Production of non-self-destructible expendable injectors, transfusion systems, blood transfusion systems, blood bags

8. Chemical Fiber Production Industry
8.1 Production of chemical fiber drawnwork of conventional chipper
8.2 Production of viscose staple fiber with an annual single thread output capacity of less than 20,000 tons
8.3 Production of polyester and spandex used for fiber and non-fiber with a daily

production capacity of less than 400 tons

9. Rubber Products
9.1 Cross-ply and old tire recondition (not including radial tire), and production of industrial rubber fittings of low-performance

10. Non-Ferrous Metal Smelting and Rolling Processing Industry
10.1 Smelting and separation of rare earth metal (joint ventures or cooperative joint ventures only)

11. Ordinary Machinery Manufacturing Industry
11.1 Manufacture of containers
11.2 Manufacture of small and medium type ordinary bearings
11.3 Manufacture of truck cranes of less than 50 tons (joint ventures or cooperative joint ventures only)

12. Special Purpose Equipment Manufacturing Industry
12.1 Production of low or middle class type-B ultrasonic displays
12.2 Manufacture of equipment for producing long dacron thread and short fiber
12.3 Manufacture of crawler dozers of less than 320 horsepower, wheeled mechanical loaders of less than 3 cubic meter (joint ventures or cooperative joint ventures only)

13. Electronic and Telecommunication Equipment Manufacturing Industry
13.1 Production of satellite television receivers and key parts

IV. Production and Supply of Power, Gas and Water
1. Construction and operation of conventional coal-fired power plants whose unit installed capacity is less than 300,000kw (with the exception of small power grid)

V. Communication and Transportation, Storage, Post and Telecommunication Services
1. Road passenger transport companies
*2. Cross-border automobile transportation companies
*3. Water Transportation companies
*4. Railway freight transportation companies
5. Railway passenger transportation companies (The Chinese party shall hold the

larger proportion of shares)

6. General aviation companies engaging in photographing, prospecting and industry (The Chinese party shall hold the larger proportion of shares)

*7. Tele communication companies

VI. Wholesale and Retail Trade Industries

*1. Commercial companies of commodity trading, direct selling, mail order selling, Internet selling, franchising, commissioned operation, sales agent, commercial management companies, and wholesale, retail and logistic distribution of grain, cotton, vegetable oil, sugar, medicines, tobaccos, automobiles, crude oil, capital goods for agricultural production

*2. Wholesale or retail trade of books, newspaper and periodicals

*3 Distributing and selling of audiovisual products (excluding movies.)

4. Commodity auctions.

*5. Leasing companies.

*6. Agencies (shipping, freight forwarding, tally for foreign vessels, advertising.)

*7. Wholesaling product oil, construction and operation of gasoline stations

8. Foreign trade companies

VII. Banking and Insurance Industries

1. Banks, finance companies, trust investment companies

*2. Insurance companies

*3. Security companies, security investment fund management companies

4. Financial leasing companies

5. Foreign exchange brokers agencies

*6. Insurance brokerage companies

VIII. Property Industry.

1. Development of land in stretches (joint ventures or cooperative joint ventures only)

2. Construction and operation of high-ranking hotels, villas, high-class office buildings and international exhibition centers

IX. Service Industry.

1. Public Facility Service Industries

1.1 Construction and operation of networks of gas, heat, water supply and water drainage in large and medium sized cities (The Chinese party shall hold the larger proportion of shares)

2. Information, Consultation Service Industries
2.1 Legal consulting

X. Public Health, Sports and Social Welfare Industries

1. Medical treatment establishments (joint ventures or cooperative joint ventures only.)
2. Construction and operation of golf courts

XI. Education, Culture and Arts, Broadcasting, Film and TV Industries

1. Education establishments for senior high school students (joint ventures or cooperative joint ventures only)
2. Construction and operation of cinemas (The Chinese party shall hold the larger proportion of shares.)

XII. Scientific Research and Poly-technical Services Industries

1. Mapping companies (The Chinese party shall hold the larger proportion of shares)
*2. Inspection, verification and attestation companies for imported and exported goods

XIII. Other industries restricted by the State or international treaties that China has concluded or taken part in

Catalogue of Prohibited Foreign Investment Industries

I. Farming, Forestry, Animal Husbandry and Fishery Industries.

1. Cultivation of China's rare precious breeds (including tine genes in plants industry, husbandry and aquatic products industry)
2. Genetically modified seeds breeding.
3. Fishing in the sea area within the Government jurisdiction and in in-land water

II. Mining and Quarrying Industries

1. Exploring, mining and dressing of radioactive mineral products

2. Exploring, mining and dressing of rare earth metal

III. Manufacturing Industry

1. Food Processing Industry

1.1 Processing of green lea and special tea with China's traditional crafts (famous tea, dark tea, etc.)

2. Medical and Pharmaceutical Products Industry

2.1 Processing of traditional Chinese medicines that have been listed as the State protection resources (musk, licorice, jute, etc.)

2.2 Application of preparing technique of traditional Chinese medicines in small pieces ready for decoction, and production of the products of secret recipe of traditional Chinese patent medicines

3. Non-Ferrous Metal Smelting and Rolling Processing Industry

3.1 Smelting and processing of radioactive mineral products

4. Weapon and Ammunition Manufacture

5. Other Manufacturing Industries

5.1 Ivory carving

5.2 Tiger-hone processing

5.3 Production of bodiless lacquerware

5.4 Production of enamel products

5.5 Production of Xuan-paper (rice paper) and ingot-shaped tablets of Chinese ink

5.6 Production of carcinogenic, teratogenic, mutagenesis and persistent organic pollutant products

IV. Production and Supply of Power, Gas and Water

1. Construction and operation of power network

V. Communication and Transportation, Storage, Post and Telecommunication Services

1. Companies of air traffic control

2. Companies of postal services

VI. Banking and Insurance Industries

1. Futures companies

VII. Service Industry

1. Development of wild animal and plant resources protected by the State.
2. Construction and operation of animal and plant natural reserves.
3. Lottery industry (including gambling in the form of horserace)
4. Pornographic services

VIII. Education, Culture and Arts, Radio, Film and TV Establishments

1. Educational institutes of basic education (compulsory education)
2. Business of publishing, master issuing, and import of books, newspaper and periodicals
3. Business of publishing, master issuing and import of audio and visual products and electronic publications
4. News agencies.
5. Radio stations, TV stations, radio and TV transmission networks at various levels (transmission stations, relaying stations, radio and TV satellites, satellite up-linking stations, satellite receiving stations, microwave stations, monitoring stations, cable broadcasting and TV transmission networks)
6. Companies producing, publishing, issuing and playing radio and TV programs
7. Companies of films producing and issuing
8. Companies of video tape playing

IX. Other Industries.

1. Projects that endanger the safety and performance of military facilities

X. Other industries restricted by the State or international treaties that China has concluded or taken part in

Note: The items marked '' are related to the commitment of China's accession to WTO. Please see the Attachment for details.*

Attachment

I. Notes for Catalogue of Encouraged Industries:

1. Prospecting and exploitation of oil and natural gas: In cooperation with Chinese partner only.

2. Exploitation of oil deposits (fields) with low osmosis: In cooperation with Chinese partner only.

3. Development and application of new technologies that can increase recovery factor of crude oil: In cooperation with Chinese partner only.

4. Development and application of new technologies for prospecting and exploitation of petroleum, such as geophysical prospecting, well drilling, well logging and downhole operation, etc.: In cooperation with Chinese partner only.

5. Manufacturing of automobile and motorcycle: The proportion of foreign investments shall not exceed 50%.

6. International liner and tramp maritime transportation business: The proportion of foreign investments shall not exceed 49%.

7. International container multi-modal transportation: The proportion of foreign investments shall not exceed 50%. Foreign majority ownership will be permitted no later than Dee. 11, 2002. Wholly foreign ownership will be permitted no later than Dec. 11, 2005.

8. Road freight transportation companies: Foreign majority ownership will be permitted no later than Dec. 11, 2002. Wholly foreign ownership will be permitted no later than Dec. 11, 2004.

9. Wholesale, retail and logistic distribution of general goods: As described in No. 5 of Notes for Catalogue of Restricted Industries of the Appendix 10 Accounting and auditing: In cooperation with Chinese partner and in the form of partnership only.

II. Notes for Catalogue of Restricted Industries:

1. Cross-border automobile transportation companies: Foreign majority ownership will be permitted no later than Dec. 11. 2002. Wholly foreign owned enterprises will be permitted no later than Dec. 11,2004.

2. Water transportation companies. The proportion of foreign investment shall not exceed 49%.

3. Rail freight transportation companies: The proportion of foreign investment

shall not exceed 49%. Foreign majority ownership will he permitted no later than Dec. 11. 2004. Wholly foreign owned enterprises will be permitted no later than Dec, 11. 2007.

4. Telecommunication Companies

4.1 Value-added services and paging services in basic telecommunication services: Foreign investments are permitted no later than Dec. 11, 2001 with the proportion of foreign investment not exceeding 30%. The proportion of foreign investment in joint venture shall not exceed 49% no later than Dec. 11. 2002, and shall be allowed to reach 50% no later than Dec. 11, 2003.

4.2 Mobile voice and data services in basic telecommunication services; Foreign investments are permitted no later than Dec. 11, 2001 with the proportion of foreign investment not exceeding 25%. The proportion of foreign investment in joint venture shall not exceed 35% no later than Dec. 11, 2002, and shall he allowed to reach 49% no later than Dec. 11,2004.

4.3 Domestic and international services in basic telecommunication services: Foreign investments will be permitted no later than Dec. 11, 2004 with the proportion of foreign investment not exceeding 25%. The proportion of foreign investment in joint venture shall not exceed 35% no later than Dec. 11, 2006 and shall be allowed to reach 49% no later than Dec. 11, 2007.

5. Commodities trade, direct selling, mail order selling. Internet selling, sales agent, franchising, commercial management; whole sale, retail and logistic distribution of grain, cotton, vegetable oil, sugar, pharmaceutical products, tobacco, automobile, crude oil, capital goods for agricultural production; whole sale and retail of books, newspapers, periodicals; whole sale of product nil, construction and operation of gasoline station

5.1 Commission agents services and wholesale trade services (excluding salt, tobacco): Foreign invested enterprises are permitted no later than Dec. 11, 2002 with foreign investment not exceeding 50%, but can not engage in the distribution of books, newspapers, magazines, pharmaceutical products, pesticides, mulching films, chemical fertilizers, processed oil and crude oil. Foreign majority ownership will be permitted no later than Dec. 11, 2003. And wholly foreign-owned enterprises will be permitted no later than Dec. 11, 2004, and can engage in the distribution of books, newspapers, magazines, medicines, farm chemical, mulching films. The distribution of chemical fertilizers, processed oil and crude oil are permitted no later than Dec. 11,2006.

5.2 Retailing services (excluding tobacco): Foreign invested enterprises are permitted but can not engage in the distribution of books, newspapers, magazines, pharmaceutical products, pesticides, mulching films, chemical fertilizers, processed oil. The proportion of foreign investment can reach 50% no later than Dec. 11, 2002, and can engage in the distribution of books, newspapers and magazines. Foreign majority ownership will be permitted no later than Dec 11, 2003. And wholly foreign-owned enterprises will be permitted no later than Dee. 11, 2004, and can engage in the distribution of pharmaceutical products, pesticides, mulching films, and processed oil. The distribution of chemical fertilizers is permitted no later than Dec. 11, 2006. Foreign investors can not take majority ownership of a Chain-store that has over 30 branch stores and engages in the distribution of automobiles (the limitation will be lift no later than Dec. 11, 2006), books, newspapers, magazines, pharmaceutical products, pesticides, mulching films, processed oil, chemical fertilizers, grain, vegetable oil, sugar, tobacco, cotton.

5.3 Franchising and wholesale or retail trade services away from a fixed location: Foreign invested enterprises are permitted no later than Dec. 11, 2004.

6. The distribution of audiovisual products (excluding movies): Foreign investments shall be permitted no later than Dee.11, 2004.

7. Goods leasing companies: Foreign majority ownership shall be permitted no later than Dec11, 2002. Wholly foreign owned enterprises shall be permitted no later than Dec. 11,2004.

8. Agencies
8.1 Ship agencies: The proportion of foreign investment shall not exceed 49%.

8.2 Freight forwarding agencies (excluding those services specially reserved for Chinese postal authorities): The proportion of foreign investment shall not exceed 50% (not exceed 49% in the case of courier services). Foreign majority ownership shall be permitted no later than Dec. 11, 2002. Wholly foreign owned enterprises shall be permitted no later than Dec. 11, 2005.

8.3 Cargo handling for foreign vessels: In forms of joint ventures or cooperative joint ventures only

8.4 Advertising agencies: Tile proportion of foreign investment shall not exceed 49%. Foreign majority ownership shall be permitted no later than Dec. 11, 2003. Wholly foreign owned enterprises shall be permitted no later than Dec. 11, 2005.

9. Insurance

9.1 Non-life insurance companies: The proportion of foreign investments shall not exceed 51%. Wholly foreign owned enterprises shall be permitted no later than Dec. 11, 2003.

9.2 Life insurance companies: The proportion of foreign investments shall not exceed 50%.

10. Securities company, securities investment fund management companies

10.1 Securities companies: Foreign investments shall be permitted no later than Dee. 11, 2004 with the proportion of foreign investment not exceeding 1/3.

10.2.Securities investment fund management companies: The proportion of foreign investment shall not exceed 33%. The proportion of foreign investment shall be allowed to reach 49% no later than Dec. 11, 2004.

11. Insurance brokerage companies: The proportion of foreign investment shall not exceed 50%. The proportion shall be allowed to reach 51% no later than Dec. 11, 2004. Wholly foreign owned enterprises shall be permitted no later than Dec. 11, 2006.

12. Companies of inspection, verification and attestation for imported and exported goods: Foreign majority ownership shall be permitted no later than Dec 11, 2003. Wholly foreign owned enterprises shall be permitted no later than Dec 11, 2005.

INTELLECTUAL PROPERTY RIGHTS

Since the end of 1970s, while taking an active part in activities regarding intellectual property rights with related international organizations and enhancing contacts and cooperation with other countries of the world, China has started to draw up laws and statutes in this regard. Although the interval is only a score of years between that time and the present day, the system of intellectual property rights China has established is already a comparatively complete legal system.

LAWS AND STATUTES CONCERNING INTELLECTUAL PROPERTY RIGHTS

The intellectual property rights stipulated in the General Principles of the Civil Law of the People's Republic of China mainly include copyright, patent right, exclusive right to use a registered trademark, discovery right, invention right and right of achievement in scientific and technological research. The current legislative system concerning intellectual property rights includes patent law, trademark law, copyright law and anti-unfair competition law. China has also promulgated the Customs Regulations on Protection of Intellectual Property Rights, Regulations on Protection of New Plant Species, etc. The new Criminal Law taking effect in 1997 has specially added in it stipulations concerning crimes in connection with intellectual property rights. Taking the above laws and regulations as a whole, we can say that China has basically been in line with international standard in the protection of intellectual property rights.

Trademark law

The Trademark Law of the People's Republic of China and its regulations for implementation are in conformity with international principles in trademark registration procedures including application, examination and registration, etc. In 1993, China revised the Trademark Law and its Regulations for implementation in which the scope of trademark protection is expanded and stipulations on registration and management of service marks added. In the revised Trademark Law in 2001, the subject of the exclusive right to use a registered trademark is specified as including natural persons such as a farmer, who is entitled to apply for trademark registration for the farm pro-

Microsoft's activity to popularize "Scheme for solving E-government affairs"

duce he has grown. At the same time, visible signs including color combination, three-dimensional symbol, etc. are also protected. Ill intentioned rush for registration of other's trademark is prohibited and economic compensation for infringement of trademark stipulated.

In 1993, China enacted the Complementary Stipulations on Punishment of Fake Registered Trademarks, which further stepped up the work in punishing fake registered trademark and handling trademark infringement behavior. In 1996, the Interim Measures for Authentication and Management of Famous Trademarks and Measures for the Implementation of International Registration of Marks Under Madrid Agreement were promulgated.

Patent law

The Patent Law of the People's Republic of China and its regulations for implementation becoming effective in 1985 has extended the scope of protecting intellectual property rights to patent rights for inventions-creations. In 1992, China revised its Patent Law. In 2001 China as a developing country combined its state conditions with the patent system universally adopted in the world and revised again its Patent Law in such a way that it came up to the standard for the protection of the patent rights stipulated in the Agreement Regarding Trade-Related Intellectual Property Rights (TRIPS). Meanwhile a lot of revision was made with respect to administration of justice and enforcement of law.

China's Patent Law provides that any invention for which patent rights may be granted must possess novelty, inventiveness and practical applicability. The term of patent right for invention shall be 20 years whereas that for utility model and design shall be 10 years, both counted from the date of filing. China practices the principles of "the first to file an application", "national treatment", "right of priority", "independence of patent" and the system of examination, cancellation of patent right after authorization, and declaration of invalidity. China's Patent Law protects all kinds of materials and processing technology including chemicals and medicines.

Copyright

The Copyright Law of the People's Republic of China was issued in1990. This Law and its regulations for implementation define clearly the protection of the copyright of authors in their literary, artistic and scientific works and copyright-related rights. According to the Law, not only written or oral works, musical, dramatic, *quyi* (folk performing art), choreographic works, works of fine arts, photographic works,

In front of the cinema.

cinematographic works and works created by virtue of an analogous method of film production, drawing of engineering design, and product design, maps, sketches and other graphic works, but also computer software are included in the scope of copyright protection. The Regulations on Computer Software Protection issued in 1991 is a coordinated document stipulating specific measures for implementation of computer software protection. The Regulations for the Implementation of the International Copyright Treaties issued in 1992 stipulates specifically the rights enjoyed by the copyright owners of foreign works in the light of international treaties. In 1994, Decisions on Punishment on Infringement of Copyright was issued.

The revised 2001 Copyright Law has already been in line with international practices. It has strengthened protection for copyright owners, improved procedures of copyright protection, established collective copyright management organization, enhanced the power of administrative and law enforcing departments, and added new measures for judicial procedures such as temporary prohibitions.

China applies automatic protection principles on copyrights, which means that a piece of work once completed, no matter in what form it is created, if it is original and can be duplicated in a certain form, shall be protected by the Copyright Law. No registration is needed except for computer software.

International conventions and treaties with respect to intellectual property rights China has acceded to

In order to be in line with international practices in the protection of intellectual property rights, China has actively joined a number of international organizations and acceded to treaties concerning intellectual property rights since 1980.

1980   Became a member country of world intellectual property right organization.

1985   Became a member country of Paris Convention for the Protection of Industrial Property.

1989   The World Intellectual Property Rights Organization passed the Treaty for the Protection of Intellectual Property Rights of Integrated Circuits. China was one of the first signatory states of the treaty.

1989   Became a member country of Madrid Agreement Concerning the International Registration of Marks.

1992   Became a member country of Bern Pact for the Protection of Literary and Artistic Works and World Copyright Convention.

1993   Became a member country of Convention for the Protection of Recording Product Makers to Guard Against Duplicating the Products Without Permission.

1994   Became a member country of Treaty of Patent Cooperation. China Patent

Bureau became acceptance country of the treaty, an international retrieval unit and a preliminary examination country.

1994   Became a member country of Nice Agreement Concerning International Classification of Service and Commodities Used for Trademark Registration.

1995   Became a member country of Budapest Treaty for the Protection of Microbe Used for Patent Procedures Internationally Recognized.

1995   Submitted Instrument of Accession of Madrid Agreement Concerning the International Registration of Marks.

1996   Became a member country of Locarno Agreement Concerning the Establishment of International Classification of Industrial Product Designing.

1996   Submitted Instrument of Accession of Strasburg Agreement for International Patent Classification.

China has taken part in the TRIPS talks and initialed the final text.

China has also cooperated with Asian-Pacific Organization for Economic Cooperation on intellectual property rights. In China's Unilateral Program of Action for the Implementation of Trade and Investment Liberalization and Facilitation regularly submitted to this organization, the status quo and objective of intellectual property rights in China are included. China has also entered into agreements and treaties concerning cooperation and protection of intellectual property rights with European Union, the United States, Russian and France.

The law enforcement organization of China adheres to the principles of the most favored country and national treatment in the protection of expatriates' intellectual property rights in accordance with the laws of China and related international conventions China has acceded to.

APPLICATION FOR TRADEMARK AND PATENT RIGHTS

Trademark registration

As is stipulated in the Trademark Law, any application for the registration of a trademark by a foreigner or a foreign firm shall be in accordance with the agreement entered into between China and the country the applicant belongs to or the international treaties both countries acceded to. Otherwise the principle of reciprocity shall be followed. Accordingly, China's principle on foreign trademark registration is 1. Handling trademark registration according to the agreement concluded. China has concluded trademark registration agreements with several dozens of countries through signing official documents or exchange of notes; 2. Handling the matter according to international treaties acceded to such as the Paris Convention for the Protection of Industrial Property, the basic principle of which is national treatment. China as a member country is obliged to abide by the principle; 3. Adhering to the principle of reciprocity China has adopted starting from January1, 1978 in flexibly handling foreign trademark registration.

Meanwhile, China's Trademark Law provides that foreigners or foreign firms applying for trademark registration or handling matters concerning trademark in China, shall entrust the organization appointed by the state with the work.

Application for patent rights

The Patent Law of China follows the stipulations specified in the Paris Convention for the Protection of Industrial Property in protecting foreigners' patent rights. Foreigners having regular residence or business offices shall be granted the same treatment as that granted to Chinese citizens and legal persons, that is, the national treatment. Foreigners without regular residence or business offices applying for patent rights shall be handled in line with specific conditions as below:

1. If the country that the applicant belongs to has concluded a bilateral treaty with China concerning patent affairs, the matter shall be conducted in the light of the treaty.

Brand competition.

2. If China and the country the applicant belongs to have both acceded to an international treaty concerning patent law, the matter shall be conducted in accordance with such treaty.

3. In the absence of the above conditions, the matter shall be conducted following the principle of reciprocity, which means that China shall permit unconditionally the nationals of a country to apply for and be granted patent rights in accor-

dance with China's Patent Law on condition that the Patent Law of the corresponding country also grants unconditionally patent protection to foreigners. If the country the applicant belongs to provides in its Patent Law that a mutual favored treatment for foreigners applying for patent rights is granted by a corresponding country as a pre-requisite for applying for patent rights in that country, China shall act on the same prerequisite in handling the matter.

China's Patent Law provides that foreigners, foreign firms or other organizations without regular residence or business offices applying for patent rights or handling patent-related affairs shall entrust a patent agency appointed by the State Council of China with the work.

COMMITMENT FOR THE PROTECTION OF INTELLECTUAL PROPERTY RIGHTS

In the legal documents regarding China's accession to WTO, China has made commitment for intellectual property protection. Main points are as follows:

Regulate and amend laws and regulations with respect to intellectual property protection

China's legislation in relation to intellectual property rights is basically in con-formity with the Agreement Regarding Trade-Related Intellectual Property Rights (hereinafter called TRIPS). Prior to China's entry into WTO, China already amended its Patent Law and committed to complete, at the time of entering the WTO, the amendment of the Copyright Law, the Trademark Law and related regulations for implementation covering different aspects of the "TRIPS" so as to implement in an all-round way the TRIPS agreement.

National treatment and most favored treatment applying to foreign nationals

China is to protect foreigners' intellectual property rights in line with the agree-ment China has entered into with the country involved, or any international conven-tion to which both countries have acceded to, or the principle of reciprocity.

China is committed to the amendment of related laws and regulations, and the adoption of other measures to ensure that the national treatment and most favored treatment granted to foreign rights holders in connection with every aspect of intel-lectual property are fully in conformity with the TRIPS, including that the local Copyright Bureau is entitled to handle legal affairs involving foreign copyright holders without authorization from the State Copyright Bureau in Beijing.

Copyright protection

China has made commitment for amendment of copyright system, including the Regulations for the Implementation of the Copyright Law and Regulations for the Implementation of International Copyright Treaties so as to ensure that China's copyright system is fully in conformity with its obligation specified in the TRIPS.

The amended Copyright Law shall define clearly the remuneration payment mechanism for sound recordings broadcasted by radio or television stations; the right to rent computer software and cinematographic works; machine performance right; and the right to communicate to the public. It shall also define clearly related protection measures, interim measures for database compilation protection, and measures for raising statutory compensatory damages and intensifying check on acts of infringement.

Note: The TRIPS provides that the term of copyright protection shall not be shorter than 50 years. The term for performance and sound recordings shall be at least 50 years, and that for mass media at least 20 years.

Trademark (including service marks) protection

The Trademark Law shall be amended mainly as follows: three-dimensional sign, color combination, letter of the alphabet and number may be applied for registration as a trademark. Collective marks and certification marks (including geographical indication) shall be included in the Law. The protection of official signs and well-known trademarks shall be added. Preference shall be added. Amend current trademark right confirmation system and offer opportunities for the party involving gains or losses to seek judicial examination. Crack down on serious infringement acts and improve trademark infringement compensation system.

Geographic indication (including the protection of names of place of origin)

China is committed to abiding by the stipulations specified in the TRIPS with respect to geographic indication.

Note: Stipulations specified in the TRIPS with respect to the protection of geographic indication include that registration application for trademarks with phony geographic indication shall be refused or declared invalid so as to avoid misunderstanding about the real origin of the commodity and prevent unfair competition; and that more efficient protection shall be given to the geographic indication of grape wine and liquor so as to prevent the use of geo-graphic indication exclusively used for some specific grape wine and liquor for similar com-modities from other places of origin.

Patent rights

1. Patent rights are refused for inventions that go against social ethics.

China pledges that the revised Regulations for the Implementation of the Patent Law is in complete conformity with Clause 2 of Article 27 of the TRIPS. The Clause 2 of Article 27 of the TRIPS provides that the member countries are entitled to refuse the application for patent rights for an invention of some products or process in mak-ing the products if the commercial development of them may cause serious damage to public order or social ethics, including damage to the environment and lives of humans or animals or plants.

2. Compulsory license for exploitation of the patent

China has amended the Regulations for the Implementation of the Patent Law to ensure that (1) In special cases a patent can be used without authorization from the patentee (including used by the government or with the authorization of the government.) That is called compulsory license or non-voluntary license; (2) The entity or individual that is granted a compulsory license for exploitation shall pay to the patentee a reasonable exploitation fee; (3) The compulsory license for exploita-tion of the patent is granted mainly for the service for domestic market in China; (4) In case semi-conducting technique is involved, the patent is limited to non-commer-cial public use, or is used to make up for the restriction in competition as determined by judicial or administrative procedures.

Protection of unrevealed data with respect to agricultural chemicals and medicines using new chemical composition

To guard against illicit commercial use, China affords effective protection for unrevealed experimental data or other data submitted as required for applying for marketing license for agricultural chemicals and medicines using new chemical composition, except for the fact that the revealing of the data is indispensable for the protection of public interest or that protective measures have already taken to prevent illicit use of the data. The protection includes enacting laws and regulations to ensure that in a period of at least 6 years from the date of granting marketing license to the data submitter, nobody shall apply for marketing license based on that data without permission of the data submitter. During this period of time, any second applicant for marketing license has to submit his own data before the application can be accepted.

All those using new chemical-composition medicines or agricultural chemical materials are entitled to data protection, whether they have been granted patent protection or not.

Kodak color printing chain store at metro station

Measures curbing abuse of intellectual property rights

China shall abide by the stipulation set forth in the TRIPS and fulfill the obligation to control competition activities under restriction as specified in the permission contract. China shall satisfy in particular the requirements for negotiation with other member countries. Such stipulations shall be applicable for all categories of intellectual property rights.

Note: The TRIPS stipulates the obligation of the member countries to control the restricted competition activities specified in international technology permission contract. As such restricted competition activities may have negative effect on trade and may even impede the transfer and dissemination of technology, member countries may take appropriate measures to forestall or control such activities. At the same time, they may conduct negotiations on restricted competition activities and litigation in progress and work in cooperation with one another in controlling these activities.

Crackdown on activities infringing on intellectual property rights

The measures China has adopted for crackdown on piracy include: as far as judicature is concerned, law courts at all levels shall attach importance to hearing cases concerning intellectual property rights; as far as administration is involved, executive authorities at all levels shall place stress on the work of anti-piracy and moreover, competent authorities shall increase the publication of legal writings catering to the needs of the general public so as to ensure that China's legal environment is adequate to satisfy the requirements of the TRIPS.

Civil procedure and related measures

China is committed to the effective implementation, in the light of judicial rules of civil procedure, of fair and reasonable procedure set forth in the TRIPS and the requirements for evidence submitted by both parties involved.

China is committed to the amendment of related regulations for implementation. Thereby when it is known or has reasons to know that the act of an individual is an infringement on other's intellectual property rights, the infringer shall compensate the right holder a compensation that is sufficient to make up for the losses the right holder has suffered owing to the infringement.

Interim measures adopted by the judicial department

China has promised that the provisions of Article 61 in its Patent Law shall be in conformity with related stipulation prescribed in the TRIPS. The Article 61 states that when the patentee or any interested party has evidence to show that someone is engaging in or is about to engage in an act of infringement and that his legal rights shall be damaged irreparably without checking in time, he may request the people's court to order the infringer to stop the act of infringment and protect the property from being damaged before instituting legal proceedings in the people's court. The interim measures the judicial department adopts shall be implemented in a form in complete compliance with the interim measure clause set forth in the TRIPS. The term "reasonable evidence" refers to any reasonably acquired evidence sufficient to convince the judicial department that the applicant is the right holder, that the applicant's right is being infringed or the infringement is on the point of occurrence, and that the judicial department is entitled to order the applicant to provide earnest money or equal guarantee sufficient to protect the defendant and to prevent abuse of the rights.

Note: The TRIPS states that under the circumstances that any delay may bring the patentee irreparably losses or cause the destruction of evidence, the judicial authorities should adopt prompt and effective measures to protect the evidence accusing infringement, and to check the infringement from happening through prohibiting the imported products from entering the commercial channel within its jurisdiction. At the same time, the judicial authorities are entitled to ask the applicant to produce reasonable and effective evidence and provide earnest money or adequate guarantee to protect the defendant and prevent abuse of the right. The measures that have been adopted shall be re-examined if requested by the defendant.

Measures for administrative punishment

China has promised to enforce the law strictly including inflicting more effective administrative punishment on the infringers. The departments involved such as the State Administration of Industry and Commerce, State Bureau of Quality Supervision, Inspection and Quarantine and the State Copyright Bureau shall be encouraged to exercise the power of finding out, handing in and keeping infringement evidence of infringement such as goods in stock and documents. The competent administrative authorities shall have the power to take punishment measures to prevent infringements and are encouraged to do so. Infringement acts involving repeated offences, willful piracy and imitations shall be turned over to the competent authorities to prosecute in accordance with the regulations set forth in the criminal law.

Measures adopted by the Customs in the protection of intellectual property rights

China shall let intellectual property rights holders know about all procedures with reference to frontier measures that are in complete compliance with the TRIPS.

Stipulations set forth in the TRIPS include that member countries should draw up relevant procedures in the light of related stipulations in which a right holder with justified reasons to suspect that imitated trademarks or piratic goods are likely to be imported, are permitted to submit written application to related judicial or administrative department for suspension of these goods from free circulation. The TRIPS also specifies other measures to be executed when the above procedures are applied, which include application, earnest money or adequate guarantee, notice of suspension from clearance, time limit of suspension, compensation for importers and commodity owners, the right to test and acquire information, actions within the scope of one's powers, relief and importing in very small quantities.

Criminal procedure

China's competent administrative authorities shall propose that the judicial organizations bring down the minimum limit of infringement money beyond which the infringer shall be prosecuted for his criminal liability so that subsequent piracy and imitation acts shall be prevented or reduced. China shall adopt all-roundly the stipulations set forth in the TRIPS starting from its accession to it.

AROUND CHINA

A SURVEY

Judging from its geographical position, social and economic development, China can be divided into three main parts: the central, the eastern and the western. The eastern part consists of 11 provinces (cities, regions): Beijing, Tianjin, Hebei, Liaoning, Shanghai, Jiangsu, Shandong, Zhejiang, Fujian, Guangdong and Hainan. It occupyies an area accounting for 12 per cent with a population accounting for 36 per cent of the national total respectively, and enjoys convenient traffic and high-quality labor resources.

For a fairly long period of time since reform and opening up, the eastern coastal area has been the state's key investment region. The majority of reform measures unveiled in recent years has been executed on a trial basis first in this region. All five special economic zones as well as most open cities in the country are situated here, which have attracted the overwhelming amount of foreign investment. Thanks to an early start in its economic development, the eastern coastal region has become the most flourishing area at home. In 2001, its GDP made up 60 per cent of the national total.

The central and western regions, in contrast, have a weaker economic foundation, a slower progress in industrialization and urbanization, and are scarce in the use of foreign capital. In view of the above situation, the Chinese government has drawn up investment policies tilted in favor of these regions. Under similar conditions priority shall be given to them with respect to resource-tapping and infrastructure projects. Projects using foreign loans, multi-lateral and bi-lateral aid-receiving projects, unless special requirements are involved, are basically arranged there. As a result of the construction of a large number of transportation, communication and energy projects as well as the transformation of some basic industrial areas, the investment environment in the central and western regions has been greatly improved in which the resources superiority have been gradually turned into economic superiority. Meanwhile, the Chinese government has increased loan propertion to these regions granted by the policy bank while guiding some primary resource-processing industris and labor-intensive industries in the eastern region to shift westwards. Foreign business people are encouraged to invest there to explore and make use of local agricultural, energy and mineral resources to boost processing industry. For some foreign invested projects that are restricted in the eastern region, in particular the labor-intensive processing projects and resource-tapping projects, preferential treatment shall be granted with respect to project setting, enterprise income taxation and means of transport, etc.

Beijing municipality

Beijing is located on the north China plain, covering an area of 16,800 square kilometers with a population of 13.83 million in 2001.

Beijing is the nation's capital where the nation's central organizations and foreign embassies are located, making the city more conspicuous than others. It therefore becomes a policy and information center enjoying favorable international communication environment. As the largest information collecting and distribution center in the country, Beijing has gathered an array of information firms and media such as Xinhua News Agency, Central Television, State Statistics Bureau, State Information Center, and some branches of international media. The ministries and commissions of the State Council have also set up respective professional information networks radiating across the country.

Beijing is the scientific and cultural center of the country, a city where scientific, educational, cultural and sports institutions assemble, among which all manners of colleges, universities and research institutes number over 200. In Beijing the proportion of technology-intensive personnel comes first in the country. Currently there are about 1.15 million professionals and technicians in specialized fields, making up 10 per cent of the national total. Its talent competitiveness ranks first at home. According to Beijing's Tenth Five Year Talent Program, the number of professionals and technicians in the Beijing region will come to 2 million by 2005. By then managing personnel in large number who are well versed in modern enterprise management, knowledgeable about international laws, international finance, international business, assets administration and operation will show up.

The overwhelming majority of the head-offices of nationwide financial institutions and large investment groups are concentrated in Beijing. At the Financial Street of Xicheng District are located China's central bank, policy banks, chief commercial

Major Indices of Beijing Municipality

Index	2000	2001	The national total in 2001
Population			
Total by the end of the year (10,000 persons)	1,382	1,383	127,627
Birthrate (‰)		6.10	13.38
Mortality (‰)		5.30	6.43
Proportion of urban population (%)	77.54		37.7
Proportion of rural population (%)	22.46		62.3
National economy assessment			
GDP (100 million yuan)	2,478.8	2,817.6	95,933
Growth rate over the previous year (%)	11.0	11.0	7.3
GDP per capita (yuan/person)	22,460	25,300	7,543
Proportion of the first industry (%)	3.6	3.3	15.2
Proportion of the second industry (%)	38.1	37.8	51.1
Proportion of the third industry (%)	58.3	58.9	33.6
Residents' level of consumption (yuan/person)	7,326		3,608
Growth rate over the previous year (%)	24.5		6.2
Volume of retail sales of consumer goods (100 million yuan)	1,443.3	1,593.5	37,595.2
Foreign trade and economy			
Export volume (USD100 million)	76.7	79.1	2,661.6
Import volume (USD100 million)	165.8	197.2	2,436.1
Foreign direct investment (10,000 US dollars)	168,368	176,818	4,687,759
People's life			
Per-capita disposable income of urban households (yuan)	10,349.7	11,577.8	6,859.6
Per-capita consumer spending of urban households (yuan)	8,493.5	8,922.7	5,309
Average net income per capita in the rural areas (yuan)	4,604.55	5,025.5	2,366.4
Average annual salary of an employee (yuan)		19,155	10,870
In HK, Macao and Taiwan invested enterprises (yuan)		21,210	12,544
In foreign invested enterprises (yuan)		34,481	16,101

banks and a batch of non-banking firms such as insurance companies, trust and investment companies, financial companies and leasing companies. Nationwide financial settlements are conducted in Beijing. The construction of Financial Street, started in 1993, is to be basically completed by 2005 and totally completed by 2008. Currently there are already 530 entities settled in the street including state organs, financial firms and noted enterprises. As the management and service center for banking business, together with other services such as lawyer's offices, accountant's offices and communication centers, the Financial Street is capable of providing employment of 100,000 persons after its completion.

Beijing is one of the cities with most highly modernized infrastructure facilities in China. Being a transport hub as well as transfer center, Beijing enjoys convenient airway and railway traffics linking up all parts of the nation (Taiwan Province not included), and leading to 56 cities in 39 countries and regions. Beijing is also a pivot of post and telecommunication connecting China with all other countries in the world. It possesses an integral communication network in pace with world technological development in the field of telecommunication. Currently its communication capacity has come up to the level of medium-developed countries. As the number one city, Beijing enjoys a beneficial location where gas and power supply from surrounding areas can be used.   Following completion of the South-to-North water diversion project in the future, adequate supply of fuel, power and water needed for the city's development can be ensured.

In the industrial system complete with all categories established during the previous scores of years, electronics, machine building, chemical and medical industries take the lead in the country. But now hi-tech industries have become the nucleus of the capital's economy. Some state-class economic and technological development zones have been set up in Beijing with a view to attract investment from transnational corporations in particular the 50 top ones in the world and at the same time place emphasis on the development of a batch of large-scaled hi-tech industrial projects.

The eye-catching Zhongguancun is a district where technological and intellectual resources concentrate. Starting from 1999, Beijing has planned the construction of the Zhongguancun Scientific and Technological Park with the slogan, "Take ten years' time to build Zhongguancun into a first-rate scientific and technological park in the world." To attain this goal, overseas risk investment is actively used to support small and medium-sized pioneering enterprises so as to boost the development of industry. In other respects, efforts are made to encourage financing from overseas stock markets, to facilitate investment in technology; and to give hi-tech enterprises incentives to set up research institutes. To date, there are already over 2,000 foreign invested enterprises and nearly half of research institutions run by foreign firms in China are settled in Zhongguancun.

The International Central Business Center (CBD) under construction in Beijing is located in Chaoyang District, adjacent to the diplomatic quarter. The CBD, integrating office, convention center, restaurant, residence and recreation into a whole, is attracting more and more transnational corporations to set up regional headquarters, research centers and representative offices there.

As China's capital, Beijing is a center for domestic as well as overseas contacts with not only market potential of its own, but also enormous influence on outside markets. To facilitate foreign investment, the Beijing municipal government has enacted a series of preferential policies to simplify formalities in doing business, reduce the number of intermediate links in examination and approval and speed up the construction of electronic system in handling government affairs. As is planned, by the end of 2002, all procedures of public examination and approval shall be conducted on line.

The Olympics Games to be held in 2008 will signify not just further acceleration of Beijing's development, but provide Chinese business people home and overseas with ample business opportunities which those who are inclined to grasp may have a try by joining in public bidding. To prepare for the Olympic Games, the municipal government has planned to build 32 sports fields including stadiums and gyms and at the same time extend or reconstruct large-scaled infrastructure facilities such as airports, railway stations, roads and streets, telecommunication system, and information center. Moreover, an Olympic Community and its accompanying projects are also under construction. In addition to an investment of 90 billion yuan for urban infrastructure construction, the Beijing municipal government, with a view to realizing "green Olympic Games", is planning to invest another 45 billion yuan in creating a favorable environment. In the mean time, in order to realize the "scientific and technological Olympic Games" program, the government plans to invest 30 billion yuan more in informatization construction.

The unique advantage of the capital's political position, its modernized and informatized infrastructure and rapidly developed commercial services help to attract talents, resources and enterprises home and overseas to gather in Beijing. Currently there are already 158 of the top 500 global corporations invested in Beijing together with 9,500 Beijing representative offices set up by foreign enterprises in various lines of business including production, exploration, trading, service, consultation, investment, cargo agency, project contracting, etc.

Tianjin municipality

Tianjin, a municipality directly under the central government, is located on the North China plain. It covers an area of 11,300 square kilometers with a population of 10.04 million in 2001.

Tianjin, within the Beijing-Tianjin-Tanggu metropolitan area, is only 120 kilometers to Beijing in the northwest, and 50 kilometers to the seacoast in the east. The surrounding area of the two metropolises, Beijing and Tianjin, has formed a group of densely distributed satellite cities and towns in the shape of a concentric circle along the communication lines radiated from the two cosmopolitan cities. Under construction is a hi-tech industrial belt which, centered on Beijing and Tianjin and along

Beijin-Tianjin-Tanggu expressway, consists of Beijing Hi-Tech Industrial Zone, Beijing Economic and Technological Development Zone, Tianjin New Technological Park, Tianjin Economic and Technological Development Zone, Tianjin Port Bonded Area, etc. It is the largest hi-tech industrial belt in the country, comprising one third of the nation's total hi-tech enterprises.

Tianjin is Noth China's major comprehensive industrial base. Boasting solid foundation of processing and manufacturing industries, low investment cost and high profit returns, it is an ideal location for transnational corporations to invest and transfer business. The industries in Tianjin mainly include electronics, automobile, metallurgy, medicines, oceanic and petroleum chemical engineering, machine building,

Major Indices of Tianjin Municipality

Index	2000	2001	The national total in 2001
Population			
Total by the end of the year (10,000 persons)	1,001	1,004	127,627
Birthrate (‰)		7.58	13.38
Mortality (‰)		5.94	6.43
Proportion of urban population (%)	71.99		37.7
Proportion of rural population (%)	28.01		62.3
National economy assessment			
GDP (100 million yuan)	1,639.4	1,826.7	95,933
Growth rate over the previous year (%)	10.8	12.0	7.3
GDP per capita (yuan/person)	17,993	19,986	7,543
Proportion of the first industry (%)	4.5	4.3	15.2
Proportion of the second industry (%)	50.0	48.8	51.1
Proportion of the third industry (%)	45.5	46.9	33.6
Residents' level of consumption (yuan/person)	6,117		3,608
Growth rate over the previous year (%)	8.0		6.2
Volume of retail sales of consumer goods (100 million yuan)	736.6	832.7	37,595.2
Foreign trade and economy			
Export volume (USD100 million)	76.7	88.7	2,661.6
Import volume (USD100 million)	94.8	94.0	2,436.1
Foreign direct investment (10,000 US dollars)	116,601	213,348	4,687,759
People's life			
Per-capita disposable income of urban households (yuan)	8,140.5	8,958.7	6,859.6
Per-capita consumer spending of urban households (yuan)	6,121.0	6,987.2	5,309
Average net income per capita in the rural areas (yuan)	3,622.4	3,947.7	2,366.4
Average annual salary of an employee (yuan)		14,308	10,870
In HK, Macao and Taiwan invested enterprises (yuan)		13,042	12,544
In foreign invested enterprises (yuan)		15,564	16,101

etc. Textiles, garments, machinery and electronic products are major exporting commodities. Electronic information technology, biological and medical engineering, new energy and new material have been designated new pillar industries of Tianjin municipality in which foreign invested enterprises are encouraged to cooperate in all forms. Of foreign invested enterprises already approved, industrial enterprises constitute 50 per cent of the total, including a large number of transnational corporations such as Motorola, Toyota and Samsung.

Tianjin is rich in oceanic resources, including primarily sea salt, petroleum, aquatic products and two oilfields: the Dagang Oilfield and the Bohai Oilfield. The Tianjin Port is the largest man-made port in China and the largest modernized, international, multi-functional trading port in North China. It is Beijing's sea outlet with a freeway of 142 kilometers in between. Tianjin also has excellent urban infrastructure facilities, well-established transport network extending in all directions and the largest airport for freight transport in North China.

Tianjin is North-China's largest foreign trade port city with an annual import-export volume constituting one tenth of the nation's total. The China Tianjin Export Commodities Fair co-sponsored by a dozen or so provinces and cities in North China is one of the most significant regional fairs held every year in spring. As one of China's chief commercial ports in the past, Tianjin is now being developed into a trading center in North China. In recent years there have been built a number of nationwide and regional wholesale trading markets, which perform a vital function of commodities and materials collecting and distributing. On either side of the city's modern commercial streets, franchised stores dealing in famous-brand commodities from all over the world, chain stores, supermarkets, banks, securities companies, insurance companies, lawyer's offices, hotels and restaurants can be seen everywhere, which render reliable services for trading activities.

Located in a region where intellectuals gather, Tianjin has a multitude of scientific research institutions, colleges and universities. The total volume of scientific and technological products there is among the greatest in China. The future development objective of Tianjin is to build itself into a modernized industrial base centering on its new coastal zone, a flourishing commercial and financial center in North China, a high-level scientific- and educational-based city, a comprehensively developed sea-land-air transport hub, a northern information port, a modernized port city and an important northern economic center.

Hebei Province

Hebei Province in North China faces the sea on the east, covering an area of

188,000 square kilometers with a population of 66.99 millions in 2001.

Hebei is a major agricultural province as well as an important base of aquatic products where the output of wheat, beans and peanuts ranks foremost in the country. Boasting rich mineral resources, the province's iron ore reserves rank second and petroleum reserves rank third in the country, which provide favorable conditions for the construction of industrial bases of iron and steel industry, building material industry and chemical industry. It also has favorable conditions and sound foundations for developing coal-chemical, salt-chemical and oil-chemical industries. Cultural resources include multiple historic sites and ancient architectural complex. As for well-known tourist attractions there are Summer Resort in Chengde and Holiday Vil-

Major Indices of Hebei Province

Index	2000	2001	The national total in 2001
Population			
Total by the end of the year (10,000 persons)	6,744	6,699	127,627
Birthrate (‰)		11.16	13.38
Mortality (‰)		6.18	6.43
Proportion of urban population (%)	26.08		37.7
Proportion of rural population (%)	73.92		62.3
National economy assessment			
GDP (100 million yuan)	5.089.0	5,577.7	95,933
Growth rate over the previous year (%)	9.5	8.7	7.3
GDP per capita (yuan/person)	7,663	8,337	7,543
Proportion of the first industry (%)	16.2	16.4	15.2
Proportion of the second industry (%)	50.3	49.2	51.1
Proportion of the third industry (%)	33.5	34.4	33.6
Residents' level of consumption (yuan/person)	2,534		3,608
Growth rate over the previous year (%)	9.8		6.2
Volume of retail sales of consumer goods (100 million yuan)	1,613.9	1,778.3	37,595.2
Foreign trade and economy			
Export volume (USD100 million)	32.8	34.7	2,661.6
Import volume (USD100 million)	21.1	23.5	2,436.1
Foreign direct investment (10,000 US dollars)	67,923	66,989	4,687,759
People's life			
Per-capita disposable income of urban households (yuan)	5,661.2	5,984.8	6,859.6
Per-capita consumer spending of urban households (yuan)	4,348.5	4,479.8	5,309
Average net income per capita in the rural areas (yuan)	2,478.9	2,603.6	2,366.4
Average annual salary of an employee (yuan)		8,730	10,870
In HK, Macao and Taiwan invested enterprises (yuan)		10,283	12,544
In foreign invested enterprises (yuan)		9,166	16,101

lage in Beidaihe.

Quite a few railway trunk lines pass through the province. The rotation volume of goods transported through railways and highways, and the length of operating expressways are both among the forefront in the country. With chief seaports from north to south such as Qinhuangdao, Jingtang, Tianjin and Huanghua, the province has convenient ocean shipping.

Pillar industries such as chemicals, metallurgy, building material, machine building and foodstuff, traditional dominant industries such as light and textiles industries have taken shape in the province. The output of key products including plate glass, yarn, cloth, steel, cement, all rank among the foremost in the country. Services such as tourism, information, banking and real estate are rapidly developing.

Hebei Province faces Japan and ROK across the sea. Together with Beijing and Tianjin, both located inside the province, the three have formed a Beijing-Tianjin-Hebei Economic Zone, being closely linked geographically and ethnically. Funds, talents, technology, information from Beijing and Tianjin are used in Hebei Province, and enterprises can be transferred thither. Hebei in turn supplies for Beijing and Tianjin commodities, materials and energy. The Beijing-Tianjin-Hebei Economic Zone, with 100 million consumers, is one of the regions having the largest market capacity in the country.

There are three state-level development zones in Hebei: Qinhuangdao Economic and Technological Development Zone, Shijiazhuang High-Tech Industrial Development Zone and Baoding High-Tech Industrial Development Zone in which complete infrastructure facilities ensure the availability of roads, electricity, water, gas, heat and communication, making foreign-related services convenient and highly-efficient.

Major cities in Hebei include the provincial capital Shijiazhuang, well-known for its cotton textile and medicine industries; Tangshan, called "capital of porcelain in the north"; and Qinhuangdao, a sea-side tourist city, key open port as well as important port exporting coal and petroleum.

Shanxi Province

North-China's Shanxi Province covers an area of 156,000 square kilometers with a population of 32.72 million in 2001.

Always known as "home of coal and iron", Shanxi Province boasts abundant reserves of coal, iron and alumina, in particular coal, of which the proven deposits have topped 270 billion tons, making up one-third of the national total. With an annual output value of the coal industry accounting for over half of the province's total, Shanxi's coal base has been listed as one of the nation's large-scale key projects in the next 15 years.

As one of China's primary bases of energy and heavy chemical industry, Shanxi has for many years been dependant on natural resources in its economic development in which coal, electricity, metallurgy, chemicals, charcoal and building materials form its industrial framework. In recent years, Shanxi has been endeavoring to regulate its industrial structure, purify and transform its coal industry to add its value. As a result, it has become the largest cleaning coal and high-quality industrial charcoal base in the country. Currently Shanxi tops the country in the quantity of electricity transmitted to other provinces thanks to its change from transmitting coal to transmitting electricity outwards. Over half of the counties in the province used to engage in tradi-

Major Indices of Shanxi Province

Index	2000	2001	The national total in 2001
Population			
Total by the end of the year (10,000 persons)	3,297	3,272	127,627
Birthrate (‰)		13.06	13.38
Mortality (‰)		5.90	6.43
Proportion of urban population (%)	34.91		37.7
Proportion of rural population (%)	65.09		62.3
National economy assessment			
GDP (100 million yuan)	1,643.8	1,774.6	95,933
Growth rate over the previous year (%)	7.8	8.3	7.3
GDP per capita (yuan/person)	5,137	5,444	7,543
Proportion of the first industry (%)	10.9	9.0	15.2
Proportion of the second industry (%)	50.3	51.7	51.1
Proportion of the third industry (%)	38.7	39.3	33.6
Residents' level of consumption (yuan/person)	2,037		3,608
Growth rate over the previous year (%)	11.2		6.2
Volume of retail sales of consumer goods (100 million yuan)	629.1	679.9	37,595.2
Foreign trade and economy			
Export volume (USD100 million)	20.9	25.9	2,661.6
Import volume (USD100 million)	7.0	6.8	2,436.1
Foreign direct investment (10,000 US dollars)	22,472	23,393	4,687,759
People's life			
Per-capita disposable income of urban households (yuan)	4,724.1	5,391.1	6,859.6
Per-capita consumer spending of urban households (yuan)	3,941.9	4,123.0	5,309
Average net income per capita in the rural areas (yuan)	1,905.6	1,956.1	2,366.4
Average annual salary of an employee (yuan)		8,122	10,870
In HK, Macao and Taiwan invested enterprises (yuan)		7,796	12,544
In foreign invested enterprises (yuan)		8,072	16,101

tional coal mining and grain growing have now turned into new-type industrial counties in which cattle and sheep raising, fruits and vegetable growing have developed into four feature industries of non-staple food grain, dried and fresh fruits, anti-seasonal vegetables and herbivorous livestock meat and milk processing.

Taking advantage of abundant coal and iron resources, Shanxi has established the nation's important special-type steel base and is building the nation's largest stainless steel base. The largest aluminum factory in Asia has been built in Shanxi where the alumina resources account for 40 per cent of the national total.

Shanxi is abundant in tourism resources in which the number of ancient architectures ranks first in the whole country. There have formed three feature tourism regions representing three different cultures, namely the northern Buddhist culture, the central commercial culture and the southern Yellow River ancestral culture.

The key industries confirmed as having great potentiality of development in the following several years are as follows: 1. Coal deep processing and clean energy industry, centering on coal washing, selecting, mixing, type coal, coal chemicals and coal-bed gas; 2. High-tech industries; 3. Tourism and 4. Metallurgy, in particular that of stainless steel, special steel, aluminum, magnesium and alloy of aluminum and magnesium. In a certain period of time from now on, the state will offer favorable investment policies to Shanxi in the fields of energy, raw and processed materials.

Chief cities in Shanxi include the provincial capital Taiyuan, an important energy, alloy steel and heavy chemicals base; Datong, a well-known coal industrial base; Yangquan, an industrial and mining city mainly developing coal mining and iron smelting.

Inner Mongolia Autonomous Region

Inner Mongolia Autonomous Region lies on the northern frontier, covering an area of 1.18 million square kilometers that constitutes 11.9 per cent of China's total territory. Bounded Mongolia and Russian on the north it spans over 2,400 kilometers from east to west and over 1,700 kilometers from north to south. The region had a population of 23.77 million in 2001.

Geographically Inner Mongolia features large area of level land high above sea level. A vast expanse of prairie lies in the east while desert stretches far and wide in the west. Grassland, historic sites, desert, lakes, forests and folklore make up unique tourist attractions. During July-August every year *nadam* (traditional festival of the Mongols) will take place at different locations celebrated with such events as wrestling, horse race, archery and bartering.

The Inner Mongolia Autonomous Region, rich in natural resources, is reputed for

Major Indices of Inner Mongolia Autonomous Region

Index	2000	2001	The national total in 2001
Population			
Total by the end of the year (10,000 persons)	2,376	2,377	127,627
Birthrate (‰)		10.77	13.38
Mortality (‰)		5.79	6.43
Proportion of urban population (%)	42.68		37.7
Proportion of rural population (%)	57.32		62.3
National economy assessment			
GDP (100 million yuan)	1,401.0	1,545.5	95,933
Growth rate over the previous year (%)	9.7	9.6	7.3
GDP per capita (yuan/person)	5,872	6,458	7,543
Proportion of the first industry (%)	25.0	23.4	15.2
Proportion of the second industry (%)	39.7	40.4	51.1
Proportion of the third industry (%)	35.3	36.2	33.6
Residents' level of consumption (yuan/person)	2,425		3,608
Growth rate over the previous year (%)	5.1		6.2
Volume of retail sales of consumer goods (100 million yuan)	484.0	537.3	37,595.2
Foreign trade and economy			
Export volume (USD100 million)	11.1	9.0	2,661.6
Import volume (USD100 million)	12.7	12.9	2,436.1
Foreign direct investment (10,000 US dollars)	10,568	10,703	4,687,759
People's life			
Per-capita disposable income of urban households (yuan)	5,129.1	5,535.9	6,859.6
Per-capita consumer spending of urban households (yuan)	3,927.8	4,195.6	5,309
Average net income per capita in the rural areas (yuan)	2.038.2	1,973.4	2,366.4
Average annual salary of an employee (yuan)		8,250	10,870
In HK, Macao and Taiwan invested enterprises (yuan)		5,936	12,544
In foreign invested enterprises (yuan)		6,882	16,101

"forests in the east, iron in the west, grain in the south, herd in the north, and mineral resources everywhere." It is also praised in four Chinese characters *yang-mei-tu-qi* (literally 'feeling proud and elated') referring in a narrow sense to four resources including cashmere, coal, rare earth and natural gas; but in a broad sense the non-polluting prairie, the grassland ecological and cultural resources and immeasurable mineral resources. The grassland, cultivated land and forest area possessed per capita there rank first in the country. Mineral reserves, which rank third in the country, consist of 5 minerals of which the proven deposits rank first and 65 minerals whose possessing quantity rank among the top 10 in the country. The comprehensive production capacity of animal husbandry is the highest among the nation's 5 largest pastoral areas. Coal reserves are the second greatest in the country. As the coal there is of high quality suitable to be used in generating electricity, the capital Beijing, North China and Northeast China regions are inclined to choose Inner Mongolia as an ideal electricity provider for its low cost and short transmitting route. Inner Mongolia's rare earth deposits account for two-thirds of the world's total. Currently there are a dozen or so key enterprises and research institutes engaging in exploiting rare earth resources. The Sugeli Natural Gas Field in the Erdos basin under prospecting is the largest integrated gas field. Such resources are what Inner Mongolia is based on in the development of its feature economy.

Inner Mongolia has a late start in industrial development. So far it has only initially formed an industrial system comprising metallurgy, energy, machine building, forest industry and wool spinning. During the two decades since reform and opening-up, Inner Mongolia has experienced great changes. Today, driving along the freeway from its capital Hohhot to Baotou the "steel city on grassland", tidy, well-arranged streets, luxurious hotels, high-grade shopping centers can be seen everywhere together with de luxe cars speeding along broad avenues.

To carry out the western development strategy, the central government has increased input in the fields of infrastructure construction, ecological environmental protection, science, technology and education, and has offered preferential policies as well. In a certain period of time in days to come, Inner Mongolia will take advantage of its local superiority to control the desert, speed up construction of energy and raw material production base. At the same time it will set up development zones for farm produce, animal products and green products.

Major cities of Inner Mongolia Autonomous Region include the capital Hohhot, which is the administrative, economic, cultural and educational center of the region and a city featuring wool spinning, animal product processing and electronic industries; and Baotou, the largest industrial city of Inner Mongolia and top rare earth production base in the country.

Liaoning Province

Liaoning Province is located in the south of Northeast China, covering an area of 145,800 square kilometers, with a population of 41.94 million in 2001.

Liaoning has a coastal line as long as 2,178 kilometers, accounting for 12 per cent of the total length of Chinese mainland's coastal line. Being adjacent to DPRK and close to Russia, it is an important passage for the northeastern region to conduct foreign trade and international contacts.

Liaoning has now formed at an initial stage a commodity grain base in the central and northern part, a forestry and medicinal materials base in the eastern mountaineous area, an animal husbandry and fruit-growing base in the northwestern part and a fruit and aquatic product base in Liaodong Peninsula. As the province borders on the Bohai Sea and the Yellow Sea, it has rich ocean resources and tourism resources that can be well developed. Geologically Liaoning Province belongs to the Pacific ore-forming belt where there are considerable reserves of ferrous and non-ferrous metal, energy, chemicals and building materials. Liaoning is also China's heavy industrial base as well as raw and processed material base, with state-owned large and medium-sized enterprises accounting for one-tenth of the national total. Metallurgy, machine building, petroleum, chemicals and building materials constitute its backbone industries; me-

Major Indices of Liaoning Province

Index	2000	2001	The national total in 2001
Population			
Total by the end of the year (10,000 persons)	4,238	4,194	127,627
Birthrate (‰)		7.74	13.38
Mortality (‰)		6.10	6.43
Proportion of urban population (%)	54.24		37.7
Proportion of rural population (%)	45.76		62.3
National economy assessment			
GDP (100 million yuan)	4,669.1	5,033.1	95,933
Growth rate over the previous year (%)	8.9	9.0	7.3
GDP per capita (yuan/person)	11,226	12,070	7,543
Proportion of the first industry (%)	10.8	10.8	15.2
Proportion of the second industry (%)	50.2	48.6	51.1
Proportion of the third industry (%)	39.0	40.6	33.6
Residents' level of consumption (yuan/person)	4,490		3,608
Growth rate over the previous year (%)	8.4		6.2
Volume of retail sales of consumer goods (100 million yuan)	1,847.6	2,034.9	37,595.2
Foreign trade and economy			
Export volume (USD100 million)	105.9	107.5	2,661.6
Import volume (USD100 million)	94.8	102.9	2,436.1
Foreign direct investment (10,000 US dollars)	204,446	251,612	4,687,759
People's life			
Per-capita disposable income of urban households (yuan)	5,357.8	5,797.0	6,859.6
Per-capita consumer spending of urban households (yuan)	4,356.1	4,654.4	5,309
Average net income per capita in the rural areas (yuan)	2,355.6	2,557.9	2,366.4
Average annual salary of an employee (yuan)		10,145	10,870
In HK, Macao and Taiwan invested enterprises (yuan)		12,505	12,544
In foreign invested enterprises (yuan)		12,766	16,101

chanical and electrical products are major export products; and electronics is a rising industry in the province.

Liaoning Province is highly urbanized. There are two city groups of which one is centered on the capital Shenyang, joined together by surrounding cities in central Liaoning such as Anshan, Fushun and Bengxi; and the other is centered on Dalian, together with southern coastal cities including Dandong, Yingkou, etc. The two groups, comprising most major cities and an array of large-sized enterprises in the province, constitute the largest industrial base in the country and are at the same time a region with concentrated sci-tech strength, convenient traffic and highly developed information technology. In the central city group, the distance between two cities is generally within 70 kilometers. Small towns are clustered together around large cities. The southern Liaoning coastal city group is the province's gateway to the sea.

Shenyang Municipality, North China's largest comprehensive industrial city, is a transport hub. It is also a base for the manufacturing of the state's advanced machinery equipment where aircraft and light automobile manufacturing and electricity transmitting and transforming hold an important position in the country. Dalian is an important open port city, the largest foreign exchange settlement center in the northeastern region and a significant industrial base. It is about 400 kilometers to Shenyang. The area along Shenyang-Dalian freeway has become a high-tech industrial belt where a multitude of enterprises converge. Anshan is a city located in the central south renowned for iron and steel industries. Fushun is an important city in the central part featuring coal industry. Bengxi is a city also in the central part, well known for its charcoal, iron with low phosphorous content and high-quality steel products.

The Dalian port, having favorable natural conditions, serves as a channel for trade and economic contacts between China's northeastern region and northeastern Asia countries. It is also a passageway for cargo shipping. Its urban construction and beautified environment are universally acclaimed. It has a sound industrial and technological base, a solid scientific and technical development force and an advantageous environment for investment. Dalian was the first in the country to set up an economic and technological development zone. Currently it has a high-tech park, a bonded area and a special football area. Every year large foreign-related activities such as international costume festival are held regularly. Now Dalian is planning to build itself into a commercial center, a financial center, a tourist center, an information center and Northeast Asia's pivot of transportation.

Jilin Province

Jilin Province, located in the central part of Northeast China, is bounded on the east by Russia, and on the southeast by DPRK. It covers an area of 187,400 square kilometers with a population of 26.91 million in 2001.

Jilin, having fertile black earth in its central part, is a major commodity grain base in the country producing in large quantities maize, soya bean and other economic crops. The commodity grain owned per capita in Jilin has for many consecutive years taken the first place at home. In the northwestern part of the province there are pastures suitable for grazing sheep well known throughout the country where commodity cattle and fine-hair sheep are produced. In the eastern mountainous area are Jilin's forest resources the possession rate per capita is more than double that of natioanal average. The province also abounds in specialties such as ginseng, marten

Major Indices of Jilin Province

Index	2000	2001	The national total in 2001
Population			
Total by the end of the year (10,000 persons)	2,728	2,691	127,627
Birthrate (‰)		8.76	13.38
Mortality (‰)		5.38	6.43
Proportion of urban population (%)	49.68		37.7
Proportion of rural population (%)	50.32		62.3
National economy assessment			
GDP (100 million yuan)	1,821.2	2,032.5	95,933
Growth rate over the previous year (%)	9.2	9.3	7.3
GDP per capita (yuan/person)	6,847	7,640	7,543
Proportion of the first industry (%)	21.9	20.2	15.2
Proportion of the second industry (%)	43.9	43.3	51.1
Proportion of the third industry (%)	34.2	36.5	33.6
Residents' level of consumption (yuan/person)	3,381		3,608
Growth rate over the previous year (%)	5.6		6.2
Volume of retail sales of consumer goods (100 million yuan)	810.9	909.1	37,595.2
Foreign trade and economy			
Export volume (USD100 million)	14.9	15.3	2,661.6
Import volume (USD100 million)	15.0	19.7	2,436.1
Foreign direct investment (10,000 US dollars)	33,701	33,766	4,687,759
People's life			
Per-capita disposable income of urban households (yuan)	4,810.0	5,340.5	6,859.6
Per-capita consumer spending of urban households (yuan)	4020.9	4,337.2	5,309
Average net income per capita in the rural areas (yuan)	2,022.5	2,182.2	2,366.4
Average annual salary of an employee (yuan)		8,771	10,870
In HK, Macao and Taiwan invested enterprises (yuan)		9,625	12,544
In foreign invested enterprises (yuan)		13,550	16,101

and pilose antler, known as "three treasures of Northeast China."

Jilin is one of the old industrial bases in China boasting considerable reserves of gold, nickel, copper, petroleum and numerous large and medium-sized state-owned enterprises. Machinery, petrochemicals, medicines, foodstuff, metallurgy and forest industries constitute the six core industries of the province. Automobile and petro-chemical have become two backbone industries whereas foodstuff, medicines and electronic industries are developing at a rapid pace.

Railway lines crisscross in Jilin with a total operating length ranking third in the country. Roads radiate from Changchun in every direction through the province. Border cities in the province can have access to the Sea of Japan via ports of Russia and DPRK. There are altogether 21 ports and passageways in the province, some on a national level and some on a provincial level, distributed mainly along the China-DPRK and China-Russia borderlines.

Changchun, the provincial capital city, is the largest comprehensive industrial city as well as a hub of communications in Northeast China, known as "city of auto-mobiles" and "city of forests". The First Automobile Group in Changchun, with a yearly output accounting for one-fifth of the national total, is the top automobile production and research base in China, acclaimed as "cradle of China's auto industry". Designated as one of the 25 key cities of "trade rejuvenation through science and technology", Changchun has quite a few scientific research and educational institutions. The city has already opened wider than other cities to the outside world in which a state-level economic and technological development zone and a high-tech industrial development zone have been established.

Other major cities in Jilin include Jilin City, an industrial city mainly producing dyestuff, chemical fertilizer and calcium carbide. Siping, a hub of communications in the central part of Northeast China and a rising industrial city with two priority industries: machinery and foodstuff.

Heilongjiang Province

Heilongjiang is located in the northeasternmost part of China, covering an area of 454,000 square kilometers with a population of 38.11 million in 2001.

Heilongjiang has the best soil conditions in China in which the total area of cultivated land and exploitable land resources both make up one-tenth of the national total. Its area of cultivated land per capita is three times the national average. As one of the three best black earth belts in the world boasting well-protected ecological environment, Heilongjiang is endowed with clear water, clean fields and fertile soil that are favorable for developing green food. It abounds in soya bean, wheat, maize, potato, beet, flax, and flue-cured tobacco among which the output of soya bean ranks first in the country with export volume making up two-thirds of the national total. The flourishing animal husbandry makes the total livestock and output of fresh milk both take first position in the country. The province has the largest forest area, the highest rate of forest coverage and the greatest forest storage in the country, with 50 species of high quality, high value trees and 30 species of timber trees.

Heilongjiang is abundant in petroleum, natural gas and coal reserves. It has rich water resources from numerous rivers within its territory. The province is one of the major industrial bases in which petroleum, coal, timber, machinery and foodstuff constitute the principal part whereas the output of crude oil, timber, flax textiles,

Major Indices of Heilongjiang Province

Index	2000	2001	The national total in 2001
Population			
Total by the end of the year (10,000 persons)	3,689	3,811	127,627
Birthrate (‰)		8.48	13.38
Mortality (‰)		5.49	6.43
Proportion of urban population (%)	51.54		37.7
Proportion of rural population (%)	48.46		62.3
National economy assessment			
GDP (100 million yuan)	3,253.0	3,561.0	95,933
Growth rate over the previous year (%)	8.2	9.3	7.3
GDP per capita (yuan/person)	8,562	9,349	7,543
Proportion of the first industry (%)	11.0	11.5	15.2
Proportion of the second industry (%)	57.4	56.1	51.1
Proportion of the third industry (%)	31.6	32.4	33.6
Residents' level of consumption (yuan/person)	3,669		3,608
Growth rate over the previous year (%)	8.5		6.2
Volume of retail sales of consumer goods (100 million yuan)	1,094.0	1,198.9	37,595.2
Foreign trade and economy			
Export volume (USD100 million)	24.2	21.8	2,661.6
Import volume (USD100 million)	15.7	19.3	2,436.1
Foreign direct investment (10,000 US dollars)	30,086	34,114	4,687,759
People's life			
Per-capita disposable income of urban households (yuan)	4,912.9	5,425.9	6,859.6
Per-capita consumer spending of urban households (yuan)	3,824.4	4,192.4	5,309
Average net income per capita in the rural areas (yuan)	2,148.2	2,280.3	2,366.4
Average annual salary of an employee (yuan)		8,910	10,870
In HK, Macao and Taiwan invested enterprises (yuan)		10,135	12,544
In foreign invested enterprises (yuan)		8,628	16,101

power-generating equipment, special-type steel, shaped aluminum, and machine-made paper rank in the forefront in the country. Industries such as natural gas, large and medium-sized machines and equipment, sugar refining, building, building materials, food processing and medicine all take an importat position in the country.

Heilongjiang is bounded on the north and east by Russia with a borderline as long as 3,045 kilometers. In winter snowfall is heavy in the mountains. The long snowfall period and good quality snow make the region suitable for ice-and-snow tourism. Every year the Harbin Ice-and-Snow Festival and Heilongjiang International Skiing Festival are held.

Heilongjiang has well-developed road system. The railway density ranks among the highest in the country. The Heilongjiang river system is one of the three major inland navigation systems in China. Air routes in the province lead to all major cities in China and Russia.

Harbin, the provincial capital of Heilongjiang, is the political, economic and cultural center of the north part of Northeast China. Having well-developed air-water-land transport network, it is an important trading port with Russia and east European countries. Harbin has solid industrial foundation and gigantic economic and technological strength. Machinery, power equipment and petrochemicals are backbone industries. It is competitive in talented personnel, science and technology. The quality of its workforce, proportion of scientific and technological personnel and number of scientific research institutions are in a medium or advanced position in the country.

Other major cities include Qiqihar, the second largest city in Heilongjiang, noted for heavy mining machinery and rolling stock industries, Daqing, well known for petroleum industry, Jixi, a city known for coal industry, and Mudanjiang, one of the four major rubber tire production bases in China.

Shanghai Municipality

Standing on the forward position of the Yangtze River Delta just at the middle point of the coastline from north to south, Shanghai covers an area of 6,340 square kilometers, accounting for 0.06 per cent of the national total, with a population of 16. 14 million in 2001.

Shanghai is a city having the most developed economy and greatest comprehensive strength in China. Ever since the middle of the 19th century when it took the place of Guangzhou and became the center of foreign trade, Shanghai has basically maintained its position as the largest economic center at home as well as a port city of international business. Its urban competitiveness manifests itself in industrial structure, scientific and technological creativity, human resources, influence and internationalization.

Shanghai is the birthplace of China's modern industry. The sign "Made in Shanghai" has been unrivalled over a long period of time. To date Shanghai has mounted a new highland of development from an old industrial base through ten years' regulation in its production structure. Shanghai's industries are closely in connection with international markets with lots of raw and processed materials imported from overseas and one-third of its products exported all over the world. In 2001, integrated circuits produced in Shanghai held 50 per cent of home market share, cars held 43 per cent; super wide-screen color kinescopes, 40 per cent; air conditioner compressors, 35 per cent; power plant equipment, 30 per cent; optical fibers, 25 per cent. The current gross industrial output value, added value and industrial profit in Shanghai make up 1/12, 1/14 and 1/11 respectively of the national total. In the regulation of the structure of production, Shanghai has given priority to the development of automobiles, communication and information equipment, complete-set of power plant and equipment, heavy mechanical and electrical equipment, petrochemicals and sophisticated chemicals processing, iron and steel and electrical household appliances manufacturing. At the same time, high-tech industries represented by electronic information and communication, modern biomedicine and new materials are developing at an even quicker pace.

From the 1980s onwards, the service sector centered on banking, trading, transportation and communication, and real estate has become a new growth point in the economic development of Shanghai. In respect to essential production factors Shanghai has taken lead in the country in the establishment of nationwide markets dealing in foreign exchange, securities, futures, and gold trading. In the field of means of production, trading markets dealing in metal, coal, agricultural resources, chemicals, petroleum, grain and cooking oil, automobile, and building materials have been set up among which the Shanghai Metal Exchange has become the third largest of its kind in the world.

During the 1930~40s, Shanghai was the largest financial center in China and an international financial center in the Far East. Later on it was declined for a time. In the 1990s, the central government put out a call, "Building Shanghai into one of international economic, financial and trading center as soon as possible". Now apart from a number of domestic banks and numerous foreign banks that have established branches and offices in Shanghai, Shanghai Stock Exchange, China Foreign Exchange Transaction Center and China Gold Transaction Center have also made their presence in Shanghai.

The Yangtze River Delta backing Shanghai is where China's eastern coastal eco-

Major Indices of Shanghai Municipality

Index	2000	2001	The national total in 2001
Population			
Total by the end of the year (10,000 persons)	1,674	1,614	127,627
Birthrate (‰)		5.02	13.38
Mortality (‰)		5.97	6.43
Proportion of urban population (%)	88.31		37.7
Proportion of rural population (%)	11.69		62.3
National economy assessment			
GDP (100 million yuan)	4,551.2	4,950.8	95,933
Growth rate over the previous year (%)	10.8	10.2	7.3
GDP per capita (yuan/person)	34,547	37,382	7,543
Proportion of the first industry (%)	1.8	1.7	15.2
Proportion of the second industry (%)	47.5	47.6	51.1
Proportion of the third industry (%)	50.6	50.7	33.6
Residents' level of consumption (yuan/person)	11,546		3,608
Growth rate over the previous year (%)	10.2		6.2
Volume of retail sales of consumer goods (100 million yuan)	1,722.3	1,861.3	37,595.2
Foreign trade and economy			
Export volume (USD100 million)	246.4	268.6	2,661.6
Import volume (USD100 million)	300.6	338.4	2,436.1
Foreign direct investment (10,000 US dollars)	316,014	429,159	4,687,759
People's life			
Per-capita disposable income of urban households (yuan)	11,718.0	12,883.5	6,859.6
Per-capita consumer spending of urban households (yuan)	8,868.2	9,336.1	5,309
Average net income per capita in the rural areas (yuan)	5,596.4	5,870.9	2,366.4
Average annual salary of an employee (yuan)		21,781	10,870
In HK, Macao and Taiwan invested enterprises (yuan)		19,625	12,544
In foreign invested enterprises (yuan)		28,787	16,101

nomic development belt and the Yangtze River valley economic development belt converge. It is a significant rising industrial base, a high-level collecting and distributing center of various essential factors of production, and the largest city group in China. Home and overseas business establishments, if getting access to the market in Shanghai with their products, are as good as getting a footing on the broad Chinese market. It is not only because Shanghai is the largest industrial and commercial center occupying a pivotal position in the nation's economic activities, but also because Shanghainese are practical and astute.

Shanghai as an important hub of communications and a cargo collecting and distributing center of China, has international air routes leading to 59 cities overseas and 14 international marine shipping lines. Shanghai port is the largest on China's mainland and the third largest in the world. Starting from the 1980s, its volume of freight handled has topped 100 million tons, accounting for 10 per cent of the national total at present. Its oceangoing routes lead to many places in the world, its coastal navigation lines to major ports from north to south, and its Yangtze River lines to the ports in the middle and lower reaches. Freeways connect Shanghai with Beijing and surrounding cities.

Shanghai is one of the most developed regions in science, technology and culture. There are numerous institutions of higher learning and scientific research institutes, which have made praiseworthy achievements in the fields of laser, optical fiber communication, microelectronics, ocean engineering and bioengineering.

The development and opening-up of Pudong has been a focal point in China's reform and opening-up starting from the 1990s up to a longer period of time in days to come. Pudong is a modernized new area integrated with modernized business area, free trade area, export processing area, high-tech park, tourism development area, seaport, airport and railway hub among which the Lujiazui Financial and Trade Zone with structures symbolizing new Shanghai has assembled over 100 home and overseas financial firms, regional head offices of 20-odd transnational corporations and thus established initially its position as a central business area and international convention center. The Waigaoqiao Bonded Area has become a rising port and a hub for the interflow of goods and materials with its three main functions: international trade, processing trade and modern logistics flow. The Zhangjiang High-Tech Park is now a major base for technological creation and industrialization of microelectronics, software and biomedicine. The Jinqiao Export Preocessing Area, with a high-tech dominated pillar industrial group established, has become a significant section of industrial and technological development. Shanghai Municipal Government plans to build Pudong into a basically world-level modernized export-oriented multi-functional new area by 2010.

Shanghai has excellent social and cultural facilities, brisk commercial districts known as "paradise of shopping", complete services including banking, accounting, consultation, engineering and telecommunication, and skilled and industrious labor force. In Shanghai's central business area are a bundle of office buildings available to business firms, mostly located in Hongqiao Economic Development Zone, Pudong Lujiazui Financial and Trade Zone, Nanjing Road and Huaihai Road.

To date there are already in Shanghai over 20,000 foreign invested enterprises and nearly 4,000 offices of enterprises from overseas, Hong Kong, Macao and Taiwan. Among the top 500 transnational enterprises in the world, 250 have set up factories or offices in Shanghai.

Jiangsu Province

Jiangsu Province is located in the middle of China's east coast, striding the Yangtze River in its lower reaches. Covering an area of 102,600 square kilometers, it is the most densely populated province in China with a population of 73.55 million in 2001.

Jiangsu is basically a plain with 1,000-kilometer long coastline and the Yangtze River passing through its southern part. Within the province lie the nation's third and fourth largest lakes, the Taihu Lake and the Hongzehu Lake amidst a network of rivers, rivulets and ponds where there are rich water resources including plentiful underground water worthy of tapping. Reputed as a "land of rice and fish", the province has fertile land and abundant produce such as grains, oil crops, cotton, cocoon, livestock, fowls and fish, which always rank foremost in the country. So far 12 export-oriented agricultural comprehensive development zones have been set up in the province, where green food, aquiculture and agricultural tourism are vigorously developed.

Processing is the priority industry of Jiangsu, mostly operated in small and medium-sized enterprises. Electronics, textiles, light industry, machinery, petrochemicals and building materials constitute the pillar industries among which the output of machinery ranks foremost, and auto industry ranks fourth in the country. The capacity to try-produce and develop high-tech products in the fields of communication equipment, computers, color tubes, integrated circuits, electronic components and parts also among the forefront in the country.

Three main railway lines run through the province leading to 40 large and medium cities at home. A highway network centered on Nanjing has been constructed connecting cities, towns and townships. The length of its inland waterway lines ranks first in the country. Major seaports and inland river ports include Nanjing port, Zhangjiagang port, Nantong port, etc. There are eight airports in Jiangsu. Air routes lead to the US, Europe, Africa and many large and medium-sized cities at home.

Jiangsu is one of the provinces in China having well-developed economy. Its GDP, revenue, FDI, value of export, scientific and technological force all rank among the best in the country. Foreign invested projects are mostly distributed in electronics, light industry, textiles, chemicals and machine building industries. In recent years, investment for projects involving energy, transport, basic industry and high-tech industry is on the increase.

Nanjing, the provincial capital, has priority industries including petrochemicals, electronics, automobile and light industry. It is well developed in industrial as well as in urban construction. In the lower reaches of the Yangtze River, it is both a commercial and a financial center, only next to Shanghai in importance. Nanjing is a city

Major Indices of Jiangsu Province

Index	2000	2001	The national total in 2001
Population			
Total by the end of the year (10,000 persons)	7,438	7,355	127,627
Birthrate (‰)		9.03	13.38
Mortality (‰)		6.62	6.43
Proportion of urban population (%)	41.49		37.7
Proportion of rural population (%)	58.51		62.3
National economy assessment			
GDP (100 million yuan)	8,582.7	9,514.6	95,933
Growth rate over the previous year (%)	10.6	10.2	7.3
GDP per capita (yuan/person)	11,773	12,925	7,543
Proportion of the first industry (%)	12.0	11.4	15.2
Proportion of the second industry (%)	51.7	51.6	51.1
Proportion of the third industry (%)	36.3	36.9	33.6
Residents' level of consumption (yuan/person)	3,862		3,608
Growth rate over the previous year (%)	6.6		6.2
Volume of retail sales of consumer goods (100 million yuan)	2,604.1	2,869.0	37,595.2
Foreign trade and economy			
Export volume (USD100 million)	263.8	293.9	2,661.6
Import volume (USD100 million)	228.2	250.9	2,436.1
Foreign direct investment (10,000 US dollars)	642,550	691,482	4,687,759
People's life			
Per-capita disposable income of urban households (yuan)	6,800.2	7,375.1	6,859.6
Per-capita consumer spending of urban households (yuan)	5,323.2	5,532.7	5,309
Average net income per capita in the rural areas (yuan)	3,595.1	3,784.7	2,366.4
Average annual salary of an employee (yuan)		11,842	10,870
In HK, Macao and Taiwan invested enterprises (yuan)		11,460	12,544
In foreign invested enterprises (yuan)		14,483	16,101

highly civilized and cultured where institutions of higher learning, scientific and research institutions converge, cultivating an array of high-quality talents. The unfavorable factor hindering its competitiveness is that it is not influencial, nor is it internationalized enough.

Other major cities include Suzhou, a renowned tourist city, well developed in silk, foodstuffs and electronic industries, having Suzhou Industrial Park; Wuxi, well developed in microelectronics, textiles and other light industries; Xuzhou, a city in northwest Jiangsu known for coal industry; and Nantong, a key open port city on the north bank of the Yangtze.

Zhejiang Province

Zhejiang, a coastal province in the southern part of Yangtze River Delta, occupies an area of 101,800 square kilometers with a population of 46.13 million in 2001.

Zhejiang has rich water resources. Mineral resources are mainly non-metallic among which the deposits of 12 varieties of minerals take the first three places in the country, including bone coal, alunite, pyrophyllite which take the first place, and fluorite which takes the second place. Fishing resources abound in maritime space in Zhejiang whereas its continental shelf is a vast storehouse of petroleum and natural gas.

Agriculture in Zhejiang boasts high-yielding crops, mainly grain, cooking oil and some economic crops such as cotton, mulberry, tea and fruit. The output and export volume of tea ranks first, and gross output of aquatic products ranks third in the country. Currently there are 37 locations in the provinces designated as "land of Chinese specialties". Having basically realized mechanization or semi-mechanization of farm work, Zhejiang has high labor productivity in agriculture.

Zhejiang is an economically developed province in China. Its industrial output value makes up 90 per cent of the gross output value of industry and agriculture. Machine building, electronics, chemicals and medicine constitute its backbone industries while silk, textiles, leather, garments and foodstuff industries all occupy important positions in the country.

Zhejiang is called a "major market province" for the facts that both its number of commodity markets and its volume of trade rank first in the country. The commodities traded cover almost every field of means of production and means of subsistence. In many markets online transactions are conducted and information released. Yiwu's China Small Commodities Fair and Shaoxing's China City of Textile and Light Industries are two largest specialized markets in the country. In the province nearly one-fifth of the total products are exported to world markets among which three categories of products: textiles, garments, and mechanical-electrical products account for two-thirds of the province's total volume of export. The European Union, US and Japan are three major trading partners of the province.

Zhejiang is well developed in transportation, primarily in railways and water routes. The total length of inland navigation lines ranks third in the country. There are many large ports in the province. A "four-hour highway ring" has been formed, ensuring that it will take no more than 4 hours by highway from the provincial capital to any cities within the province. There are also quite a few home and international air routes. Airports in Hangzhou, Ningbo and Wenzhou have been designated specially as airports for international air freight.

Major Indices of Zhejiang Province

Index	2000	2001	The national total in 2001
Population			
Total by the end of the year (10,000 persons)	4,677	4,613	127,627
Birthrate (‰)		10.02	13.38
Mortality (‰)		6.25	6.43
Proportion of urban population (%)	48.67		37.7
Proportion of rural population (%)	51.33		62.3
National economy assessment			
GDP (100 million yuan)	6,036.3	6,700.0	95,933
Growth rate over the previous year (%)	11.0	10.5	7.3
GDP per capita (yuan/person)	13,461	14,550	7,543
Proportion of the first industry (%)	11.0	10.3	15.2
Proportion of the second industry (%)	52.7	51.3	51.1
Proportion of the third industry (%)	36.3	38.4	33.6
Residents' level of consumption (yuan/person)	4,366		3,608
Growth rate over the previous year (%)	11.7		6.2
Volume of retail sales of consumer goods (100 million yuan)	2,298.8	2,555.5	37,595.2
Foreign trade and economy			
Export volume (USD100 million)	204.8	242.6	2,661.6
Import volume (USD100 million)	110.4	126.5	2,436.1
Foreign direct investment (10,000 US dollars)	161,266	221,162	4,687,759
People's life			
Per-capita disposable income of urban households (yuan)	9,279.2	10,464.7	6,859.6
Per-capita consumer spending of urban households (yuan)	7,020.2	7,952.4	5,309
Average net income per capita in the rural areas (yuan)	4,253.7	4,582.3	2,366.4
Average annual salary of an employee (yuan)		16,385	10,870
In HK, Macao and Taiwan invested enterprises (yuan)		14,099	12,544
In foreign invested enterprises (yuan)		14,105	16,101

Hangzhou the provincial capital is a city known for tourist attractions and cultural wealth. Its composite economic strength ranks among the top ten in the country. With well-developed transport network, it is only two hours' journey to Shanghai by highway or railway. The refined urban environment and excellent infrastructure facilities have won for the city the "United Nations Dwelling Prize". Hangzhou boasts scientific and technological talents, well-developed education, competitive social and economic order and commercial and cultural atmosphere. There are a number of economic and technological development zones and industrial parks in which a bundle of overseas-invested enterprises have made their presence. Hangzhou plans to establish a new and high-tech research and development center, an achievement trade center, an industrialized base and an export base for new and high-tech achievements prior to 2010.

Other major cities include Ningbo, a key open city on the coast developing primarily petrochemicals, machine building, textile and light industries and Wenzhou, another key open port city in the south of the province, having machine building, electronics, garments and leather industries. Besides, there are a number of medium and small-sized cities, which have relaxed economic environment, well-developed individual and private economy, specialized markets where assemble small enterprises full of strong pioneering spirit and mercantile inclination.

Anhui Province

Anhui, lying in East-China's inland region, occupies an area of 139,000 square kilometers with a population of 63.28 million in 2001.

Anhui is about 400 kilometers from the sea. The Yangtze River flows from west to east through the southern part of the province, serving as a passageway going to the sea. Anhui borders in the east the two economically developed provinces of Jiangsu and Zhejiang, and neighbors in the west the densely populated Henan, Hubei and Jiangxi provinces. It is an intermediate region linking up China's eastern and central regions.

Anhui is one of China's major agricultural provinces where the output of grain, cotton, oil products, tea, fruit, crude drugs and animal by-products rank among the top ten in the country. There are plenteous and well-concentrated mineral deposits of coal, iron, copper and chemical raw materials that are suitable for tapping on a large scale. Petrochemicals, non-ferrous metal and light industries in the province hold an important position in the country.

Anhui has well-maintained highways and railways linking large and medium-sized cities and seaports in the surrounding regions, convenient for goods collecting and distributing. Its five ports along the Yangtze River are all open ports where import and export commodities can be loaded and unloaded and apply directly to the Customs for entry or exit.

Anhui, a province between China's high- and medium-level consumption regions, has enormous potential for developing consumption market. Following the economic growth in the medium-level consumption region and the increase of residents' income, consumption is expected to increase by a wide margin.

With the focus of China's development strategy shifted gradually from the eastern coast to the central and western regions, Anhui has manifested its positional superiority in that it links east and west, and joins north to south. It is now a new region witnessing rapid economic growth and a hot spot for overseas investment. To create a favorable investment environment, Anhui has established 24 economic and technological development zones, high-tech development zones and tourism development zones, mainly for attracting foreign investment. Among them Hefei High-Tech Development Zone, Wuhu Economic Development Zone are both state-level development zones within which high-tech enterprises and foreign-invested enterprises enjoy still more preferential tax policy.

Chief cities in Anhui are the capital Hefei, the largest and most economically developed city in the province known for machine building and foodstuff industries; Huainan, a city noted for coal, power and chemical industries; Huaibei, noted north-

Major Indices of Anhui Province

Index	2000	2001	The national total in 2001
Population			
Total by the end of the year (10,000 persons)	5,986	6,328	127,627
Birthrate (‰)		12.46	13.38
Mortality (‰)		5.85	6.43
Proportion of urban population (%)	27.81		37.7
Proportion of rural population (%)	72.19		62.3
National economy assessment			
GDP (100 million yuan)	3,038.2	3,290.1	95,933
Growth rate over the previous year (%)	8.3	8.6	7.3
GDP per capita (yuan/person)	4,867	5,221	7,543
Proportion of the first industry (%)	24.1	22.9	15.2
Proportion of the second industry (%)	42.7	43.0	51.1
Proportion of the third industry (%)	33.2	34.1	33.6
Residents' level of consumption (yuan/person)	2,588		3,608
Growth rate over the previous year (%)	4.3		6.2
Volume of retail sales of consumer goods (100 million yuan)	1,054.3	1,142.8	37,595.2
Foreign trade and economy			
Export volume (USD100 million)	21.2	21.7	2,661.6
Import volume (USD100 million)	15.7	14.8	2,436.1
Foreign direct investment (10,000 US dollars)	31,847	33,672	4,687,759
People's life			
Per-capita disposable income of urban households (yuan)	5,293.6	5,668.8	6,859.6
Per-capita consumer spending of urban households (yuan)	4,233.0	4,517.7	5,309
Average net income per capita in the rural areas (yuan)	1,934.6	2,020.0	2,366.4
Average annual salary of an employee (yuan)		7,908	10,870
In HK, Macao and Taiwan invested enterprises (yuan)		7,369	12,544
In foreign invested enterprises (yuan)		10,130	16,101

ern coal city; Wuhu, a city on the south bank of the Yangtze River, known for textile and other light industries and the second largest foreign trade base in Anhui.

Fujian Province

Southeast China's seaboard province of Fujian, adjoining the Yangtze River Delta in the north, the Zhujiang River Delta in the south, and facing Taiwan across the straits, is one of the provinces nearest in distance from China's mainland to southeastern Asia. It occupies a land area of 121,400 square kilometers with a population of 34.40 million in 2001.

Fujian is one of the four major forest regions in China boasting bountiful rare tree species and precious crude drugs. Densely crisscrossed rivers and rivulets in the province contain rich water–power resources. Its sea area is at a point where subtropical oceanic cold current and warm current converge into which pours large quantity river water. Hence it abounds in marine products such as fish, shrimp, shellfish and algae. Off the curvy coastline numerous islets dot the maritime space. The province has quite a few natural good harbors and is rich in regenerable energy such as tidal energy and wave energy. The quartz reserves in the province ranks first in the country both in quality and quantity. Fujian also abounds in reserves of gold, silver, kaolin, granite, and alumstone.

Rice is the staple cereal crop of the province, and sweet potato the second. Economic crops include sugar cane, orange, tobacco, rapeseed, peanut and tea. Fujian is one of the five major sugar cane producing areas where tropical and subtropical fruits are abundant. The leading industries in Fujian include electronics, information technology, mechanical equipment, and petrochemicals. Foodstuff is one of the backbone industries. Sugar refining, tea producing and canned food industries take front places in the country. In addition, ceramics, plastic, garments and sensitive material industries are well developed.

Fujian, as one of the provinces having trade relations with foreign countries at the earliest, is China's "Home of overseas Chinese". The majority of overseas Chinese are inhabited in Philippines, Indonesia, Singapore, Malaysia, Thailand, Europe, America and Hong Kong. Among foreign investment in Fujian, that from overseas Chinese forms a considerable proportion.

Fujian's open ports include Fuzhou, Xiamen and Quanzhou from where many shipping lines lead to Singapore, Manila, Kuala Lumpur, Jakarta and a number of major cities at home.

The provincial capital Fuzhou is a key coastal open city. Its major industries include machine building, electronics, chemicals and light industries. Although not

Major Indices of Fujian Province

Index	2000	2001	The national total in 2001
Population			
Total by the end of the year (10,000 persons)	3,471	3,440	127,627
Birthrate (‰)		11.56	13.38
Mortality (‰)		5.52	6.43
Proportion of urban population (%)	41.57		37.7
Proportion of rural population (%)	58.43		62.3
National economy assessment			
GDP (100 million yuan)	3,920.1	4,258.4	95,933
Growth rate over the previous year (%)	9.5	9.0	7.3
GDP per capita (yuan/person)	11,601	12,375	7,543
Proportion of the first industry (%)	16.3	15.3	15.2
Proportion of the second industry (%)	43.7	44.7	51.1
Proportion of the third industry (%)	40.0	40.0	33.6
Residents' level of consumption (yuan/person)	4,428		3,608
Growth rate over the previous year (%)	6.9		6.2
Volume of retail sales of consumer goods (100 million yuan)	1,372.8	1,499.5	37,595.2
Foreign trade and economy			
Export volume (USD100 million)	136.2	147.9	2,661.6
Import volume (USD100 million)	93.3	96.0	2,436.1
Foreign direct investment (10,000 US dollars)	343,191	391,804	4,687,759
People's life			
Per-capita disposable income of urban households (yuan)	7,432.3	8,313.1	6,859.6
Per-capita consumer spending of urban households (yuan)	5,638.7	6,015.1	5,309
Average net income per capita in the rural areas (yuan)	3,230.5	3,380.7	2,366.4
Average annual salary of an employee (yuan)		12,013	10,870
In HK, Macao and Taiwan invested enterprises (yuan)		10,334	12,544
In foreign invested enterprises (yuan)		11,015	16,101

comprehensively competitive among the southeastern coastal cities, Fuzhou maintains a high rate of sustained economic growth, suggesting potential competitiveness. Besides, it has high capital competitiveness. Its geographical advantage of bordering on the sea and close to Taiwan has brought political and economic advantages. Helped by a large number of Fujian compatriots living abroad, the city has a high proportion of foreign investment but also a high degree of reliance on foreign trade. Fuzhou is also well developed in education.

Xiamen, designated as a special economic zone in the 1980s, is a city highly opened both at home and to the outside world, with a high proportion of foreign investment in the city's total capital. At present the city is defined as one of trade and tourism type. In industrial development it is centered on processing. A state-level foreign investment symposium is held every year in the city. As it is the closest in distance to Taiwan, once the three direct links of trade, mail, and air and shipping services across the Taiwan Straits are fully implemented, the city will reveal its unique superiority in bringing together the essential production elements home and overseas and opening overseas markets.

Quanzhou is a noted city inhabited by a multitude of returned overseas Chinese and relatives of overseas Chinese. Its major industries are electronics, garments and building materials.

Jiangxi Province

Jiangxi, a province in the central part of Southeast China, is on the south bank of the middle and lower reaches of the Yangtze River and close to the well-developed southeastern coastal provinces. Occupying an area of 166,900 square kilometers, it had a population of 41.86 million in 2001.

Currently Jiangxi is carrying out the strategy of "three bases and a back garden" in its social and economic development. The "three bases" refer to building the province into a base for receiving the industrial transfer from coastal nucleus cities, a base for supplying high-quality farm and sideline products and a base for export of labor services. The "back garden" refers to that the province will serve as a garden for tourism and holiday taking catering to the coastal nucleus cities.

Geographically the province, though some distance to the sea, is at the intersection of Zhujiang River Delta, Yangtze River Delta and South Fujian Delta. It is only an hour's flight to Shanghai, Guangzhou or Hong Kong. The transport construction in Jiangxi is proceeding at a rapid pace. The freeway leading to Shanghai and Zhejiang has been completed and the freeway across Guangdong and Fujian is well under way. Its positional advantage and convenient transportation have provided more favorable conditions together with accompanying services for cooperation with well-developed regions.

Forests cover 60 per cent of Jiangxi' total land area. The Boyanghu Lake is the largest freshwater lake in China, occupying an area of 5,100 square kilometers, equivalent to the total area of Shanghai Municipality. With favorable climate, verdant hills and emerald water, Jiangxi Province produces high-quality farm and sideline products.

Jiangxi is famed as "red cradle" as well as "green homeland", both referring to tourist resources. The "porcelain" culture and the Taoist culture coexist with natural landscape and cultural spectacles. Rich tourism resources and low commodity prices make it possible for Jiangxi to become the "back garden" of coastal regions in South-

Major Indices of Jiangxi Province

Index	2000	2001	The national total in 2001
Population			
Total by the end of the year (10,000 persons)	4,140	4,186	127,627
Birthrate (‰)		15.44	13.38
Mortality (‰)		6.06	6.43
Proportion of urban population (%)	27.67		37.7
Proportion of rural population (%)	72.33		62.3
National economy assessment			
GDP (100 million yuan)	2.003.1	2,173.8	95,933
Growth rate over the previous year (%)	8.0	8.8	7.3
GDP per capita (yuan/person)	4,851	5,217	7,543
Proportion of the first industry (%)	24.2	23.3	15.2
Proportion of the second industry (%)	35.0	36.1	51.1
Proportion of the third industry (%)	40.8	40.6	33.6
Residents' level of consumption (yuan/person)	2,396		3,608
Growth rate over the previous year (%)	16.6		6.2
Volume of retail sales of consumer goods (100 million yuan)	704.9	763.3	37,595.2
Foreign trade and economy			
Export volume (USD100 million)	11.9	10.9	2,661.6
Import volume (USD100 million)	8.6	7.1	2,436.1
Foreign direct investment (10,000 US dollars)	22,724	39,575	4,687,759
People's life			
Per-capita disposable income of urban households (yuan)	5,103.6	5,506.0	6,859.6
Per-capita consumer spending of urban households (yuan)	3,623.6	3,894.5	5,309
Average net income per capita in the rural areas (yuan)	2,135.3	2,231.6	2,366.4
Average annual salary of an employee (yuan)		8,026	10,870
In HK, Macao and Taiwan invested enterprises (yuan)		6,721	12,544
In foreign invested enterprises (yuan)		8,331	16,101

east China.

There are a dozen or so minerals whose reserves come first in the country. Rich in non-ferrous metals, rare metals and precious metals, Jiangxi boasts the "five golden flowers" —— copper, tungsten, tantalum, uranium and rare earth. Compared with the coastal region, Jiangxi has sufficient land supply, which is lower in price. Its raw and processed materials and energy are also cheaper. Its labor force costs only one third that of Shanghai and Guangdong whereas the quality of the labor force in Jiangxi is by no means inferior. Traditionally Jiangxi has always attached great importance to education where talents come forth in large numbers up to this day. To date Jiangxi has 48 institutions of higher learning among which more than 30 are located in

Nanchang. From the low cost of land and manpower Jiangxi has derived another advantage: low cost of infrastructure such as freeways and factory buildings, etc.

Major cities in Jiangxi include Nanchang the capital, well developed in metallurgy, machine building, aviation, foodstuffs, textiles and light industries; Jiujiang, an open port on the Yangtze, well developed in oil refinery, petrochemicals, textiles and light industries; and Jingdezheng, a central city in the northeastern part known as the "porcelain city."

Shandong Province

Shandong Province is located on East China coast, facing Korean Peninsula and Japanese Islands across the sea, covering an area of 157,000 square kilometers with a population of 90.41 million in 2001.

Shandong has more than 30 varieties of minerals the deposits of which rank among the top 10 in the country. Among them the deposits of gold, natural sulfur and gypsum come first, petroleum, diamond, magnesite, cobalt, hafnium, granite come second, sylvite, graphite, talcum, porphyry and limestone come third. Shandong is also one of the major energy bases in China in which the Shengli Oilfield is the country's second largest petroleum base. Its coal and power resources are abundant. Shandong's offshore space occupies 37 per cent of the total area of the Bohai Sea and the Yellow Sea where the output of quite a number of aquatic products rank first in the country.

Shandong is well developed in economy. Its chief indices of national economy come in the forefront in the country. The gross annual value of agricultural output ranks first and grain output ranks second in China. Wheat output, which accounts for 50 per cent of Shandong's total grain output, comes first in the country. Chief economic crops include cotton, peanut, flue-cured tobacco and hemp of which the output of peanut accounts for 40 per cent of the country's total with its volume of export accounting for 90 per cent of the country's total. The growing area and output of hemp both rank in the forefront in the country. Shandong is also one of the major producing areas of fruits, vegetables, cocoon and crude drugs.

Chief industries in Shandong include energy, machinery, electronics, chemicals, textiles, and foodstuffs. The output of foodstuffs ranks first in the country. Beer and peanut oil sell well home and abroad. The production of heavy-duty automobiles, machine tool, household appliances and timepieces is well known.

Shandong has a well-developed transportation system. Its operating freeways are the longest in the country. Seaports open to foreign ships include Qingdao, Yantai, Weihai and Rizhao.

Shandong has numerous foreign invested firms. The key lines of business encouraged by local governments include information technology, biology and medicine, new-type materials, advanced manufacturing, advanced energy, advanced environmental protection and comprehensive utilization of resources, modern agriculture, modern transportation and urban infrastructure.

The capital Jinan is the province's political, economic, cultural, scientific, technological and educational center. Qingdao is a chief open port and one of the five major foreign trade ports in China. It is the largest industrial city in Shandong known for the textile industry. In the fields of information industry, electrical household appliances, marine organism engineering and medicine there are many brand name enterprises.

Major Indices of Shandong Province

Index	2000	2001	The national total in 2001
Population			
Total by the end of the year (10,000 persons)	9,079	9,041	127,627
Birthrate (‰)		11.12	13.38
Mortality (‰)		6.24	6.43
Proportion of urban population (%)	38.00		37.7
Proportion of rural population (%)	62.00		62.3
National economy assessment			
GDP (100 million yuan)	8,524.4	9,438.3	95,933
Growth rate over the previous year (%)	10.5	10.1	7.3
GDP per capita (yuan/person)	9,555	10,465	7,543
Proportion of the first industry (%)	14.9	14.4	15.2
Proportion of the second industry (%)	49.7	49.3	51.1
Proportion of the third industry (%)	35.5	36.3	33.6
Residents' level of consumption (yuan/person)	3,467		3,608
Growth rate over the previous year (%)	7.7		6.2
Volume of retail sales of consumer goods (100 million yuan)	2,545.9	2,834.9	37,595.2
Foreign trade and economy			
Export volume (USD100 million)	160.9	184.8	2,661.6
Import volume (USD100 million)	121.6	138.5	2,436.1
Foreign direct investment (10,000 US dollars)	297,119	352,093	4,687,759
People's life			
Per-capita disposable income of urban households (yuan)	6,490.0	7,101.1	6,859.6
Per-capita consumer spending of urban households (yuan)	5,022.0	5,252.4	5,309
Average net income per capita in the rural areas (yuan)	2,659.2	2,804.5	2,366.4
Average annual salary of an employee (yuan)		10,008	10,870
In HK, Macao and Taiwan invested enterprises (yuan)		7,914	12,544
In foreign invested enterprises (yuan)		9,526	16,101

Other major cities include: Zibo, an industrial and mining city in central Shandong, well known for petrochemicals, porcelain, and glass production; Yantai, a state-level key open port with foodstuff, textile and light industries well developed; and Weifang, an industrial city centered on textiles, machine building, electronics, chemical, building material and light industries.

Henan Province

Henan Province is located in the Mideast China covering an area of 167,000 square kilometers with a population of 95.55 million in 2001. The majority of its land lies to the south of the Yellow River.

Henan links the coastal regions that are more developed in economy and the central and western regions that are relatively backward. It has several railways running from north to south and from east to west, giving the province regional advantages. The capital city Zhengzhou is where the Beijing-Guangzhou and Lanzhou-Lianyungang railways intersect. It is also the largest passenger and freight transport transfer post of Lianyungang-Rotterdam continental bridge. The Zhengzhou north railway station is the largest marshalling yard in Asia, which is first-rate in transfer and handling capacity as well as operation measures.

Henan is a major agricultural province where the cultivated area is the second largest in the country. Its output of cotton, jute, bluish dogbane, sesame, wheat, beans, peanut and beef rank in the forefront in the country. It is abundant in mineral resources including large-scale coalmines and oilfields. Textiles, coal, petroleum and light industries constitute pillar industries of the province.

Henan has fully developed market economy where a commercial, financial and information center geared to the needs of the whole nation has gradually formed. Zhengzhou as a core, supported by cities along the Yellow River, threading together urban areas and countryside, radiates in every direction towards the Central Plains. There are in the province quite a number of nationwide and regional commodity distributing centers, trading centers and specialized wholesale markets. Zhengzhou Commodity Fair is held annually and Henan Economic and Trade Symposium held once every two years. Zhengzhou Commodity Trading Center is the largest grain futures market in the country while Henan Sci-Tech Market is one of the seven permanent technological trading centers in the country.

In addition to the state stipulated policies, Henan has formulated an industrial catalogue and corresponding policies to encourage investment in which special priorities are given to the tertiary industry, agriculture, infrastructure, new and high-tech industries and environmental protection industries.

Major Indices of Henan Province

Index	2000	2001	The national total in 2001
Population			
Total by the end of the year (10,000 persons)	9,256	9,555	127,627
Birthrate (‰)		13.20	13.38
Mortality (‰)		6.26	6.43
Proportion of urban population (%)	23.20		37.7
Proportion of rural population (%)	76.8		62.3
National economy assessment			
GDP (100 million yuan)	5,137.7	5,645.0	95,933
Growth rate over the previous year (%)	9.4	9.1	7.3
GDP per capita (yuan/person)	5,444	5,929	7,543
Proportion of the first industry (%)	22.6	21.9	15.2
Proportion of the second industry (%)	47.0	47.2	51.1
Proportion of the third industry (%)	30.4	31.0	33.6
Residents' level of consumption (yuan/person)	2,208		3,608
Growth rate over the previous year (%)	13.5		6.2
Volume of retail sales of consumer goods (100 million yuan)	1,786.7	1,979.8	37,595.2
Foreign trade and economy			
Export volume (USD100 million)	15.9	18.4	2,661.6
Import volume (USD100 million)	15.4	15.8	2,436.1
Foreign direct investment (10,000 US dollars)	56,403	45,729	4,687,759
People's life			
Per-capita disposable income of urban households (yuan)	4,766.3	5,267.4	6,859.6
Per-capita consumer spending of urban households (yuan)	3,830.7	4,110.2	5,309
Average net income per capita in the rural areas (yuan)	1,985.8	2,097.9	2,366.4
Average annual salary of an employee (yuan)		7,916	10,870
In HK, Macao and Taiwan invested enterprises (yuan)		9,558	12,544
In foreign invested enterprises (yuan)		8,924	16,101

Chief cities in Henan include Zhengzhou the capital city, a railway hub and trading center, known for cotton textiles, textile machinery and aluminum industry; Loyang, a city noted for tractor manufacturing, mining machinery and bearing-making industry; Pingdingshan, a rising city in the central part of the province, famous for producing high-quality charcoal and special-type steel plates; Xinxiang, a rising North-Henan city with well-developed textiles, electronics and light industries; Kaifeng, an important industrial and commercial city; and Anyang, well-developed in steel and textile industries.

Hubei Province

Hubei, a Central-China's province in the middle reaches of the Yangtze River, occupies an area of 185,900 square kilometers with a population of 59.75 million in 2001.

Hubei, with a water area accounting for one-tenth of the province's total area, is known as a "province of thousand lakes". Enjoying the good reputation as a "land of fish and rice", it is abundant in water energy, biological, mineral and tourism resources. It is also a major production base of commodity grain, cotton, oil and fresh-water aquatic products.

Hubei's priority industries include steel and iron, automobiles, heavy-duty ma-

Major Indices of Hubei Province

Index	2000	2001	The national total in 2001
Population			
Total by the end of the year (10,000 persons)	6,028	5,975	127,627
Birthrate (‰)		8.51	13.38
Mortality (‰)		6.07	6.43
Proportion of urban population (%)	40.22		37.7
Proportion of rural population (%)	59.78		62.3
National economy assessment			
GDP (100 million yuan)	4,276.3	4,662.3	95,933
Growth rate over the previous year (%)	9.3	9.1	7.3
GDP per capita (yuan/person)	7,188	7,813	7,543
Proportion of the first industry (%)	15.5	14.8	15.2
Proportion of the second industry (%)	49.7	49.6	51.1
Proportion of the third industry (%)	34.9	35.5	33.6
Residents' level of consumption (yuan/person)	2,857		3,608
Growth rate over the previous year (%)	5.8		6.2
Volume of retail sales of consumer goods (100 million yuan)	1,789.4	1,975.2	37,595.2
Foreign trade and economy			
Export volume (USD100 million)	19.0	18.0	2,661.6
Import volume (USD100 million)	19.9	23.7	2,436.1
Foreign direct investment (10,000 US dollars)	94,368	118,860	4,687,759
People's life			
Per-capita disposable income of urban households (yuan)	5,524.5	5,856.0	6,859.6
Per-capita consumer spending of urban households (yuan)	4,644.5	4,804.8	5,309
Average net income per capita in the rural areas (yuan)	2,268.6	2,352.2	2,366.4
Average annual salary of an employee (yuan)		8,619	10,870
In HK, Macao and Taiwan invested enterprises (yuan)		8,592	12,544
In foreign invested enterprises (yuan)		10,959	16,101

chine tools, hydropower and textiles. Among the enterprises well known throughout the country are the Gezhouba Hydropower Station, Wuhan Steel Company, China Second Auto Works, etc. Along the Yangtze River there have been established three industrial bases: the East-Hubei industrial base centered on the three cities of Wuhan, Huangshi and Ezhou, chiefly developing metallurgy, machine building, textile, chemicals and building materials; the West-Hubei industrial base centered on Yichang, Jingzhou, Jingmen chiefly developing power, petroleum, chemical and textiles; and the North-Hubei industrial base centered on Xiangfan, Shiyan, chiefly developing autos, electronics, textiles and light industries.

Hubei is Central-China's land and water transportation hub. The capital Wuhan is known as "thoroughfare of nine provinces". Competitive in the fields of science and technology, the province has numerous scientific research and educational institutions. Its scientific research level and production capacity in laser, optical communication, bioengineering, and new materials rank in the forefront in the country.

Wuhan, the provincial capital, is the largest industrial and commercial city and transport hub in the middle reaches of the Yangtze River, well known for steel, auto and communication industries. It has enormous manpower reserves that are rapidly on the increase. It is superior in capital competitiveness, capital strength and financial control capacity. The Yangtze River, Beijing-Guangzhou railway and highways radiating in all directions give the province a positional advantages in transport. As an economic, financial, scientific and technological center in China's central south region as well as the political center of the province, Wehan has a strong urban cohesive power, a large-scale economic structure, immense overall strength and large population.

Other major cities include Xiangfan, an industrial, commercial and transport center in the north of the province; Jingzhou, a central south city known for textiles and light industries; Huangshi, an industrial and mining port in southeast Hubei; and Yichang, a major industrial and transport center in west Hubei.

Hunan Province

Hunan Province is situated in South China's central part, to the south of the middle reaches of the Yangtze River. Occupying an area of 210,000 square kilometers, it had a population of 65.96 million in 2001.

As one of China's "lands of fish and rice", Hunan ranks in the forefront in the country in the output of grains and economic crops such as rice, ramie, tea, oil and tung oil. Hunan has abundant non-ferrous metals and non-metal mineral deposits, of which antimony, tungsten and manganese are among the largest in the country. Among

Major Indices of Hunan Province

Index	2000	2001	The national total in 2001
Population			
Total by the end of the year (10,000 persons)	6,440	6,596	127,627
Birthrate (‰)		11.80	13.38
Mortality (‰)		6.72	6.43
Proportion of urban population (%)	29.75		37.7
Proportion of rural population (%)	70.25		62.3
National economy assessment			
GDP (100 million yuan)	3,691.9	3,983.0	95,933
Growth rate over the previous year (%)	9.0	9.0	7.3
GDP per capita (yuan/person)	5,639	6,054	7,543
Proportion of the first industry (%)	21.3	20.7	15.2
Proportion of the second industry (%)	39.6	39.4	51.1
Proportion of the third industry (%)	39.1	39.8	33.6
Residents' level of consumption (yuan/person)	2,723		3,608
Growth rate over the previous year (%)	3.2		6.2
Volume of retail sales of consumer goods (100 million yuan)	1,364.7	1,511.1	37,595.2
Foreign trade and economy			
Export volume (USD100 million)	16.3	17.4	2,661.6
Import volume (USD100 million)	13.6	11.8	2,436.1
Foreign direct investment (10,000 US dollars)	67,833	81,011	4,687,759
People's life			
Per-capita disposable income of urban households (yuan)	6,218.7	6,780.6	6,859.6
Per-capita consumer spending of urban households (yuan)	5,218.8	5,546.2	5,309
Average net income per capita in the rural areas (yuan)	2,197.2	2,299.5	2,366.4
Average annual salary of an employee (yuan)		9,623	10,870
In HK, Macao and Taiwan invested enterprises (yuan)		9,489	12,544
In foreign invested enterprises (yuan)		9,769	16,101

its mainstay industries are machine building, foodstuffs, chemicals, metallurgy, ramie textiles, energy and building materials.

Lying between South China's coastal opening belt and Yangtze valley opening belt, Hunan is a transport hub where container train can reach Hong Kong on the same day of departure. To make transport more convenient and speedy, a freeway network connecting the provincial capital Changsha and a number of cities within and without the province is under construction together with a batch of railway, shipping and civil aviation projects.

Lines of business which encourage foreign investment include agriculture, energy industry, communication and transportation, metallurgy of ferrous metals, machinery, electronics, building materials, chemicals, foodstuffs and new and high-tech industries.

Chief cities include Changsha the capital, a comprehensive industrial city focusing on textile and light industries, foodstuffs, machine building and electronics; Hengyang, a major industrial and commercial city and railway hub; Zhuzhou, a scientific research and manufacturing base for aero-engine and electric locomotives in central south region, well developed in machine building, textiles and light industry, tobacco and building material industries; Xiangtan, a city in central Hunan known for raw and processed material industries and a base for electrical machinery, low-pressure electrical appliances and manganese production; and Yueyang, a city chiefly developing petrochemicals, textiles and light industries.

At present, the economic strength of the three cities of Changsha, Zhuzhou and Hengyang accounts for one third of the province's sum total. The provincial government plans, in the few years to come, to construct a riverside economic and scenic belt centered on an area of 1,200 square kilometers by the Xiangjiang River in which new and high-tech industries, commercial and banking, high-grade residential quarters and holiday centers assemble. And thus the three cities are expected to develop into an area of considerable importance in Central China.

Guangdong Province

Guangdong Province, situated in the south of China's mainland, adjoins Hong Kong and Macao and faces Southeast Asia, occupying an area of 178,000 square kilometers with a population of 77.83 million in 2001.

A province earliest in reform and opening-up, Guangdong is one of the most economically vital and highly export-oriented regions. It has three special economic zones located in Shenzhen, Zhuhai and Shantou respectively; four state-level economic and technological development zones in Guangzhou, Zhanjiang and two other cities, 6 bonded areas, 10 state- or provincial- level high-tech development zones, and more than 50 development zones. In 2001 about 40 per cent of the provincial GNP realized its value in world market. About 40 per cent of Guangdong's construction funds came from overseas. Of the 500 top transnational companies, more than 250 have made investment in Guangdong.

Guangdong is a major commodity grain base in the country. Boasting varieties of economic crops, it is one of the three sugarcane-growing areas in China, a famous silkworm breeding area and a land rich in tropical and subtropical flowers and fruits. In the development of agriculture, according to the provincial government's planning, priority is given to popularizing practical advanced techniques in high-quality, high-

Major Indices of Guangdong Province

Index	2000	2001	The national total in 2001
Population			
Total by the end of the year (10,000 persons)	8,642	7,783	127,627
Birthrate (‰)		13.95	13.38
Mortality (‰)		5.12	6.43
Proportion of urban population (%)	55.00		37.7
Proportion of rural population (%)	45.00		62.3
National economy assessment			
GDP (100 million yuan)	9,662.2	10556.5	95,933
Growth rate over the previous year (%)	10.8	9.5	7.3
GDP per capita (yuan/person)	12,885	13,612	7,543
Proportion of the first industry (%)	10.4	9.6	15.2
Proportion of the second industry (%)	50.4	50.2	51.1
Proportion of the third industry (%)	39.3	40.2	33.6
Residents' level of consumption (yuan/person)	5,007		3,608
Growth rate over the previous year (%)	1.6		6.2
Volume of retail sales of consumer goods (100 million yuan)	4,071.9	4,515.3	37,595.2
Foreign trade and economy			
Export volume (USD100 million)	934.3	958.3	2,661.6
Import volume (USD100 million)	820.6	814.8	2,436.1
Foreign direct investment (10,000 US dollars)	1,128,091	1,193,203	4,687,759
People's life			
Per-capita disposable income of urban households (yuan)	9,761.6	10,415.2	6,859.6
Per-capita consumer spending of urban households (yuan)	8,016.9	8,099.6	5,309
Average net income per capita in the rural areas (yuan)	3,654.5	3,769.8	2,366.4
Average annual salary of an employee (yuan)		15,682	10,870
In HK, Macao and Taiwan invested enterprises (yuan)		13,601	12,544
In foreign invested enterprises (yuan)		18,192	16,101

yield, high-efficient agriculture, eco-agriculture, agriculture earning foreign exchange through export, high-quality economic crops and green foods such as fruits, vegetables, flowers and medicinal materials. At the same time the province is to carry on comprehensive oceanic exploitation, focusing on deep-sea fishing and seawater aquiculture.

Guangdong has gradually moved on towards the middle stage of industrialization. Currently its industrial output value comes first in the country. Its leading industries include electric household appliances, daily-use chemicals, textiles and medicines of which output of many products top the country. In industry Guangdong aims to vigorously develop the three rising mainstay industries: information technology, electrical machinery and petrochemicals; to renovate the three traditional cornerstone industries: textile and apparel, foodstuff and beverage, and building materials; and to help the growth of industries with great potentiality such as autos, medicines, paper making, and environmental protection. In the tertiary sector, efforts will be made to enlarge the use of foreign capital and private capital.

Guangdong has a rapid growth in the service sector. It is a nationwide trade center as well as a commodity-distributing center, flourishing in particular in wholesale trade where non-state economy has become the main body. Guangdong has always been in the van of financial reform and opening up to the outside world where there are the first stock market, first securities company, the first financial electronic settlement center, the largest inter-bank ATM network and the first real-time asset transfer system in the country. A large number of foreign funded financial firms have set up branches or representative offices in Guangdong.

Guangdong boasts convenient transport. Its highway network has the highest density in the country, with high-grade highways leading to numerous cities in and out of the province, including through buses and freight wagons to Hong Kong and Macao.The Baiyun International Airport in Guangzhou, offering regular flights to various cities home and abroad, ranks second in the country in its passenger handling capacity. There are key railways on which through trains carry passengers to Beijing, Shanghai and Kowloon regularly. A number of seaports and rivers provide water transport services. At present, construction of a high-speed track transport system linking up the cities in the Zhujiang River Delta is well under way.

As Guangdong's capital, Guangzhou is the second economic center as well as scientific and technological, educational, transport and information center in South China. It has a large-scale three-dimensional water-land-air transport network and well-developed textile, apparel, electronics and light industries. It leads the country in financial regulatory strength and capital competitiveness. Guangzhou is good at turning advanced technology into productive force. Its economic structure manifests obvious superiority in the country where the proportion of the tertiary sector is the largest among the nation's large and medium-sized cities. Guangzhou is also a manufacturing center in South China. Its long history of trade has enabled local people to cultivate a strong sense of mercantilism whereas its reform and opening up has nurtured in them a pioneering and adventuristic spirit. Lying in a forward position of opening up, Guangzhou takes the lead in economic internationalization. The provincial government is highly efficient in handling affairs and flexible and creative in implementing policies.

Shenzhen, separated from Hong Kong by a mere river, is the first special economic zone in China. In 1980s, it seemed that Shenzhen suddenly turned from a petty frontier township into an international metropolis overnight. This was indispensably attributive to introducing foreign investment and developing foreign trade. Now Shenzhen has well-equipped infrastructure facilities, numerous industrial districts, port districts, entry-exit check points, the largest land passenger transport check point in China's mainland —— Lohu Check Point, the largest land freight transport check point — Huanggang Check Point, the second largest container seaport — Shenzhen Port, and the fourth largest airport — Huangtian International Airport where transportation, communication, commerce and warehousing are all well developed. The electronic industry has an early start in Shenzhen where the tertiary industry has also developed rapidly. New and high-tech industries are growing steadily which include computer and software, communication and network, microelectronics and components, optical, mechanical and eletronic integration, digital audio-visual technique, biotechnology and new materials. Every year in October the China International High-Tech Achievements Fair is held in Shenzhen. There is in Shenzhen a relaxed economic system and favorable market environment with economic operational mechanism basically in line with international practice. There the banking market, securities market, futures market, real estate trading market, bonded means-of-production market, technology market, and talent market are bustling in business. Shenzhen occupies a dominant position in urban innovation and development of high-tech industries. Its capital competitiveness in particular its ability to secure funds ranks among the forefront in the country. Shenzhen is especially capable of turning advanced technology into productive force. As an immigration city, it is strongly trade-conscious and competition-conscious, and in it a cultural atmosphere of opening, tolerance and innovation has come into shape. Apart from traditional industries which lure foreign investors such as electronics, textiles, machinery and building materials, Shenzhen places stress on attracting foreign investment to develop high-tech industries and encourages investment in tertiary industries such as infrastructure, logistics and banking.

Other chief cities include Shantou, a major port on the eastern coast, a special economic zone and an industrial and commercial center well developed in textiles and light industries, sensitive material, and supersonic electronics industries; and Zhuhai, a special economic zone with fantastic environment, chiefly developing export processing industries such as electronics, apparel and foodstuffs.

Guangxi Zhuang Nationality Autonomous Region

Guangxi Zhuang Nationality Autonomous Region is situated on Southwest China coast, adjacent to Guangdong in the east, leading to Hong Kong and Macao via the

Xijiang River and adjoining Viet Nam in the southwest. It occupies a land area of 236,000 square kilometers with a population of 47.88 million in 2001.

Economic crops dominate agriculture of Guangxi, which is a major producing area of tropical and subtropical fruits. There are more than 60 bases growing famous, high quality and special subtropical fruits including sugarcane, banana, pineapple and litchi the output of which is among the highest in the country. The Beibu Gulf is one of China's four major tropical fisheries abundant in sea fishes.

With numerous rivers flowing through the province, Guangxi boasts water energy resources with potential installed capacity ranking sixth in the country. Among mineral deposits, non-ferrous metal species attain a large proportion. Manganese and

Major Indices of Guangxi Zhuang Nationality Autonomous Region

Index	2000	2001	The national total in 2001
Population			
Total by the end of the year (10,000 persons)	4,489	4,788	127,627
Birthrate (‰)		13.80	13.38
Mortality (‰)		6.07	6.43
Proportion of urban population (%)	28.15		37.7
Proportion of rural population (%)	71.85		62.3
National economy assessment			
GDP (100 million yuan)	2,050.1	2,231.2	95,933
Growth rate over the previous year (%)	7.3	8.2	7.3
GDP per capita (yuan/person)	4,319	4,697	7,543
Proportion of the first industry (%)	26.3	24.9	15.2
Proportion of the second industry (%)	36.5	36.6	51.1
Proportion of the third industry (%)	37.2	38.5	33.6
Residents' level of consumption (yuan/person)	2,147		3,608
Growth rate over the previous year (%)	5.6		6.2
Volume of retail sales of consumer goods (100 million yuan)	859.2	935.9	37,595.2
Foreign trade and economy			
Export volume (USD100 million)	16.4	13.5	2,661.6
Import volume (USD100 million)	6.4	7.3	2,436.1
Foreign direct investment (10,000 US dollars)	52,466	38,416	4,687,759
People's life			
Per-capita disposable income of urban households (yuan)	5,834.4	6,665.7	6,859.6
Per-capita consumer spending of urban households (yuan)	4,852.3	5,224.7	5,309
Average net income per capita in the rural areas (yuan)	1,864.5	1,944.3	2,366.4
Average annual salary of an employee (yuan)		9,075	10,870
In HK, Macao and Taiwan invested enterprises (yuan)		6,637	12,544
In foreign invested enterprises (yuan)		10,309	16,101

stannum reserves account for one third and antimony, one fourth, of the national total, and aluminum and zinc also assume a considerable proportion of deposits. Already Guangxi has formed its own dominating and special industries such as nonferrous metal industry centered on aluminum and stannum, energy industry centered on hydropower, processing industry centered on sugar refining, building material industry centered on cement and machine building industry centered on auto manufacturing.

Guangxi is a region on the frontiers, on the sea and on the river. Possessing the geographic advantages of "having Southwest China behind and Southeast Asia in front", it is a hub linking up southeast coastal region with southwest hinterland, and a convenient passage for the southwestern provinces to go to sea. It has formed a three-dimensional transport network consisting of water, railway, highway and air routes with railways as a mainstay. There are in the region 5 river ports and seaports, 20 berths for 10,000-tonnage ships. Railways run crisscross, some leading to seaports directly. Land routes lead to Hanoi. All townships in every county now have transport service.

Guangxi exports chiefly minerals, textiles, apparel, mechanical and electrical products to Asia, Europe and North America in the form of general trade. Currently Guangxi imports commodities from more than 60 countries and regions, chiefly from Viet Nam, Japan, ROK, South Africa, Finland, the US and Taiwan. Guangxi attracts foreign investment primarily from Hong Kong, Macao and Taiwan, secondly from European countries such as the Great Britain and France. There is a borderline as long as over 1,000 kilometers between Guangxi and Vietnam along which there are quite a few trading ports and frontier trading posts.

Guangxi boasts vagarious peaks and clear waters. As the saying goes, "The mountains and waters of Guilin are the finest under heaven." In the region there live 48 nationalities including Zhuang and Han ethnic groups, giving the area a strong flavor of ethnic culture. Great efforts have been made to develop tourism and holiday industry. So far five tourism areas have been established in Guilin, Nanning, Liuzhou, southeast Guangxi and along the coast respectively.

Guangxi enjoys preferential policies granted by the state to coastal and frontier open regions. It enjoys special favorable treatment granted to western regions and to minority nationality regions as well.

Chief cities in Guangxi include the capital Nanning, a coastal open city and a comprehensive industrial city mainly developing light industries, having a state-level high-tech development zone; Guilin, a key nationwide tourism city, having a state-level high-tech development zone, with machine building, electronics and handicrafts constituting mainstay industries; Liuzhou, the largest industrial base in the region; and Beihai, a coastal open city and state-level tourism and holiday area.

Hainan Province

Situated at the southern tip of China, Hainan is a province with the largest maritime space and the smallest land area in China. Bordering on Vietnam in the west, facing Taiwan in the east, and adjoining the Philippines, Brunei and Malaysia in the southeast and south, it covers a land area of 35,400 square kilometers with a population of 7.96 million in 2001.

A province within the tropical zone, Hainan is full of sunshine, heat and water and abundant in rice, sugarcane, rubber and coconuts among which the area of rubber plantation accounts for 70 per cent of the country's total. Currently Hainan has become China's most important "orchard" and "vegetable basket in winter". Great varieties of plants have won for it the name of "natural herbal medicine warehouse."

Hainan is extremely rich in offshore petroleum gas and land mineral resources. The area of proven petroleum gas in South China Sea comes to more than 120,000 square kilometers. The deposits of rich iron ore, titanium, zirconium and quartz rank in the forefront in the country. The largest rich iron ore field in Asia is found in Hainan. The round-the-island coastline of Hainan stretches as long as over 1,500 kilometers. With coastal fisheries covering an area of nearly 300,000 square kilometers, Hainan has immense potentiality in developing seawater aquiculture and sea fishing.

Relying on resources and environmental advantages, Hainan has a rapid development in agricultural and marine products processing, offshore petroleum gas industry, biological pharmacy, machine building and high-tech industries. Tourism has become one of the motive forces bringing along Hainan's economic growth.

Ever since the founding of Hainan Province and Hainan Special Economic Zone in 1988, a great number of large-scale infrastructure projects have been constructed among which the majority have been completed and put to use. Now the whole round-the-island freeway is opened to traffic; a score or so of seaports have been constructed; satisfactory infrastructure facilities available; electricity more than needed. It means that there are adequate conditions for the province to start large-scale construction and development.

Hainan has the unique advantage of being the sole "eco-island" and "sunshine island" in the country, which offers favorable geographical conditions especially suitable for developing high-efficient tropical agriculture, island tourism and modern industries. Therefore, the local government plans to build the island into a rising industrial province, high-efficient tropical agricultural base and a holiday resort. In

Major Indices of Hainan Province

Index	2000	2001	The national total in 2001
Population			
Total by the end of the year (10,000 persons)	787	796	127,627
Birthrate (‰)		15.23	13.38
Mortality (‰)		5.76	6.43
Proportion of urban population (%)	40.11		37.7
Proportion of rural population (%)	59.89		62.3
National economy assessment			
GDP (100 million yuan)	518.5	545.3	95,933
Growth rate over the previous year (%)	8.8	8.9	7.3
GDP per capita (yuan/person)	6,894	7,110	7,543
Proportion of the first industry (%)	37.9	36.7	15.2
Proportion of the second industry (%)	19.8	20.2	51.1
Proportion of the third industry (%)	42.3	43.0	33.6
Residents' level of consumption (yuan/person)	2,904		3,608
Growth rate over the previous year (%)	5.6		6.2
Volume of retail sales of consumer goods (100 million yuan)	172.5	187.5	37,595.2
Foreign trade and economy			
Export volume (USD100 million)	6.1	6.4	2,661.6
Import volume (USD100 million)	4.9	9.9	2,436.1
Foreign direct investment (10,000 US dollars)	43,080	46,691	4,687,759
People's life			
Per-capita disposable income of urban households (yuan)	5,358.3	5,838.8	6,859.6
Per-capita consumer spending of urban households (yuan)	4,082.6	4,367.9	5,309
Average net income per capita in the rural areas (yuan)	2,182.3	2,226.5	2,366.4
Average annual salary of an employee (yuan)		8,321	10,870
In HK, Macao and Taiwan invested enterprises (yuan)		10,088	12,544
In foreign invested enterprises (yuan)		11,296	16,101

order to lure foreign investment, no restrictions will be imposed as regards investment direction so long as no environment pollution, no resources damaging and no duplicated projects are involved. The state has granted a series of preferential policies to Hainan on fixed assets, tax revenue, finance and banking, customs duty, import and export, frontier trade, entry and exit of personnel, land use, etc. The same preferential policies are also granted to the Yangpu Development Zone, Haikou Bonded Area, and Qiongtai Agricultural Cooperative Development Experimental Zone. The provincial government has, within the limits authorized by the state, formulated various preferential and protective policies for investment for the benefit and convenience of foreign investors.

Chief cities of Hainan include the capital Haikou, a provincial economic and cultural center and an export-oriented economic port city; and Sanya, a tropical tourism seaport city on the southern tip of the island.

Chongqing Municipality

A municipality directly under the central government, Chongqing is the largest city in the country's hinterland. It occupies an area of 820,000 square kilometers with a population of 30.97 million in 2001.

The Yangtze River links twelve provinces and cities and cuts across three big economic belts: the eastern, central and western belts inhabited by hundreds of millions of people. The vast area upstream with rich resources, low-price labor force and better industrial foundation, is certainly an ideal place for foreign investment, technological and industrial transfer. With a view to speed up the development of central and western regions, the central government designated Chongqing as a municipality directly under the central government in 1997. In the development of the Yangtze River valley, Shanghai is the dragon head while Chongqing the dragon tail. As a city linking the upper reaches of the Yangtze and the central and western regions, Chongqing brings along the development of the vast and populous countryside surrounding it where there are important production bases of commodity grain, pork, traditional Chinese medicinal material, mulberry and orange.

Chongqing is the largest comprehensive industrial base in Southwest China. Machine building focusing on autos and motorcycles, chemicals focusing on natural gas and medicines have become two mainstay industries whereas new ones are taking shape such as foodstuffs, tourism, building and building materials. Currently high-tech industries are quickly developing with information engineering, bioengineering and environmental protection engineering as forerunners.

The financial sector in Chongqing has a rapid development. Having the largest foreign exchange market and inter-bank short-term loan market in the southwestern region, Chongqing is now gradually developing into a financial center of West China. Well developed in the circulation domain, Chongqing has long been a commodity distribution as well as trading center in the southwestern region and the upper reaches of the Yangtze River.

Chongqing has plentiful manpower and sufficient scientific, technological and educational strength where there are over a score of institutions of higher learning, about a thousand scientific research institutes, and technical personnel in various fields amounting to 560,000 in number.

The transportation and information sectors that used to restrict the development

of hinterland have undergone great changes. Chongqing, as the largest water-land-air transport hub in the southwestern region, has three key railways linking up the southern, northern and western provinces and regions. The highways also have a rapid development in recent years. The municipal government plans to establish a modernized transport system covering the whole area under its jurisdiction. It is expected that by 2005 it will take no more than 8 hours' journey to reach Chongqing city proper from any county town or township. Chongqing is the largest river port in the upper reaches of the Yangtze River through which ships can go abroad via Shanghai. After the completion of the Three Gorges Project, the Yangtze is navigable up to Chongqing for 10,000-tonnage steamers. To beef up the city's integral strength and optimize

Major Indices of Chongqing Municipality

Index	2000	2001	The national total in 2001
Population			
Total by the end of the year (10,000 persons)	3,090	3,097	127,627
Birthrate (‰)		9.70	13.38
Mortality (‰)		6.90	6.43
Proportion of urban population (%)	33.09		37.7
Proportion of rural population (%)	66.91		62.3
National economy assessment			
GDP (100 million yuan)	1,589.3	1,749.8	95,933
Growth rate over the previous year (%)	8.5	9.0	7.3
GDP per capita (yuan/person)	5,157	5,655	7,543
Proportion of the first industry (%)	17.8	16.7	15.2
Proportion of the second industry (%)	41.4	41.5	51.1
Proportion of the third industry (%)	40.8	41.7	33.6
Residents' level of consumption (yuan/person)	2,466		3,608
Growth rate over the previous year (%)	5.1		6.2
Volume of retail sales of consumer goods (100 million yuan)	643.4	699.3	37,595.2
Foreign trade and economy			
Export volume (USD100 million)	18.5	11.7	2,661.6
Import volume (USD100 million)	7.9	9.7	2,436.1
Foreign direct investment (10,000 US dollars)	24,436	25,649	4,687,759
People's life			
Per-capita disposable income of urban households (yuan)	6,276.0	6,721.1	6,859.6
Per-capita consumer spending of urban households (yuan)	5,569.8	5,873.7	5,309
Average net income per capita in the rural areas (yuan)	1,892.4	1,971.2	2,366.4
Average annual salary of an employee (yuan)		9,523	10,870
In HK, Macao and Taiwan invested enterprises (yuan)		10,694	12,544
In foreign invested enterprises (yuan)		12,903	16,101

investment environment, Chongqing is carrying on the construction of key projects centered on transport, communication, urban infrastructure, and eco-environmental protection.

In order to open up wider to the outside world, Chongqing has started to construct a new district in the north of the city proper where there are five zones including state-level export processing, auto manufacturing, optical and electronic, software and environmental protection. Within the zones services are provided involving customs formalities, foreign exchange management, and import and export commodities inspection. Moreover, in-zone enterprises are entitled to enjoy the same preferential treatment as that granted to the state-level economic and technological development zones and state-level high-tech industrial development zones and that granted by the municipal government. Now the Chongqing municipal government is planning to build the new district into a modern industrial base within 10 years.

Chongqing is looked upon by investors home and overseas as one of the hot spots for investment in China. Up to the end of 2001, there were already 3,000-plus enterprises from more than 50 countries and regions established in the form of joint venture, cooperative joint venture or wholly foreign invested enterprises. Canada, Japan and the Great Britain have set up consulates in Chongqing. Austria and other countries have set up representative offices of Chamber of Commerce respectively.

Chongqing, connecting western region with eastern, is planning to further develop itself into an updated industrial base, commercial center, banking center, scientific, technological, educational, and information center in the upper reaches of the Yangtze.

Sichuan Province

Sichuan, situated in Southwest China in the upper reaches of the Yangtze, occupies an area of 485,000 square kilometers with a population of 86.4 million in 2001.

The Sichuan basin is the principal part of the province in the middle of which lies the Chengdu plain, known as "Nature's storehouse" as far back as 2,000 years ago, thanks to its vast expanse of fertile land and well-developed agriculture. Later on the nice name is used to refer to the Sichuan Province as a whole.

Sichuan is the homeland of giant panda. Rich in tourism resources, the province is one having the richest world cultural and natural heritage, the most numerous state-level scenic spots and tourist attractions. Wide rivers running through gorges and canyons produce abundant water energy resources that top the country. As only 10 per cent of water energy resources have been exploited so far, further exploitation has become the primarily invested project, aiming at "transmitting electricity from

Major indices of Sichuan Province

Index	2000	2001	The national total in 2001
Population			
Total by the end of the year (10,000 persons)	8,329	8,640	127,627
Birthrate (‰)		11.16	13.38
Mortality (‰)		6.79	6.43
Proportion of urban population (%)	26.69		37.7
Proportion of rural population (%)	73.31		62.3
National economy assessment			
GDP (100 million yuan)	4,010.3	4,421.8	95,933
Growth rate over the previous year (%)	9.0	9.2	7.3
GDP per capita (yuan/person)	4,784	5,250	7,543
Proportion of the first industry (%)	23.6	22.2	15.2
Proportion of the second industry (%)	42.4	39.7	51.1
Proportion of the third industry (%)	34.0	38.1	33.6
Residents' level of consumption (yuan/person)	2,456		3,608
Growth rate over the previous year (%)	11.8		6.2
Volume of retail sales of consumer goods (100 million yuan)	1,523.7	1,680.4	37,595.2
Foreign trade and economy			
Export volume (USD100 million)	27.8	16.8	2,661.6
Import volume (USD100 million)	13.4	16.8	2,436.1
Foreign direct investment (10,000 US dollars)	43,694	58,188	4,687,759
People's life			
Per-capita disposable income of urban households (yuan)	5,894.3	6,360.5	6,859.6
Per-capita consumer spending of urban households (yuan)	4,855.8	5,176.2	5,309
Average net income per capita in the rural areas (yuan)	1,903.6	1,987.0	2,366.4
Average annual salary of an employee (yuan)		9,934	10,870
In HK, Macao and Taiwan invested enterprises (yuan)		10,167	12,544
In foreign invested enterprises (yuan)		10,408	16,101

the west to the east". When the project is completed, Sichuan will become the biggest hydropower transmission base in China.

Sichuan is a major agricultural province where the output of grain, edible oil, cocoon, live pigs, tea, and orange rank in the forefront in the country. Its medicinal plants account for three-fourth of the national total, winning for the province the good name of "treasure house of traditional Chinese medicine" though the output of medicinal materials makes up only one-tenth of the national total. Moreover, Sichuan is one of China's three major forest zones and five major pastoral areas.

The reserves of over 10 minerals including titanium, lithium and silver come first in the country. With solid industrial foundation, Sichuan has developed such pillar industries as electronics, machinery, metallurgy, chemicals, medicine, foodstuffs and building materials. Priority industries include electronics and information technology, hydroelectricity, machinery and metallurgy, medicines and chemicals, beverage and foodstuffs.

More than one thousand years ago the celebrated Tang Dynasty poet Li Bai wrote in an exaggerated way that "It is easier to climb to Heaven than to take the Sichuan Footpath." But now in Sichuan a three-dimensional transport system has taken shape comprising highway, railway, civil aviation, inland navigation and pipe transportation. To date its freeway transport takes the lead in West China. With Chengdu as a core, a network has basically formed leading to all major cities within the province and large ports along the Yangtze. Chengdu Shuangliu International Airport is the largest one of its kind in West China.

Sichuan has three major advantages for development including rich natural resources, chiefly in tourism, water energy, minerals, biology and natural gas; immense market capacity; and advanced science and technology in particular in the fields of nuclear industry, aviation, space flight, electronics and communication. Meanwhile, Sichuan is a major province rendering labor export services. The first home labor export base and training base for export of specialized labor force were established in the province.

Chengdu the provincial capital is the scientific, technological, commercial and banking center in Southwest China and a distributing center for all varieties of important goods and materials in the western region. As a banking center, Chengdu has adequate capital strength and financial regulatory ability. Agencies of banks, stock markets and insurance companies of the central government in charge of business in Southwest China all have a presence in Chengdu. Moreover, Chengdu not only has a solid foundation in industry, economy and technology with completed industrial and commercial categories, but also is a city suitable for relaxation and holiday taking.

Other chief cities include Panzhihua, a rising steel industrial city in southwestern part of the province; Mianyang, developing chiefly electronics, metallurgy, foodstuffs, building materials and textile industries; Leshan, an industrial, commercial and tourism city mainly developing foodstuffs, silk fabrics, medicines, chemicals and mechanical and electrical industries; and Yibin, a central city in the south of the province, known for power and light industries in particular liquor-making.

Guizhou Province

Guizhou, a province in Southwest China, covers an area of 176,000 square kilometers with a population of 37.99 million in 2001.

Guizhou has always been referred to as a place consisting of "80 per cent of mountains, 10 per cent of waters and 10 per cent of farmland", meaning that restricted by unfavorable traffic and natural conditions. Guizhou has suffered a slow economic growth despite of its abundant exploitable resources. However, in recent years, numerous farmers in mountainous areas have already had adequate food and clothing. Agriculture is now developing in a diversified way. No longer is the province ill informed now with program-controlled phones found everywhere in the countryside and mobile switching centers set up in all cities and towns within the province.

Guizhou has initially established an economic system centered on energy, raw materials, machinery, electronics, textile and light industries based on its natural re-

Major Indices of Guizhou Province

Index	2000	2001	The national total in 2001
Population			
Total by the end of the year (10,000 persons)	3,525	3,799	127,627
Birthrate (‰)		18.56	13.38
Mortality (‰)		7.23	6.43
Proportion of urban population (%)	23.87		37.7
Proportion of rural population (%)	76.13		62.3
National economy assessment			
GDP (100 million yuan)	993.5	1,082.2	95,933
Growth rate over the previous year (%)	8.7	8.8	7.3
GDP per capita (yuan/person)	2,662	2,865	7,543
Proportion of the first industry (%)	27.3	25.3	15.2
Proportion of the second industry (%)	39.0	39.0	51.1
Proportion of the third industry (%)	33.7	35.7	33.6
Residents' level of consumption (yuan/person)	1,608		3,608
Growth rate over the previous year (%)	1.9		6.2
Volume of retail sales of consumer goods (100 million yuan)	343.7	378.0	37,595.2
Foreign trade and economy			
Export volume (USD100 million)	8.6	5.1	2,661.6
Import volume (USD100 million)	3.7	3.5	2,436.1
Foreign direct investment (10,000 US dollars)	2,501	2,829	4,687,759
People's life			
Per-capita disposable income of urban households (yuan)	5,122.2	5,451.9	6,859.6
Per-capita consumer spending of urban households (yuan)	4,278.3	4,273.9	5,309
Average net income per capita in the rural areas (yuan)	1,347.2	1,411.7	2,366.4
Average annual salary of an employee (yuan)		8,991	10,870
In HK, Macao and Taiwan invested enterprises (yuan)		9,695	12,544
In foreign invested enterprises (yuan)		8,871	16,101

sources and technological advantages. Liquor making and cigarette are mainstay light industries in which the liquor *maotai* is reputed as "national liquor."

In 2002, Guizhou presented a series of major projects inviting investment from home and overseas among which energy resource is a key field for exploitation in the next few years. Guizhou is rich in water and thermal energies, which are complementary to each other. Currently an array of hydropower stations is under construction in light of the state plan of "transmitting electricity from the west to the east." Guizhou, having proven coal reserves amounting to 52.6 billion tons, is known as a "coal sea in the south of the Yangtze". A high-grade coal exploitation project is under planning to coordinate with the plan of "transmitting electricity from the west to the east." Guizhou is rich in high-grade, concentrated mineral reserves in particular alumina, phosphorus ore, antimony, manganese and gold. Already the largest electrolytic aluminum plant, the largest phosphate fertilizer base, the largest abrasive and synthetic diamond production and export base in the country have been constructed. Moreover, such fields as biological pharmacy and local delicacies, auto parts and electronic components, urban infrastructure facilities and services still have ample space for development.

Guizhou has basically completed an integral transport network centered on Guiyang comprising railways, highways, airlines and water routes. The railways linking up Sichuan, Yunnan, Guizhou and Guangxi have opened a passage for the southwestern region going to sea. Nevertheless, for a province featuring high mountain landforms, transport construction is still an urgent job to be carried on. During the Tenth Five-Year Plan period, the Guizhou sections of two key state routes, the Chongqing-Zhanjiang Highway and Shanghai-Ruili Highway will be completed. As such high-grade roads, some already open to traffic, some just about to start construction, are to bear heavy traffic flow, investors home and overseas are welcome to purchase part of the shares, whole of the shares, or wholly invest in the project.

Guizhou has remarkable scenery, distinctive ethnic flavor and abundant tourist resources to be exploited. It is promising to open new tourist routes, explore new tourist attractions, run service facilities and develop recreation projects. In addition there are varieties of biological resources such as traditional medicinal materials of which one of the four major producing areas in the country is in Guizhou.

In the western development, the province plans to become a passage going to sea and a land transport hub in the southeastern region, an eco-protective screen for the upper reaches of the Yangtze and the Zhujiang River, an energy and raw material base in the southern region, a base of high-tech industries represented by aviation and space flight, electronical information, biological technology, and a tourism province featuring natural landscape and ethnic charm.

Chief cities include the capital Guiyang, a political, economic and cultural center of the province, having aluminum smelting, machinery, cement, tobacco and liquor-making industries; Liupanshui, a western city known for coal industry and the largest charcoal production base in the southwestern region; Zunyi, a city having metallurgy, electrical appliances, liquor-making and tobacco industries.

Yunnan Province

Yunnan is situated in the southwestern frontier, bordering Myanmar on the west and southwest, and adjoining Laos and Vietnam in the south. It is a land passage connecting Southeast Asia with Asian hinterland. Covering an area of 394,000 square kilometers, it had a population of 42.87 million in 2001.

Yunnan is in possession of plentiful biological resources. Containing almost all plant species in the tropical, subtropical, temperate and even frigid zones, it has been reputed as a "kingdom of plants", "treasure house of crude drugs", "natural garden" and "home of perfume". Although boasting great varieties of economic crops, Yunnan is rational in exploiting its biological resources. So far, tobacco, crude drugs and tropical fruit growing has been of a grand scale whereas flowers and plants for ornamentation, coffee and perfume growing is just on the rise. The favorable geographic and climatic conditions, numerous ethnic groups and unique culture help the province to develop tourism into a rising industry.

Yunnan abounds in non-ferrous metals such as aluminum, zinc, tin, copper and nickel the deposits, of which all rank among the forefront in the country. Among the precious and rare element metals, thallium and cadmium reserves both come first, and silver, germanium and platinum family second in the country. There are also considerable water and coal energy reserves and some chemical material ore depostis in the province. To date Yunnan has established on a certain scale an industry specialized in non-ferrous metal ore mining, dressing and smelting. It is also a national production base of tin, copper and phosphate fertilizer.

Yunnan, literally meaning "south of rosy clouds" in the Chinese language, is a miniature of China's natural scenery where as the saying goes, "Four seasons appear at different parts of the same mountain; sky varies looking from places at a mere distance of 10 kilometers." It is a province inhabited by a majority of ethnic groups each presents different cultural pattern resulted from different natural environment and historical background. Yunnan, thanks to its high mountains and deep valleys, glacier of the contemporary age, highland lakes, karst landform, ornamental flowers

Major Indices of Yunnan Province

Index	2000	2001	The national total in 2001
Population			
Total by the end of the year (10,000 persons)	4,288	4,287	127,627
Birthrate (‰)		18.51	13.38
Mortality (‰)		7.57	6.43
Proportion of urban population (%)	23.36		37.7
Proportion of rural population (%)	76.64		62.3
National economy assessment			
GDP (100 million yuan)	1,955.1	2,077.5	95,933
Growth rate over the previous year (%)	7.1	6.5	7.3
GDP per capita (yuan/person)	4,637	4,872	7,543
Proportion of the first industry (%)	22.3	21.7	15.2
Proportion of the second industry (%)	43.1	42.4	51.1
Proportion of the third industry (%)	34.6	35.9	33.6
Residents' level of consumption (yuan/person)	2,530		3,608
Growth rate over the previous year (%)	9.0		6.2
Volume of retail sales of consumer goods (100 million yuan)	583.2	655.4	37,595.2
Foreign trade and economy			
Export volume (USD100 million)	18.8	11.5	2,661.6
Import volume (USD100 million)	7.9	10.0	2,436.1
Foreign direct investment (10,000 US dollars)	12,812	6,457	4,687,759
People's life			
Per-capita disposable income of urban households (yuan)	6,324.6	6,797.7	6,859.6
Per-capita consumer spending of urban households (yuan)	5,185.3	5,252.6	5,309
Average net income per capita in the rural areas (yuan)	1,478.6	1,533.7	2,366.4
Average annual salary of an employee (yuan)		10,537	10,870
In HK, Macao and Taiwan invested enterprises (yuan)		10,965	12,544
In foreign invested enterprises (yuan)		13,611	16,101

and grasses, historic sites and cultural relics, traditional gardens and ethnic charm, has set up a number of feature tourism development zones at an initial phase.

As a result of construction for many years, Yunnan has improved greatly its infrastructure facilities. A road network has taken shape, which is centered on Kunming the capital and leads to cities within and without the province and neighboring countries such as Myanmar, Laos, Vietnam and Thailand. As these countries are also accessible via railways or water routes, Yunnan, together with other southwestern provinces, holds every year a "China Kunming Export Commodities Fair." With the strengthening of the Lancangjiang River—Menam Khong River Sub-Regional Economic Cooperation, Yunnan is becoming both a passage and a forward post of the southwestern region of China in opening up to the outside world.

In the course of western development, Yunnan plans to vigorously cultivate and develop five major industries: high-tech industry, biotic resources exploiting and innovating industry, tobacco, mining and tourism industries; to build five major bases: the largest biotic resources exploiting and innovating base, the largest safety tobacco planting and cigarette production base, the largest phosphorous chemical production base, major non-ferrous metal industrial base and energy base for the "West-East electricity transmission project."

Chief cities include Kunming the capital, a rising industrial base specialized in precision machine tools, optical instruments, cigarette-making and non-ferrous metal smelting; Qujing, a central city in the northeast of the province, well developed in coal and cigarette industries; Dali, head city of Bai nationality prefecture in the west of the province; and Yuxi, a city in the central part well known for light industries featuring cigarette making.

Tibet Autonomous Region

Tibet Autonomous Region is situated in Southwest China's border area, adjoining Nepal, Sikkim, Bhutan, India and Myanmar with a total borderline as long as 4,000-plus kilometers. Occupying a land area of 1.22 million square kilometers, about one-eighth of the national total, it had a population of 2.63 million in 2001.

Tibet consists of largely a plateau called Qinghai-Tibet plateau which, at an average elevation of over 4,000 meters, is one the largest in area and highest in altitude in the world. Favored with long sunshine time, great temperature difference and long growth period, Tibet has high-yield and good-quality vegetables and crops including the staple highland barley and wheat. Most of crops in Tibet, watered with melted snow and therefore free of pollution, are fit for processing into green food. Tibet is one of the five major forest regions in China where grow plentiful highly exploitable medicinal plants.

Tibet has abundant sunshine energy. Its water reserves make up one-fifth of the country's total. Of its rich ferrous, non-ferrous and non-metallic minerals, borax and lithium deposits rank first in the country. Bountiful terrestrial heat resources bring convenience to Tibetans' daily life and production. There is great potentiality to develop geothermal power.

Agriculture and animal husbandry constitute the main body of Tibetan economy. Tibet is one of the five major pastoral areas in China. In former times there was only traditional ethnic handicrafts in Tibet, but now an industrial system has taken shape initially including mining and building materials. The traditional handicrafts have already developed into a large-scale ethnic industry.

Tibet has long been known as a "land of snow" where the "Divine Mountain", "Sacred Lake", and its unique culture, scenery and folklore are luring more and more tourists, explorers and mountaineers. For many people, Tibet is a mysterious and romantic "Pure Land" (a paradise in Buddhism). In recent years, tourism has become a mainstay industry earning most of the region's foreign exchanges.

Inadequacy in infrastructure facilities is the main factor that hinders Tibet from economic development. To make up for the deficiency, the state has taken measures to increase investment for infrastructure facilities and stepped up the construction of railways, highways, airports, power, communication and water conservancy facilities.

Major Indices of Tibet Autonomous Region

Index	2000	2001	The national total in 2001
Population			
Total by the end of the year (10,000 persons)	262	263	127,627
Birthrate (‰)		18.60	13.38
Mortality (‰)		6.50	6.43
Proportion of urban population (%)	18.93		37.7
Proportion of rural population (%)	81.07		62.3
National economy assessment			
GDP (100 million yuan)	117.5	138.6	95,933
Growth rate over the previous year (%)	9.4	12.6	7.3
GDP per capita (yuan/person)	4,559	5,302	7,543
Proportion of the first industry (%)	30.9	27.1	15.2
Proportion of the second industry (%)	23.2	23.2	51.1
Proportion of the third industry (%)	45.9	49.7	33.6
Residents' level of consumption (yuan/person)	1,823		3,608
Growth rate over the previous year (%)	7.1		6.2
Volume of retail sales of consumer goods (100 million yuan)	42.9	49.0	37,595.2
Foreign trade and economy			
Export volume (USD100 million)	1.1	0.8	2,661.6
Import volume (USD100 million)	0.4	0.2	2,436.1
Foreign direct investment (10,000 US dollars)			4,687,759
People's life			
Per-capita disposable income of urban households (yuan)	7,426.3	7,869.2	6,859.6
Per-capita consumer spending of urban households (yuan)	5,554.4	5,994.4	5,309
Average net income per capita in the rural areas (yuan)	1,330.8	1,404.0	2,366.4
Average annual salary of an employee (yuan)		19,144	10,870
In HK, Macao and Taiwan invested enterprises (yuan)			12,544
In foreign invested enterprises (yuan)		17,877	16,101

In 1949 when new China was founded, there was only a makeshift road one kilometer long for the use of autos in the whole Tibet region, not to be compared with the operating highway lines totalled 26,000 kilometers today. The chief traffic in Tibet is by roads, assisted by airlines. In 2001, the construction of Qinghai-Tibet railway from Ge'ermu in the east to Lhasa in the west, 1,118 kilometers in full length, was started and is to be completed in 2007. By that time the plentiful coal and petroleum in the northwestern region will be conveyed to the Qinghai—Tibet plateau through the economical and convenient railway line, which has far-reaching significance in regulating energy resource structure, exploiting tourist resources and protecting highland eco-environment of the Tibet region.

Tibet has a rapid development in telecommunication. Up to now telephone services, which have joined in the national automatic telephone network, are available in all counties of Tibet. Apart from traditional services, audiotext service, Internet and e-mail services have been offered. Mobile phones are available in all cities and towns at prefectural level and above and a part of county towns along the key transport lines.

Six distinctive mainstay industries in Tibet are worthy of attention by investors home and overseas. They are tourism; Tibetan medicine; highland feature biotic industry and green food (including beverage) processing; farm and livestock product processing; ethnic handicrafts; mining, building and building material industris.

In order to support Tibet in its development, the state has granted a series of preferential policies. To seek investment from overseas, the Tibet Autonomous Region government is authorized to examine and approve on its own all foreign-funded projects without scope limit or restrictions by the state industrial policies except for those projects prohibited or need to be fitted in comprehensively by the state. Meanwhile, more relaxed and favorable policies are granted to Tibet than to other hinterland provinces as regards tax revenue, finance, foreign trade and economy, entry-exit control and land use.

Lhasa is the capital of Tibet and Rikaze is the second largest city.

Shaanxi Province

Northwest China's Shaanxi Province occupies an area of 205,000 square kilometers with a population of 36.59 million in 2001.

In Shaanxi, apart from the loess plateau that covers nearly half of Shaanxi's total land area, there are the Guanzhong Basin known as "a plain stretching 800 *li*," (traditional unit of length, roughly half a kilometer) and the Hanzhong Basin, called "land of rice and fish in Shaanxi." The province is rich in fruits such as apple, soft

Major Indices of Shaanxi Province

Index	2000	2001	The national total in 2001
Population			
Total by the end of the year (10,000 persons)	3,605	3,659	127,627
Birthrate (‰)		10.50	13.38
Mortality (‰)		6.34	6.43
Proportion of urban population (%)	32.26		37.7
Proportion of rural population (%)	67.74		62.3
National economy assessment			
GDP (100 million yuan)	1,660.9	1,841.2	95,933
Growth rate over the previous year (%)	9.0	9.1	7.3
GDP per capita (yuan/person)	4,549	5,015	7,543
Proportion of the first industry (%)	16.8	15.2	15.2
Proportion of the second industry (%)	44.1	44.3	51.1
Proportion of the third industry (%)	39.1	40.5	33.6
Residents' level of consumption (yuan/person)	2,035		3,608
Growth rate over the previous year (%)	6.3		6.2
Volume of retail sales of consumer goods (100 million yuan)	607.6	665.1	37,595.2
Foreign trade and economy			
Export volume (USD100 million)	13.3	14.2	2,661.6
Import volume (USD100 million)	10.6	12.3	2,436.1
Foreign direct investment (10,000 US dollars)	28,842	35,174	4,687,759
People's life			
Per-capita disposable income of urban households (yuan)	5,124.2	5,483.7	6,859.6
Per-capita consumer spending of urban households (yuan)	4,276.7	4,637.7	5,309
Average net income per capita in the rural areas (yuan)	1,443.9	1,490.8	2,366.4
Average annual salary of an employee (yuan)		9,120	10,870
In HK, Macao and Taiwan invested enterprises (yuan)		9,788	12,544
In foreign invested enterprises (yuan)		13,524	16,101

pear, red date, and kiwi fruit. Fruit processing (chiefly apple) has become a feature industry in Shaanxi.

Over one thousand years up to two thousand years ago, Shaanxi used to be China's political center. Xi'an was then the capital for several dynasties. With plentiful historic sites and tourism resources, the province is stepping up the scope and level of tourism in recent years. Auxiliary services are also being fostered.

Boasting rich coal, natural gas and petroleum reserves, Shaanxi is a major energy base and a location of long energy continuance in days to come. Shaanxi has an industrial system dominated by machine building, electronics, textiles, medicine, chemicals, energy and foodstuff. Currently five feature industries are emphatically developed: high-tech industry, tourism, fruit industry, national defense scientific and technological industry, and energy chemicals.

Shaanxi has a great number of institutions of higher learning and scientific and research institutes. It is one of the provinces where talents gather, who manifest marked comprehensive high-tech developing and integration ability. Its high-tech industries are concentrated in the fields of electronic information technology, bioengineering, new materials, new energy, software and high-efficient agriculture. Currently there are three state-level high-tech industrial development zones located in Si'an, Baoji and Yangling respectively. In addition, there is also the Xi'an Economic and Technological Development Zone.

Shaanxi has a solid foundation of railway, highway and air transportation. State trunk highway and the Great Western Passage run crisscross through the province. On the basis of the transport framework constituted by six key state highways, a sub-network of trunk highway is under construction. It plans to link up all the cities within the province with the four state-level developments zones, the energy and heavy chemical base, farm, forest and fruit specialties base and main tourist districts. At the same time, it will connect all central cities of the surrounding provinces to form a "one-day transport circle", meaning that it takes only one day's journey to get to any of these central cities.

Xi'an the provincial capital is a political, economic, scientific and technological, cultural, transportation and commercial center in the northwestern region. It is one of China's seven ancient capitals rich in cultural heritage and is therefore a well-favored tourism city. There are numerous scientific research institutes and institutions of higher learning in the city, which is called "scientific city in West China". With comprehensive scientific and technological strength ranked in the forefront in China, it is a major machinery, textile, electronics and defense industrial base. Xi'an's defense science and technology industry is most competitive at home. It is a major production base in the fields of aviation, space flight and weapons.

Other chief cities include Xianyang, a city known for textile, electronics and foodstuff industries; Baoji, commody transfer and distributing center in Shaanxi-Gansu-Ningxia area, having machine building industry; and Tongchuan, a city with well developed coal industry in the central part of the province.

Gansu Province

Gansu Province, situated in the hinterland of Northwest China adjoining Mongolian People's Republic, occupies an area of 450,000 square kilometers with a population of 25.75 million in 2001.

Major Indices of Gansu Province

Index	2000	2001	The national total in 2001
Population			
Total by the end of the year (10,000 persons)	2,562	2,575	127,627
Birthrate (‰)		13.58	13.38
Mortality (‰)		6.43	6.43
Proportion of urban population (%)	24.01		37.7
Proportion of rural population (%)	75.99		62.3
National economy assessment			
GDP (100 million yuan)	983.4	1,074.9	95,933
Growth rate over the previous year (%)	8.7	9.4	7.3
GDP per capita (yuan/person)	3,838	4,173	7,543
Proportion of the first industry (%)	19.7	19.3	15.2
Proportion of the second industry (%)	44.7	44.9	51.1
Proportion of the third industry (%)	35.6	35.8	33.6
Residents' level of consumption (yuan/person)	1,734		3,608
Growth rate over the previous year (%)	7.1		6.2
Volume of retail sales of consumer goods (100 million yuan)	362.7	395.4	37,595.2
Foreign trade and economy			
Export volume (USD100 million)	4.2	4.8	2,661.6
Import volume (USD100 million)	2.7	4.4	2,436.1
Foreign direct investment (10,000 US dollars)	6,235	7,439	4,687,759
People's life			
Per-capita disposable income of urban households (yuan)	4,916.3	5,382.9	6,859.6
Per-capita consumer spending of urban households (yuan)	4,126.5	4,420.3	5,309
Average net income per capita in the rural areas (yuan)	1,428.7	1,508.6	2,366.4
Average annual salary of an employee (yuan)		9,949	10,870
In HK, Macao and Taiwan invested enterprises (yuan)		9,822	12,544
In foreign invested enterprises (yuan)		11,911	16,101

High-yield drought-resistant grain crops are mainly grown in Gansu where animal husbandry is well developed. It is one of the five major grassland pastoral areas in China. The output of its wild medicinal materials comes second in the country.

Gansu has bountiful mineral resources. The reserves of eleven minerals include nickel, cobalt, platinum family, and selenium rank first in the country. It has also considerable deposits of precious metals and non-ferrous metals such as lead, zinc, copper and aluminum. Leading industries in Gansu include power, non-ferrous metal smelting, petroleum processing, petrochemical and machine building. Gansu is a major raw material base and non-ferrous metal industrial base. The eastern Gansu area is now rising to become a new petrochemical base.

Jiuquan and Jiayuguan are two neighboring cities in the central part of an area called "passageway west of the Yellow River", referring to the most rich-endowed area of Gansu Province. Jiuquan is a historic and cultural city on the Silk Road, having a solid foundation for building material, papermaking, wine making, food-stuffs and machine building. Jiayuguan is known for the Jiayuguan Pass, which is the end of the Great Wall reputed as "first pass under heaven". It is a modernized city integrating industry with tourism where the Jiuquan Steel Company, the largest in-corporated steel company in Northwest China, is located. Now Jiuquan-Jiayuguan economic belt has basically taken shape.

Gansu stretches 1,650 kilometers from east to west in which the topography is peculiar and landform varied. There is Gobi desert together with green mountains and clear waters; there is ancient cultural heritage on the Silk Road and there are distinctive ethnic conditions and customs. Despite abundant tourism resources, its tourist economy remains to be developed.

In the course of western development, Gansu plans to launch a large number of engineering projects including high-grade highway construction; airport renovation, expansion and building; railways, oil, gas transmission pipes and lines and auxiliary facilities construction; rural electrified wire netting renovation; and basic tourist fa-cilities construction.

Chief cities include Lanzhou the capital, which is a geometrical center of the national domain, a hub of north-south transportation, post and telecommunication as well as a commercial center, mainly developing petrochemical, petroleum equip-ment manufacturing and non-ferrous metal industries; Tienshui, second largest city in Gansu, well developed in processing industry, in particular in machine building, electrical appliances and electronics processing industries; and Baiyin, a major coal, non-ferrous metal industrial base in the province.

Qinghai Province

Qinghai Province is situated on the Qinghai-Tibet plateau at an average elevation of over 3,000 meters. It occupies an area of more than 720,000 square kilometers, the fourth largest in the country, with a population of 5.23 million in 2001.

Qinghai is the source of the Yangtze, the Yellow River and the Lancangjiang River. As one of the five major grassland pastoral areas in China, it chiefly develops animal husbandry and planting. Its output of yak and Tibetan sheep ranks in the fore-front in the country. Having a long history in artificial planting of Tibetan medicinal materials, Qinghai now has adequate conditions to develop it into a feature industry. With both distinctive highland natural resources and cultural resources rich in ethnic flavor, the region has established Qinghai Lake Tourism Zone, Hehuang Tourism Zone, Kunlun Cultural and Tourism Zone and the Source of Three Rivers Tourism Zone.

Qinghai is a province scarce in population but large in area and rich in resources. There are eleven varieties of minerals including potash fertilizer, lithium, magnesium, chemical limestone, silica and asbestos, the deposits of which come first in the country. Petroleum, natural gas, gold and non-ferrous metals are well worthy of exploitation.

In recent years, Qinghai has invested substantially in infrastructure construction including renovation of state highways and provincial trunk highways, the "roads leading to every village" project, renovation and expansion of airports and develop-

Major Indices of Qinghai Province

Index	2000	2001	The national total in 2001
Population			
Total by the end of the year (10,000 persons)	518	523	127,627
Birthrate (‰)		19.06	13.38
Mortality (‰)		6.44	6.43
Proportion of urban population (%)	34.76		37.7
Proportion of rural population (%)	65.24		62.3
National economy assessment			
GDP (100 million yuan)	263.6	300.8	95,933
Growth rate over the previous year (%)	9.0	12.0	7.3
GDP per capita (yuan/person)	5,087	5,732	7,543
Proportion of the first industry (%)	14.6	13.7	15.2
Proportion of the second industry (%)	43.2	44.1	51.1
Proportion of the third industry (%)	42.1	42.3	33.6
Residents' level of consumption (yuan/person)	2,255		3,608
Growth rate over the previous year (%)	6.4		6.2
Volume of retail sales of consumer goods (100 million yuan)	82.1	90.4	37,595.2
Foreign trade and economy			
Export volume (USD100 million)	1.3	1.7	2,661.6
Import volume (USD100 million)	0.9	0.9	2,436.1
Foreign direct investment (10,000 US dollars)		3,649	4,687,759
People's life			
Per-capita disposable income of urban households (yuan)	5,170.0	5,853.7	6,859.6
Per-capita consumer spending of urban households (yuan)	4,185.7	4,698.6	5,309
Average net income per capita in the rural areas (yuan)	1,490.5	1,557.3	2,366.4
Average annual salary of an employee (yuan)		12,906	10,870
In HK, Macao and Taiwan invested enterprises (yuan)		5,727	12,544
In foreign invested enterprises (yuan)			16,101

ment of branch airlines. As a result, transportation has been greatly improved. At the same time telephone system and network communication have developed even more rapidly.

In a considerably long process of western development, Qinghai will give priority to eco-environmental protection, infrastructure construction, feature economy promotion, and technological and educational development. In the field of industries, five feature industrial chains will be shaped. They are the salt chemical industry chain which integrates salt lake sylvite exploitation with comprehensive use of magnesium, potash, selenium and borax resources; the power and high power-consumption industries chain which integrates hydropower resources exploitation with non-ferrous metallurgy industry; the oil-gas tapping and oil-gas chemical industry chain integrating prospecting and recovery with processing and utilization of petroleum and natural gas; the bio-resources exploitation and utilization industry chain centered on Chinese and Tibetan medicine, green food, bio-products which integrates protection and planting with processing to add value to highland bio-resources; and the tourist economic chain integrating tourism resources exploitation with food, accommodation, recreation and shopping services. With respect to areas, priority will be given to "one district, two belts, and three parks." By one district it refers to Chaidamu Resource Exploitaton District, primarily dealing with salt lake chemicals, petroleum gas and non-ferrous metals. By two belts it refers to two passageways: the non-polluting industry passage headed by the hydropower industry in the upper reaches of the Yellow River, and the power consumption industry and farm and livestock products processing industry passage in Huangshui valley. By three parks it refers to Xining State-level Economic and Technological Development parks, Highland Biological Scientific and Technological Demonstration Parks and Ganhetan Industrial Park.

Chief cities include the capital Xining, the province's political, administrative and cultural center, the east gate to the Qinghai-Tibet plateau; and Ge'ermu, the second largest city in the province, having extremely abundant mineral resources and therefore called "a treasure bowl."

Ningxia Hui Nationality Autonomous Region

Ningxia Hui Nationality Autonomous Region is located in the east of Northwest China, covering an area of 66,400 square kilometers with a population of 5.63 million in 2001. It is a region where the largest number of Hui people lives in compact communities. The Hui ethnic group there has a population of 1.9 million plus, accounting for one-third of the region's total.

The Yellow River winds about Ningxia in nine turns, irritating a large area of its

Major Indices of Ningxia Hui Nationality Autonomous Region

Index	2000	2001	The national total in 2001
Population			
Total by the end of the year (10,000 persons)	562	563	127,627
Birthrate (‰)		16.55	13.38
Mortality (‰)		4.84	6.43
Proportion of urban population (%)	32.43		37.7
Proportion of rural population (%)	67.57		62.3
National economy assessment			
GDP (100 million yuan)	265.6	298.1	95,933
Growth rate over the previous year (%)	9.8	10.1	7.3
GDP per capita (yuan/person)	4,839	5,338	7,543
Proportion of the first industry (%)	17.3	16.6	15.2
Proportion of the second industry (%)	45.2	45.2	51.1
Proportion of the third industry (%)	37.5	38.2	33.6
Residents' level of consumption (yuan/person)	2,290		3,608
Growth rate over the previous year (%)	13.9		6.2
Volume of retail sales of consumer goods (100 million yuan)	90.2	98.9	37,595.2
Foreign trade and economy			
Export volume (USD100 million)	3.5	3.9	2,661.6
Import volume (USD100 million)	1.8	2.4	2,436.1
Foreign direct investment (10,000 US dollars)	1,741	1,680	4,687,759
People's life			
Per-capita disposable income of urban households (yuan)	4,912.4	5,544.2	6,859.6
Per-capita consumer spending of urban households (yuan)	4,200.5	4,595.4	5,309
Average net income per capita in the rural areas (yuan)	1,724.3	1,823.1	2,366.4
Average annual salary of an employee (yuan)		10,442	10,870
In HK, Macao and Taiwan invested enterprises (yuan)		6,469	12,544
In foreign invested enterprises (yuan)		10,797	16,101

fields, hence the saying "The Yellow River under heaven enriches but Ningxia." The region develops planting in agriculture and sheepraising in animal husbandry. It is the primary producing area of beach-sheep, a species known for its fine thick wool. Among its leading industries are Chinese medicinal materials, high-quality beef, mutton and fur processing, grape wine making and potato processing. Already have a Yellow River irrigation area commodity grain base and a base for planting Chinese medicinal material been established.

Ningxia abounds in energy resources, particularly coal. Green food, feature medicine, new-type materials, natural gas, chemicals, deep processing of coal, forest and paper making integration, and environmental protection monitoring instruments are leading industries. Currently Ningxia is constructing a state-level large-scaled energy heavy chemical base along the Yellow River. It is also developing bio-medical industry; exploring and producing new series of special medicine and health products such as the fruit of Chinese wolfberry, Chinese ephedra and sheep placenta essence. While speeding up the growth of special rare metal material and products such as tantalum, niobium and beryllium, the region is renovating and upgrading by means of new and high technology its leading traditional industries, primarily metallurgical industry that produces high power consumption products, chemical industry that is based on rubber products and oil deep processing, and machine building industry centered on NC machine tools and automation instruments.

The vast desert, the Yellow River, the site of the Western Xia Dynasty, and the Hui ethnic villages are the most distinctive tourist attractions.

The western development is conducive to the rapid development of Ningxia. The central and local governments have put in dedicated funds for infrastructural and ecological construction. Electricity, telephone, radio and television services are available in every administrative village. Railways, highways and airlines lead to all large and medium-sized cities in the country.

Chief cities include the capital Yinchuan, a rising industrial city and administrative, commercial, cultural and educational center of the region and Shizuishan, a rising city in the north of the region known as a "coal city beyond the Great Wall."

Xinjiang Uygur Autonomous Region

Xinjiang Uygur Autonomous Region is located in Northwest China. Occupying an area of 1.6 million square kilometers, it is the largest in area of regions (provinces) in China. In 2001, it had a population of 18.76 million.

Xinjiang abounds in natural resources where petroleum and natural gas reserves make up 30 per cent and 34 per cent respectively of the total of national petroleum and natural gas reserves on land. It is also rich in non-ferrous, rare and precious metal deposits, in particular copper, gold, and sylvite.

Xinjiang has plentiful light, heat and biotic resources. With a long history of agriculture and oasisgrassland stockraising, the region is known as "Land of melons and fruits." In recent years, the "red industry" represented by tomato, safflower, wolfberry and pomegranate, and the "green industry" represented by grape and pear have rapidly developed on a large scale. Having a natural superiority for the development of green food, Xinjiang has the prospect of becoming China's key green animal product production base and a most competitive stockbreeding region.

Xinjiang has unique geographical advantages. It has a land border of 5,600 kilo-

Major Indices of Xinjiang Uygur Autonomous Region

Index	2000	2001	The national total in 2001
Population			
Total by the end of the year (10,000 persons)	1,925	1,876	127,627
Birthrate (‰)		16.82	13.38
Mortality (‰)		5.69	6.43
Proportion of urban population (%)	33.82		37.7
Proportion of rural population (%)	66.18		62.3
National economy assessment			
GDP (100 million yuan)	1,364.4	1,483.5	95,933
Growth rate over the previous year (%)	8.2	8.0	7.3
GDP per capita (yuan/person)	7,470	7,898	7,543
Proportion of the first industry (%)	21.1	19.4	15.2
Proportion of the second industry (%)	43.0	43.1	51.1
Proportion of the third industry (%)	35.9	37.6	33.6
Residents' level of consumption (yuan/person)	3,207		3,608
Growth rate over the previous year (%)	6.2		6.2
Volume of retail sales of consumer goods (100 million yuan)	374.5	406.3	37,595.2
Foreign trade and economy			
Export volume (USD100 million)	11.5	6.7	2,661.6
Import volume (USD100 million)	14.4	17.0	2,436.1
Foreign direct investment (10,000 US dollars)	1,911	2,035	4,687,759
People's life			
Per-capita disposable income of urban households (yuan)	5,644.9	6,359.0	6,859.6
Per-capita consumer spending of urban households (yuan)	4,422.9	4,931.4	5,309
Average net income per capita in the rural areas (yuan)	1,618.1	1,710.4	2,366.4
Average annual salary of an employee (yuan)		10,278	10,870
In HK, Macao and Taiwan invested enterprises (yuan)		10,873	12,544
In foreign invested enterprises (yuan)		10,153	16,101

meters bounded by eight countries: Mongolia, Russia, Kazakstan, Kyrgyrzstan, Tajikistan, Afganistan, Pakistan and India. To date there are in Xinjiang already 16 ports opened to the outside world. With the second Eurasian continental bridge passing through its frontier, Xinjiang has the favorable condition to become an international trade passage and a world business center in West China.

Xinjiang was an important section of the ancient Silk Road. The three ancient civilizations of China, India and Greece once blended in this region where the world's three major religions spread. In Xinjiang, the magical landscape, strong flavor of folkways and profound cultural background have provided bounteous resources for tourist industry. So far there have already set up a Kanasi Lake Ecotourist Zone, a

Turpan Historic Sites Tourist Zone, a Kashi Folklore Tourist Zone and an Ili Grassland Tourist Zone.

In the development of the country's western regions, Xinjiang has further improved its investment environment while the local inhabitants' market concept is strengthened. Vast desert having little rainfall is certainly a disadvantage not to be evaded. However, the local people, having managed successfully to plant on the desolate land licorice and saline cistanche, have started to develop sand industry, tourism and fruit industry. Always known for "One black and one white", meaning petroleum and cotton, Xinjiang is the country's largest cotton producing area, the largest pastoral area, and an area richest in petroleum and natural gas reserves. However, such resources are not yet well exploited. In recent years, the local people have changed their old ways of selling primary products into developing distinctive industries. So far some brand names have been developed.

Chief cities in Xinjiang include: the regional capital Urumqi, a rising city and a regional administrative, industrial, commercial, transport, cultural and educational center; Shihezi, second largest city in the region, having cotton and wool textiles industry; and Kelamayi, a city in the northern part of the region known for petroleum industry.

Note: The data of the year 2000 refer to those of the census conducted at zero hour of November 1 quickly gathered covering all provinces, autonomous regions, and municipalities directly under the central government including non-natives but exclusive of those away from home. The data of 2001 indicate figures calculated based on sample survey of changes in population.

URBAN DEVELOPMENT

Since 1978, China's urbanization level has raised by fifteen percentage points, double the growth rate of the world's average for the period.

In 2001, China had an urban population of 458.44 million, accounting for 36.22 per cent of the country's total. At present, over 50 per cent of the nation's industrial creation, over 70 per cent of GNP, nearly 80 per cent of national tax revenue, 85 per cent of added value in the tertiary industry and over 90 per cent of higher education and scientific researches are concentrated in urban areas.

Currently there are in China altogether 668 cities of which 13 each has a population of over 2 million, 24 each has a population of between 1-2 million, 48 each has a population of between 0.5-1 million, 205 each has a population of 0.2-0.5 million and 378 each has a population of less than 200,000.

Affected by various factors involving history, geography and social and economic development, China's cities are spaced in an uneven density —— much more closely distributed in the east than in the west. Average urbanization ratio is 37 per cent in the eastern part, 30 per cent in the central part and 24 per cent in the western part. Apart from Beijing, Tianjin, Shanghai and Chongqing, Liaoning Province has the highest urbanization level, double the national average. Tibet is the lowest in urbanization, only about 14 per cent of the nation's average. In the resent 20 years, Guangdong, Zhejiang, Jiangsu, Shandong, Hebei and Guangxi have a more rapid development in urbanization whereas Heilongjiang, Inner Mongolia, Jilin, Qinghai, Xinjiang and Tibet are lagging behind.

To develop small cities and towns is a major strategy of the Chinese government to bring along rural social and economic growth. In the process of urbanization, the rapid rising of small cities and towns has become an important motive force to realize rural industrialization and change the binary social structure in China. In the past 10 years, about 800 small cities and towns have appeared, with 10 million rural population transferred every year on an average. Altogether there has a rural population of over 100 million settled down in small cities and towns in the period.

Night scene in Beijing streets.

At the same time, city groups and city belts centered on metropolises have further taken shape. Among those broad in scale are round-the-Bohai-Sea city group centered on Beijing, Tianjin, Dalian and Qingdao; the Yangtze River Delta city group centered on Shanghai, Suzhou, Wuxi, Nanjing, Hangzhou, and Ningbo; the Zhujiang River Delta city group centered on Guangzhou, Shenzhen, Zhuhai, Dongguan and Zhongshan. These city groups are highly urbanized, well developed in economy and have complete urban facilities.

Urbanization has accelerated the transfer of rural population to cities and towns. With more employment opportunities provided, the pressure of inadequate land for the populous rural area is relieved. The rapid urban infrastructure and housing construction have greatly improved the prople's living conditions and economic environment. Pushing forward by the policy of opening up to the outside world, economic contacts and mutual influence between Chinese cities and other parts of the world are continuously promoted. Large cities such as Shanghai and Beijing are stepping into the line of international metropolitan cities.

Owing to historic and natural conditions, and the long-pursued strategy for economic development and the policy to keep cities and rural area apart in specific circumstances after the founding of the People's Republic of China, urbanization and urban development in China fail to satisfy the need for the economic and social development. For instance, the level of urbanization lags behind that of industrialization, urban industrial structure is not rational, and the tertiary sector is slow in growth. So far traditional services still constitute the main body of the tertiary sector, information and financial element market not yet well developed, urban infrastructure facilities input not enough to meet the need of development.

According to the Tenth Five-Year Plan, during the 2000-2005 period, the country's urbanization level is to increase by 0.8 ~ 1 percentage point annually. In improving urban functions and enhancing urban radiant force and competitiveness, main points are as below:

1. Cities having well equipped infrastructure facilities and social services and capable of converting their pillar industries to other uses shall enhance their urban competitiveness. International metropolises such as Shanghai and Beijing shall be guided by knowledge economy and develop high-tech and foreign exchange earning industries such as electronic information, biotechnology and new materials. They shall give priority to the development of modern services including finance, insurance, information, logistics flow, and professional services, so as to take part in international economic competition and become the country's economic, cultural, scientific and educational centers. Coastal open cities such as Shenzhen, Guangzhou, Dalian,

Tianjin, Xiamen, Qingdao, Yantai, Ningbo, Shantou and Qinhuangdao shall base on economic development zones to develop export-oriented economy and leading industries guided by technology. As such cities are mostly located in the populous areas with inadequate land resources, projects using large quantity of water or causing serious pollution or occupying large area of land shall be restricted strictly.

2. Important industrial bases established over a long period of development such as Harbin, Shenyang, Changchun, Wuhan, Xi'an, Lanzhou, Chongqing and Chengdu shall further amplify their

A corner of Qingdao: a city coordinated in running 2008 Beijing Olimpic Games.

urban functions. Depending on their solid economic foundation and galaxy of talents, these cities shall optimize industrial structure; renovate traditional industries using new and high technology; develop technology-intensive new products, high-tech industries and establish rising leading industries. They shall give full play to the advantages of regional resources, low land and labor cost, advanced technology to develop resource deep processing and small and medium sized labor-intensive industrial enterprises. They shall also step up the growth of the tertiary industry to become commodity flow, scientific, technological, cultural, and information centers.

3. Cities and towns, where pillar industries are on the decline owing to industrial structural regulation by the state and changes in the market, should adjust their simplistic industrial structure at the proper time. Such cities and towns include those developing primarily traditional processing industries such as textile and general machinery, and those developing primarily coal and forest resource processing.

4. All-sidedly enhance cities' and towns' radiating and leading function in regional development. In the light of the characteristics of their function, their radiating power and the regional development conditions, the cities and towns of the country can be divided into six levels: national central cities and cities having international significance; trans-provincial central cities; provincial central cities; prefectural central cities; central county towns; and central towns under county jurisdiction. Among them, national central cities and cities having international significance include Beijing, Shanghai and Hong Kong; trans-provincial central cities include Shenyang, Tianjin, Wuhan, Guangzhou, Xi'an, Chongqing, Dalian, Harbin, Jinan, Qingdao, Zhengzhou, Changsha, Nanjing, Hangzhou, Shenzhen, Xiamen, Lanzhou, Urumqi, Chengdu and Kunming; provincial central cities refer mainly to provincial capitals including Changchun, Hohhot, Shijiazhuang, Taiyuan, Hefei, Nanchang, Fuzhou, Haikou, Yinchuan, Xining, Nanning and Guiyang; others include cities significant in provincial development such as Baotou, Tangshan, Ningbo and Liuzhou.

All these cities should give priority to the replenishment of region-oriented trade, information, and financial, educational, scientific, technological and cultural services. They should set up convenient intercity transport network to integrate central cities with surrounding cities. They should regulate and rationally ease up urban functions so as to bring about a radical change in the over populous situation and over crowded traffic, to optimize the urban layout, improve environment, and boost radiating and leading power.

THE WESTERN DEVELOPMENT

A survey

The vast western area of China covers 12 provinces (municipalities, autonomous regions): Sichuan, Chongqing, Guizhou, Yunnan, Guangxi, Tibet, Shaanxi, Gansu, Qinghai, Ningxia, Xinjiang and Inner Mongolia. It had a population of 355 million in 2000, accounting for 28.1 per cent of the national total, with GDP reaching 1665.5 billion yuan, accounting for 17.1 per cent. It is a multi-ethnic region inhabited by 51 ethnic groups apart from the Han, China's majority ethnic group.

The region is adjacent to 14 countries including Russia, Mongolia, Kazakstan, Kyrgyzstan, Tajikistan, Afghanistan, Pakistan, India, Nepal, Sikkim, Bhutan, Myanmar, Laos, and Vietnam. It has a land border of 12,747 kilometers connecting 15 trading ports leading to some European and Asian countries, giving the area a locational advantage to develop economic and trading cooperation with surrounding areas. In 1990, when construction of the railway line from the Alatav Pass

(Xinjiang) to Alma-Ata (Kazakstan) was completed, a new Eurasia continental bridge starting from Lianyungang passing through the Alatav Pass, Kazakstan, Russia, Belarus, Poland, German, and ended at Holland's Rotterdam has been

Billboard giving publicity to the western development.

wholly linked up. This new continental bridge serves to connect the Pacific and the Atlantic, joining the Round-the-Pacific Economic Circle in the east and the European Unified Market in the west, and at the same time, radiating in the direction of the Central Asian, Western Asian and Southern Asian Economic Circles. As a tie as well as a passage joining Asia and Europe, the new continental bridge has formed an entirety with the western area of China. Its total length within China's territory exceeds 4,000 kilometers of which over 3,000 kilometers lie in the western regions, favorable for the development of the area. In recent years, infrastructure facilities serving the new continental bridge such as railways, expressways, optical cable communications, pipelines for conveying, aerodromes, and ports have been constructed at a rapid speed. Compared with the northwestern regions, the southwestern area has the advantage of going to sea via the Yangtze in the east, and via Guangxi, Vietnam and Myanmar in the south.

Restricted by multiple factors like natural conditions, history, culture, policy and structure, the western area lags far behind the eastern regions of the country in economic and social development. Its industrial structure is not adequately rational, industrial and services still underdeveloped, enterprise mechanism inflexible, marketization and urbanization hardly started, poverty-stricken and outlying ethnic minority districts and old industrial bases confronting many difficulties, and social undertakings remaining at a lower level of development.

However, the western area contains ample investment opportunities, market as well as development potential. In 1999, the central government made a strategic decision to develop the vast western area and implemented a series of favorable policies and measures. During 2000 – 2001, the GDP of the 12 provinces (autonomous regions and municipalities directly under the central government) in the western re-

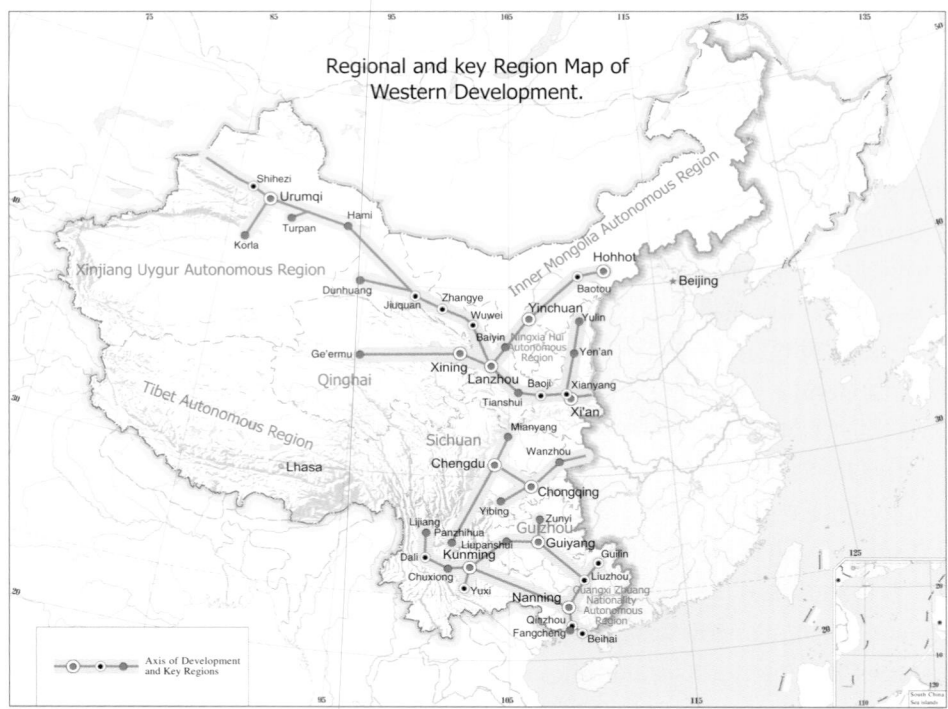

Regional and key Region Map of
Western Development.

Axis of Development
and Key Regions

gions increased by 8.6 per cent on the average, the fixed assets investment increased by 17 per cent, both higher than the national average. There already appears a trend towards accelerated development of economic and social undertakings in the western area.

Natural resources

Boasting a vast expanse of land, the western region occupies an area of 6.85 million square kilometers, accounting for 71.4 per cent of the nation's total. It has a forest area of 5.642 million hectares, accounting for 45.3 per cent and a grassland area of 323.471 million hectares, accounting for 97.78 per cent, both of the national total. It has a cultivated area of 31.6 million hectares.

The western region has considerable resources of water energy, petroleum, natural gas, coal, rare earth, potash, phosphorous, and non-ferrous metals. The proven deposits indicate that coal accounts for 36 per cent, petroleum, 12 per cent, natural gas, 53 per cent, and water energy, 82.5 per cent respectively of the national total. Among the 10 state programmed hydropower bases, 7 are located in the western region. Over 120 of the 140 varieties of proven minerals are distributed in the western regions where the deposits of some kinds of rare earth rank not only among the forefront at home but also in the world. As is culculated, about 41 per cent of oil fields with deposits beyond 100 million tons are distributed in this area. Non-ferrous metals, salt and some non-metal minerals are particularly bounteous. In the southwest of the region, exploitable water energy reserves amount to 232 million kilowatts, accounting for 60 per cent of the nation's total. In the vast forests over 15,000 species of trees are grown. Alumina, copper, lead and zinc are rich in reserves.

Human resources

The western region has well-developed education system and solid scientific and technological force. In both Xi'an and Chengdu there are nearly 50 institutions of higher learning, over 160 scientific research institutes, and a multiple of large and medium-sized industrial enterprises and defense industrial enterprises. It therefore has a sound scientific and technological foundation. With a population of 287 million, the region enjoys low labor cost. The average wage of an employee there is only half that in the Zhujiang Delta region in East China.

Tourism resources.

Shrouded in a mysterious hue, the western region possesses the richest tourism resources in China. Great varieties of biological reserves, multiple places of historic interest and scenic beauty appealing to tourists home and overseas include Jiuzhaigou in Sichuan, Three Gorges on the Yangtze River, the Qin tombs with cotta terra soldiers and horses, Mogao grottoes on the Silk Road in Gansu, karst formation in Guizhou and Yunnan, vast prairie in Inner Mongolia and colorful ethnic customs in Yunnan, Xinjiang and Tibet. All the western provinces and autonomous regions have now placed tourism as a key sector for development in which foreign investment is encouraged.

Market environment

With accelerated progress in urbanization and industrialization in addition to the continuous improvement of people's living standard, the populous western region is a potential consume market, in particular each provincial capital where local inhabitants' consumption has reached a comparatively high level. There are in the region highways and railway lines connecting surrounding countries. Fifteen trade ports give positional advantage for developing trade and economic relations with Russian, Mongolia, Central Asia, West Asia and Southeast Asian countries. Now border transactions are flourishing, in particular in the southwest of the region, which not only maintains traditional economic and cultural contacts with neighboring countries but also is mutually complementary with them in resources structure as well as economic and technological structure. As viewed from traditional economic links, minority nationalities in the southwestern area are mostly cross-border inhabitants who are closely associated with people of the same nationalities living in the other side of the borderline in language as well as in customs. And judged in the light of economic mutual complementarity, cotton, silk, famous brand liquor, and medicinal material produced in the western area, and rubber, jade, petroleum, timber, coconut oil, precious metals produced in Southeast Asian countries can be used to make up for the other's deficiency from their own surplus. Such complementarity and geographical as well as ethnic relationship constitute the social and economic basis for economic and technological exchanges and cooperation between the two sides. The China Kunming Export Commodities Fair and Urumqi Foreign Trade Symposium held in August and September respectively every year aiming at enlarging exports to southeastern Asian area have provided favorable conditions and opportunities for trade with neighboring countries.

Industrial and Agricultural foundation

As China's major agricultural and stockraising center, the western region is also a base of energy, raw material and heavy industries. It has a solid foundation of transportation, communication, science, technology, education and industrial system centered on the aircraft industry in Xi'an, auto and motorcycle industry in Chongqing, petrochemical industry in Gansu and Xinjiang, iron and steel industry in Inner Mongolia and Sichuan, electronics in Sichuan, coal industry in Guizhou, and woolen fabrics industry in Inner Mongolia. Quite a number of the country's large -and-medium-sized enterprises are set up in the western region in particular in Xi'an, Chongqing and Chengdu, which are the nation's important industrial bases. In recent years many state-level military industrial enterprises have been transformed for civil use, adding vitality to the industrial development in the region. At the same time provincial capitals in the region have set up economic and technological development zones of preliminary size with a view to provide favorable conditions and environment for investors home and overseas.

The western region as a major agricultural and stockbreeding center, is an important commodity grain producing area and cotton out-transfer area. Plentiful agricultural and plant resources can be used for processing such as fruit and cotton in Xinjiang, livestock in Inner Mongolia. Chinese medicinal materials in Yunnan and Sichuan, which account for over 50 per cent of the nation's total discovered species, can be used for developing Chinese medicines.

Policies on Western Development

In December 2000, the State Council promulgated Notice on the Enforcement of Several Policies and Measures for the Western Development. Below are the main points.

Focal points

1. Key task and strategic objective. At a certain period of time henceforth, the

key task in enforcing the western development is to speed up infrastructure construction, enhance eco-environmental protection and construction, consolidate agricultural foundation, regulate industrial structure, develop feature tourism, and promote scientific, technological, educational, cultural, and health undertakings. Strive by all means to make a breakthrough in a period of 5 – 10 years in the development of infrastructure and eco-environment construction. Build the region into an economically prosperous, socially advanced, stable in life, all ethnic groups united new area with fantastic mountains and waters by the mid-2000s.

2. Priority areas. Policies on the western development are applicable to the areas including Chongqing Municipality, Sichuan Province, Guizhou Province, Yunnan Province, Tibet Autonomous Region, Shaanxi Province, Gansu Province, Ningxia Hui Nationality Autonomous Region, Qinghai Province, Xinjiang Uygur Autonomous Region (exclusive of Xinjiang Production and Construction Corps, which has independent budgetary status), Inner Mongolia Autonomous Region and Guangxi Zhuang Nationality Autonomous Region. Autonomous prefectures of minority nationalities in other regions such as Xiangxi Tujia Nationality and Miao Nationality Autonomous Regions in Hunan Province, Enshi Tujia Nationality and Miao Nationality Autonomous Regions in Hubei Province and Yanbian Korean Nationality Autonomous Region in Jilin Province shall be given appropriate preferential treatment in the light of relevant policies and measures.

Policies to increase funds input

1. Step up the input of construction fund. Raise the proportion of the central government's finance-related construction fund used in the western region. State policy-based bank loans, preferential loans granted by world financial firms and foreign governments, shall be placed as far as possible in projects in the western region in accordance with loan policies. Capital needed for significant infrastructure projects in the region newly planned by the state shall be fully contributed with the central government's finance-related construction funds, other dedicated funds, bank loans or foreign capital. The central government shall adopt various means to collect specialized funds for the western development. The competent departments concerned, when drafting trade development program, enacting policies and allocating specialized funds, shall give full expression to the support to the western region. Enterprises are encouraged to invest in weighty construction projects.

2. Give priority to construction projects. Infrastructure facilities involving water conservancy, exploitation and use of key resources, distinctive high-tech projects and industrialized projects using technology converted from military to civilian production shall be distributed in favor of the western region. Accelerate the construc-

tion of the systems of corporate responsibility, the system of project capital funds, the system for public bidding for projects, the system of supervision and management of work quality, the system of environment supersision and management, and do well related work at the early stage.

3. Boost financial transfer payment capacity. Following the growth of the state's financial resources, gradually extend the scope of general transfer payment. In allocating specialized subsidies involving agriculture, social security, education, science, technology, health, family planning, culture and environmental protection, preferential treatment shall be granted to the western region. The central government's poverty-alleviation funds are mainly used in the poverty-stricken area in the western region. Cereals, seed and seedling allowance and subsidies needed for converting cultivated land and woodland to grassland, natural forest protection and sand curb projects approved by the state, shall be paid by the financial department of the central government. Decresed local revenue caused by such projects shall be subsidized appropriately by the central government.

4. Enhance the support of bank loan. In line with the principle of independence in commercial credit management, banks shall enhance credit input for basic industrial construction in the western region. Stress shall be placed on supporting construction of railway lines, key roads, large and medium-sized energy projects involving power, petroleum and natural gas. Speed up assessment and examination of national debt complementary loan projects and ensure that the loans will be in place at an earlier time in the light of the progress rate of the construction. As regards infrastructure projects with large investment that takes a long period of time for construction, loan term shall be appropriately extended according to the construction cycle and loan pay-off capacity. The State Development Bank shall raise the proportion of new added loans used in the western region. Enlarge the scope of pledge loans on fee-collecting right or earning right of infrastructure projects. Increase credit amount for agriculture, eco-environmental protection construction, key industries, small-town construction, enterprise technological renovation, high-tech enterprises and medium and small-sized enterprises. Extend credit to students and grant loans for the construction of students' apartment. The village power network renovation loan and large loans involved in key projects in priority industries shall be granted specifically by the head office of the Agricultural Bank of China or by the head office of commercial banks directly. Take proper steps to introduce shareholding banks to set up branches in the western region.

Policies to improve investment environment

1. Improve soft environment. Intensify state-owned enterprise renovation, speed

up establishment of modern corporate system and carry out strategic regulation of national economy and assets reorganization in state-owned enterprises. Give substantial support to the state-owned enterprises in burden-alleviation, poverty-relief, reorganization and renovation. Strengthen cultivation and construction of commodity and element markets. Guide non-state owned economy such as private-run and individual enterterprise forward to a rapid development. All types of ownership at home are permitted in principle to get access to all investment fields open to foreign business people in line with relevant laws and regulations. Set up at a quicker pace credit guaranty system and services for medium and small-sized enterprises. Except for important state projects and projects specially stipulated, enterprises using equity capital or bank loans to invest in industrial projects under the permission category or encouraged by the state can submit project proposal together with feasibility study for approval in line with stipulated procedures. To simplify the procedure, the initial designing and operation report submitted by foreign-invested enterprises can be free from governmental examination and approval. Further transform governmental functions, separate governmental functions from enterprise management, simplify procedures in handling affairs, strengthen service consciousness, remove administrative monopoly, regional blockade and protectionism, administer government affairs in conformity with legal provisions and protect the legitimate interest of investors. Intensify environmental protection, avoid duplication of similar projects, close down in accordance with the law factories, mines and firms that waste resources, pollute seriously environment, produce low quality products or fail to satisfy the requirements for safety production.

2. Carry out preferential policies on taxation. The income tax is levied at a reduced rate of 15 per cent for a certain period of time on both domestic and foreign invested enterprises set up in the western region engaging in state encouraged projects. Enterprises in nationality autonomous regions shall be exempted from income tax or allowed a reduction for a specific period of time with the approval of the provincial government. Newly run enterprises engaging in transportation, power, water conservancy, radio and television shall be exempted from income tax for the first two years and allowed a 50 per cent reduction for the subsequent three years. For special agricultural products grown from farmland-reverted eco-woodland and eco-grassland, the growers shall be exempted from tax for 10 years. For the land used in the construction of state highways or provincial highways in the western region the land-use tax shall be exempted following the example of railway and civil aviation land use. As for land used in the construction of other roads, the governments of provinces, autonomous regions and municipalities directly under the central government shall

decide on their own whether or not to charge land use fee. Home and foreign invested enterprises engaging in state encouraged projects and priority projects importing advanced technical equipment for their own use with fund included in the total investment shall be exempted from importing link value-added tax except for those to which no tax exemption is granted as stipulated by the state.

3. Put into effect preferential policies on land and mineral resources. For afforestation and planting grass on waste land and barren hills or reverting cultivated land on slopes to woodland or grassland, the policy shall be effected that whoever plants trees or grass or reverts the cultivated land to woodland or grassland shall be entitled to operate and own the land use right and the woods or grass grown on that piece of land. Economic organizations of any kind and individuals can apply for the use of state-owned wasteland or barren hills in accordance with the law for eco-environmental protection such as recovery of woods, grassland or vegetation. The land use right can be obtained in the form of buying at reduced price or free of charge on condition that the construction fund and greening work have both been in place. The duration of the land use right shall be 50 years and can be applied for extension following its expiration. The right can also be inherited or transferred with compensation. In case the state needs to take back the land for construction use, compensation shall be given in accordance with the law. Eco-woods reverted from farmland, which enjoy state cereals subsidy, are not permitted to have the trees felled. Basic farmland shall be strictly protected so as to keep balance between farmland, woodland and grassland. Simplify the procedure of examination and approval to ensure that the land can be used in time for construction. The proceeds from compensation for urban construction land use shall be used mainly in urban infrastructure construction. Enhance policy-related support for the survey, assessment, exploitation, protection and rational utility of mineral resources. Draw up policies and measures to accelerate sales and transfer of ore prospecting right and mining right in accordance with the law so that a mining right market can be established.

4. Regulating using price and fee-collection mechanism. Deepen price reform. Further raise the proportion of market regulating price. Fix rational prices for "electricity transmitted from the western region to East China" and "natural gas transported from the western region to East China" and establish a price-fixing mechanism for natural gas, power, petroleum and coal in production and marketing. Accelerate water price reform to improve the system of water resources management and fee-collection in which water price shall be gradually raised to a reasonable level in conformity with the principle of water saving. Intensify unified management of water resources of great river valleys and strictly adhere to the system of planned water

use and water amount allocation so that water resources can be rationally exploited and utilized. Apply widely the fee collection system for sewage and garbage disposal. The fee so collected shall be used specifically in sewage and garbage disposal. Intensify curbs on pollution and protection of the upper reaches and river sources. The ticket price of inter-province, provincial and regional flights shall be fixed by the operators on their own. Special transport price can be set for newly built railway lines. Enhance general postal and telecommunication services.

Specialty trade.

Policies to further open up internally and externally

1. Further enlarge the sphere for foreign investment. Encourage overseas business people to invest in infrastructure construction and resources exploitation in the fields of agriculture, water conservancy, ecology, transport, energy, municipal works, environmental protection, minerals and tourism, and in setting up technological research and development centers. Widen the scope of opening up in the service and trade sectors. Extend the sphere of pilot foreign investment in banks and retail business to municipalities directly under the central government, provincial capital and regional capital cities. Permit overseas banks to engage in RMB business step by step, and to invest in conformity with relevant regulations in telecommunication, insurance, tourism, joint venture accounting firms, lawyer's offices, engineering design companies, railway and highway cargo services, municipal utilities enterprises and firms in other fields China has taken commitment for opening. A certain fields can be opened up first in the western region on an experimental basis.

2. Further broaden the channel of using foreign capital. Conduct experiments in financing in the form of BOT and at the same time try using the form of TOT. Permit foreign invested projects to engage in project financing including RMB financing. Support foreign invested enterprises that are up to the requirements in their efforts to be listed in stock markets home and abroad. Support enterprises engaging in state encouraged or permitted projects in seeking foreign investment by means of transference of management power, sales of stock ownership, merging or reorganization. Probe the feasibility of luring foreign investment in the form of joint venture industrial funds and VC funds. Encourage joint ventures to reinvest in the western region in which the new projects with the proportion of foreign investment exceeding 25 per cent shall enjoy the same preferential treatment as that granted to foreign invested firms. For the infrastructural and key industrial projects invested by foreign business people, limit to stock ratio for foreign investors and proportion of RMB loans on fixed assets investment granted by home banks can be properly relaxed. Permit the proportion of overseas loans on favorable terms in the total investment to be increased properly in certain projects. Key industries and foreign exchange earning projects importing advanced technology and equipment shall be supported by the state in allocating overseas commercial loan quotas. Give priority to projects in the western region in allocating multi-lateral or bi-lateral donations.

3. Devote major efforts in the development of foreign trade and economic relations. Further enhance industrial enterprises' power in making management decision in foreign trade. Encourage them to develop competitive export products, to contract for export projects and labor cooperation, and to invest in running factories overseas in particular in neighboring countries. Relax exit-entry restrictions. Give appropriate preferential treatment to the import of technology and equipment urgently needed in the development of the western region. Exercise the policy of issuing visa-on-arrival and other convenient entry visas in the light of specific conditions for overseas tourists entering China via chief tourist cities in the western region. Execute more favorable policies on border trade. Relax restrictions in export rebate, scope of export commodity business, import-export commodity quotas, license management, entry and exit of personnel, etc. in a bid to promote mutual opening of markets between the western region and neighboring countries and regions, and thus boost sound development of regional economic and technological cooperation between the two sides of the borderline.

4. Promote regional coordination and mutual support between counterparts. Under the prerequisite of no duplication of similar projects and no transfer of backward technology that causes environmental pollution, forceful measures shall be adopted

in the fields of investment, finance, taxation, credit, trade, economy, industry, commerce, labor and statistics to help enterprises in the eastern and central regions to foster cooperation with their counterparts in the western region in various forms such as running factories, purchasing enterprise shares, merging, technology transfer, etc. Under the guidance of the central and local governments, mobilize social strength to promote support given by similar entities in the eastern regions. Further intensify support for the poverty-stricken and minority nationality area in the western region. Continue to carry along the action of "invigorating the border area and enriching its people." Develop multiple forms of regional economic cooperation around the key development areas in the western region.

Policy to attract talents and develop science and technology

1. Attract and make proper use of talents. Enact policies on luring talents, keeping talents, encouraging talents to start business in the western region. Following the reform of wage system, grant subsidy for outlying areas and places where conditions are hardest. Raise the payment of government functionaries and public institution personnel in the western region step by step to the same level or above the average of the national standard. Based on the key tasks, key construction projects and major research topics in connection with the western development, attract professionals home and overseas to the western region with favorable work and living conditioons. Reform household registration system. Permit people from other regions starting businesses or taking part in the development in the western region to retain their original household registration. Those who have legal permanent dwelling place, stable occupation or source of income in small towns or cities at or below preferential level, are entitled to apply for permanent urban residence registration as they wish. Encourage spare rural labor to transfer and trans-regional population to flow rationally. Enhance the interflow of cadres between the eastern and western regions. Departments of the central government involved, institutions of higher learning and scientific research institutes in the eastern region shall provide intelligence services and talent support to the western region. Make efforts to import overseas talents to the western region. Backed by departments of the central government involved and the more economically developed coastal region, cultivate leading cadres and minority nationality cadres in the western region and train civil servants, specialized technical personnel and management personnel of enterprises

2. Bring into play the dominant role of science and technology. Preferential treatment shall be given to the western region with regard to allocating funds for various technological projects. Around the key tasks in the western development, endeavor to promote technological capacity. Organize technical personnel to over-

Village scene.

come key technical difficulties and speed up popularization and application of major technological achievements. Speed up industrialization. Support the conversion of technology from military to civilian production. Support scientific research institutes and institutions of higher learning in conducting distinctive application study and basic researches. Intensify the reform of scientific and technological system, and speed up the process of transforming scientific research institutes engaging in application study into business companies. Combine production, education and research together to bring along close linking between economy and technology. Permit the enterprises in the western region to draw development funds from their turnover and raise the proportion of the funds to be drawn. Give more support to projects that are up to the requirements with innovation funds specially used for technology-based medium and small-sized enterprises. For technological personnel running technology-based enterprises, registration procedures shall be simplified and the upper limit for stock ownership, futures ownership and proportion of buying shares with intellectual property rights shall be raised.

3. Increase educational funds input. Continue carrying out the compulsory education project in poverty-stricken area, increase the impact of the state's support for the compulsory education in the western region, raise fund input and speed up implementation of the system of nine-year compulsory education. Give support to the establishment of institutions of higher learning in the western region and increase the number of students in the western region to be enrolled by institutions of higher learning in the central and eastern regions. Carry out the project under which schools

in the eastern region will suppor their counterparts in the poverty-stricken areas in the western region, and the project under which schools in large and medium-sized cities in the western region will support their counterparts in poverty-stricken rural areas. Build the system of distance learning in the western region. Train enthusiastically rural cadres at the grassroots level and teach farmers scientific and cultural knowledge.

4. Speed up cultural and health construction. The funds arranged by the state to subsidize local cultural, radio and television construction and cultural relics protection should be allocated in favor of the western region. Further implement the state's economic policy towards cultural and propaganda units so as to promote literary creation. Bring along the project of "radio and TV in every natural village" to extend the effective coverage of radio and TV network. Promote the development of cultural undertakings in the border areas and minority nationality areas. Accelerate cultural and ideological progress. Enhance health and family planning focusing on establishment of primary rural healthcare system.

The above policies and measures are applicable for the 2001 – 2010 period and shall be further improved following the implementation of the western development strategy. The rules for implementation became effective from January 1, 2001.

Preferential Treatment for Foreign Investment in the Central and Western Regions

Preferential industrial policies

In November 2001, the related department of the state promulgated a catalogue of priority industries for foreign investment in the central and western regions, listing the priority industries in the 20 provinces, autonomous regions and municipalities directly under the central government. Basic industries and infrastructure involving agriculture, forestry, water conservancy, transport, energy, municipal utilities, environmental protection; resources to be exploited involving minerals and tourism; technological research and development centers, new-type electronic component development and manufacturing are included as major fields in which foreign investment is encouraged and preferential treatment granted. All foreign invested projects included in this catalogue are entitled to enjoy the policies under the encouragement category of "Provisions on Guiding the Orientation of Foreign Investment" and other preferential treatment.

Major preferential treatment for tax revenue

In 1999, the state stipulated that all foreign invested enterprises under the encouragement category established in the western region shall pay a reduced 15 per cent income tax for three years following the expiration of duration for current tax preferential treatment. The current tax preferential treatment referred to indicates that foreign invested production enterprises whose operation lasts over 10 years shall be exempted from income tax for the first two profit-making years and allowed a half reduction during the following three years. Technologically advanced enterprises run by foreign business people if remain advanced enterprises after exemption for two years and reduction for three years, shall be allowed to pay income tax for three extended years at the rate stipulated in the tax law.

In the three years mentioned above, the enterprise, if confirmed as an export enterprise with export turnover of the current year coming to 70 per cent of its total output value, shall be allowed a half reduced rate of income tax stipulated in the tax law. However, the reduced rate shall not be lower than 10 per cent, as is the same with the special economic zones and the economic and technological development zones.

Foreign invested enterprises under the encouragement category established in the western region shall pay a reduced 15 per cent income tax during 2001 - 2010. The enterprises mentioned above refer to enterprises engaging in industrial projects under the encouragement category of the "Guidance Catalog of Industry with Foreign Investment" and "List of Advantageous Industries for Foreign Investment Directly under the Central Government in the Central and Western Parts" with income from chief business topping 70 per cent of the total income. Foreign invested enterprises in nationality autonomous regions, with the approval of provincial government, shall be exempted from local income tax or allowed a reduction.

Enterprises in nationality autonomous regions, with the approval of the provincial government, shall enjoy income tax exemption or reduction for a fixed period of time. Enterprises newly run in the western region involving transport, power, water conservancy, postal service, radio and TV, shall be exempted from income tax for the first two years and half reduction for the following three years. The income from special farm produce involving eco-environmental protection and eco-woods and eco-grassland reverted from farmland, shall be exempted from special farm produce tax for 10 years. Land used in the construction of state and provincial highways shall be exempted from land use tax in line with the land used in railway lines and airdromes. Whether or not levy tax on land used in construction of other roads, it shall be decided by governments of provinces, autonomous regions and municipalities directly under the central government.

Other policies

If a foreign invested enterprise reinvests in the western region with an investment accounting for no less than 25 per cent of the total registered capital of the newly

invested company, the newly invested company can enjoy the treatment for foreign invested firms.

Foreign invested enterprises in the eastern region can contract for managerial right of foreign invested enterprises in the western region. They can also contract for the management of state-owned or collectively owned domestic enterprises.

Requisite qualifications for joint ventures in the western region involving some specific industries can be properly relaxed. Restrictions on capital shares apportionment for foreign investment in infrastructure and priority industries in the western region can be properly loosed in the light of the conditions of the industry. Relax the proportion of RMB loans granted by domestic banks for fixed assets investment. The operation period of commercial projects in the western region invested by foreign business people can be extended to 40 years, 10 years longer than in the eastern region; and the registered capital can be reduced to 30 million yuan, 20 million yuan less than in the eastern region.

More favorable policies are put into effect for border trade in the western region. Restrictions are relaxed as regards export rebate, scope of import-export commodity business, import-export commodity quotas, etc.

For other stipulations please consult data involved.

List of Advantageous Industries for Foreign Investment in Provinces, Autonomous Regions and Municipalities Directly under the Central Government in the Central and Western Parts

Shanxi Province

1. Storage, preservation and processing of grain, vegetables, fruits, and poultry products

2. Plantation of forests and introduction of improved varieties of tree

3. Production of non-phosphate washing powder

4. Technical transformation of cotton manufacturing, printing and dyeing enterprises

5. Manufacturing of new-type textile machinery

6. Construction and operation of highways, independent bridges and tunnels

7. Development of coal processing and application technologies and production of coal products

8. Deep-processing of coal tar

9. Exploration, exploitation and utilization of coal-bed gas resources

10. Construction and operation of thermal power stations with a unit capacity above 300,000 KW

11. Exploration and exploitation of copper resources no sole foreign investment permitted

12. Development and manufacturing of high-performance neodymium-iron-boron material and rare-earth electric motors

The Inner Mongolian Autonomous Region

1. Storage, preservation and processing of grain, vegetables, fruits, and poultry products

2. Plantation of forests and introduction of improved varieties of tree

3. Production of health care wine

4. Post-trimming of leather and production of high-grade leather products

5. Processing of dairy products

6. Technical transformation of wool manufacturing, wool knit goods manufacturing enterprises

7. Construction and operation of highways, independent bridges and tunnels

8. Development of coal processing and application technologies and production of coal products

9. Exploration, exploitation and utilization of coal-bed gas resources

10. Construction and operation of thermal power stations with a unit capacity above 300,000 KW

11. Construction and operation of wind power stations

12. Processing of rare-earth ore and production of rare-earth products

13. Exploration and exploitation of copper resources no sole foreign investment permitted.

14. Processing of Chinese and Mongolian medicinal crop

Heilongjiang Province

1. Storage, preservation and processing of grain, vegetables, fruits, poultry and aquatic products

2. Plantation of forests and introduction of improved varieties of tree

3. Deep-processing of soybean and corn and development and production of their products

4. Technical transformation of wood pulp and papermaking enterprises

5. Flax processing and production of lingerie

6. Construction and operation of highways, independent bridges and tunnels

7. Development of coal processing and application technologies and production of coal products

8. Exploration, exploitation and utilization of coal-bed gas resources

9. Exploration and exploitation of copper resources no sole foreign investment permitted

10. Technical transformation of highly refined aluminium processing enterprises

11. Manufacturing of electrotechnical instrument and electric network intelligent administration and control systems and devices

12. Development of computer software

13. Development and production of new-type electronic components

14. Exploitation and processing of graphite and production of graphite products

15. Production of raw material for antibiotic medicine

16. Production of frozen, dry, powder and injection agent of traditional Chinese medicine

Jiling Province

1. Storage, preservation and processing of grain, vegetables, fruits, poultry and aquatic products

2. Construction and operation of good-quality crops and livestock and fowl breed-

ing bases

3. Plantation of forests and introduction of improved varieties of tree

4. Comprehensive utilization of by-products of crops such as corn straw.

5. Technical transformation and comprehensive utilization of chemical fibre wood pulp production enterprises

6. Construction and operation of highways, independent bridges and tunnels

7. Construction and operation of wind power stations

8. Production of down-stream deep-processing products of ethylene and fine chemical products

9. Manufacturing of automobile components and parts

10. Manufacturing of automobile electronic components

11. Development and manufacturing of high-performance neodymium-iron-boron material and rare-earth electric motors

12. Development and manufacturing of displayer LCD

13. Development of computer software

14. Plantation and processing of medicinal plants and development of new pharmaceutical technologies

15. Pharmaceuticals with biological engineering technologies

Anhui Province

1. Storage, preservation and processing of grain, vegetables, fruits, poultry and aquatic products

2. Plantation of forests and introduction of improved varieties of tree

3. Comprehensive utilization of bamboo resources

4. Technical transformation of cotton manufacturing enterprises

5. Development and production of carbon fibre

6. Construction and operation of highways, independent bridges and tunnels

7. Development of coal processing and application technologies and production of coal products

8. Exploration, exploitation and utilization of coal-bed gas resources

9. Exploration and exploitation of nonmetalic mines and deep-processing of non-metal products

10. Manufacturing of agricultural machinery

11. Manufacturing of copper-related electronic products

12. Development, construction and operation of tourist areas spots. and their supporting facilities

 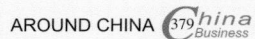

Jiangxi Province

1. Storage, preservation and processing of grain, vegetables, fruits, poultry and aquatic products

2. Plantation of forests and introduction of improved varieties of tree

3. Comprehensive utilization of bamboo resources

4. Production of high-grade domestic ceramics except blue and white porcelain

5. Ramie spinning and production of ramie products

6. Construction and operation of highways, independent bridges and tunnels

7. Development of coal processing and application technologies and production of coal products

8. Exploration, exploitation and utilization of coal-bed gas resources

9. Refining and processing of rare metals such as rubidium, cesium, cobalt, tantalum and niobium

10. Production of wet phosphoric acid and high concentration NPK composite fertilizer

11. Development and manufacturing of new-type electronic components and electronic luminescent materials

12. Processing of Chinese medicinal crop and Chinese patent drugs

13. Development and production of pharmaceuticals with fermentation technologies

14. Development, construction and operation of tourist areas spots. and their supporting facilities

Henan Province

1. Storage, preservation and processing of grain, vegetables, fruits, poultry and aquatic products

2. Plantation of forests and introduction of improved varieties of tree

3. Technical transformation of cotton manufacturing, printing and dyeing enterprises

4. Construction and operation of highways, independent bridges and tunnels

5. Development of coal processing and application technologies and production of coal products

6. Construction and operation of thermal power stations with a unit capacity above 300,000 KW

7. Technical transformation of copper processing enterprises

8. Exploitation and processing of native soda ore

9. Development and manufacturing of new-type electronic components

10. Manufacturing of new-type digital products and accessories

11. Manufacturing of electric energy comprehensive management automation and electrotechnical instrument

12. Processing of fine-quality float glass

13. Plantation and processing of Chinese medicinal crop

Hubei Province

1. Storage, preservation and processing of grain, vegetables, fruits, poultry and aquatic products

2. Plantation of forests and introduction of improved varieties of tree

3. Comprehensive utilization of bamboo resources

4. Rational exploitation, utilization of water resources and protective works

5. Cultivation and deep-processing of aquatic products

6. Technical transformation of cotton manufacturing, printing and dyeing enterprises

7. Processing of high-grade clothing lining and garment

8. Construction and operation of highways, independent bridges and tunnels

9. Construction and operation of wind power stations

10. Exploitation of phosphorus deposit and production of high-concentration phosphate fertilizer, products of phosphorus and salt chemical industry

11. Manufacturing of automobile components and parts

12. Manufacturing of large-size environmental protection equipment

13. Development and manufacturing of new-type electronic components

14. Exploitation and deep-processing of graphite

Hunan Province

1. Storage, preservation and processing of grain, vegetables, fruits, poultry and aquatic products

2. Plantation of forests and introduction of improved varieties of tree

3. Comprehensive utilization of bamboo resources

4. Reclamation projects of red earth

5. Rational exploitation and utilization of water resources and protective works

6. Production of high-grade domestic ceramics

7. Ramie spinning and production of ramie products

8. Construction and operation of highways, independent bridges and tunnels

9. Development of coal processing and application technologies and production of coal products

 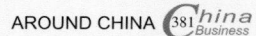

10. Mining and dressing of iron and manganese ore and deep-processing of manganese serial products

11. Design and packaging of large scale integrated circuit

12. Production of semi-finished and finished products of Chinese medicinal crop and Chinese patent drugs

The Guangxi Zhuang Nationality Autonomous Region

1. Storage, preservation and processing of grain, vegetables, fruits, poultry and aquatic products

2. Plantation of forests and introduction of improved varieties of tree

3. Comprehensive utilization of bamboo resources

4. Deep-processing of rosin

5. Cultivation and processing of aquatic products

6. Comprehensive utilization of cane sugar production

7. Construction and operation of highways, independent bridges and tunnels

8. Exploitation, construction and operation of hydroelectric resources

9. Exploitation of indium and zinc non-ferrous metal deposit No sole foreign investment permitted

10. Technical transformation of salt fluoride, salt chloride and phosphate polymeride production enterprises

11. Development and manufacturing of new-type electronic components

12. Processing of semi-finished and finished products of Chinese medicinal crop and Chinese patent drugs

13. Development, construction and operation of tourist areas spots. and supporting facilities

Sichuan Province

1. Storage, preservation and processing of grain, vegetables, fruits, poultry and aquatic products

2. Plantation of forests and introduction of improved varieties of tree

3. Construction and operation of fine-quality agricultural products

4. Comprehensive utilization of bamboo resources

5. Transformation of production lines of cotton, bast fibre and silk manufacturing enterprises

6. Construction and operation of highways, independent bridges and tunnels

7. Development of coal processing and application technologies and production of coal products

8. Development, construction and operation of hydroelectric resources

9. Exploitation and processing of schreyerite ore no sole foreign investment permitted

10. Exploitation of natural gas resources and production of products of gas chemical industry

11. Development of computer software and manufacturing of network products

12. Manufacturing of new-type digital products and accessories

13. Manufacturing of new-type electronic components

14. Development and production of Chinese medicinal crop, Chinese patent drugs and phytochemical materials

15. Development, construction and operation of tourist areas spots. and their supporting facilities

Chongqing Municipality

1. Storage, preservation and processing of grain, vegetables, fruits, poultry and aquatic products

2. Plantation of forests and introduction of improved varieties of tree

3. Comprehensive utilization of bamboo resources

4. Rational exploitation and utilization of water resources and protective works

5. Protection and renovation projects for the ecological environment in the reservoir region

6. Technical transformation of ramie spinning and ramie products production enterprises

7. Construction and operation of highways, independent bridges and tunnels

8. Construction and operation of city metro, light rail communications the Chinese side holds the controlling share or takes the dominant position.

9. Exploration and exploitation of natural gas and production of products of gas chemical industry

10. Manufacturing of components and parts for automobiles and motor cars and electronic components

11. Manufacturing of large-size environmental protection equipment

12. Manufacturing of large-size complete automatic control systems

13. Production of semi-finished and finished products of Chinese medicinal crop and Chinese patent drugs

Yunnan Province

1. Storage, preservation and processing of grain, vegetables, fruits, poultry and

aquatic products

2. Plantation of forests and introduction of improved varieties of tree

3. Introduction, development and operation of flowers and plants and floristry; construction and operation of modern flowers and plants gardens

4. Comprehensive utilization of bamboo resources

5. Plantation and processing of natural perfume material edible mushroom

6. Rational exploitation and utilization of water resources and protective works

7. Pollution administration and environmental protection projects for Dianchi

8. Development and production of green food and health care food

9. Comprehensive utilization of cane sugar production

10. Construction and operation of highways, independent bridges and tunnels

11. Development of coal processing and application technologies and production of coal products

12. Exploitation of phosphorus deposit and production of high-concentration phosphate fertilizer, products of phosphorus chemical industry

13. Development and production of traditional Chinese medicine and biological medicine

14. Development, construction and operation of tourist areas spots. and their supporting facilities

Guizhou Province

1. Storage, preservation and processing of grain, vegetables, fruits, poultry and aquatic products

2. Plantation of forests and introduction of improved varieties of tree

3. Comprehensive utilization of bamboo resources

4. Rational exploitation and utilization of water resources and protective works

5. Construction and operation of highways, independent bridges and tunnels

6. Development of coal processing and application technologies and production of coal products

7. Technical transformation of titanium refining and processing enterprises

8. Exploitation of low-grade and hard-to-dress metallurgical mines

9. Technical transformation of barium salt production enterprises

10. Exploitation of phosphorus deposit and production of high-concentration phosphate fertilizer, products of phosphorus chemical industry

11. Development and manufacturing of new-type electronic components

12. Production of semi-finished and finished products of Chinese medicinal crop and Chinese patent drugs

13. Development, construction and operation of tourist areas spots. and their supporting facilities

The Tibet Autonomous Region

1. Storage, preservation and processing of grain, vegetables, fruits, and poultry products

2. Plantation of forests and introduction of improved varieties of tree

3. Production of products with national characteristics, arts and crafts, packing and container materials

4. Construction and operation of highways, independent bridges and tunnels

5. Construction and operation of electrical infrastructure and new-energy power stations

6. Exploitation and processing of chrome mineral No sole foreign investment permitted

7. Exploitation and utilization of salt lake resources

8. New-type dry cement production lines

9. Development and production of finished products of Tibetan medicine

10. Development, construction and operation of tourist areas spots. and their supporting facilities

Shaanxi Province

1. Storage, preservation and processing of grain, vegetables, fruits, poultry and aquatic products

2. Plantation of forests and introduction of improved varieties of tree

3. Technical transformation of cotton manufacturing, printing and dyeing enterprises

4. Construction and operation of highways, independent bridges and tunnels

5. Development of coal processing and application technologies and production of coal products

6. Exploration, exploitation and utilization of coal-bed gas resources

7. Exploration and exploitation of copper resources no sole foreign investment permitted

8. Exploitation of natural gas resources and production of products of gas chemical industry

9. Manufacturing of on-site bus intelligent instrument

10. Development and manufacturing of new-type electronic components

11. Production of natural drugs, health care medicine and health products

12. Design and manufacturing of civil aircraft the Chinese side holds the controlling share or takes the dominant position

13. Development, construction and operation of tourist areas spots. and their supporting facilities

Gansu Province

1. Storage, preservation and processing of grain, vegetables, fruits, poultry and aquatic products

2. Plantation of forests and introduction of improved varieties of tree

3. Construction of fine-quality vinifera base and brewing of fine- quality wine

4. Deep-processing of potato flour and cornstarch

5. Rational exploitation and resources of water resources and protective works

6. Technical transformation of wool manufacturing enterprises, development and production of industrial textile

7. Construction and operation of highways, independent bridges and tunnels

8. Production of ultra high graphite electrode and carbon products

9. Production of products of gas chemical industry

10. Manufacturing of drilling machine and oil-field equipment

11. Packaging of IC-component integrated circuit and manufacturing of dedicated electronic equipment and instrument

12. Development, construction and operation of tourist areas spots. and their supporting facilities

Qinghai Province

1. Storage, preservation and processing of grain, vegetables, fruits, poultry and aquatic products

2. Plantation of forests and introduction of improved varieties of tree

3. Rational exploitation and utilization of water resources and protective works

4. Construction and operation of highways, independent bridges and tunnels

5. Exploitation, refining and processing of copper, aluminium and zinc deposit no sole foreign investment permitted

6. Exploitation and processing of potassium resources

7. Comprehensive utilization of salt lake resources and production of its products

8. Manufacturing of new-type building materials

9. Plantation and processing of Chinese and Tibetan medicinal crop

10. Development, construction and operation of tourist areas spots, and their supporting facilities

The Ningxia Hui Nationality Autonomous Region

1. Storage, preservation and processing of grain, vegetables, fruits, poultry and aquatic products

2. Plantation of forests and introduction of improved varieties of tree

3. Rational exploitation and utilization of water resources and protective works

4. Plantation of grapes and brewing

5. Plantation and deep-processing of corn and potato

6. Breeding of silkworm and processing of cocoon

7. Construction and operation of highways, independent bridges and tunnels

8. Refining and processing of tantalum and niobium ore

9. Manufacturing of tantalum capacitor and tantalum powder

10. Development, construction and operation of tourist areas spots, and their supporting facilities

The Xinjiang Uygure Autonomous Region

1. Storage, preservation and processing of grain, vegetables, fruits, poultry and aquatic products

2. Plantation of forests and introduction of improved varieties of tree

3. Plantation and deep-processing of fine-quality tomato

4. Plantation of fine-quality grapes and brewing

5. Rational exploitation and utilization of water resources and protective works

6. Construction and operation of highways, independent bridges and tunnels

7. Technical transformation of cotton manufacturing enterprises and development of new products

8. Construction and operation of wind and solar power stations

9. Exploitation of lithium salt no sole foreign investment permitted

10. Development, construction and operation of tourist areas spots and their supporting facilities

COMMERCIAL ACTIVITIES

ACQUISITION OF COMMERCIAL INFORMATION

Channel of information

The more rapidly the market economy develops, the more important market study becomes. In China, the primary access to information is through either governmental channels or non-governmental commercial channels.

Governmental channels mainly refer to statistics organizations of the central and local governments. The State Statistical Bureau is the largest specialized organization engaging in survey, gathering, processing, arrangement, analysis, study, compilation and publication of the country's statistical data. Under it are specialized general investigation teams, general survey centers, economic thriving monitor centers, statistical information services and publishers. Next are the statistics agencies of the ministries and commissions of the State Council and those of provinces, regional autonomous regions and municipalities. The governmental statistics agencies provide services for domestic and overseas firms and organizations through the consulting centers and information centers they have set up. The information provided covers a wide range including economically GDP, energy and mineral resources, production conditions and results in the fields of industry, agriculture, architecture, transportation, postal and telecommunication, commerce, and data on foreign trade, tourism, urban utilities, finance, banking, insurance and price index. Socially it includes primarily population, employment, salary, people's living standard, education, culture, health and sports. Such data can be used for the study of market, profession and consumption.

Life in China

Generally speaking, the advantage of governmental data is that while covering all walks of life and a long period of time, it is conducive to long-term dynamic analysis of the overall situation of the country, market, profession and population. However, as a large part of the indices set are not market-oriented, the data collected reflects much more production results and conditions than market sales.

With the development of market economy, there have appeared in society a large number of non-governmental market survey firms. The commercial data they provide involves consumption study such as data collecting centered on large cities involving consumers' demand for daily necessities, cosmetics, food, beverage, tobacco and medicine; retail study such as monitoring electric household appliances sales in large- and-medium-sized shopping centers in major cities in the country; media monitor such as viewing rate of TV programs monitor and advertisement monitor; enterprise credit investigation; and financial data, which commercialize governmental data.

Prior to entering the WTO, China's information market was restricted to a certain degree because the information resources possessed by the government was not open to the public. Since China's accession of the WTO, the situation of government monopoly has gradually changed. Now the information resources are shared and exploited by the general public, some information services extensive in scope, seeking the favorable opportunity, have started to set up sub-companies and agencies in large cities as channels of information. Meanwhile, as there is no policy-related restriction

Street convenience stand rendering information service with multimedia facilities

on information and consultation business in connection with opening up and competition, overseas large-scaled information and consulting firms have started to set foot in China one after another.

Consulting centers, information centers and guild associations subordinate to government institutions, though having various advantages in acquiring information, are not satisfactory in response to the market demand flexibly and timely. However, professional information services established by government institutions or by associations and research institutes may have marked advantages in acquiring government data and materials while at the same time, being entities established in the light of corporate law, enjoy the rights granted to independent legal persons and operate according to market rules.

Foreign business people conducting market survey in China may have two options: either doing so independently or doing so through domestic Chinese firms. The experience of many companies has shown that the most effective way in a country you have newly arrived is to cooperate with local market study companies. This is particularly true in China in that it helps to solve lots of difficulties a company may come across working alone, helps to increase knowledge about local situations, helps to cultivate market study ability and reduce cost.

If domestic market study firms can come up to the standard required by clients, clients may cooperate directly with Chinese firms without resorting to foreign agencies. In this way efficiency can be raised, cost reduced and quality improved by, for instance, reducing information losses in contacts. As for projects relying on large-scale official data, the sources of information should be taken into consideration and the information firms should be chosen that are within easy reach of government data. Among all sorts of institutions conducting market study or in connection with commercial information, the companies having government background and the information services jointly run with professional overseas companies should be followed with interest. Such companies and services have the following advantages: the Chinese side, backed by the government, may have easy access to data, make use of existing data collecting network and know well China's state conditions whereas the foreign side, as professional firms, is rich in experience and well-versed in technology. High cost is their disadvantage.

Publications and network

The State Statistical Bureau publishes every year China Statistical Yearbook (in Chinese and English), China Rural Statistical Yearbook, China Urban Statistical Yearbook, China Market Statistical Yearbook, China Labor Statistical Yearbook, China Population Statistical Yearbook, China Industrial Economy Statistical Yearbook, China Price and Urban Household Income and Expenses Survey Statistical Yearbook, China Building Statistical Yearbook and China Fixed Assets Investment Statistical Yearbook. Likewise, each province, municipality and county compiles and publishes local Statistical Yearbook. Ministries and commissions of the State Council and statistics institutions of provincial competent business departments also compile and publish specialized statistical yearbooks.

More dynamic publications include China Economic Thriving Monthly (in Chinese and English) compiled by the State Statistical Bureau, which publishes monthly China's latest major economic statistical data. The journal contains 1,000-plus basic statistical indices reflecting China's national conditions and national strength involving social production, enterprise economic returns, fixed assets investment, import-export trade, urban and rural household income, consumption, and purchase of durable commodities, price index, finance, banking, all sorts of thriving indices and experts' predicted results.

The yearbooks mentioned above have a common characteristic that they are all compiled and published for government decision making and social and economic studies but not for market sales and business decision making. Judging from the angle of commerce and market information they do not much fit in with the needs though they are of considerable value. In view of this, many information firms have compiled and published professional analysis reports, which are significant for reference in ascertaining each profession's development trend, analyzing its operational and financial conditions, assessing and evaluating its position on Chinese market, and studying the regional distribution of all professions.

Network has greater advantages in information coverage and timeliness. The min-

istries and commission of the State Council, local governments and their competent departments have basically set up their own websites, some of which are large scaled such as China Economic Information Web. All provincial entities have also set up websites of similar kinds, some are professional, which can be either run by government departments, or run by guild associations or research institutes. As for websites involving economic and trade cooperation and investment inviting, they are mainly run by foreign economic and trade departments and supported by the government for free use. In addition, there are commercial websites available.

In 2001, the Huatong Data Center exclusively authorized by the State Statistical Bureau started services to the general public, which signifies that state statistical data are no longer used laying special emphasis on serving government departments but used for serving the general public in an all-rounded way. Currently Huatong Data Center Website (http://acmr.com.cn) has six channels including China Microeconomic Statistical Data, China Customs Import-Export Statistical Data, China Industrial and Commercial Enterprise Information, China Statistics Analysis Report, China Professional Data and Huatong People Publications.

The government websites provide a wealth of information about policies, inside news, business instructions, etc. However, like publications, they are not meant for market. If more or detailed professional and market information is needed, there are websites run by some information firms available for the purpose, of which quite a number charge fees. In this book is attached a detailed list of websites, which are run by government institutions, professional organizations and entities subordinate to government departments or relevant organizations.

WORK AND LIFE

Visa

A foreigner intending to enter China has to hold valid passport and apply for visa to China's foreign representative institution, consulate or other Chinese diplomatic entity overseas authorized by the Ministry of Foreign Affairs of China.

To provide necessary convenience for foreigners coming to China on matters of urgency, China has opened a number of port visa institutions in some open port cities and regions. A foreigner holding a letter or fax from China's authorized domestic unit and a general passport of a country which has official trade contacts or diplomatic relations with China, is in urgent need to come to China but without enough time to apply for a visa in a Chinese diplomatic entity overseas, may apply for a visa at a port visa institutions appointed by competent government authorities.

Foreign investors wish to come to China to hold trade talks, may contact directly their Chinese trade partner unit, stating purpose and time for coming to China. The unit, if agreed, may apply on behalf of them for visa advice note or fax to a local foreign affairs organization authorized by the Ministry of Foreign Affairs. The foreign investors, on receipt of the note or fax from authorized domestic organization, can apply to China's embassy or consulate in that country for visiting visa with the note or fax.

Life

Foreigners coming to China doing business or working are mostly in large or medium sized cities where they need not worry about everyday life. Transport, communication, catering service, recreation, shopping, public health and medical care in larger cities are generally satisfactory. Nowadays even small cities are developing at a high speed. Firms offering commercial and daily-life services special for foreigners are available in most places.

If a person intends to stay in China for a short period of time, the best option is to make a reservation for a room at a hotel. Before arrival at China, better make confirmation for the reservation and any special personal requirements through the receptive unit, travel agency, or friends or send fax directly to the hotel.

Facilities and services in grand hotels in China are up to international standard.

Making dumplings – When in Rome, do as the Romans do.

Santa Claus coming on stage a month prior to Christmas.

Hotels are star-rated as high, medium and low grades. Needless to say, high-grade hotels, of which many are China-foreign joint ventures, offer convenient and comfortable services. Even medium-grade hotels are satisfactory in every respect and are often favored by package tour organizers. Low-grade hotels with low price look somewhat like motels in foreign countries. Generally in hotels in China no tips are accepted though the situation has changed in some cities and regions. For instance, in Guangdong Province, accepting tips or not is determined by the hotels themselves.

In the streets and lanes in Chinese cities restaurants providing local delicacies can be seen everywhere. Wherever you are from, whatever suits your taste, you can always find the uniqueness of "eating in China." If you are one adhering to western food, there are still various options open to you such as French-style food, Russian-style food and the US fast food. Of course you can also cook for yourself if you like.

Business trips are convenient in a majority of regions in China. The most time saving way is traveling by air. It takes only two hours' flight from Beijing in the north to Shenzhen in the south. Neighboring cities are often linked with freeways. To travel longer distances trains are available, which usually "depart in the morning and arrive in the evening," or "depart in the evening and arrive the next morning." Moreover, train's moving speed per hour is to be accelerated gradually as planned.

It is always fantastic traveling in China. It seems awkward trying to recommend in limited writing China's history and culture, national customs and traditions, nature and scenery, cities and countryside. We have included in the last chapter of this book a list of tourism websites. Seeing is believing. Better go and see for yourself.

Language and media

It is wrong to think that there will be no language barrier if only you have a little command of spoken Chinese. In China there are many dialects, which are different in pronunciation. Besides, some minority nationalities have their own languages. If speaking in respective dialects, communication would be difficult even among Chinese people themselves. However, there is no need for expatriates to worry about since Chinese people would like to talk to you in *putonghua*, that is, a common speech of the Chinese language using standard pronunciation, which has been popularized nationwide. People living in outlying area or a few elderly people may not speak *putonghua*. But you are not likely to do business with these people. Nowadays in China, more and more people know and speak English, in particular young people in large and medium sized cities.

There are in China an array of English language newspapers, magazines, webs, radio and TV channels and a number of professional media the largest of which include the Xinhua web, people's web, China web, China Daily, China International Radio Station, CCTV English language channel, etc.

Foreign newspapers and magazines are also available in China. In some grand hotels in large cities, foreign TV programs can be viewed though web media are the most convenient.

Nationalities

Foreigners living in cities are not likely to see the rich and colorful ethnic culture and life in China, which, in fact, is one of the charms China possesses.

There are 56 ethnic groups in China. In 2001, the population of the Han nationality accounted for 91.6 per cent of the national total, distributed countrywide. The other 55 ethnic minorities accounted for 8.4 per cent of the total population of the country, distributed chiefly in southwest, northwest, and northeast China, mostly in border areas. There are 18 ethnic minorities whose population each exceeded 1 million. The Zhuang ethnic group has the largest population among the ethnic minorities, exceeding 15 million.

The areas where ethnic minorities live in compact communities were usually underdeveloped in the past. With a view to boost social and economic development in these areas and protect the culture and features of ethnic minorities, China has

Bodybuilding in a leisure way.

established a number of ethnic autonomous regions. The rich and colorful natural landscape and cultural spectacles, in particular the unique customs and lifestyles in the ethnic minorities areas have attracted a multitude of tourists. To date, means of modern transportation and communication have emerged in many outlying areas where the local governments have placed emphasis on the development of tourism and feature economy for which domestic and overseas investment is encouraged.

Owing to differences in natural environment, social and economic conditions, minority nationalities in China are different in their respective development. They also have different customs and habits in eating and drinking, dress and living, etc. Travelers visiting there are expected to mind that when in Rome, do as the Romans do.

Religion

Chinese culture has always assumed an all-inclusive attitude towards religions. There are in China five major religions: Buddhism, Taoism, Islamism, Catholicism and Christianity (Protestantism) with more than 100 million believers, accounting for 10 per cent of the country's total population. Among them there are 18 million people believing in Islamism, 4 million in Catholicism and 10 million in Christianity. Totally different from other places in the world, in the majority of regions inhabited mainly by the Han nationality, where the number of believers in the truth sense occupies only a small proportion, religions make far less impact on society and politics as they do in other countries and regions. However, there are nearly 20 ethnic groups in which almost everyone believes in religion, such as the Tibet and Mongolia nationalities who extensively believe in Tibet-based Buddhism; and Hui and Uygur nationalities who believe overwhelmingly in Islamism. In these regions religion plays a much more significant role in social life than in other places in China. There some religious festivals or religious ceremonies have become traditional national holidays.

In China religion is separated from politics. Religion is not permitted to interfere with state power, education or marriage. Different forms of beliefs enjoy equality in law. There is no religion holding dominating position. Religious belief is the citizens' personal affair. Every citizen enjoys the freedom of religious beliefs. The Chinese government respects foreigners' freedom of worship in China. No matter whether they believe in religion or not, what religion they believe in, whether there is such a religion in China or not, China will respect and protect their justified religious activities. For details please consult Rules of People's Republic of China on the Management of Foreigners' Religious Activities Within China's Territory promulgated by the State Council.

Festivals and Holidays

There are 5 working days per week in China. The office hours of government departments are usually from 8 o'clock in the morning to 5 o'clock in the afternoon, but in some cities they are from 9 to 6.

National holidays include New Year's Day (January 1), having 1 day off; Spring Festival (Lunar New Year's Day), having 3 days off; International Labor Day (May 1) having 3 days off; and National Day (October 1), having 3 days off.

Major traditional festivals include Spring Festival, Lantern Festival, Lantern Festival, Dragon Boat Festival, Mid-Autumn Festival, Double Ninth Festival, etc. Moreover, minority nationalities also have their own festivals such as Dai ethnic group's Water Splashing Festival, Mongolians' Nadam Fair, Yi people's Torch Festival, Tibet people's Tibetan New Year's Day and Fruit Expecting Festival.

Generally, there will be a seven-day holiday for Spring Festival, Labor Day and National Day as arranged by the Central Government when there will be sudden increase in the number of outgoing people. Tourist holiday areas will become hot spots for market consumption though transport and accommodation can be less convenient.

Central Organs

Ministry of Foreign Affairs
http://www.fmprc.gov.cn
　　The Ministry of Foreign Affairs is one of the component departments of the State Council in charge of foreign affairs.

State Development and Reform Commission
http://www.sdpc.gov.cn
　　The State Development and Reform Commission is a macro readjustment and control department responsible for researching and putting forward strategy, plan, aggregate volume balance and restructuring national economy and social development.

Ministry of Education
http://www.moe.edu.cn
　　The Ministry of Education is one of the component departments of the State Council in charge of educational undertaking and language.

Ministry of Science and Technology
http://www.most.gov.cn
　　The Ministry of Science and Technology is one of the component departments of the State Council responsible for science and technology.

Commission of Science, Technology and Industry for National Defense
http://www.costind.gov.cn

State Nationalities Affairs Commission
http://www.seac.gov.cn
　　The State Nationalities Affairs Commission is one of the component departments of the State Council responsible for state nationalities affairs.

Ministry of Civil Affairs
http://www.mca.gov.cn

The Ministry of Civil Affairs is one of the component departments of the State Council in charge of social administrative affairs.

Ministry of Finance
http://www.mof.gov.cn
The Ministry of Finance, one of the component departments of the State Council, is a macro readjustment and control department responsible for financial revenues and expenditures, financial and taxation policies, and state-owned capital funds.

Ministry of Personnel
http://www.mop.gov.cn
The Ministry of Personnel is one of the component departments of the State Council responsible for personnel work and promotion of personnel system reforms.

Ministry of Labor and Social Security
http://www.molss.gov.cn
The Ministry of Labor and Social Security is one of the component departments of the State Council responsible for the administrative affairs of labor and social security.

Ministry of Land and Resources
http://www.mlr.gov.cn
The Ministry of Land and Resources is one of the component departments of the State Council responsible for the planning, management, protection and rational utilization of land resource, mineral resource, marine resource and other natural resources.

Ministry of Construction
http://www.cin.gov.cn
The Ministry of Construction is one of the component departments of the State Council responsible for administrative management of construction.

Ministry of Railways
http://www.chinamor.cn.net
The Ministry of Railways is one of the component departments of the State Council responsible for the work related to railways.

Ministry of Communications

http://www.moc.gov.cn

The Ministry of Communications is one of the component departments of the State Council responsible for the sector of highway and waterway communications.

Ministry of Information Industry
http://www.mii.gov.cn

The Ministry of Information Industry, one of the component departments of the State Council, is in charge of national manufacturing industry of electronic information products, the industry of telecom and software, and responsible for promoting the informatization of social service of national economy.

Ministry of Water Resources
http://www.mwr.gov.cn

The Ministry of Water Resources is one of the component departments of the State Council responsible for water administration.

Ministry of Agriculture
http://www.agri.gov.cn

The Ministry of Agriculture is one of the component departments of the State Council responsible for agriculture and rural economic development.

Ministry of Commerce
http://www.mofcom.gov.cn

The Ministry of Commerce is one of the component departments of the State Council responsible for domestic and foreign trade and economic cooperation with foreign countries

Ministry of Culture
http://www.ccnt.gov.cn

The Ministry of Culture is one of the component departments of the State Council in charge of cultural and art undertakings.

Ministry of Public Health
http://www.moh.gov.cn

The Ministry of Public Health is one of the component departments of the State Council responsible for public health.

State Population and Family Planning Commission
http://www.sfpc.gov.cn
   The State Population and Family Planning Commission is one of the component departments of the State Council responsible for population and family planning.

People's Bank of China
http://www.pbc.gov.cn
   The People's Bank of China, one of the component departments of the State Council, is the central bank of the People's Republic of China. It is a macro readjustment and control department under the leadership of the State Council, responsible for laying down and implementing monetary policy and supervising and managing the financial sector.

General Administration of Customs
http://www.customs.gov.cn
   The General Administration of Customs, an organization directly under the State Council, is an administrative enforcement organization responsible for customs.

State Administration of Taxation
http://www.chinatax.gov.cn
   The State Administration of Taxation, an organization directly under the State Council, is responsible for taxation.

State Administration of Environmental Protection
http://www.zhb.gov.cn/sepa
   The State Administration of Environmental Protection, an organization directly under the State Council, is responsible for environmental protection.

General Civil Aviation Administration of China
http://www.caac.gov.cn
   The General Civil Aviation Administration of China, an organization directly under the State Council, is responsible for national civil aviation affairs.

State Administration of Radio, Film and Television
http://www.sarft.gov.cn
   The State Administration of Radio, Film and Television, an organization directly under the State Council, is responsible for radio and television propaganda and the

undertaking of radio, film and television.

State Administration of Physical Culture
http://www.sport.gov.cn
　　The State Administration of Physical Culture, an organization directly under the State Council, is responsible for physical culture.

State Administration of Industry and Commerce
http://www.saic.gov.cn
　　The State Administration of Industry and Commerce, an organization directly under the State Council, is responsible for market supervision and management, and administrative enforcement.

State Administration of Press and Publication
http://www.ncac.gov.cn
　　The State Administration of Press and Publication, an organization directly under the State Council, is responsible for press and publication undertaking and copyright management. In the respect of copyright management, it exercises exclusively the authority of office at home and abroad in the name of the State Copyright Bureau.

State Administration of Quality Supervision, Inspection and Quarantine
http://www.ciq.gov.cn

State Statistical Bureau
http://www.stats.gov.cn
　　The State Statistical Bureau, an organization directly under the State Council, is responsible for statistics and national economical accounting.

State Administration of Food and Drug
http://www.sda.gov.cn
　　The State Administration of Food and Drug, an organization directly under the State Council, is responsible for the comprehensive supervision, organization and coordination of security management of foodstuffs, healthcare, food and cosmetics and responsible for investigation of major incidents as well as for administrative and technical supervision of researches, production, circulation, use and other links of medicines and chemical reagents.

State Administration for Safety Production Supervision (State Bureau of Coal Mine Safety Supervision)

http://www.chinasafety.gov.cn

The State Administration for Safety Production Supervision, an organization directly under the State Council, is responsible for comprehensive supervision and administration of safety production and safety supervision of coalmine.

State Bureau of Intellectual Property

http://www.sipo.gov.cn

The State Bureau of Intellectual Property, an organization directly under the State Council, is responsible for patent work and making overall coordination for foreign-related intellectual property affairs.

State Tourism Bureau

http://www.cnta.com

The State Tourism Bureau, an organization directly under the State Council, is responsible for nationwide tourism sector.

State Grain Bureau

http://www.chinagrain.gov.cn

The State Grain Bureau, an administrative organization under the management of the State Development and Planning Commission, is responsible for detailed macro readjustment and control of national grain circulation (including edible oils), sector guidance and administration of central grain reserve.

State Tobacco Monopoly Bureau

http://www.tobacco.gov.cn

The State Tobacco Monopoly Bureau, an administrative enforcement organization under the Ministry of Commerce, is responsible for national tobacco sector and implementing tobacco monopoly system.

State Bureau of Foreign Experts Affairs

http://www.safea.gov.cn

The State Bureau of Foreign Experts Affairs, an administrative organization, is responsible for recruiting talents from foreign countries for the state, mainly in charge of the administration of foreign experts working in China and the state personnel and personnel of enterprises and institutions of China to be trained in foreign countries, as well as in Hong Kong Special Administrative Region, Macao Administrative Region and Taiwan Area.

State Bureau of Oceanography
http://www.soa.gov.cn

The State Bureau of Oceanography, an administrative organization under the management of the Ministry of Land and Resources, is responsible for supervising and managing maritime space use and marine environmental protection, for maintaining marine rights and interests in accordance with the law and for organizing marine scientific and technical researches.

State Bureau of Surveying and Mapping
http://www.sbsm.gov.cn

The State Bureau of Surveying and Mapping, an administrative organization under the management of the Ministry of Land and Resources, is responsible for nationwide surveying and mapping undertakings, for undertaking various kinds of responsibilities of governmental surveying and mapping administration and sector management entrusted by the State Council and for planning, coordination and organizing implementation of nationwide surveying and mapping production, scientific researches, education, and publication.

State Postal Bureau
http://www.chinapost.gov.cn

The State Postal Bureau, an organization under the management of the Ministry of Information Industry, is responsible for the nationwide postal sector and for managing nationwide postal enterprises.

State Cultural Relics Bureau
http://www.nach.gov.cn

The State Cultural Relics Bureau, an administrative organization under the management of the Ministry of Culture, is responsible for state cultural relics and museums.

State Administration of Traditional Chinese Medicine
http://www.satcm.gov.cn

The State Administration of Traditional Chinese Medicine, an administration under the management of the Ministry of Public Health, is responsible for the enterprises of nationwide traditional Chinese medicine.

State Administration of Foreign Exchange

http://www.safe.gov.cn

The State Administration of Foreign Exchange, an administration under the management of the People's Bank of China, is responsible for foreign exchange in accordance with the law.

Development and Research Center under the State Council

http://www.drc.gov.cn

The Development and Research Center under the State Council, an organization of policy researches and consultation directly under the State Council, is mainly responsible for researching national economy, social development, and overall, comprehensive, strategic and long-term issues in the reform and opening as well as for providing policy proposals and ideas for consultation.

China Seismological Bureau

http://www.eq-csi.ac.cn

The China Seismological Bureau, a functional organization, is responsible for nationwide anti-seismic and earthquake relief work.

China Meteorological Administration

http://www.cma.gov.cn

The China Meteorological Administration, an undertaking directly under the State Council and authorized by the State Council, is responsible for government administration of nationwide meteorological work.

China Securities Regulatory Commission

http://www.csrc.gov.cn

The China Securities Regulatory Commission, an undertaking directly under the State Council, is a department responsible for nationwide securities and forward market.

Local Information

Beijing Municipal Government   http://www.beijing.gov.cn

Beijing Window   http://www.beijingwindow.com

Being Economic Information Net   http://www.beinet.net.cn
Beijing Statistical Information Net   http://www.stats-bj.gov.cn
Beijing Agricultural Information Net   http://www.agri.ac.cn
Beijing Scientific and Educational Information Net   http://www.bestinfo.gov.cn
Capital Scientific and Technical Net   http://www.bast.cn.net
Beijing Educational Information Net   http://www.bjedu.gov.cn

Tianjin Municipal Government   http://www.tj.gov.cn
Tianjin Window   http://www.tianjin-window.com
Tianjin Information Net   http://www.tinet.tj.cn
Tianjin Statistical Net   http://www.stats-tj.gov.cn
Tianjin Agricultural Information Net   http://www.tianjin-agri.gov.cn
Tianjin Industrial Online   http://www.tjbbc.com.cn
Tianjin Science and Technology   http://www.tstc.ac.cn
Tianjin Educational Information Net   http://www.tj.edu.cn

Hebei Internet   http://www.hebnet.gov.cn
Hebei Window   http://www.hebeiwindow.com
Hebei Enterprise Online   http://www.heeol.com
Hebei Statistical Information Net   http://www.stats-he.gov.cn
Hebei Agricultural Information Net   http://www.agri.hebnet.gov.cn
Hebei Constructional Information Net   http://www.cin.hebnet.gov.cn
Hebei Science and Technology Net   http://www.heinfo.gov.cn
Hebei Educational Net   http://www.hee.com.cn
Hebei China   http://www.china-hebei.com

Shanxi Provincial Government   http://www.sxpublic.gov.cn
Shanxi Window   http://www.china-window.com/Shanxi_w
Shanxi Economic Information Net   http://www.sx.cei.gov.cn
Shanxi Statistical Information Net   http://www.stats-sx.gov.cn
Shanxi Agricultural Information Net   http://www.sxagri.gov.cn
Shanxi China   http://www.shanxi.gov.cn

Inner Mongolia Window   http://china-window.com.cn/Neimenggu_w
Inner Mongolia Economic Information Net   http://www.nmg.cei.gov.cn
Inner Mongolia Agricultural Information Net   http://www.nmagri.gov.cn
Inner Mongolia Scientific and Technical Information Net   http://host.nmsti.com

Liaoning Provincial Government   http://www.ln.gov.cn
Liaoning Window   http://www.liaoning-window.com
                           http://china-window.com/Liaoning_w
Liaoning Economic Information Net   http://www.ln.cei.gov.cn
                           http://www.lnnet.gov.cn
Liaoning Statistical Information Net   http://www.stats-ln.gov.cn
Liaoning Agricultural Information Net   http://www.e-no1.net
Liaoning Industry On-line   http://www.industry-ln.ln.cn
Liaoning Constructional Information Net   http://www.cc.ln.gov.cn
Liaoning Scientific and Technical Information Net   http://www.lninfo.gov.cn
Liaoning Educational Information Net   http://www.lnein.edu.cn

Jilin Provincial Government   http://www.jilin.gov.cn
Jilin Window   http://www.china-window.com/Jilin_w
Jilin Economic Information Net   http://www.jilin.cei.gov.cn
Jilin Statistical Information Net   http://www.stats-jl.gov.cn
Jilin Agricultural Information Net   http://www.jlagri.gov.cn
Jilin Science and Technology   http://www.jilinsi.com
Jilin Provincial Educational Information Net   http://edu.jl.cninfo.net

Heilongjiang Provincial Government   http://www.hlj.gov.cn
Heilongjiang Window   http://www.china-window.com/
Heilongjiang_w Heilongjiang Economic Information Net
      http://www.hlj.cei.gov.cn
Heilongjiang Statistics   http://hlj.stats.gov.cn
Heilongjiang Agricultural Information Net   http://www.e-gov.hl.cn/agriculture
Heilongjiang Scientific and Technical Information Net   http://www.dragon.net.cn
Heilongjiang Educational Net   http://www.hljedu.com

Shanghai Municipal Government   http://www.shanghai.gov.cn
Shanghai Window   http://china-window.com/shanghai
Shanghai Economic Information Net   http://www.sheinet.com
Shanghai Statistical Information Net   http://www.stats-sh.gov.cn
Shanghai Agricultural Net   http://www.shac.gov.cn
Shanghai Constructional Net   http://www.shucm.sh.cn
Shanghai Industry   http://www.shec.gov.cn
Shanghai Science and Technology   http://www.stcsm.gov.cn

Shanghai Education   http://www.shec.edu.cn

Jiangsu China Net   http://www.jschina.com.cn
Jiangsu Window   http://china-window.com/Jiangsu_w
Jiangsu Economic Information Net   http://www.js.cei.gov.cn
Jiangsu Statistical Information Net   http://www.stats-js.gov.cn
Jiangsu Agricultural Net   http://www.jsagri.gov.cn
Jiangsu Engineering Construction Net   http://www.jscetcc.com
Jiangsu Scientific and Technical Information   http://www.jsinfo.gov.cn
Jiangsu Educational Information Net   http://www.jsinfo.net/education

Zhejiang Provincial Government   http://zhejiang.gov.cn
Zhejiang Window   http://china-window.com/Zhejiang_w
Zhejiang China   http://www.cnzj.org.cn
Zhejiang Economic Information Net   http://www.zei.gov.cn
Zhejiang Economic Construction Net   http://www.zjeconomic.com
Zhejiang Statistical Information Net   http://www.stats-zj.gov.cn
Zhejiang Agriculture   http://www.agzj.com
Zhejiang Scientific and Technical Information Net   http://www.zjinfo.gov.cn
Zhejiang Educational Net   http://www.zj.edu.cn

Anhui Provincial Government   http://www.ah.gov.cn
Anhui Window   http://www.anhui-window.com.cn
Anhui Economic Information Net   http://www.in.ah.cn
Anhui Statistical Information Net   http://www.stats-ah.gov.cn
Anhui Agriculture   http://www.ahnw.gov.cn
Anhui Scientific and Technical Information Net   http://www.ahinfo.gov.cn
Anhui Educational Net   http://ahsjw.ah.gov.cn

Fujian Provincial Government   http://www.fujian.gov.cn
Fujian Window   http://www.Fujian-window.com
Fujian Economic Information Net   http://www.fjic.gov.cn
Fujian Constructional Information Net   http://www.fjjs.gov.cn
Fujian Agricultural Information Net   http://www.fjagri.gov.cn

Jiangxi Provincial Government   http://www.jiangxi.gov.cn
Jiangxi Window   http://www.china-window.com/Jiangxi_w

Jiangxi Economic Information Net   http://www.jxeinet.gov.cn
Jiangxi Agricultural Information Net   http://www.jx-agri.gov.cn
Jiangxi Constructional Information Net   http://www.jxjst.com
Jiangxi Scientific and Technical Information Net   http://www.jxinfo.gov.cn

Shandong Provincial Government   http://www.sd.gov.cn
Shandong Window   http://www.shandong-window.com
Shandong China   http://www.sd-china.com
Shandong Net   http://www.china-sd.net
Shandong Economic Information Net   http://www.sd.cei.gov.cn
Shandong Statistical Information Net   http://www.stats-sd.gov.cn
Shandong Agricultural Information Net   http://www.sdny.gov.cn
Shandong Science and Technology   http://www.sdstc.gov.cn
Shandong Educational Information Net   http://www.sdpec.edu.cn

Henan Provincial Government   http://www.henan.gov.cn
Henan China   http://www.henanews.org.cn
Henan Window   http://www.henan-window.com
Henan Economic Information Net   http://www.hnei.gov.cn
Henan Statistical Information Net   http://www.ha.stats.gov.cn
Henan Agricultural Information Net   http://www.hnagri.org.cn
Henan Scientific and Technical Information Net   http://www.sti.ha.cn

Hubei Provincial Government   http://www.hubei.gov.cn
Hubei Window   http://www.hubei-window.com
Hubei Economic Information Net   http://www.hub.cei.gov.cn
Hubei Statistical Information Net   http://www.stats-hb.gov.cn
Hubei Agricultural Information Net   http://www.hbagri.gov.cn
Hubei Enterprise Net   http://www.goldenter.com
Hubei Science and Technology   http://www.hbstd.gov.cn

Hunan Provincial Government   http://www.hunan.gov.cn
Hunan Window   http://www.hunan-window.com
Hunan Economic Information Net   http://www.hun.cei.gov.cn
Hunan Statistical Information Net   http://www.hntj.gov.cn
Hunan Agricultural Information Net   http://www.hnagri.gov.cn
Hunan Science and Technology   http://www.hninfo.gov.cn

Guangdong Provincial Government   http://www.gd.gov.cn
Guangdong Window   http://www.Guangdong-china.com
Guangdong Economic Information Net   http://www.gd.cei.gov.cn
Guangdong Rural Economic Information Net   http://www.agri.gd.gov.cn
Guangdong Constructional Information Net   http://www.gdcic.net
Guangdong Scientific and Technical Information Net   http://www.sti.gd.cn
Guangdong Educational Net   http://www.gd.edu.cn

Guanxi Zhuang Nationality Autonomous Region Government
    http://www.gxi.gov.cn
Guangxi Window   http://www.china-window.com/Guangxi_w
Guangxi Economic Information Net   http://www.gx.cei.gov.cn
Guangxi Agricultural Information Net   http://www.gxny.gov.cn
Guangxi Scientific and Technical Information Net   http://www.gxsti.net.cn
Guangxi Statistical Information Net   http://www.gxtj.gov.cn

Hainan Provincial Government   http://www.hainan.gov.cn
Hainan Window   http://www.hainan-window.com.cn
Hainan Economic Information Net   http://www.han.cei.gov.cn
Hainan Statistical Information Net   http://www.statistical.hainan.gov.cn
Hainan Science and Technology   http://www.dost.hainan.gov.cn

Chongqing Municipal Government   http://www.cq.gov.cn
Chongqing Window   http://www.cqi.com.cn
Chongqing Economic Information Net   http://www.cq.cei.gov.cn
Chongqing Agricultural Information Net   http://www.cqagri.gov.cn
Chongqing Constructional Window   http://www.ccc.gov.cn
Chongqing Constructional Engineering Information Net   http://www.cqjsxx.com
Chongqing Scientific and Technical Information Net   http://www.ctin.ac.cn
Chongqing Educational Information Net   http://www.spbemis.net.cn

Sichuan Provincial Government   http://www.sc.gov.cn
Sichuan China   http://www.sichuan.gov.cn
Sichuan Window   http://china-window.com/Sichuan_w
Sichuan Economic Information Net   http://www.sc.cei.gov.cn
Sichuan Agricultural Information Net   http://www.scagri.gov.cn
Sichuan Construction Net   http://www.sccin.com.cn

Sichuan Science and Technology   http://www.sckw.sichuan.net.cn

Sichuan Educational Net   http://www.scedu.net

Guizhou Provincial Government   http://www.gzgov.gov.cn

Guizhou Window   http://www.china-window.com/Guizhou_w

Guizhou China   http://www.chinabus.com

Guizhou Comprehensive Information Net   http://www.guz.cei.gov.cn

Guizhou Statistical Information Net   http://www.gz.stats.gov.cn

Guizhou Agricultural Economy   http://www.gznw.gov.cn

Guizhou Scientific and Technical Information Net   http://gzkw.gy.gz.cn

Yunnan Provincial Government   http://www.yn.gov.cn

Yunnan Window   http://www.Yunnan-window.com.cn

Yunnan China   http://www.e-yunnan.com.cn

Yunnan Economic Information Net   http://www.yn.cei.gov.cn

Yunnan Science and Technology   http://www.istiy.yn.cn

Yunnan Educational Information Net   http://ynnu.yn.cninfo.net

Yunnan Provincial Engineering Construction Net   http://www.ynzb.com.cn

Tibet Net   http://www.tibet-Net.com

Tibetan Construction Net   http://www.com668.com

Tibetan Window   http://china-window.com.cn/Xizang_w

Tibet China   http://www.tibetinfor.com

Tibet Guide   http://www.tibetguide.com.cn

Tibetan Government Procurement   http://www.ccgp-xizang.gov.cn

Shaanxi Provincial Government   http://www.shaanxi.gov.cn

Shaanxi Window   http://china-window.com/Shaanxi_w

Shaanxi Economic Information Net   http://www.sei.sn.cn

Shaanxi Agriculture   http://www.agri.sn.cn

Shaanxi Provincial Construction Department   http://jst.shaanxi.gov.cn

Shaanxi Science and Technology   http://www.sninfo.gov.cn

Gansu Provincial Government   http://www.gansu.gov.cn

Gansu Window   http://www.china-window.com/Gansu_w

Gansu Economic Information Net   http://www.gsei.gansu.gov.cn

Gansu Statistical Information Net   http://www.gs.stats.gov.cn

Gansu Information Net   http://www.gansuchina.com
Gansu Scientific and Technical Information Net   http://www.gsinfo.net.cn
Gansu Educational Net   http://www.gsedu.gov.cn

Qinghai Provincial Government   http://www.qh.gov.cn
Qinghai Window   http://www.china-window.com/Qinghai_w
Qinghia Economic Information Net   http://www.qhei.gov.cn
Qinghai Agriculture   http://www.qhsjyagri.gov.cn
Qinghai Constructional Engineering   http://www.qhbid.com

Ningxia Window   http://www.china-window.com/Ningxia_w
Ningxia Economic Information Net   http://www.nx.cei.gov.cn
Ningxia Statistical Information Net   http://www.nx.stats.gov.cn
Ningxia Agricultural Information Net   http://www.nxny.gov.cn
Ningxia Scientific and Technical Information Net   http://www.nxinfo.gov.cn

Xinjiang Uygur Autonomous Region   http://www.xj.gov.cn
Xinjiang Window   http://china-window.com/Xinjiang_w
Xinjiang Economic Information Net   http://www.xj.cei.gov.cn
Xinjiang Statistical Information Net   http://www.xj.stats.gov.cn
Xinjiang Scientific and Technical Information Net   http://www.xjinfo.gov.cn

Sector Information

China Economic Information Net   http://www.cei.gov.cn
China Macroeconomic Information Net   http://www.macrochina.com.cn
China Industrial Economic Information Net   http://www.cinic.org.cn
China Statistical Information Net   http://www.stats.gov.cn
China Western Development   http://www.chinawest.gov.cn
China Agricultural Information Net   http://www.agri.gov.cn
China Agricultural Products Supply and Demand Information Net
    http://www.agrisd.gov.cn
China Agricultural Guide   http://www.agro-guide.com.cn
China Northern Agriculture Information Net   http://www.agri.net.cn
China Agricultural Foreign Economy and Foreign Trade Information Net

http://www.cafte.gov.cn

China Agricultural Foreign Economic Information Net
http://www.fecc.agri.gov.cn

China Council for Promotion of International Trade, Agricultural Branch
http://www.ccpit-ssa.org.cn

China Foodstuff Net   http://www.foodchina.com

China Feed Sector Information Net   http:// www.feedtrade.com.cn

China Supply and Marketing Cooperation Net   http://www.chinacoop.com

China Planting Sector Information Net   http://zzys.agri.gov.cn

China Aquatic Market Information Net   http://www.agri.gov.cn/_fish

China Cotton Net   http://www.cncotton.com

China Electronic Sector Information Net   http://www.ceic.gov.cn

China Electronic Sector Investment Information Net   http://www.ceiinet.gov.cn

China Electronic Information of 100 Top Firms Net   http://www.ittop100.gov.cn

China Mobile Telecom Sector Net   http://www.chinamobile.gov.cn

China Machinery Information Net   http://www.machineinfo.gov.cn

China Machinery Industry Economic Information Net   http://www.mei.gov.cn

China Mechanical and Electrical Equipment Bidding Information Net
http://www.machinebidding.gov.cn

China Auto Industry Information Net   http://www.autoinfo.gov.cn

China Auto Information Net   http://www.cnauto.com.cn

China Bearing Sector Net   http://www.cnbearing.com

China Sophisticated Chemical Industry Net   http://www.china-finechem.com.cn

China Metallurgical Net   http://www.mmi.gov.cn

China Metallurgical Economical Information Net   http://www.chinaesteel.com.cn

China Nonferrous Metal Information Net   http://www.atk.com.cn

China Chemical Industry Information Net   http://www.cheminfo.gov.cn

China Fertilizer Information Net   http://www.sinofi.com

China Construction Net   http://www.chinacon.com.cn

China Construction Window   http://www.c-window.com.cn

China Engineering Construction and Architectural Sector Information Net
http://www.cein.gov.cn

China Building Material Information Net   http://www.bm.cei.gov.cn

China Communication Net   http://www.iicc.ac.cn

China Civil Aviation Information Net   http://www.caac.cn.net

China Energy Information Net   http://www.energy-china.com

China Coal Industry Net   http://www.chinacoal.org.cn

State Power Information Net   http://www.sp.com.cn
China Light Industry Information Net   http://www.clii.com.cn
China Electrical Household Appliances Net   http://www.cheaa.com
China Sewing Machine Information Net   http://www.sewinginfo.com
China Textile Economic Information Net   http://www.ctei.gov.cn
China Garment Information Net   http:// www.cnapparel.org
China Footwear Net   http://www.china-footwear.com.cn
China Pharmaceutical Economy and Trade Net   http://www.yyjm.net.cn
China Pharmaceutical Information Net   http://www.cpi.ac.cn
China Pharmaceutical Market Net   http://www.chinapharmarket.com
China Traditional Chinese Medicine Information Net   http://www.cintcm.ac.cn
China Technology and Investment Net   http://www.techcn.com/technew
                                                            http://www.techcn.com/etechnew
China Technology Trade Net http://www.ctmnet.com.cn
China Engineering Technical Information Net   http://www.cetin.net.cn

Information Net of China National Industrial and Commercial Chamber of Commerce
    http://www.chinachamber.com.cn
All-China Industrial and Commercial Chamber of Commerce Net
    http://www.chinachamber.com
China State-Owned Enterprises Net   http://www.chinabbc.com.cn
China Enterprise Information Net   http://www.cen.com.cn
China Small and Medium Enterprises Information Net
    http://www.chinasmb.gov.cn
China Township Enterprises Information Net   http://www.cte.gov.cn
China Enterprise Joint Conference of APEC   http://www.apec-cea.org.cn

All-China Federation of Industry and Commerce   http://www.acfic.org.cn
China Federation of Industrial Economyhttp:// www.cfie.org.cn
China Enterprise Federation   http://www.cec-ceda.org.cn
China Small and Medium Enterprise International Cooperation Association
    http://www.chinasme.org.cn
China Foodstuff Industry Association   http://www.cfiin.com
China Quality Association   http://www.cqca.org
China Packing Technology Association   http://www.pack.org.cn
China Chain Business Association   http://www.ccfa.org.cn
China Federation of Enterprises with Commercial Stock Cooperative System Economy

http://www.ejcccse.org.cn

China Federation of Logistics and Procurement   http://www.chinawuliu.com.cn

China Association of Coal Industry   http://www.chinacoal.org.cn

China Federation of Mechanical Industry   http://www.mei.cei.gov.cn

China Association of Electrical Household Appliances   http://www.cheaa.org

China Federation of Light Industry   http://www.clii.com.cn

China Association of Textile Industry   http://www.cnfti.com.cn

China Association of Power Enterprises   http://www.cec.org.cn

China Textile Import and Import Chamber of Commerce
    http://www.texchamber.org.cn
    http://www.ccct.org.cnPeople's

Bank of China   http://www.pbc.gov.cn Bank of China
            http://www.bank-of-china.com

China Construction Bank   http://www.ccb.cn.ne

Industrial and Commercial Bank of China   http://www.icbc.com.cn

Agricultural Bank of China   http://www.intl.abocn.com

China Bank of Communications   http://www.bankcomm.com

Merchants' Bank   http://www.cmb.com.cn

China Insurance Net   http://www.china-insurance.com

China Association of Security Industry   http://www.s-a-c.org.cn

Shanghai Stock Exchange   http://www.sse.com.cn

Shenzhen Stock Exchange   http://www.sse.org.cn

Shanghai Forward Exchange   http://www.shfe.com

Zhengzhou Commodities Exchange   http://www.czce.com.cn

Dalian Commodities Exchange   http://www.dce.com.cn

Trade and Investment

Ministry of Commerce   http://www.mofcom.gov.cn

China Business Guide   http://www.cbg.org.cn

China Trade   http://www.chinatradeworld.com

China Export Commodities Fair   http://www.cecf.com.cn

China Goods Net   http://www.goods-china.com

China Technical Export Fair   http://www.techfair.com.cn

China Electromechanical Trade Net   http://www.chinamet.com

UN Technical, Economic and Trade Information Net   http://www.tipschina.gov.cn

China International Investment Promotion Net   http://www.chinafdi.org.cn

China Business Invitation   http://www.chinainvest.com.cn

China Window of Development Zones   http://www.sezo.gov.cn

China Procurement and Bidding Net   http://www.chinabidding.gov.cn

China Bidding Invitation and Bidding Net   http://www.cec.gov.cn

China Government Procurement   http://www.ccgp.gov.cn

China Foreign Investment Net   http://www.chinafiw.com

CCPIT/China International Chamber of Commerce   http://www.ccpit.org

CCPIT Beijing Municipal Branch   http://www.ccpitbj.com

CCPIT Tianjin Municipal Branch   http://www.tianjinccpit.com

CCPIT Shanghai Municipal Branch   http://www.ccpitsh.org

CCPIT Pudong Shanghai Branch   http://ccpit.pudong.gov.cn

CCPIT Shanxi Provincial Branch   http://www.ccpitsx.org

CCPIT Hebei Provincial Branch   http://www.ccpithb.com

CCPIT Liaoning Provincial Branch   http://www.liaoning-window.com.cn

CCPIT Shenyang Municipal Branch   http://www.ccpit-sy.org.cn

CCPIT Dalian Municipal Branch   http://www.ccpitdl.org

CCPIT Jilin Branch   http://www.jl.org/ccpit

CCPIT Heilongjiang Provincial Branch   http://www.hlj.ccpit.org

CCPIT Harbin Municipal Branch   http://www.hrbccpit.com.cn

CCPIT Jiangsu Provincial Branch   http://ccpitjs.asiansources.com

CCPIT Anhui Provincial Branch   http://anhui.ccpit.org

CCPIT Shandong Provincial Branch   http://www.ccpitsd.org

CCPIT Qingdao Municipal Branch   http://www.ccpitqd.com

CCPIT Zhejiang Provincial Branch   http://www.ccpitzj.com

CCPIT Hangzhou Municipal Branch   http://www.ccpit-hangzhou.com

CCPIT Ningbo Municipal Branch   http://www.ccpitnb.org

CCPIT Fujian Provincial Branch   http://www.ccpitfujian.org

CCPIT Xiamen Municipal Branch   http://www.ccpitxiamen.org

CCPIT Hunan Provincial Branch   http://www.ccpithn.com

CCPIT Hubei Provincial Branch   http://www.hbccpit.org

CCPIT Henan Provincial Branch   http://www.ccpit-henan.org

CCPIT Guangdong Provincial Branch   http://www.getgd.net

CCPIT Guangzhou Municipal Branch   http://www.ccpitgz.com.cn

CCPIT Shenzhen Municipal Branch   http://www.ccpitsz.org

CCPIT Zhuhai Municipal Branch   http://www.zhuhai.org/ccpit

CCPIT Shantou Municipal Branch   http://www.ccpitst.org

CCPIT Hainan Provincial Branch   http://www.ccpit.hq.cninfo.net

CCPIT Guangxi Zhuang Nationality Autonomous Region Branch
    http://www.ccpitgx.org

CCPIT Sichuan Provincial Branch   http://www.ccpit-sichuan.org

CCPIT Yunnan Provincial Branch   http://yunnan.ccpit.org

CCPIT Shaanxi Provincial Branch   http://www.ccpit.xaonline.com

CCPIT Gansu Provincial Branch   http://www.ccpitgs.org

CCPIT Machinery Sector Branch   http://www.chinamachine.org

CCPIT Electronic Information Sector Branch   http://www.ccpitecc.com

CCPIT Light Industry Sector Branch   http://www.chinafoodadditives.com

CCPIT Textile Sector Branch   http://www.ccpittex.com

CCPIT Agricultural Sector Branch   http://www.ccpit-ssa.org.cn

CCPIT Auto Sector Branch   http://www.auto-ccpit.org

CCPIT Commercial Sector Branch   http://csc.ccpit.org

CCPIT Metallurgical Sector Branch   http://www.metallurgy-china.com

CCPIT Chemical Industry Sector Branch   http://www.ccpitscci.org.cn

CCPIT Building Material Sector Branch   http://www.chinabuilding.cn.net

CCPIT Construction Sector Branch   http://www.realstate.cei.gov.cn

CCPIT Grains Sector Branch   http://grain.ccpit.org

China Metals, Minerals and Chemicals Import and Export Chamber of Commerce
    http://www.cocmc.org.cn

China Electromechanical Products Import and Export Chamber of Commerce
    http://www.cccme.cn.net

China Contracting Foreign Engineering Chamber of Commerce
    http://www.moftec.gov.cn/dwchb.shtml

China Textiles Import and Export Chamber of Commerce   http://www.ccct.org.cn

China Light Industry and Arts and Crafts Import and Export Chamber of Commerce
    http://www.moftec.gov.cn/qggy.shtml

China Foodstuffs, Native Produce and Animal By-products Import and Export Chamber of Commerce
    http://www.cccfna.org.cn

China Medical and Healthcare Stuffs Chamber of Commerce
    http://www.cccmhpie.org.cn

Beijing Municipal Development and Planning Commission
  http://www.bjpc.gov.cn
Beijing Municipal Foreign Economic and Trade Commission
  http://www.moftecbj.gov.cn
Beijing Economy and Trade   http://www.bjec.gov.cn
Beijing Investment Platform   http://www.bjinvest.gov.cn
Beijing Foreign Fund Net   http://www.bj-invest.com
Beijing International Investment Promotion Net   http://www.fdibeijing.org.cn
Beijing Economical and Technical Development Zone   http://www.bda.gov.cn
Beijing Government Procurement   http://www.bj-procurement.gov.cn

Tianjin Municipal Development and Planning Commission
  http://www.tjjw.tinet.tj.cn
Tianjin Municipal Economic and Trade Commission
  http://www.goldentianjin.net.cn
Foreign Investment Office of Tianjin Municipal People's Government
  http://tjfisc.onlime.tj.cn
Tianjin Foreign Economy and Trade Net   http://www.tjfisc.gov.cn
Tianjin Economic and Technical Development Zone   http://www.teda.gov.cn
Tianjin Government Procurement   http://www.ccgp-tianjing.gov.cn

Hebei Provincial Development and Planning Commission
  http://www.dpc.hebnet.gov.cn
Hebei Provincial Economic and Trade Commission   http://www.etc.hebnet.gov.cn
Hebei Provincial International Investment Promotion Net
  http://www.hebei.chinafdi.org.cn
Hebei Provincial Foreign Trade and Economic Cooperation Department
  http://www.doftec.gov.cn
Hebei Provincial Business Invitation Cooperation Net   http://www.hebiic.gov.cn
Hebei Government Procurement   http://www.ccgp-hebei.gov.cn

Shanxi Provincial Development and Planning Commission
  http://www.sx.cei.gov.cn/jiwei
Shanxi Provincial Economic and Trade Commission   http://www.sxetc.gov.cn
Shanxi Provincial Foreign Trade and Economic Cooperation Department
  http://www.sxwjm.net.cn
Shanxi Business and Investment Invitation   http://www.sxpublic.gov.cn/zgsx/zsyz

Shanxi Government Procurement   http://www.ccgp-shanxi.gov.cnInner

Mongolian Autonomous Region Development and Planning Commission
    http://www.nmjw.gov.cnInner
Mongolia Foreign Economy and Trade   http://www.gov.nm.cninfo.net/users/zhfm
Inner Mongolia Business and Investment Invitation Net
    http://www.iminvest.comInner
Mongolia Government Procurement   http://www.ccgp-neimeng.gov.cn

Liaoning Provincial Development and Planning Commission
    http://www.lndp.gov.cn
Liaoning Provincial Trade and Economic Cooperation Department
    http://www.china-liaoning.org
Liaoning Provincial Economic and Trade Information Net
    http://www.lnbbc.com.cn
Investment in Liaoning   http://china.china-liaoning.org
Liaoning International Business Net   http://www.liaoning-window.com.cn
Liaoning Government Procurement   http://www.ccgp-liaoning.gov.cn
Liaoning Foreign Enterprises Online   http://www.lnfesco.com

Jilin Provincial Development and Planning Commission
    http://www.jilin.cei.gov.cn/jwzl
Jilin Provincial Economic and Trade Commission   http://jmw.jl.gov.cnJilin
Provincial Foreign Traded and Economic Cooperation Department
    http://wmt.jl.gov.cn
Jilin Foreign Investment Information Net   http://www.investment.jl.cn
Jilin Provincial Foreign Investment Management Service Center
    http://www.investment.jl.cn
Jilin Government Procurement
    http://www.ccgp-jilin.gov.cn

Heilongjiang Provincial Planning Commission   http://www.hl.dpc.gov.cn
Heilongjiang Provincial Economic and Trade Commission
    http://www.hletc.gov.cn
Heilongjiang Provincial Foreign Trade and Economic Cooperation Department
    http://www.hl-doftec.gov.cn
Heilongjiang Government Procurement   http://www.ccgp-heilongj.gov.cn

Shanghai Municipal Development and Planning Commission
    http://www.shpc.gov.cn
Shanghai Municipal Foreign Economic and Trade Commission
    http://www.smert.gov.cn
Shanghai Municipal Foreign-Funded Enterprises Association
    http://www.safete.org.cn
Shanghai Foreign Investment   http://www.investment.gov.cn
Shanghai Government Procurement   http://www.ccgp-shanghai.gov.cn

Jiangsu Provincial Development and Planning Commission
    http://www.jsdpc.gov.cn
Jiangsu Provincial Economic and Trade Commission   http://www.jsetc.gov.cn
Jiangsu Investment   http://www.jsinvest.net
Jiangsu Government Procurement   http://www.ccgp-jiangsu.gov.cn

Zhejiang Provincial Development and Planning Commission
    http://www.zjdpc.gov.cn
Zhejiang Provincial Economic and Trade Commission   http://www.zjjmw.gov.cn
Zhejiang Provincial Foreign Trade and Economic Cooperation Department
    http://www.zftec.gov.cn
Zhejiang International Investment Promotion Net   http://www.zhejiangchina.com
Zhejiang Government Procurement   http://www.ccgp-zhejiang.gov.cn

Anhui Provincial Planning Commission   http://www.ahpc.gov.cn
Anhui Provincial Economic and Trade Commission   http://www.ahetc.gov.cn
Anhui Provincial Foreign Trade and Economic Cooperation Department
    http://www.ahmoftec.gov.cn
Anhui Business and Investment Invitation Information Net
    http://www.anhuionline.com
Anhui Government Procurement   http://www.ccgp-anhui.gov.cn
Anhui Provincial Foreign-Funded Businesses Net   http://www.ahinvest.gov.cn

Fujian Provincial Development and Planning Commission
    http://www.fjdpc.gov.cn
Fujian Provincial Economic and Trade Commission   http://www.fjetc.gov.cn
Fujian Provincial Foreign Trade and Economic Cooperation Department
    http://www.fiet.gov.cn

Fujian Economy and Trade   http://www.fjge.com
Fujian Government Procurement   http://www.ccgp-fujian.gov.cn

Jiangxi Provincial Development and Planning Commission
   http://www.jxdpc.gov.cn
Jiangxi Provincial Foreign Trade and Economic Cooperation Department
   http://www.jxdoftec.gov.cn
Jiangxi Business and Investment Invitation   http://www.jiangxi.gov.cn/zhaoshangyz
Jiangxi Government Procurement   http://www.ccgp-jiangxi.gov.cn

Shandong Provincial Development and Planning Commission
   http://server.sd.cei.gov.cn/mrjj/jiwei
Shandong Provincial Economic and Trade commission   http://www.sdetn.gov.cn
Shandong Provincial Foreign Trade and Economic Cooperation Department
   http://www.trade.gov.cn
Shandong Foreign Trade   http://www.sd-trade.com
Shandong Government Procurement   http://www.ccgp-shandong.gov.cn

Henan Provincial Planning Commission   http://www.hndpc.gov.cn
Henan Provincial Economic and Trade Commission
   http://www.hajm.henan.gov.cn
Henan Provincial Foreign Trade and Economic Cooperation Department
   http://www.trade.henan.gov.cn
Henan Economic and Trade Net   http://ectr.zz.ha.cn
Henan Government Procurement   http://www.ccgp-henan.gov.cn

Hubei Provincial Planning Commission   http://www.hbjw.gov.cn
Hubei Business Invitation Net   http://www.hbinvest.gov.cn
Hubei Government Procurement   http://www.ccgp-hubei.gov.cn
Hubei Provincial Foreign Investment Association   http://www.hbaefi.com

Hunan Provincial Development and Planning Commission
   http://www.hunan.gov.cn/hnzf/zfjg/jiwei
Hunan Provincial Economic and Trade Commission   http://www.hnjmw.gov.cn
Hunan Provincial Foreign Trade and Economic Cooperation Department
   http://www.hninvest.gov.cn
Hunan Business and Investment Invitation Information

http://www.hunan.gov.cn/zs/hnzs
Hunan Government Procurement   http://www.ccgp-hunan.gov.cn

Guangdong Provincial Development and Planning Commission
    http://www.gddpc.gov.cn
Guangdong Provincial Economic and Trade Commission   http://www.gdet.gov.cn
Guangdong Provincial Foreign Trade and Economic Cooperation Department
    http://www.gddoftec.gov.cn
Guangdong Economic and Trade Window   http://www.getgd.net
Guangdong Business Invitation   http://www.invest.gd.gov.cn
Guangdong Government Procurement   http://www.ccgp-guangdong.gov.cn
Guangdong Government Investment Promotion Center   http://www.gdccfi.gov.cn
Guangdong Provincial Foreign Investment Service Center   http://www.gdfisc.com

Guangxi Zhuang Nationality Autonomous Region Development and Planning Com-
mission   http://www.gxi.gov.cn/jw
Guangxi Zhuang Nationality Autonomous Region Economic and Trade Commission
    http://www.gxjm.gov.cn
Guangxi Zhuang Nationality Autonomous Region Foreign Economic and Trade Co-
operation Department   http://wjmt.gxi.gov.cn
Guangxi Zhuang Nationality Autonomous Region Foreign Investment Management
Office   http://www.gxofipc.gov.cn
Guangxi Business Invitation   http://www.gxinvest.gov.cn
Guangxi Government Procurement   http://www.ccgp-guangxi.gov.cn
Guangxi Foreign-Funded Enterprises Association   http://www.gaefi.org.cn

Hainan Provincial Development and Planning Department
    http://plan.hainan.gov.cn
Hainan Provincial Economic and Trade Department   http://industry.hainan.gov.cn
Hainan Provincial Foreign Trade and Economic Cooperation Department
    http://doftec.hainan.gov.cn
Hainan Government Procurement   http://www.ccgp-hainan.gov.cn

Chongqing Municipal Development and Planning Commission
    http://www.cqdpc.gov.cn
Chongqing Municipal Foreign Economic and Trade Commission
    http://www.ft.cq.cn

 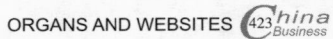

Chongqing Economy and Trade   http://www.cqec.gov.cn
Chongqing Business Invitation   http://www.cqinvest.gov.cn
Chongqing Municipal Government Procurement
    http://www.ccgp-chongqing.gov.cn
Chongqing Municipal Foreign-Funded Enterprises Association
    http://www.cqaefi.org

Sichuan Provincial Economic and Trade Commission   http://www.scjm.gov.cn
Sichuan Provincial Foreign Trade and Economic Cooperation Department
    http://www.scbg.org.cn
Sichuan Provincial Business and Investment Invitation Bureau
    http//www.investment-sc.org
Sichuan Economy and Trade   http://www.scjm.gov.cn
Sichuan Business and Investment Invitation   http://www.sichuaninvest.gov.cn
Sichuan Government Procurement   http://www.ccgp-hainan.gov.cn

Guizhou Provincial Development Commission   http://www.gzdpc.gov.cn
Guizhou Provincial Economic and Trade Commission
    http://www.gzgov.gov.cn/china/department/jmw
Guizhou Provincial Trade and Cooperation Department   http://www.gzfdi.org
Guizhou Business Information Net   http://www.investgz.com
Guizhou Provincial International Investment and Promotion Net
    http://www.gzfdi.org
Guizhou Government Procurement   http://www.ccgp-guizhou.gov.cn

Yunnan Provincial Development and Planning Commission
    http://www.yn.gov.cn/jw
Yunnan Provincial Economic and Trade Commission   http://www.ynetc.gov.cn
Yunnan Provincial Foreign Economic and Trade Cooperation Department
    http://www.boftec.gov.cn
Foreign Investment Office of Yunnan Provincial People's Government
    http://www.invest-yunnan.com
Yunnan Government Procurement   http://www.ccgp-yunnan.gov.cn

Shaanxi Provincial Development and Planning Commission
    http://sjw.shaanxi.gov.cn
Shaanxi Provincial Economic and Trade Commission   http://jmw.shaanxi.gov.cn

Shaanxi Provincial Trade and Economic Cooperation Department
http://www.sx-trade.com
Shaanxi Business and Investment Invitation   http://www.ewit.gov.cn
Shaanxi Government Procurement   http://www.ccgp-shaanxi.gov.cn

Gansu Provincial Development and Planning Commission
http://www.gspc.gov.cn
Gansu Provincial Economic and Trade Commission
http://www.gsetc.gansu.gov.cn
Gansu Trade Net   http://www.gstrade.com
Gansu Government Procurement   http://www.ccgp-gansu.gov.cn

Qinghai Provincial Development and Planning Commission
http://www.qhei.gov.cn
Qinghai Provincial Economic and Trade Commission   http://www.qhetc.gov.cn
Qinghai Provincial Foreign Trade and Economic Cooperation Department
http://www.qhwjmt.gov.cn
Qinghai Provincial Investment Promotion Net   http://qinghai.chinafdi.org.cn
Qinghai Government Procurement   http://www.ccgp-qinghai.gov.cn

Ningxia Hui Nationality Autonomous Region Development and Planning Commission
http://www.nx.cei.gov.cn/jw
Foreign Trade and Economic Cooperation Department of Ningxia Hui Nationality
Autonomous Region   http://www.nxdoftec.gov.cn
Ningxia Government Procurement   http://www.ccgp-ningxia.gov.cn

Xinjiang Investment Information Net   http://www.xjnet.com.cn
Xinjiang Government Procurement   http://www.ccgp-xinjiang.gov.cn

China Expo General Net   http://www.2t2.net
China Trade Fair Net   http://chinafair.com.cn
China Trade Fair Expo Net   http://www.cce.net.cn
China Meeting Net   http://www.chinameeting.com
World Fair Net   http://www.dcoem.com
China Investment and Trade Fair   http://www.chinafair.org.cn
China Export Commodities Trade Fair (Guangzhou Trade Fair)
http://www.cantonfair.org.cn

China Beijing International Scientific and Technical Industry Expo
http://www.hightechbj.com
China International High-Tech Achievements Trade Fair   http://www.chtf.com
Shanghai International Industrial Expo   http://www.sif-expo.com
China Kunming Export Commodities Trade Fair   http://www.kunmingfair.com
China East-China Import and Export Commodities Trade Fair
http://www.east-china-fair.com
China Dalian Import and Export Commodities Trade Fair
http://www.dalianfair.com
Zhengzhou National Commodities Trade Fair   http://www.zzfair.com
China Daily-Use Commodities Trade Fair   http://china-dnf.com
China International Daily-Use Consumer Goods Expo   http://www.cicgf.com
China International Small and Medium Enterprises Commodities Expo
http://www.czcicf.org
China International Agricultural Expo   http://www.ciae.com.cn
China International Electronic and Household Electrical Appliances Expo
http://www.qingdaoexpo.org
Beijing China International Household Electrical Appliances Expo
http://www.cheaa-elec.com
China International Telecom Equipment and Technology Expo
http://www.expocommcn.com
China International Electronic Products Expo   http://liufang.gongkong.com
Beijing International Auto Industry Expo   http://www.autochina.com.cn
International Industrial Automation and Control Technology Expo
http://iac.gongkong.com
China International Space and Aviation Expo   http://www.airshow.com.cn
China International Energy and Environmental Protection World Expo
http://www.ciscexpo.orgcn.net
China International Water Technology and Equipment Expo
http://www.waterchina.net
China Hotel Expo   http://www.hotelchinaexpo.comInternational
Franchise Symposium and Expo   http://www.franchisechina.com
China International Biological Technology Expo   http://chinabio.org
China International Printing Equipment and Materials Expo
http://print.ciec-exhibition.com.cn
China International Packing Technology Expo   http://cip.ciec-exhibition.com.cn
Beijing International Broadcasting, Film and TV Equipment Expo

http://www.birtv.com

Shanghai International Ad Technology and Equipment Expo
http://www.apppexpo.com

China International Foodstuff Industry Expo   http://www.2t2.net/cfi

Shanghai International Foodstuffs Expo   http://chinafood2002.ifood1.com

China Gardening Expo   http://www.china-gardening.com

China Textiles Expo   http://www.ctcte.com

China International Garment and Dress Adornment Expo
http://www.chic.com.cn/chic

Dalian International Garment Expo and China Garment Export Trade Fair
http://www.e-clothing.com.cn/fznew

China National Furniture Expo   http://www.cnfa.com.cn

China Watch and Jewelry Commodities Fair
http://www.cbwchina.com/business/exhib/jewel

China Plastics Expo   http://www.21cp.net

China Dyes Fair   http://www.cndyes.com

China Internet Expo   http://chinainet.chtf-expo.com

China International Education Expo   http://www.chinaeducationexpo.com

Beijing International Books Fair   http://www.bibf.net

China International Sports Goods Expo   http://www.sportshow.com.cn

Society, Media and Tourism

China Reform Net   http://www.chinareform.com

China Law Online   http://www.chinalaw.com.cn

Beijing University Law Information Net   http://www.chinalawinfo.com
http://www.chnlaw.com

China Population http://www.cpirc.org.cn China Science and Technology Net
http://www.cstnet.net.cn

State Scientific and Technical Achievements Net   http://www.nast.org.cn

National Defense Scientific and Technical Achievements for Turning into Commercial Production Net   http://www.techinfo.gov.cn

China Science and Technology Online   http://www.chinatech.com.cn

China University Science and Technology Net   http://www.unitech.net.cn

China Education and Scientific Research Computer Net   http://www.edu.cn

China Educational Information Net   http://www.ceinn.net

China Basic Education Information Net   http://www.chinaevedu.com

China Returned Talents Information Net   http://www.chinatalents.gov.cn

China Cultural Information Net   http://www.ccnt.com.cn

                   http://www.ccnt.com

China National Library   http://www.nlc.gov.cn

China Intellectual Property Net   http://www.cnipr.com

China Copyright Protection   http://www.ccopyright.com.cn

China Sustainable Development Information Net   http://www.sdinfo.coi.gov.cn

China *Jinwei* Net   http://www.2919.net

Xinhua Net   http://www.xinhua.org

             http://www.xinhuanet.com

             http://www.xhnet.com

People's Net   http://www.peopledaily.com.cn

China United Report of Local News Net   http://www.unn.com.cn

                        http://www.unn.people.com.cn

China International Radio Broadcasting Station   http://www.cri.com.cn

CCTV International Network   http://www.cctv.com

                 http://www.cctv.com.cn

Central People's Radio Broadcasting Station   http://www.cnradio.com

China Net   http://www.china.org.cnEconomic Daily

    http://ww.economicdaily.com.cn

China Financial Net   http://www.fec.com.cn

China Economic Times   http://www.cet.com.cn

China Industrial and Commercial Times   http://www.cbt.com.cn

International Business Newspaper   http://www.chinapages.com/interbusi/gisb

China Securities Newspaper   http://www.cs.com.cn

China Industrial and Commercial Newspaper   http://www.cicn.com.cn

China Enterprise Newspaper   http://www.cennews.com.cn

China Daily   http://www.chinadaily.com.cn

People's Liberation Army Daily   http://www.pladaily.com.cn

Guangming Net   http://www.gmdaily.com.cnLegal Daily

                 http://www.legaldaily.com.cn

Science and Technology Daily   http://www.stdaily.com

Radio and TV Online   http://www.sarft.com

China News Net   http://www.chinanews.com.cn

China News Agency Hong Kong Branch   http://www.chinanews.com.hk
China News Agency Tokyo Branch   http://www.cnsjp.net
China News Agency Shanxi Net   http://www.sx.chinanews.com.cn
Chins News Agency Liaoning Net   http://www.lnnews.net
China News Agency Jilin Net   http://www.jl.chinanews.com.cn
China News Agency Northeast Asia News Net   http://www.northeastasia.net
China News Agency Shanghai Net   http://www.sh.chinanews.com.cn
China News Agency Jiangsu Net   http://www.js.chinanews.com.cn
China News Agency Anhui Net   http://www.ah.chinanews.com.cn
China News Agency Fujian Net   http://www.fj.chinanews.com.cn
China News Agency Hubei Net   http://www.hb.chinanews.com.cn
China News Agency Guangxi Net   http://www.gx.chinanews.com.cn
China News Agency Chongqing Net   http://www.cqnews.com.cn
China News Agency Sichuan Net   http://www.sc.chinanews.com.cn
China News Agency Shaanxi Net   http://www.shx.chinanews.com.cn
China News Agency Xinjiang Net   http://www.xj.chinanews.com.cn
China Youth Online   http://www.cyol.net Beijing Review
    http://www.bjreview.com.cn
China Today   http://www.chinatoday.com.cn
Huasheng Longmai Net   http://www.chineseinternetnews.com.cn
China Culture Daily   http://www.ccnt.com.cn/chinaculturedaily
China Education Newspaper   http://www.jyb.com.cn
Science Times   http://www.sciencetimes.com.cn
China Media Net   http://www.media-china.com
Qianlong News Net   http://www.beijingnews.com.cn
Beijing Daily   http://www.bjd.com.cnNorth Net http://www.enorth.com.cn
Tianjin Daily   http://www.tianjindaily.com.cn
Hebei Daily   http://www.hebeidaily.com.cn
Shanxi Daily   http://www.sxrb.comLiaoning Daily http://www.lndaily.com.cn
Jilin Daily   http://www.jlrb.com.cn
Heilongjiang Daily   http://www.hljdaily.com.cn
East Net   http://www.eastday.com
Liberation Daily   http://www.jfdaily.com
Zhejiang Daily   http://www.zjdaily.com.cn
Anhui News Net   http://www.ahnews.com.cn
Anhui Daily   http://www.ahrb.com.cn
Fujian Daily   http://www.fjdaily.com.cn

Dajiang News Net   http://www.canno.com
Shandong News Net   http://www.shandongxinwen.com
Dazhong Daily   http://www.dzdaily.com.cn
Henan Daily   http://www.hnby.com.cn
Jingchu News Net   http://www.99sky.com/
Hubei Daily   http://www.hbdaily.com.cn
Hunan News Net   http://www.rednet.com.cn
Hunan Daily   http://www.hnrb.com.cn
South Net   http://www.southcn.com
Nanfang Daily   http://www.nanfangdaily.com.cn
Guilong News Net   http://www.gxnews.com.cn
Guangxi Daily   http://www.gxrb.com.cn
Hainan Daily   http://www.hndaily.com.cn
Hualong Net   http://www.cqnews.net
Sichuan News Net   http://www.newssc.net
Sichuan Daily   http://www.sichuandaily.com
Guizhou Daily   http://www.gog.com.cn
Yunnan Daily   http://www.yndaily.com
Shaanxi Daily   http://www.sxdaily.com.cn
Gansu Daily   http://www.gansudaily.com.cn
Ningxia Daily   http://www.nxdaily.com.cn

China Tour Net   http://www.cnta.com
Huaxia Tour Net   http://www.ctn.com.cn
China Tour News Net   http://www.ctnews.com.cn
Beijing Tour Information Net   http://www.bjta.gov.cn
Tianjin Travel Information Net   http://www.tianjin-travel.com.cn
Hebei Travel Information Net   http://www.travel.hebnet.gov.cn
Shanxi Tour Information Net   http://www.sxta.com.cn
Liaoning Tour http://travel.ln.cninfo.netJilin Tour   http://www.jlcta.com.cn
Shanghai Tour Information http://www.tourinfo.sh.cn
Jiangsu Tour Net   http://www.jstour.com
Zhejiang Tour   http://www.tourzj.com
Anhui Tourism Net   http://www.ahtourism.com
Fujian Tour Window   http://www.fjta.com
Jiangxi Travel Net   http://www.travel-jx.com
Shandong Tour Information Net   http://www.sdta.gov.cn

Henan Tour Service Net   http://www.hnly.com.cn
Hunan Tour Information Net   http://202.103.68.38
Guangdong Travel Net   http://www.gdtravel.com
Guangxi Travel Net   http://www.gx-travel.com
Hannan Tour   http://www.100t.com
Hannan International Tour Net   http://www.ctrs.com.cn
Chongqing Tour Information Net   http://www.visitcq.net
Sichuan Tour   http://www.scsti.ac.cn
Yunnan Tour Information Net   http://www.tourinfo.com.cn
                                   http://www.traveloyunnan.com.cn
Tibet Tour   http://www.tibettour.org
Tibet Tour   http://www.tibettour.net.cn
Shaanxi Tour   http://www.sxtour.com.cn
Gansu Tour Information Net   http://www.joingansu.com
Ningxia Tour Net   http://www.nxtour.com
Xinjiang Tour Net   http://www.xinjiangtour.gov.cn

Embassies in China

Embassy of the Islamic State of Afghanistan
Office: No. 8 Dong Zhi Men Wai Avenue, Beijing
Tel: 65321582

Embassy of the Islamic Republic of Pakistan
Office: No. 1 Dong Zhi Men Wai Avenue, Beijing
Tel: 65322504

Embassy of the Democratic People's Republic of Korea (DPRK)
Office: Ri Tan Rd. (N.), Jian Guo Men Wai, Beijing
Tel: 65321186

Embassy of the Republic of Korea (ROK)
Office: No. 3 4th St. (E.), San Li Tun, Beijing
Tel: 65320290
Website: www.koreaemb.org.cn

Embassy of the Republic of the Philippines
Office: No. 23 Xiu Shui St. (N.), Jian Guo Men Wai, Beijing
Tel: 65321872
Website: www.philembassy-china.org

Embassy of the Kingdom of Cambodia
Office: No. 9 Dong Zhi Men Wai Avenue, Beijing
Tel: 65321889

Embassy of Lao People's Democratic Republic
Office: No. 11 4th St. (E.), San Li Tun, Beijing
Tel: 65321224

Embassy of Malaysia
Trade Representative's Office: S119 Office Building of Yan Sha Center, Beijing
Tel: 84515109

Embassy of the State of Mongolia
Office: No.2 Xiu Shui St. (N.), Jian Guo Men Wai, Beijing
Tel: 65321203

Embassy of the People's Republic of Bangladesh
Office: No. 42 Guang Hua Rd., Beijing
Tel: 65322521

Embassy of the Union of Myanmar
Office: No. 6 Dong Zhi Men Wai Avenue, Beijing
Tel: 65321425

Embassy of the Kingdom of Nepal
Office: No. 1 6th St. (W.), San Li Tun, Beijing
Tel: 65321795

Embassy of Japan
Office: No. 7 Ri Tan Rd., Jian Guo Men Wai, Beijing
Tel: 65322361
Website: www.japan.org.cn

Embassy of the Democratic Socialist Republic of Sri Lanka
Office: No. 3 Jian Hua Rd., Jian Guo Men Wai, Beijing
Tel: 65321861
Website: www.slemb.com

Embassy of the Kingdom of Thailand
Office: No. 40 Guang Hua Rd., Beijing
Tel: 65321749

Embassy of Negava Brunei Darusslam
Office: No. 3 Villa of Diplomatic Apartment, Qi Jia Yuan, Jian Wai, Chao Yang District,
     Beijing
Tel: 65324094

Embassy of the Republic of Singapore
Trade Representative's Office: No. 1 Guang Hua Rd., F/27 North Tower, Jia Li Center,
                          Beijing
Tel: 85296241
Website: www. mfa.gov.sg/beijing

Embassy of the Republic of India
Office: No. 1 Ri Tan Rd. (E.), Beijing
Tel: 65321856
Website: www.indianembassybeijing.org.cn

Embassy of the Republic of Indonesia
Office: Tower B of Diplomats' Office Building, San Li Tun, Beijing
Tel: 65325488
Website: www.indonesianembassy-china.com

Embassy of the Socialist Republic of Vietnam
Office: No. 32 Guang Hua Rd., Jian Guo Men Wai, Beijing
Tel: 65321155

Embassy of the Democratic People's Republic of Algeria
Office: No. 7 San Li Tun Rd., Beijing
Tel: 65321231

Embassy of the Arab Republic of Egypt
Office: No.2 Ri Tan Rd (E.), Beijing
Tel: 65321825

Embassy of the United Arab Emirates
Office: No. 2-6-2 Diplomats' Office Building, Ta Yuan, Beijing
Tel: 65327650
Website: www.uaeemb.com

Embassy of the Syrian Arab Republic
Office: No. 6 4th St. (E.) San Li Tun, Beijing
Tel: 65321372

Embassy of the Sultanate of Oman
Office: No. 6 Liang Ma He Rd. (S.), Beijing
Tel: 65323692

Embassy of the State of Palestine
Office: No. 2 3rd St. (E.), Beijing
Tel: 65321361

Embassy of the State of Bahrain
Office: Rm. 312 & 313, Business Building of Yan Sha Center, Beijing
Tel: 64635385

People's Office of the Great Socialist People's Libyan Arab Jamahiriya
Office: No. 3 6th St., San Li Tun, Beijing
Tel: 65323666

Embassy of the State of Qatar
Office: No. 5-1 Villa of Diplomatic Apartment, Qi Jia Yuan, Jian Guo Men Wai Avenue,
        Beijing
Tel: 65322231

Embassy of the State of Kuwait
Office: No. 21 Guang Hua Rd., Beijing
Tel: 65322216

Embassy of the Republic of Lebanon
Office: No. 10 6th St. (E.) San Li Tun, Beijing
Tel: 65321560

Embassy of the Islamic Republic of Mauritania
Office: No. 9 3rd St. (E.), Beijing
Tel: 65321346

Embassy of the Kingdom of Morocco
Office: No. 16 San Li Tun Rd., Beijing
Tel: 65321796

Embassy of the Republic of Cyprus
Office: No. 2-13-2 Diplomats' Office Building, Ta Yuan, Beijing
Tel: 65325057

Embassy of the Kingdom of Saudi Arabia
Office: No. 1 Bei Xiao St., San Li Tun, Beijing
Tel: 65324825

Embassy of the Republic of the Sudan
Office: No. 1 2nd St. (E.), San Li Tun, Beijing
Tel: 65323715
Website: www.sudanembassychina.com

Embassy of the Republic of Tunisia
Office: No. 1 East St., San Li Tun, Beijing
Tel: 65322435

Embassy of the Republic of Turkey
Office: No. 9 5th St. (E.), San Li Tun, Beijing
Tel: 65321715, 65322490

Embassy of the Republic of Yemen
Office: No. 5 3rd St. (E.), San Li Tun, BeijingTel: 65321558

Embassy of the Republic of Iraq

Office: No. 25 Xiu Shui St. (N.), Jian Guo Men Wai, Beijing
Tel: 65323385

Embassy of the Islamic Republic of Iran
Office: No. 13 6th St. (E.), San Li Tun, Beijing
Tel: 65322040, 65324870

Embassy of the State of Israel
Office: F/4 West Office Building of World Trade Center, No. 1 Jian Guo Men Wai
      Avenue, Beijing
Tel: 65052970
Website: www.israeltrade.org.cn

Embassy of the Hashemite Kingdom of Jordan
Office: No. 5 6th St. (E.), San Li Tun, Beijing
Tel: 65323906

Embassy of the Democratic Republic of Ethiopia Federation
Office: No.3 Xiu Shui St. (S.), Jian Guo Men Wai, Beijing
Tel: 65325258

Embassy of the Republic of Angola
Trade Representative's Office: No. 3-1-32 Diplomatic Apartment, Ta Yuan, Beijing
Tel: 65326562

Embassy of the Republic of Benin
Office: No. 38 Guang Hua Rd., Beijing
Tel: 65322741

Embassy of the Republic of Botswana
Office: No. 811 IBM Tower, Ying Ke Center, No. A-2 Gong Ti Rd. (N.), Beijing
Tel: 65391616

Embassy of the Republic of Burundi
Office: No. 25 Guang Hua Rd., Beijing
Tel: 65321801

Embassy of the Republic of Equatorial Guinea
Office: No. 2 4th St. (E.) San Li Tun, Beijing
Tel: 65323679

Embassy of the Republic of Togo
Office: No. 11 Dong Zhi Men Wai Avenue, Beijing
Tel: 65322202

Embassy of the State of Eritrea
Office: No. 2-10-1 Diplomats' Office Building, Ta Yuan, Beijing
Tel: 65326534

Embassy of the Republic of Cape Verde
Office: No. 6-2-121 Diplomatic Apartment, Ta Yuan, Beijing
Tel: 65327547

Embassy of the Republic of the Congo
Office: No. 7 4th St. (E.), San Li Tun, Beijing
Tel: 65321658

Embassy of the Democratic Republic of the Congo
Office: No. 6 5th St. (E.), San Li Tun, Beijing
Tel: 65323224

Embassy of the Republic of Djibouti
Office: No. 2-2-102 Diplomatic Apartment, Ta Yuan, Chao Yang District, Beijing
Tel: 65327857

Embassy of the Republic of Guinea-Bissau
Office: No. 1-1-101 Diplomatic apartment, Ta Yuan, Chao Yang District, Beijing
Tel: 65327106

Embassy of the Republic of Guinea
Office: No. 2 6th St. (W.), San Li Tun, Beijing
Tel: 65323649

Embassy of the Republic of Ghana

Office: No. 8 San Li Tun Rd., Beijing
Tel: 65321319

Embassy of the Gabonese Republic
Office: No. 36 Guang Hua Rd., Beijing
Tel: 65322810

Embassy of the Republic of Zimbabwe
Office: No. 7 3rd St. (E.), Beijing
Tel: 65323795

Embassy of the Republic of Cameroon
Office: No. 7 5th St. (E.) Beijing
Tel: 65321771

Embassy of the Republic of Côte d'lvoire
Office: No. 9 Xiao St. (N.), San Li Tun, Beijing
Tel: 65321482

Embassy of the Republic of Kenya
Office: No. 4 6th St. (W.), San Li Tun, Beijing
Tel: 65323381

Embassy of the Kingdom of Lesotho
Office: Rm. 302 Diplomatic Office, Dong Zhi Men Wai, Beijing
Tel: 65326842

Embassy of the Republic of Rwanda
Office: No. 30 Xiu Shui St. (N.), Beijing
Tel: 65322193

Embassy of the Republic of Madagascar
Office: No. 3 East St., San Li Tun, Beijing
Tel: 65321353

Embassy of the Republic of Mali
Office: No. 8 4th St. (E.) San Li Tun, Beijing

Tel: 65321704

Embassy of the Republic of Mauritius
Office: Rm. 202 Diplomatic Office, Dong Wai, No. 23 Dong Zhi Men Wai Avenue,
    Beijing
Tel: 65325695

Embassy of the Republic of Mozambique
Office: Rm. 2 F/7 Unit 1 of Diplomats' Office Building, Ta Yuan, Beijing
Tel: 65323664

Embassy of the Republic of Namibia
Office: No. 2-9-2 Diplomats' Office Building, Ta Yuan, Beijing
Tel: 65324810

Embassy of the Republic of South Africa
Office: No. 5 Dong Zhi Men Wai Avenue, Beijing
Tel: 65320171 /2/3/4/5/6

Embassy of the Republic of Niger
Office: 3-2-12 San Li Tun Apartment, Beijing
Tel: 65324279

Embassy of the Federal Republic of Nigeria
Office: No. 2 5th St. (E.), San Li Tun, Beijing
Tel: 65323631

Embassy of the Republic of Sierra Leone
Office: No. 7 Dong Zhi Men Wai Avenue, Beijing
Tel: 65321222

Embassy of the Somalia Republic
Office: No. 2 San Li Tun Rd., Beijing
Tel: 65321752

Embassy of the United Republic of Tanzania
Office: No. 8 Liang Ma He Rd. (S.), San Li Tun, Beijing

Tel: 65321491

Embassy of the Republic of Uganda
Office: No. 5, San Li Tun St. (E.), Beijing
Tel: 65321708
Website: www.uganda.cn777.com.cn

Embassy of the Republic of Zambia
Office: No. 5 4th St. (E.), San Li Tun, Beijing
Tel: 65321554

Embassy of the Central African Republic
Office: 1-1-132 Diplomatic Apartment, Ta Yuan, No. 1 Xin Dong Rd., Chao Yang `
        District, Beijing
Tel: 65327353

Embassy of the Republic of Albania
Office: No. 28 Guang Hua Rd., Beijing
Tel: 65321120

Embassy of the Azerbaijani Republic
Office: 1-91 Diplomats' Office Building, San Li Tun, Beijing
Tel: 65324614

Embassy of the Republic of Estonia
Office: Rm. C-617/618 Office Building of Kempinski Hotel, Yan Sha Center, Beijing
Tel: 64637913

Embassy of the Republic of Belarus
Office: No. 1 1st Ri Tan St. (E.), Beijing
Tel: 65326505

Embassy of the Republic of Bulgaria
Trade Representative's Office: No. 4 Xiu Shui St. (N.), Jian Guo Men Wai, Beijing
Tel: 65322969

Embassy of the Republic of Poland

Office: No. 1 Ri Tan Rd., Jian Guo Men Wai, Beijing
Tel: 65321235

Embassy of Bosnia-Herzegovena
Office: Rm.1 F/5 Unit 1 of Diplomats' Office Building, Ta Yuan, Beijing
Tel: 65326587

Embassy of the Russian Federation
Office: No. 4 Bei Zhong St., Dong Zhi Men Nei, Beijing
Tel: 65322051
Website: www.russia.org.cn

Embassy of the Republic of Kazakhstan
Office: No. 9 6 St. (E.), San Li Tun, Beijing
Tel: 65326182

Embassy of the Republic of Kirghizstan
Office: Rm. 1 F/7 Unit 2 of Diplomats' Office Building, Ta Yuan, Beijing
Tel: 65326458

Embassy of the Czech Republic
Office: No. 2 Ri Tan Rd., Jian Guo Men Wai, Beijing
Tel: 65326902
Website: www.mfa.cz/beijing

Embassy of the Republic of Croatia
Office: 2-72 Diplomats' Office Building, San Li Tun, Beijing
Tel: 65326241

Embassy of the Republic of Latvia
Office: No. 71 Villa of Jia Lin Garden, No. A-1 Jia Lin Rd., Chao Yang District,
        Beijing
Tel: 64333863

Embassy of the Republic of Lithuania
Office: E-18 Jing Run Shui Shang Garden, No. 18 Xiao Yun Rd., Beijing
Tel: 64681150

Embassy of Romania
Office: 2nd St. (E.), Ri Tan Rd., Beijing
Tel: 65323442

Embassy of the Republic of Macedonia
Office: 3-2-21 Diplomatic Apartment, San Li Tun, Beijing
Tel: 65327846

Embassy of the Republic of Moldova
Office: 2-9-1 Diplomats' Office Building, Ta Yuan, Beijing
Tel: 65325494

Embassy of the Federal Republic of Yugoslavia
Office: No. 1 6th St. (E.), Beijing
Tel: 65323516

Embassy of the Republic of Slovakia
Office: Ri Tan Rd., Jian Guo Men Wai, Beijing
Tel: 65321531

Embassy of the Republic of Slovenia
Office: No. 57 F-Area Ya Qu Garden, Jing Run Shui Shang Garden Villa, No. 18
        Xiao Yun Rd., Chao Yang District, Beijing
Tel: 64681030

Embassy of the Republic of Tadzhikistan
Office: 5-1-41 Diplomatic Apartment, Ta Yuan, Beiing
Tel: 65322598

Embassy of the Republic of Turkmenistan
Office: D-26 Jing Run Shui Shang Garden, Ya Qu Garden, No. 18 Xiao Yun Rd.,
        Chao Yang District, Beijing
Tel: 65326975

Embassy of Ukraine
Office: No. 11 6th St. (E.) San Li Tun, Beijing
Tel: 65326314

Website: www.ukrembcn.org

Embassy of the Republic of Uzbekistan
Office: No. 11 Bei Xiao St., San Li Tun, Beijing
Tel: 65326305

Embassy of the Republic of Hungary
Trade Representative's Office: No. 41 Unit 1 Bldg.3 of Diplomatic Apartment, Ta
                              Yuan, Beijing
Tel: 65323845
Website: www.huemb.org.cn

Embassy of the Republic of Armenia
Office: 9-2-62 Diplomatic Apartment, Ta Yuan, Beijing
Tel: 65325677

Embassy of Ireland
Trade Representative's Office: No. 3 Ri Tan Rd. (E.), Beijing
Tel: 65322280

Embassy of the Republic of Austria
Trade Representative's Office: Rm. 2280 Sheng Fu Tower, No. 37 Mai Zi Dian St.,
                              Chao yang District, Beijing
Tel: 85275050

Embassy of the Kingdom of Belgium
Office: No. 6 San Li Tun Rd., Beijing
Tel: 65321736

Embassy of the Republic of Iceland
Office: Rm. 802 Seat 1 Liang Ma He Tower, No. 8 Dong San Huan Rd. (N.), Beijing
Tel: 65907795 65907796

Embassy of the United Kingdom of Great Britain and Northern Ireland
Office: No. 11 Guang Hua Rd., Beijing
Tel: 65321961
Website: www.britishembassy.org.cn

Embassy of the Kingdom of Denmark
Office: No. 1 5th St. (E.), San Li Tun, Beijing
Tel: 65322431
Website: http://www.dk-embassy-cn.org

Embassy of the Federal Republic of Germany
Office: No. 17 Don Zhi Men Wai Avenue, Beijing
Tel: 65322161
Website: www.deutschebotschaft-china.org

Embassy of the Republic of France
Trade Representative's Office: Rm. 1015 Ying Ke Center, No. A-2 Gong Ti Rd. (N.),
Beijing
Tel: 65391300
Website: www.ambafrance-cn.org

Embassy of the Republic of Finland
Trade Representative's Office: F/26 South Tower, Beijing Jia Li Center, No. 1 Guang
Hua Rd., Beijing
Tel: 85298625
Website: www.finland-in-china.com

Embassy of the Kingdom of the Netherlands
Office: No. 4 Liang Ma He Rd. (S.), Beijing
Tel: 65321131
Website: www.nlembassypek.org

Embassy of the Grand Duchy of Luxembourg
Office: No. 21 Nei Wu Bu St., Beijing
Tel: 65135937

Embassy of the Republic of Malta
Office: 1-52 Diplomats' Office Building, San Li Tun, Beijing
Tel: 65323114

Embassy of the Kingdom of Norway
Trade Representative's Office: No. 1 1st St. (E.), San Li Tun, (100600) Beijing

Tel: 65322262

Embassy of the Republic of Portugal
Trade Representative's Office: No. 8 5th St. (E.), San Li Tun, Beijing
Tel: 65320401

Embassy of Sweden
Trading Department: Rm. 205A Diplomatic Office, Dong Wai, Beijing
Tel: 65321857
Website: www.swedemb-cn.org

Embassy of Switzerland
Office: No. 3 5th St. (E.), San Li Tun, Beijing
Tel: 65322736

Embassy of Spain
Trade Representative's Office: No. 2 F/2 Unit 2 of Diplomatic Office, Ta Yuan, Beijing
Tel: 65322072

Republic of the Hellenic Republic
Trade Representative's Office: F/1 of No. 35 Office Dong Zhi Men Wai Avenue,
Beijing
Tel: 64639394

Embassy of the Italian Republic
Trade Representative's Office: No. 2 2nd St. (E.), San Li Tun, Beijing
Tel: 65321378
Website: www.italianembassy.org.cn

Embassy of Australia
Trade Representative's Office: No. 21 Dong Zhi Men Wai Avenue, San Li Tun, Beijing
Tel: 65324606
Website: www.austemb.org.cn

Embassy of Papua New Guinea
Office: No. 2 F/11 Unit 2 of Diplomats Office, Ta Yuan, Beijing
Tel: 65324312

Embassy of the Republic of Fiji Islands

Office: 1-15-2 Diplomatic Office, Ta Yuan, Beijing

Tel: 65327305

Embassy of Canada

Trade Representative's Office: No. 19 Dong Zhi Men Wai, Chao Yang District,
Beijing

Tel: 65323536

Website: www.canada.org.cn

Embassy of the United States of America

Office: No. 3 Xiu Shui St. (N.), Jian Guo Men Wai, Beijing

Tel: 65323831

Website: www.usembassy-china.org.cn

Embassy of the Kingdom of New Zealand

Trade Representative's Office: No. 1 2nd St. (E.), Ri Tan Rd., Beijing

Tel: 65324064

Website: www.immigration.govt.nz

Embassy of the Republic of Argentina

Office: No. 11, 5th St. (E.), San Li Tun, Beijing

Tel: 65321406

Embassy of Antigua and Barbuda

Office: No. 1 F/12 Unit 1 of Diplomatic Office, Ta Yuan, Beijing

Tel: 65326518

Embassy of the Federative Republic of Brazil

Office: No. 27 Guang Hua Rd., Beijing

Tel: 65322881

Embassy of the Republic of Bolivia

Office: No. 2-3-2 Diplomats' Office Building, Ta Yuan, Beijing

Tel: 65323074

Embassy of the Republic of Ecuador

Trade Representative's Office: No. 62 Unit 2 of Diplomats' Office Building, San Li Tun, Beijing

Tel: 65320410

Embassy of the Republic of Columbia
Office: No. 34 Guang Hua Rd., Beijing
Tel: 65323377

Embassy of the Republic of Cuba
Trade Representative's Office: No. 1 Xue Shui St. (S.), Jian Guo Men Wai, Beijing
Tel: 65321990
Website: www.embacubachina.com

Embassy of the Cooperative Republic of Guyana
Office: No. 1 Xiu Shui St. (E.), Jian Guo Men Wai, Beijing
Tel: 65321337

Embassy of the Republic of Peru
Trade Representative's Office: No 91 Unit 1 of Diplomats' Office Building, San Li Tun, Beijing
Tel: 65322976
Website: www.embperu.cn.net

Embassy of the United Mexican States
Office: No. 5 5th St. (E.), San Li Tun, Beijing
Tel: 65322574

Embassy of the Republic of Surinam
Office: 2-2-22 Diplomatic Apartment, Jian Guo Men Wai, Beijing
Tel: 65322939

Embassy of the Republic of Venezuela Bolivar
Office: No. 14 San Li Tun Rd., Beijing
Tel: 65321295
Website: www.venezuela.org.cn

Embassy of the Oriental Republic of Uruguay

Office: 1-11-2 Diplomats' Office Building, Ta Yuan, Beijing
Tel: 65324445

Embassy of the Republic of Chili
Office: No. 1 4th St. (E.), San Li Tun, Beijing
Tel: 65321591

Long Distance Call Area Codes
of Main Cities and Regions in China

   When making phone calls outside the boundary of China or from Hong Kong, Macao and Taiwan areas to the Chinese mainland, please dial successively the international code (00) + the national code (86) + the area code + the user's phone number.
   When making calls inside the Chinese mainland, please dial successively 0 + the area code + the user's phone number.

Fire 119   Ambulance 120   Time Inquiry 117   Weather Forecast 121
Police 110   Operator 114   Traffic Accident 122

Beijing Municipality 10   Cangzhou 317
Shanghai Municipality 21   Hengshui 318
Tianjin Municipality 22   Xingtai 319
Chongqing Municipality 23   Qinhuangdao 335

Hebei Province   Shanxi Province
Shijiazhuang 311   Taiyuan 351
Handan 310   Shuozhou 349
Baoding 312   Xinzhou 350
Zhangjiakou 313   Datong 352
Chengde 314   Yangquan 353
Tangshan 315   Jinzhong 354
Langfang 316   Changzhi 355

Jincheng 356
Linfen 357
Luliang 358
Yuncheng 359

Inner Mongolian Autonomous Region
Hohhot 471
Hunnlunbei'er 470
Manzhouli 470
Baotou 472
Wuhai 473
Wulanchabu 474
Ji'ning 474
Tongliao 475
Chifeng 476
Ordos 477
Bayannao'er 478
Xilin Guole 479
Xilinhot 479
Erenhot 479
Xing'an 482
Alashan 483

Liaoning Province
Shenyang 24
Tieling 410
Dalian 411
Anshan 412
Fushun 413
Benxi 414
Dandong 415
Jinzhou 416
Yingkou 417
Fuxin 418
Liaoyang 419
Zhaoyang 421
Panjin 427

Huludao 429

Jilin Province
Changchun 431
Jilin 432
Yanbian 433
Yanji 433
Tumen 433
Siping 434
Tonghua 435
Baicheng 436
Liaoyuan 437
Songyuan 438
Baishan 439
Huichun 440

Heilongjiang Province
Harbin 451
Qiqihar 452
Mudanjiang 453
Suifenhe 453
Jixi 453
Jiamusi 454
Suihua 455
Hegang 468
Heihe 456
Daxinganling 457
Yichun 458
Daqing 459
Quitaihe 464
Shuangyashan 469

Jiangsu Province
Nanjing 25
Wuxi 510
Zhenjiang 511
Suzhou 512

Zhangjiagang 512
Nantong 513
Yangzhou 514
Yancheng 515
Xuzhou 516
Huai'an 517
Lianyungang 518
Changzhou 519
Taizhou 523
Suqian 527

Zhejiang Province
Hangzhou 571
Quzhou 570
Huzhou 572
Jiaxing 573
Ningbo 574
Shaoxing 575
Taizhou 576
Wenzhou 577
Lishui 578
Jinhua 579
Zhoushan 580

Anhui Province
Hefei 551
Chuzhou 550
Bangbu 552
Wuhu 553
Huai'nan 554
Ma'anshan 555
Anqing 556
Suzhou 557
Fuyang 558
Haozhou 558
Huangshan 559
Huaibei 561

Tongling 562
Xuancheng 563
Lu'an 564
Chaohu 565
Chizhou 566

Fujian Province
Fuzhou 591
Xiamen 592
Ningde 593
Putian 594
Quanzhou 595
Zhangzhou 596
Longyan 597
Sanming 598
Nanping 599

Jiangxi Province
Nanchang 791
Yingtan 701
Xinyu 790
Jiujiang 792
Shangrau 793
Fuzhou 794
Yichun 795
Ji'an 796
Ganzhou 797
Jingdezhen 798
Pingxiang 799

Shandong Province
Ji'nan 531
He'ze 530
Qingdao 532
Zibo 533
Dezhou 534
Yantai 535

Weifang 536
Ji'ning 537
Tai'an 538
Linyi 539
Binzhou 543
Dongying 546
Weihai 631
Zaozhuang 632
Rizhao 633
Laiwu 634
Liaocheng 635

He'nan Province
Zhengzhou 371
Shangqiu 370
Anyang 372
Xinxiang 373
Xuchang 374
Pingdingshan 375
Xinyang 376
Nanyang 377
Kaifeng 378
Luoyang 379
Jiaozuo 391
Hebi 392
Puyang 393
Zhoukou 394
Luohe 395
Zhumadian 396
Sanmenxia 398

Hubei Province
Wuhan 27
Xiangfan 710
E'zhou 711
Xiaogan 712
Huanggang 713
Huangshi 714
Xianning 715
Jingzhou 716
Yichang 717
Enshi 718
Shiyan 719
Suizhou 722
Jingmen 724

Hunan Province
Changsha 731
Yueyang 730
Xiangtan 732
Zhuzhou 733
Hengyang 734
Binzhou 735
Changde 736
Yiyang 737
Loudi 738
Shaoyang 739
Xiangxi 743
Zhangjiajie 744
Huaihua 745
Yongzhou 746

Guangdong Province
Guangzhou 20
Jiangmen 750
Shaoguan 751
Huizhou 752
Meizhou 753
Shantou 754
Shenzhen 755
Zhuhai 756
Foshan 757
Zhaoqing 758
Zhanjiang 759

Zhongshan 760
Heyuan 762
Shanwei 660
Yangjiang 662
Jieyang 663
Maoming 668
Qingyuan 763
Shunde 765
Yunfu 766
Chaozhou 768
Dongguan 769

Guangxi Zhuang Nationality Autonomous Region
Nanning 771
Fangchenggang 770
Dongxing 770
Pingxiang 771
Liuzhou 772
Guilin 773
Wuzhou 774
Hezhou 774
Yuelin 775
Guigang 775
Beise 776
Qinzhou 777
Hechi 778
Beihai 779

Hainan Province
Haikou 898
Sanya 898

Sichuan Province
Chengdu 28
Panzhihua 812
Zigong 813
Mianyang 816

Nanchong 817
Dazhou 818
Suining 825
Guang'an 826
Bazhong 827
Luzhou 830
Yibin 831
Neijiang 832
Ziyang 832
Leshan 833
Meishan 833
Xichang 834
Liangshan 834
Ya'an 835
Ganzi 836
A'ba 837
Deyang 838
Guangyuan 839

Guizhou Province
Guiyang 851
Zunyi 852
Anshun 853
Qiannan 854
Duyun 854
Qiandongnan 855
Kaili 855
Tongren 856
Bijie 857
Liupanshui 858
Qianxi'nan 859

Yunnan Province
Kunming 871
Xishuangbanna 691
Dehong 692
Ruili 692

Wanding 692
Zhaotong 870
Dali 872
Honghe 873
Geyang 873
He'kou 873
Qujing 874
Baoshan 875
Wenshan 876
Yuxi 877
Chuxiong 878
Si'mao 879
Lincang 883
Nujiang 886
Diqing 887
Lijiang 888

Tibet Autonomous Region
Lhasa 891
Rikaze 892
Shannan 893
Linzhi 894
Changdu 895
Nagqu 896
Ngali 897

Shaanxi Province
Xi'an 29
Xianyang 910
Yan'an 911
Yulin 912
Weinan 913
Shangluo 914
Ankang 915
Hanzhong 916
Baoji 917
Tongchuan 919

Gansu Province
Lanzhou 931
Linxia 930
Dingxi 932
Pingliang 933
Qingyang 934
Wuwei 935
Zhangye 936
Jiayuguan 937
Jinchang 937
Jiuquan 937
Tianshui 938
Longnan 939
Gannan 941
Baiyin 943

Qinghai Province
Xining 971
Haidong 972
Huangnan 973
Hainan 974
Guoluo 975
Yushu 976
Haixi 977
Ge'ermu 979

Ningxia Hui Nationality Autonomous Region
Yinchuan 951
Shizuishan 952
Wuzhong 953
Guyuan 954

Xinjiang Uygur Autonomous Region
Urumchi 991
Tacheng 901
Hami 902

Hetian 903

Altay 906

Kezilesu 908

Bo'ertala 909

Bole 909

Kelamayi 990

Yili 992

Shihezi 993

Changji 994

Turpan 995

Bayin'guoleng 996

Ku'erle 996

Akesu 997

Kashi 998

Yi'ning 999